This volume provides, by far, the most comprehensive and in-depth coverage of the topic of bridge employment I have ever seen. Leading scholars in the area of bridge employment and retirement provide incomparable coverage of how bridge employment is playing out in developed countries across the globe. It represents an absolute must read for students and scholars alike.

Kenneth S. Shultz, *Professor, California State University, San Bernardino, USA*

Flexible retirement patterns are a dream for any pension policy-maker. They are a superior alternative to compulsory increases in retirement age and enhance both workers' welfare and firms' efficiency. The rich comparative analysis of experiences in the field makes this book an innovative and crucial read.

Elsa Fornero, *Professor, University of Turin and CeRP, Italy*

Routledge is to be commended for having the vision to synthesize decades of research from around the world into one comprehensive volume on bridge employment. This book is an essential tool for any researcher interested in retirement transitions. Each chapter is well structured and provides an in-depth country-specific description of the essential elements regarding the prevalence and determinants of bridge employment. As a whole, the book leaves the reader with a deep understanding of labor force participation later in life with different perspectives from Europe, North America and the Asia-Pacific region.

Kevin E. Cahill, *PhD, Research Economist, The Sloan Center on Aging & Work at Boston College, USA*

At last we have a book that brings a global perspective, by authors from Australia, Canada, eight European countries and Japan on a rapidly emerging concern for employers and baby boomers – bridge employment.

Gary Latham, *University of Toronto, Canada*

Bridge Employment

With the long-term trend toward earlier retirement slowing, and the majority of older workers remaining in employment up to and beyond statutory retirement age, it is increasingly important that we understand how to react to these changes. Bridge employment patterns and activities have changed greatly over the past decade, yet there is little information about the benefits of the various different forms this can take, both for employees and employers.

This comparative international collection provides the first comprehensive summary of the literature on bridge employment, bringing together experiences from Europe, the United States, Canada, Australia and Japan. It identifies the opportunities, barriers and gaps in knowledge and practice, whilst offering recommendations on how organizations and individuals can cope with future challenges in aging and work. Written by international experts in the field, each chapter also makes substantive and contextualized suggestions for public policy and organizational decision-makers, providing them with a roadmap to implement and integrate bridge employment into policies and practices designed to prolong working life – a priority for workers, organizations and societies in the coming decades.

This unique research handbook will be useful to a wide range of readers with an interest in the new concept of bridge employment and the extension of working life, and of interest to researchers and practitioners in organizational behavior, labor market analysis, human resource management, career development/counselling, occupational health, social economy and public policy administration.

Carlos-María Alcover is Senior Lecturer of Social and Organizational Psychology, Rey Juan Carlos University, Spain.

Gabriela Topa is Associate Professor of Psychology at the Spanish University for Distance Teaching (UNED), Spain.

Emma Parry is Reader in Human Resource Management at Cranfield School of Management, Cranfield University and a Visiting Fellow at Westminster Business School, UK.

Franco Fraccaroli is Full Professor of Work and Organizational Psychology, University of Trento, Italy.

Marco Depolo is Professor of Work and Organizational Psychology, University of Bologna, Italy.

Routledge studies in human resource development
Edited by Monica Lee
Lancaster University, UK

HRD theory is changing rapidly. Recent advances in theory and practice, how we conceive of organizations and of the world of knowledge, have led to the need to reinterpret the field. This series aims to reflect and foster the development of HRD as an emergent discipline.

Encompassing a range of different international, organizational, methodological and theoretical perspectives, the series promotes theoretical controversy and reflective practice.

1 **Policy Matters**
   Flexible learning and organizational change
   Edited by Viktor Jakupec and Robin Usher

2 **Science Fiction and Organization**
   Edited by Warren Smith, Matthew Higgins, Martin Parker and Geoff Lightfoot

3 **HRD and Learning Organisations in Europe**
   Challenges for professionals
   Edited by Saskia Tjepkema, Jim Stewart, Sally Sambrook, Martin Mulder, Hilde ter Horst and Jaap Scheerens

4 **Interpreting the Maternal Organisation**
   Edited by Heather Höpfl and Monika Kostera

5 **Work Process Knowledge**
   Edited by Nick Boreham, Renan Samurçay and Martin Fischer

6 **HRD in a Complex World**
   Edited by Monica Lee

7 **HRD in Small Organisations**
   Research and practice
   Edited by Jim Stewart and Graham Beaver

8 **New Frontiers in HRD**
Edited by Jean Woodall, Monica Lee and Jim Stewart

9 **Human Resources, Care Giving, Career Progression, and Gender**
A gender neutral glass ceiling
Beulah S. Coyne, Edward J. Coyne, Sr. and Monica Lee

10 **The Industrial Relations of Training and Development**
Jason Heyes and Mark Stuart

11 **Rethinking Strategic Learning**
Russ Vince

12 **Critical Thinking in Human Resource Development**
Edited by Carole Elliott and Sharon Turnbull

13 **Aesthetics and Human Resource Development**
Connections, concepts and opportunities
Stephen Gibb

14 **Action Learning, Leadership and Organizational Development in Public Services**
Edited by Clare Rigg and Sue Richards

15 **Human Resource Development in the Public Sector**
The case of health and social care
Edited by Sally Sambrook and Jim Stewart

16 **Management Development**
Perspectives from research and practice
Edited by Rosemary Hill and Jim Stewart

17 **Workplace Learning**
Concepts, measurement, and application
Edited by Marianne van Woerkom and Rob Poell

18 **Managing Healthy Organizations**
Worksite health promotion and the new self-management paradigm
Mikael Holmqvist and Christian Maravelias

19 **New Ways of Organizing Work**
Developments, perspectives, and experiences
Edited by Clare Kelliher and Julia Richardson

20 **Human Resource Development as We Know It**
Speeches that have shaped the field
Edited by Monica Lee

21 **Bridge Employment**
A research handbook
*Edited by Carlos-María Alcover, Gabriela Topa, Emma Parry,
Franco Fraccaroli and Marco Depolo*

Also published in the series in paperback:

Action Research in Organisations
Jean McNiff, accompanied by Jack Whitehead

Understanding Human Resource Development
A research-based approach
Edited by Jim Stewart, Jim McGoldrick and Sandra Watson

Bridge Employment
A research handbook

Edited by Carlos-María Alcover,
Gabriela Topa, Emma Parry,
Franco Fraccaroli and Marco Depolo

LONDON AND NEW YORK

First published 2014
by Routledge
2 Park Square, Milton Park, Abingdon, Oxon OX14 4RN

and by Routledge
711 Third Avenue, New York, NY 10017

Routledge is an imprint of the Taylor & Francis Group, an informa business

© 2014 selection and editorial matter, Carlos-María Alcover, Gabriela
Topa, Emma Parry, Franco Fraccaroli and Marco Depolo; individual
chapters, the contributors

The right of the editors to be identified as the authors of the editorial
material, and of the authors for their individual chapters, has been asserted
in accordance with sections 77 and 78 of the Copyright, Designs and
Patents Act 1988.

All rights reserved. No part of this book may be reprinted or reproduced or
utilized in any form or by any electronic, mechanical, or other means, now
known or hereafter invented, including photocopying and recording, or in
any information storage or retrieval system, without permission in writing
from the publishers.

Trademark notice: Product or corporate names may be trademarks or
registered trademarks, and are used only for identification and explanation
without intent to infringe.

British Library Cataloguing in Publication Data
A catalogue record for this book is available from the British Library

Library of Congress Cataloging in Publication Data
Bridge employment: a research handbook / edited by Carlos-María
Alcover, Gabriela Topa, Marco Depolo, Franco Fraccaroli and
Emma Perry.
    pages cm. – (Routledge studies in human resource development)
    Includes bibliographical references and index.
    1. Older people–Employment. 2. Age and employment. 3. Retirees–
Employment. 4. Post-retirement employment. I. Alcover, Carlos-María.
    HD6279.B75 2014
    331.3'98–dc23   2013036914

ISBN: 978-0-415-82909-0 (hbk)
ISBN: 978-0-203-38310-0 (ebk)

Typeset in Times New Roman
by Wearset Ltd, Boldon, Tyne and Wear

Printed and bound in the United States of America by Publishers Graphics,
LLC on sustainably sourced paper.

Contents

List of figures	xii
List of tables	xiv
Notes on contributors	xvi
Foreword	xx
Preface	xxii
Acknowledgments	xxiv
List of abbreviations	xxvi

Introduction 1

1 Bridge employment: an introduction and overview of the handbook 3

CARLOS-MARÍA ALCOVER, GABRIELA TOPA, EMMA PARRY,
FRANCO FRACCAROLI AND MARCO DEPOLO

PART I
Bridge employment in Europe 25

2 Bridge employment in the Netherlands: who, what and why? 27

KÈNE HENKENS AND HANNA VAN SOLINGE

3 Bridge employment, a Swedish perspective 51

KERSTIN ISAKSSON, GUNN JOHANSSON AND SOFIE PALM

4 Bridge employment in Belgium: between an early retirement culture and a concern for work sustainability 70

DONATIENNE DESMETTE AND PATRICIA VENDRAMIN

x   *Contents*

5 Flexible transitions from work to retirement: evidence from Poland   90
PIOTR ZIENTARA

6 Bridge employment in Spain: a possible option to postpone retirement   115
CARLOS-MARÍA ALCOVER AND GABRIELA TOPA

7 Career transitions at retirement age in the United Kingdom: bridge employment or continued career progression?   138
EMMA PARRY AND DIANNE BOWN WILSON

8 No bridge and no employment? Problems and challenges for older workers in Italy   154
MARCO DEPOLO AND FRANCO FRACCAROLI

9 Flexible transitions from work to retirement in Germany   167
JÜRGEN DELLER AND LEENA PUNDT

PART II
Bridge employment in North America   193

10 Bridge employment in the United States   195
MO WANG, LEE THOMAS PENN, AGUSTINA BERTONE, AND SLAVIANA STEFANOVA

11 Promoting active aging: the Canadian experience of bridge employment   216
TANIA SABA

PART III
Bridge employment in the Asia-Pacific region   237

12 The role of partial retirement in organizational policy-making in Australia   239
PHILIP TAYLOR, CHRISTOPHER McLOUGHLIN AND CATHERINE EARL

13 The Japanese approach to bridge jobs   252
CHIKAKO USUI, RICHARD A. COLIGNON AND DAN ROSEN

Contents xi

Conclusions 267

**14 Bridge employment: lessons learned and future prospects
for research and practice** 269
CARLOS-MARÍA ALCOVER, GABRIELA TOPA, EMMA PARRY,
FRANCO FRACCAROLI AND MARCO DEPOLO

Author index 291
Subject index 300

Figures

2.1	Relationship to the labor market in 2011 by age (N = 1,528)	31
2.2	Probability of taking up bridge employment by level of education and sex (N = 1,310 retired employees)	34
2.3	Probability of taking up bridge employment by health status (N = 1,310 retired employees)	35
2.4	Probability of taking up bridge employment by sex and marital status (N = 1,310 retired employees)	35
2.5	Probability of entering bridge employment by sex and age at retirement (N = 1,310 retired employees)	37
2.6	Probability of entering bridge employment by reasons for involuntary retirement (N = 1,310 retired employees)	37
2.7	Bridge employees by level of education and type of bridge employment (N = 318 people who are or used to be in bridge employment)	40
2.8	Job satisfaction in old and new job (N = 141 people active in bridge employment in 2011)	41
2.9	Bridge employees by level of education and reasons for working beyond retirement age (N = 350 people who are or used to be in bridge employment)	46
3.1	Reasons for retirement	56
3.2	Working conditions related to planned retirement before 65, at 65 or after 65	58
4.1	Do you think you will be able to do the same job you are doing now when you are 60 years old? All employees who answered: 'Yes, I think so'	74
4.2	Does your work affect your health? All employees. Answer: 'Yes, mainly negatively'	77
6.1	Population structure by major age groups, EU-27, 1990–2060	116
6.2	Population pyramid forecasts for Spain	117
6.3	Evolution of retirement discharges, 2005–2011, Total System	123
6.4	Evolution of retirement discharges, 2005–2011, General System (salaried employees, excluding self-employed workers)	124

Figures xiii

9.1	Persons in paid employment, 2007, aged 65 to 75	173
9.2	Percentage of all professional groups among persons in paid employment of the respective age group in 2007	174
9.3	Development of gainful employment of women aged 65–69, according to education groups, 1996–2010	175
9.4	Development of gainful employment of men aged 65–69, according to education groups, 1996–2010	176
11.1	Employment rate trend for people aged 55 and over reversed in the mid-1990s	220
11.2	Years of employment before retiring and average retirement age, by gender	222
11.3	Bridge employment increased more or less steadily from 1999 to 2004	227
12.1	Percentage of organizations that had adopted policies relating to workforce aging	242
12.2	Percentage of responding organizations by the number of older-worker-oriented policies used by the organization	243
12.3	Percentage of responding organizations that had adopted, would consider adopting and would not consider adopting a part-time retirement by the number of older-worker-oriented policies adopted	244
12.4	Percentage of the total number of organizations that had adopted each of the older worker friendly policies that had also employed a part-time retirement policy	245
12.5	Percentage of each industry group that had adopted part-time retirement	248
12.6	Percentage of employers that are encouraging employees to retire later by the adoption of part-time retirement policies	249

Tables

1.1	Estimated percentage of population aged 65 and over in developed and developing (BRICS group) countries in 2014 and 2050	4
2.1	Interest in finding work after retirement, by cohort (N = 1,310 retired employees)	32
2.2	Characteristics of bridge employment	39
2.3	Perceived quality of the work in career job and bridge job, in percentages (N = 141 people active in bridge employment in 2011)	42
2.4	Results of the logit regression explaining bridge employment decisions among older workers in the Netherlands, marginal effects and standard errors (N = 1,296 retired employees)	44
3.1	The Swedish labor market 1987–2010 for ages 55–74 divided by age and gender	53
3.2	Summary of factors influencing the motivation to continue working in old age	65
4.1	Sub-dimensions of job quality (able to do the same job when 60 years old). All employees in the 50+ age category	76
4.2	Health and sustainability (able to do the same job when 60 years old). All employees in the 50+ age category	77
5.1	Findings from the interviews	105
6.1	Evolution of the average retirement age in Spain, 2005–2011	123
9.1	Employment and pension receipt by age and gender	177
9.2	Reasons for working	180
9.3	Development of post-retirement activities	182
9.4	Reasons for post-retirement activities	183
9.5	Framework for post-retirement activities	184
10.1	Motives to engage in bridge employment	201
11.1	Average effective age of retirement of men in selected OECD countries	219
11.2	Changes in average retirement age, Canada, men and women	221

12.1	Probability that an employer that used part-time retirement would have adopted another of the older-worker-friendly policies, 95% confidence interval for the probability and the variance explained in adoption of each policy by the adoption of part-time retirement	246
12.2	Principle components analysis structure: human resource strategies	247
13.1	Labor-force-participation rates among older persons (male and female combined)	253
13.2	Prevalence of re-employment system until age 65 measured by % firms with re-employment system until age 65, 2011	255
13.3	Older workers by employment status	257
13.4	Unemployment rate (%)	263

Contributors

Editors

Carlos-María Alcover received a PhD in social psychology from the Complutense University of Madrid, Spain. He is currently a Senior Lecturer in Social and Organizational Psychology in the Department of Psychology at the Rey Juan Carlos University, Madrid. His research has been focused on psychological contract and exchange relationships in organizations, early retirement and psychological well-being, and membership and temporal matters in work teams. His work has been published in *European Psychologist, Journal of Vocational Behavior, Work and Stress, Research on Aging, Personnel Review, European Journal of Psychological Assessment, Journal of Managerial Psychology, Career Development International, Social Science Information* and *Economic and Industrial Democracy*, among others. He is author, co-author and editor of ten books and of 30 book chapters, and editor of special issues of academic journals such as *Journal of Managerial Psychology* and the Spanish *Journal of Work and Organizational Psychology* about *Varieties of Work Retirement in Europe: Psychological Well-Being and Associated Psychosocial Factors.*

Marco Depolo is Full Professor (Work and Organizational Psychology), University of Bologna, Department of Psychology, Cesena, Italy. He is Dean of the 'WOP-P', Erasmus Mundus Master, University of Bologna, Faculty of Psychology. His work has been published in international journals (such as *Journal of Vocational Behavior, Research on Aging, Career Development International, Relations Industrielles, International Archives of Occupational and Environmental Health, Journal of Occupational Medicine and Toxicology, Journal of Workplace Learning*). He is co-author, with Franco Fraccaroli, of the chapter 'Career and ageing at work', in *An Introduction to Work and Organizational Psychology*, (Blackwell, 2008), and author of several books and book chapters about work and organizational psychology and human resources development. He has served as referee for national and international scientific journals.

Franco Fraccaroli is Full Professor (Work and Organizational Psychology) at the Department of Psychology and Cognitive Science at the University of

Trento (Rovereto, Italy). He has been Dean of the Faculty of Cognitive Science (2010–2012). He is past-President of the EAWOP (European Association of Work and Organizational Psychology). His research interests include psychosocial transitions to work and within work, elderly workers and the work exit phase, psychological experience of joblessness, quality of organizational life and evaluation of training programs and the work accompaniment of adults. He has published articles in international journals (such as *Work and Stress, European Journal of Work and Organizational Psychology, Anxiety, Stress and Coping, Industrial and Organizational Psychology, European Journal of Psychological Assessment, Career Development International, Travail Humain*) on work socialization, organizational justice, late career and transition to retirement. He is co-editor (with Donald Truxillo) of the special issue *Age in the Workplace: Challenges and Opportunities* of the *European Journal of Work and Organizational Psychology*, 22 (2013).

Emma Parry is a Reader in Human Resource Management (HRM) at Cranfield School of Management, Cranfield University, United Kingdom and a Visiting Fellow at Westminster Business School. Her research focuses on the impact of context on the way that we manage people, specifically the impact of national context, demographic changes and technological advancements on HRM. She has conducted many research projects in the public, private and not-for-profit sectors. Emma leads 'Cranet', a network of over 40 academic institutions worldwide that conducts research into HRM, and is a Co-director of '5C', another global academic network that researches the impact of national culture on careers. Emma is also a member of the global team for the Center of Aging and Work in Boston, USA. Emma is the co-author, with Shaun Tyson, of *Managing People in the Contemporary Context* (Routledge, 2013) and co-editor of *Managing an Age-Diverse Workforce* and *Global Trends in Human Resource Management* (both Palgrave Macmillan). She is also the author of numerous journal articles in the field of HRM.

Gabriela Topa received a PhD in social psychology from the Spanish University for Distance Teaching (UNED), where she is currently an Associate Professor of Work and Organizational Psychology in the Department of Social and Organizational Psychology. Her research interests include early retirement, financial preparation for retirement, psychological contracts, antecedents and consequences of mobbing, and quality of work-life. Her work has been published in top international academic journals. Recent publications include 'Antecedents and consequences of retirement planning and decision-making: A meta-analysis and model', *Journal of Vocational Behavior*, 75: 38–55 (2009) and 'Retirement and wealth relationships: Meta-analysis and SEM', *Research on Aging*, 33: 501–28 (2011).

xviii *Contributors*

Authors

Carlos-María Alcover, Department of Psychology, Rey Juan Carlos University, Madrid, Spain.

Agustina Bertone, Department of Management, University of Florida, Gainesville, Florida, USA.

Dianne Bown Wilson, School of Management, Cranfield University, Bedfordshire, United Kingdom.

Richard A. Colignon, Department of Sociology and Anthropology, St. Louis University, Missouri, USA.

Jürgen Deller, Institute of Strategic Human Resource Management Research and Development, Leuphana University, Luneburg, Germany.

Marco Depolo, Department of Psychology, University of Bologna, Cesena, Italy.

Donatienne Desmette, Department of Psychology, Catholic University of Louvain, Louvain-La-Neuve, Belgium.

Catherine Earl, Faculty of Business and Economics, Federation University Australia, Churchill, Victoria, Australia.

Franco Fraccaroli, Department of Psychology and Cognitive Science, University of Trento, Rovereto, Trento, Italy.

Kène Henkens, Netherlands Interdisciplinary Demographic Institute (NIDI), The Hague, Department of Sociology and Anthropology, University of Amsterdam, the Netherlands.

Kerstin Isaksson, Division of Psychology, Mälardalen University, Västerås, Sweden.

Gunn Johansson, Department of Psychology, Stockholm University, Stockholm, Sweden.

Christopher McLoughlin, Faculty of Business and Economics, Monash University, Churchill, Victoria, Australia.

Sofie Palm, Division of Psychology, Mälardalen University, Sweden, Västerås, Sweden.

Emma Parry, School of Management, Cranfield University, Bedfordshire, United Kingdom.

Lee Thomas Penn, Department of Management, University of Florida, Gainesville, Florida, USA.

Leena Pundt, Institute of Strategic Human Resource Management Research and Development, Leuphana University, Luneburg, Germany.

Contributors xix

Dan Rosen, Department of Law, Chuo University, Tokyo, Japan.

Tania Saba, School of Industrial Relations, University of Montreal, Quebec, Canada.

Hanna van Solinge, Netherlands Interdisciplinary Demographic Institute (NIDI), The Hague, the Netherlands.

Slaviana Stefanova, Department of Management, University of Florida, Gainesville, Florida, USA.

Philip Taylor, Faculty of Business and Economics, Federation University Australia, Churchill, Victoria, Australia.

Gabriela Topa, Department of Social and Organizational Psychology, Spanish University for Distance Teaching, Madrid, Spain.

Chikako Usui, Department of Sociology, University of Missouri–St. Louis, St. Louis, Missouri, USA.

Patricia Vendramin, Fondation Travail-Université de Namur, Namur, Belgium.

Mo Wang, Department of Management, University of Florida, Gainesville, Florida, USA.

Piotr Zientara, Department of International Economic Relations, University of Gdansk, Poland.

Foreword

The increase of life expectancy, low fertility rates and migrations are demographic trends that produce, in advanced societies, high rates of older people in the composition of their populations. In this context, policy-makers and governments aim to delay workers' age of retirement and to extend the active period at work as a way of making economic progress and pension schemes sustainable.

The extension of the working life is already in place for some groups of workers and sectors in developed countries. It presents a wide array of forms that combine in different trajectories from full-time standard work to final retirement. Retirement is less and less a defined event occurring at a given point in time and at an institutionalized age. It rather becomes an extended process over time. The limits between work and retirement are becoming blurry and the combination of situations of work activity and its temporary cessations during the final period of the occupational career may be complex and differ among individuals and across settings and contexts.

To identify and describe the patterns and profiles of work arrangements, and eventually unemployment periods, during the now-extended span from work to retirement is an empirical issue. Likely it is also a question for empirical research to identify the main antecedents and effects of those retirement paths in a context where its occurrence will probably increase and generalize.

This handbook represents a major contribution to this task. It focuses on the study of bridge employment, one of the most flexible and widely used work arrangements from work to retirement. The approach to this phenomenon takes the country as the basic context of analysis. The handbook recollects an excellent bundle of contributions from a dozen of countries, targeted and selected for the purpose of the book. In all of them bridge employment is present and its analysis provides rich knowledge.

Bridge employment is a complex phenomenon that requires a multi-level approach. In its emergence and forms adopted, a large number of antecedents play a role and the country appears to be a productive context for their analysis. Specific combinations of legal and economic factors, retirement policies and pension schemes, labor-market conditions, demographic composition of the population, migration patterns and political traditions (liberal, social welfare

Foreword xxi

state, etc.) are important determinants for the development and types of bridge employment and their outcomes for the stakeholders involved.

Country is also a useful context to deepen understanding of the meso- and micro-level antecedents. Meso-level variables include company policies and practices on retention or dismissal of older employees, working conditions and jobs offered, and cultural norms and values in the close social context. It also includes family expectations and behavioral patterns. Micro-level variables include individual antecedents. Factors such as age and gender, education, socio-cultural and economic conditions, health, work ability, cognitions, personality, values and motives also have an influence on bridge employment practices.

The chapters in the handbook provide an excellent picture of bridge employment in its multiple forms, their antecedents as well as the main consequences for different interest groups. The research reported, often qualitative, extends the understanding of this multifaceted phenomenon and the ways it is implemented in different countries. It also identifies relevant boundary conditions for its successful implementation. The comparative analysis of the information provides relevant trends and raises important questions for further research. Especially interesting will be the study of this phenomenon in BRICS countries, where the growth of aged population expected within the next decades is really large.

Economic, demographic and policy analysis point out that extending work activities beyond the institutionalized age of retirement is needed to make economic development and pension schemes sustainable. Nevertheless, the implications and boundary conditions to make it successful for different groups and their effects on individuals' health and well-being and on the family and other spheres of life are still largely unknown. Likely, the understanding of the forms and contingencies for an effective, valuable and productive bridge employment in companies is also limited.

The contributions of this handbook also point out the value of a work and organizational psychology perspective to understand the study of bridge employment. Contributions from this discipline are significant for policy interventions at country and organization level, and to improve the design and implementation of specific forms and conditions of bridge employment. The analysis of employees' behaviors and attitudes and of company practices enhances the positive outcomes for the parties involved and prevents the negative direct or side-effects. This is especially important given that this practice most probably will be extended in the near future to other countries, sectors, organizations and groups of workers. The analysis carried out, the policy recommendations and the inputs for interventions presented in the chapters are important assets for professionals aiming to introduce new bridge employment programs and for researchers looking to further their understanding. I hope the readership will find the contribution of the book stimulating and will profit from it to further advance practice, research and the understanding of the fascinating phenomenon of aging and work.

José M. Peiró
University of Valencia, Spain
President of the International Association of Applied Psychology (IAAP)

Preface

In its inception, this volume grew out of the experiences of three of the contributing authors and editors (Carlos-María, Gabriela and Marco) in the course of our research into the psychosocial factors involved in early retirement processes in Spain and Italy, a project carried out between 2006 and 2007 with funding from the national Research and Education Agencies of both countries. In the spring of 2011, the idea of an ambitious publication offering a broad international outlook on the issue of bridge employment, took shape out of our collaboration on this research project and subsequent research stays at the University of Bologna. The project began to unfold and a primary version crystallized from personal contacts made at the Small Group Meeting, *Age Cohorts in the Workplace: Understanding and Building Strength through Differences*, organized by the University of Trento and held on November 11–13, 2011 in Rovereto (Trento), Italy, with the support of the European Association of Work and Organizational Psychology (EAWOP). At the end of the meeting, Franco and Emma joined the project as editors to complete the team. An initial proposal (which included analysis of several European countries and the United States) was then submitted to Routledge, and after a rigorous evaluation process and review by leading scholars in this field, it was suggested that the analysis should be extended to other countries and contexts, resulting in the project presented here.

It might be asked why we have focused on bridge employment when our basic research referred to early retirement? The answer lies in the rapid pace of demographic, economic, financial and social change, which is already transforming the concept of retirement and the meaning of workforce participation by older people. Work, pensions, the welfare state, the well-being of the elderly and social cohesion are today undergoing a process of far-reaching change, which will only intensify in the future. Research carried out in developed countries shows that the early retirement trends characteristic of the last two decades of the twentieth century have halted and even gone into reverse. Meanwhile, the retirement context in both developed and developing countries has changed rapidly over the last decade, shifting away from the encouragement of retirement toward the prolongation of working life through a variety of flexible working practices. This has lead to the increasing prevalence of diverse forms of transitional or gradual retirement in older workers' lives today, including 'phased

Preface xxiii

retirement', 'partial retirement', 'bridge employment' and 're-entry'. Bridge employment is probably the most widespread of these options and the most attractive for the future labor market, as the chapters in this book will show.

The most common definition of bridge employment refers to jobs that follow career or full-time employment and precede complete labor-force withdrawal or retirement from work. The transitions characterizing bridge employment occur both within the individual's own profession and in other occupations, and they can take the form of (full- or part-time) salaried work, permanent or temporary jobs and self-employment.

The purpose of this handbook is to review, analyze, summarize and integrate existing knowledge and practices based on a range of bridge employment and late retirement experiences from around the world. The issues are addressed by a select interdisciplinary group of researchers and experts (social psychologists, sociologists, demographers, economists, business and human resource management specialists) in 12 chapters providing an overview of the situation in eight European countries, the United States, Canada, Australia and Japan. Our intention is to present the first comprehensive, all-round view of the past, present and future of bridge employment, analyzing key features, commonalities and differences across different cultural, economic, legal and social contexts. A more detailed overview of the content of each chapter in the handbook is provided by the editors in Chapter 1.

We hope this book will be useful to a wide range of readers with an interest in the new concept of retirement and the alternatives available for the prolongation of working life associated with bridge employment. We also trust that its contents will be helpful for both researchers and practitioners in the fields of organizational behavior, labor-market analysis, human resource management, career development and career counseling, occupational health, older workers' well-being, public policy administration and social economy.

As they gradually percolate through to a wider audience of graduate students, researchers, managers, experts and practitioners in all of the relevant disciplines, we hope the ideas and conclusions contained this book will help develop a broader, more imaginative and more applicable vision of this undeniably important field. Many of our conclusions are partial and provisional, and research and practice will of course continue to evolve in new, more refined ways. However, the numerous interesting ideas that emerge from these chapters will surely steer both academics and practitioners working in the field of bridge employment and late retirement in productive new directions.

Carlos-María Alcover, Gabriela Topa, Emma Parry, Franco Fraccaroli and
Marco Depolo

Acknowledgments

This handbook represents the hard work of many individuals through more than two years. We wish to thank the many persons, organizations and institutions that made this book possible, and who provided support and assistance in various phases of the development and completion of this book. First and foremost, we would like to thank Jacqueline Curthoys, Commissioning Editor – Routledge Research, Business and Management at Routledge/Taylor & Francis, who trusted early on in our book proposal and encouraged us to expand the initial objectives to achieve a larger international vision. She has truly been a warm support and a reliable guidance throughout the process of completing the book. We would also like to thank editorial assistants Alexander Krause, in the first phases, and Sinead Waldron, in the last ones, for their patience and valuable help in preparing the typescript; we would have been lost without your support.

We are, of course, foremost indebted to the authors who accepted the invitation to write chapters for this handbook and are appreciative of their timeliness in submitting drafts, making changes after our reviews and comments and submitting the final versions of their chapters. We would like to thank José M. Peiró for agreeing to write a foreword, and for his sincere endorsement of our project. We extend deep appreciation to Routledge and Taylor & Francis Group, Lifelong Learning Programme/Erasmus Programme of the European Commission, Rey Juan Carlos University, Spanish University for Distance Teaching, Cranfield University, University of Trento and University of Bologna for their respective editorial support, financial support in form of grants for international research stays of several of the editors of this book, and bibliographical and material resources that their respective institutions have provided to the editors. Last, but certainly not least, we would like to thank the European Association of Work and Organizational Psychology (EAWOP) for supporting the Small Group Meeting *Age Cohorts in the Workplace: Understanding and Building Strength through Differences*, organized by the University of Trento and held November 11–13, 2011 in Rovereto (Trento), Italy, which allowed many of the researchers in this book to meet in person and exchange their knowledge, so that subsequently they were invited to participate as authors in the handbook. In sum, this book has been a labor of commitment and dedication with many participants (included our respective families, friends and colleagues), and we are grateful for their efforts in helping us to achieve our goal.

Carlos-María Alcover, Gabriela Topa, Emma Parry,
Franco Fraccaroli and Marco Depolo

Abbreviations

AOW	basic pension for the over-65s in the Netherlands
BRICS	Brazil, Russia, India, China and South Africa, or the five major emerging national economies
CCTM	conseil consultatif sur la main-d'œuvre et le travail
CPP	Canada Pension Plan
ELSA	English Longitudinal Study of Ageing
EU	European Union
EWCS	European Working Conditions Survey
DEAS	German Aging Survey
FER	flexible early retirement in the Netherlands
GDP	gross domestic product
HCE	Higher Council for Employment in Belgium
HR	human resource
HRM	human resource management
HRS	Health and Retirement Study in the United States
ILO	International Labour Office
INE	Spanish National Bureau of Statistics
ISTAT	Italian National Bureau of Statistics
LFS	Labor Force Survey
NEETs	Not in Employment, Education and Training (applied to young people)
NIDI	Netherlands Interdisciplinary Demographic Institute
OADR	Old-Age Dependency Ratio
OECD	Organization for Economic Cooperation and Development
OHS	Occupational Health and Safety
SHARE	Survey of Health, Aging and Retirement in Europe
SOEP	German Socio-Economic Panel
TAEN	The Age and Employment Network
TFR	total fertility rate
TTR	Transition to Retirement Federal Government's scheme in Australia
VUT	voluntary early retirement in the Netherlands
WEF	World Economic Forum
ZUS	Social-Security Institution in Poland

Introduction

1 Bridge employment

An introduction and overview of the handbook

Carlos-María Alcover, Gabriela Topa,
Emma Parry, Franco Fraccaroli and
Marco Depolo

The changing nature of retirement in the twenty-first century

Progressively increasing life expectancy and attendant aging of the population is a worldwide phenomenon, particularly in Western economically advanced countries. Forecasts for the coming decades suggest that the trend is likely to intensify, reaching hitherto unimagined proportions. The proportion of the world's people aged 60 or more in 2011 will double in percentage terms by 2050, when this age group will account for some two billion people and 22 percent of the population (United Nations 2011). These changes in population structure are a consequence of declining fertility and mortality rates (known as the *demographic transition*) and shifting migration trends. Fertility decline reduces family size and produces smaller cohorts at younger ages, while mortality decline raises life expectancy. The combined outcome is population aging (Alley and Crimmins 2007). Table 1.1 shows the percentage of the population aged 65 and over in selected developed and developing countries in 2014 and 2050.

As may be observed in Table 1.1, countries like Japan, Germany and Italy will reach percentages close to 25 percent by 2014, although the percentages are significantly lower among the BRICS group, with the exception of Russia. Meanwhile, the forecast for 2050 points to a major increase in the number of people aged 65 and over in the developed countries, and even faster growth in the BRICS resulting in a tripling of the percentages in Brazil, China and India.

These marked population trends will eventually require a reassessment of the balance between the period of people's working lives and the length of their retirement (Engelhardt 2012), taking into account also the better health condition of people over 55 in relation to the past, in order to maintain pension systems and welfare programs for the elderly (Börsch-Supan *et al.* 2009; de Preter *et al.* 2013). As leading experts have warned for years now, for most developed countries, the traditional pay-as-you-go social security system includes promises that cannot be kept without significant system reforms; and in the absence of true reforms, current systems are fiscally unsustainable (see, e.g., Gruber and Wise 2005). Retirement is a matter of global significance which influences and determines the sustainable financial and social development of countries and societies

4   *C.-M. Alcover* et al.

Table 1.1 Estimated percentage of population aged 65 and over in developed and developing (BRICS group) countries in 2014 and 2050

	2014			2050		
	Total (%)	Male (%)	Female (%)	Total (%)	Male (%)	Female (%)
Developed countries						
Australia	15.1	13.9	16.3	22.5	20.5	24.5
Canada	17.3	15.5	19.1	26.3	23.5	29.0
France	18.3	16.0	20.5	25.8	23.0	28.5
Germany	21.1	18.8	23.4	30.1	27.2	32.7
Italy	21.0	18.7	23.2	31.0	28.1	33.6
Japan	25.8	23.0	28.3	40.1	36.1	43.7
United Kingdom	17.5	15.7	19.3	23.6	21.5	25.6
United States	14.2	12.6	15.7	20.5	18.9	22.2
Developing countries (BRICS Group)						
Brazil	7.6	6.5	8.6	21.1	18.6	23.5
China	9.6	9.0	10.3	26.8	24.0	29.5
India	5.8	5.3	6.4	14.7	13.3	16.1
Russia	13.3	8.8	17.1	25.7	20.0	30.6
South Africa	6.3	5.0	7.5	11.4	10.1	11.7

Source: US Census Bureau, International Data Base, June 2010 version.

as a whole (Wang 2013). Consequently, these international trends require a reformulation and further research on aging and work, and mid and late career structures (Peiró *et al.* 2013; Shultz and Adams 2007; van der Heijden *et al.* 2008; Wang *et al.* 2012).

Research carried out mainly in the United States, Canada, Australia, the United Kingdom and the countries of northern Europe has shown that the trend toward the early retirement options, promoted by governments in order to avoid high unemployment rates mainly among young people, characteristic of the latter two decades of the twentieth century has halted and even gone into reverse (Cahill *et al.* 2006a; Kantarci and van Soest 2008; Lee *et al.* 2011; Peiró *et al.* 2013; Phillipson and Smith 2005; Quinn 2010; Saba and Guerin 2005). The context for retirement in developed and developing countries is rapidly changing with a shift from 'pro-retirement' to 'pro-work' (Wang and Shultz 2012). Meanwhile, Japan traditionally has followed a different pattern (Raymo *et al.* 2009), as retirement in Japan is a particularly lengthy, gradual process, especially for male workers (Shimizutani 2011), and the participation of older people in the workforce has usually been high among men and women, both in the 60–64 age bracket and among those aged over 65 years, which are the higher rates among OECD countries.

The trend to prolong working life has even been detected in countries where early retirement has been used as an organizational strategy to handle challenges

Introduction and overview 5

in the labor market (Schalk *et al*. 2010), making it an involuntary option forced upon retirees by organizational policies so that they are bereft of any influence over the decision. Such a situation may lead to adverse psychological outcomes, lower levels of household income and lower well-being and life satisfaction (Alcover *et al*. 2012; Bender 2012; Dorn and Sousa-Poza 2007; Hershey and Henkens in press; Noone *et al*. 2013). Recent studies show that in the United States the majority of older workers are employed, or plan to work, part-time and in temporary jobs (Giandrea *et al*. 2009; Raymo *et al*. 2010), while the data from European countries suggest that paid work between the ages of 60 and 70 is the domain of persons with high socio-economic status (Komp *et al*. 2010). Though older workers' motives for wishing to stay in the labor market may differ, the results of a recent meta-analysis suggest that they do so basically to satisfy intrinsic interests, such as the nature of the work, the satisfaction it provides and the motivation of success, for social reasons and to gain financial security (Kooij *et al*. 2011). All of this is redefining the conventional concepts of career and retirement.

Comparisons of extensive international surveys (Topa *et al*. in press) such as SHARE (Survey of Health, Ageing and Retirement in Europe; Börsch-Supan and Jürges 2005), HRS (Health and Retirement Study) from the United States and ELSA (English Longitudinal Study of Ageing) from the United Kingdom, have shown that the rate of employment among older workers (i.e., those aged over 50) is much higher in the United States than in Europe, but the difference is even more pronounced among workers aged 60–64 and over. For instance, data from the first eight waves of HRS reveal that 47 percent of retirees experienced post-retirement employment, with 43 percent of retired women making the transition compared to 50 percent of retired men (Pleau 2010). However, longitudinal data for the last 33 years display a modest curvilinear trend in post-retirement employment in the United States (Pleau and Shauman 2013). Despite the existence of considerable differences between countries, labor markets in Europe are characterized by low employment and labor-force participation rates among older workers due to early retirement from work (Engelhardt 2012; von Nordheim 2004). Nevertheless, there is a general trend to prolong working life through a variety of flexible working practices in the majority of the developed nations, as the contents of this book will show.

Over the past two decades the conceptualization of work and retirement as opposite states among older workers has become obsolete in most developed countries (Cahill *et al*. 2013), and models conceived within the work/non-work dichotomy can no longer accommodate the new, creative forms of living that many men and especially women now aspire to (Everingham *et al*. 2007). One of the main consequences of this trend to prolong working life using alternative working practices has been the replacement of the concept of *trajectory* by that of *transition* to define the work–life cycle (Elder and Johnson 2003). Thus, a consensus has arisen among researchers that retirement is not a single event but rather a process that older individuals go through over a variable period of years (Marshall *et al*. 2001; Shultz and Wang 2011; Szinovacz 2003), with dozens of

6   C.-M. Alcover et al.

possible combinations of paid work and time out from the labor force (Pleau and Shauman 2013). Retirement, then, represents a longitudinal developmental process through which workers tend to reduce their psychological attachment to work and behaviorally withdraw from the workforce (Wang 2013; Wang *et al.* 2011). Above the age of 50 both men and women face a series of work-related, family, personal, financial and leisure events that condition their decisions to stay in the labor market and to seek alternatives to the conventional *full-time job* in order to prolong their activity beyond the normal retirement age.

This development has substantially altered the linearity of a long period in people's lives that is given over to work followed by definitive retirement and the passage to complete and irreversible labor-force withdrawal. Retirement from work has changed from a landmark event to a gradual process (Cahill *et al.* 2006b; Calvo *et al.* 2009; Vickerstaff 2007), or from total into partial retirement (Beehr and Bennett 2007). As underlined by Wang and Schultz (2012: 13), for many old workers 'retirement is no longer synonymous with the end of one's career'.

Diverse modalities of transitional or gradual retirement, including 'phased retirement', 'partial retirement', 'bridge employment' and 're-entry', are increasingly prevalent in older workers' lives today (Cahill *et al.* 2013).

'Phased retirement' refers to the alternative of working shorter hours for the same employer. 'Partial retirement' refers to a job change from a career job to a new full-time or part-time position (Kantarci and van Soest 2008). 'Bridge jobs' involve a change in employer and sometimes a switch from wage-and-salary work to self-employment (Cahill *et al.* 2013). Finally, 're-entry' into the labor force after retiring can come about in one of two ways (Cahill *et al.* 2011). It can be either (1) planned as a way to move out of career employment gradually by taking a break from full-time work before moving to another job, which may or may not be part-time; or (2) unplanned, acting as a fallback where an individual's standard of living in retirement fails to meet expectations, or as a way to reinforce or ensure retirement income in anticipation of future contingencies. In short, 're-entry' has now become relatively common, and as Shultz and Wang (2011: 171) recently noted, 'there are individuals now who retire multiple times throughout their lives'.

Though different forms of bridge employment and gradual retirement began to emerge in the 1990s (Doeringer 1990; Ruhm 1990, 1994), these transitions have become ever more complex in the twenty-first century as a consequence of the increasing 'negotiation' and 'de-institutionalization' of these options, with the result that workers and organizations now commonly agree the terms defining employment relations on a flexible, individual basis (Peterson and Murphy 2010; Phillipson 2002; Vickerstaff 2007). In short, the lives of people above the age of 50 have become less predictable (Henretta 2003), and variable, complex and contingent transition experiences lasting in some cases into an individual's seventies have come to define what was traditionally a clearly delineated stage in the life course of almost everyone.

To sum up, the available alternatives for the postponement of retirement labor-force re-entry tend to blur the work/non-work boundary and what it means to retire.

Introduction and overview 7

Conceptualization of bridge employment

The most common definition of bridge employment refers to jobs that follow career or full-time employment and precede complete labor-force withdrawal or retirement from work (Cahill *et al.* 2013; Feldman and Kim 2000; Shultz 2003a). Bridge employment alternatives may therefore be considered forms of retirement that prolong working life, allowing the term *full retirement* to be used to refer to final withdrawal from the workforce (Gobeski and Beehr 2009). The transitions characterizing bridge employment occur both within the individual's own profession and in other occupations, and they can take the form of (full- or part-time) salaried work, permanent or temporary jobs and self-employment (Beehr and Bennett 2007).

In short, bridge employment can be conceptualized in two primary ways (Gobeski and Beehr 2009; Wang *et al.* 2008), namely *career-consistent* bridge employment and *non-career* bridge employment. Bridge employment in the career field may occur either within the same organization as the career job or in a different organization where the older person works in the same occupation (Raymo *et al.* 2004). However, it is *non-career* bridge employment (i.e., bridge employment in a different field) that is most common among older workers, who usually accept lower pay and status in return for the flexibility of a bridge job (Feldman 1994; Shultz 2003b).

Bridge employment involving some form of self-employment appears to be the most common alternative as people grow older, because it allows greater freedom to satisfy needs like flexible working hours and personal autonomy, whereas salaried jobs tend to be more restrictive. This shows that entrepreneurial attitudes and behavior are in no way incompatible with old age (Davis 2003). The option of self-employment as a form of bridge working has positive consequences not only for older workers, but also for political leaders and employers, as it allows older workers to continue earning and paying social security dues and taxes, while providing organizations with the benefit of their knowledge, skills and experience via contingent agreements (Giandrea *et al.* 2008; Kim and DeVaney 2005; Zissimopoulos and Karoly 2009). In fact, the motivation and capacity to engage in a bridge job can be considered a measure of *work ability*, as Ilmarinen (2009a) defines this construct. *Work ability* describes the relation and balance between individual resources (health, competence, work values and attitudes, and motivation) and work demands (work arrangements, work load, work environment, co-workers and management or leadership) (Ilmarinen 2009b). In this sense, bridge employment can be considered a form of *work ability* that concerns the ability of older workers to maintain their employability as they age and beyond mandatory retirement ages. In sum, *work ability* may play an important role in the psychological analysis of the changing nature of retirement in the twenty-first century (Shultz and Wang 2011), and in the theoretical foundations of bridge employment as well.

It has become increasingly common in recent years for early retirees (i.e., those under 65 years of age) in countries like the United States and Canada to

8   C.-M. Alcover et al.

re-enter working life (Alley and Crimmins 2007; Armstrong-Stassen and Staats 2012). In this regard, the longitudinal data from the HRS reveal that approximately 15 percent of older North Americans who once had a full-time professional career re-enter the labor force after retiring (Cahill *et al.* 2011). Meanwhile, longitudinal data from a large Australian sample (Griffin *et al.* 2012) showed that a longer subjective life expectancy increases the odds that retirees return to paid work.

The rising popularity of bridge employment among older workers has been helped by certain changes in human resource management practices and the organization of the labor market (Henretta 2001; Saba and Guerin 2005), but are still underutilized by older workers in some European countries (Bredgaard and Tros 2006).

To begin with, ever fewer people work for a single employer throughout their working lives and ever more people are therefore likely to have undergone fluctuations in their earnings and/or periods without making social security contributions over the course of their working lives. As a consequence, levels of personal income and pensions make it necessary to go on working, or to opt against early retirement. In the second place, many organizations have begun to bolster their early retirement programs with partial pension systems and mixed structures allowing older workers to re-enter the labor market in temporary or part-time jobs if they wish or need to do so, at the same time as receiving early-retirement benefits. Finally, the variability of pension benefits encourages many older workers to prolong their working lives at least for a few years in jobs with short or intermittent working hours in order to maintain an expected (subjective) level of income and reduce the likelihood that the transition to retirement will involve a fall in their standard of living and quality of life (Topa *et al.* 2011). The data obtained from a study of this factor in the United States reveal that seven out of ten older workers expect to work full- or part-time after reaching the *normal* retirement age of 62 or 65 years (Taylor and Geldhauser 2007). Furthermore, the majority of these people do not view retirement as a one-off event but as the last phase of their working lives, in which they will move and change jobs several times before final retirement (Cahill *et al.* 2011).

According to Shultz's (2003a) model, bridge employment decisions are determined by individual attributes, contextual conditions and organizational factors. Prior research has shown that acceptance of bridge employment depends on numerous factors, including the perception of good health, age in the late fifties and early sixties, length of service to the employer, high job satisfaction, organizational and/or career commitment, the perception of being in possession of a high level of career competences and skills, the flexibility of working arrangements, a significant entrepreneurial bent, family background including a working partner and children or other dependants, the need to maintain a certain level of income beyond retirement age or make the requisite contributions to receive a later retirement pension, absence of defined benefits compensation and pension systems, economic perceived stress, and the wish to reduce the stress and workload inherent in a full-time job (see, for instance, Beehr and Bennett 2007; Cahill

Introduction and overview 9

et al. 2005; Davis 2003; Feldman 2007; Gobeski and Beehr 2009; Kim and Feldman 1998, 2000; Lim and Feldman 2003; Shacklock and Brunetto, 2011; Šimová 2010; von Bonsdorff *et al.* 2009; Wang *et al.* 2008; Weckerle and Shultz 1999; Zhan *et al.* 2013). In addition, a recently proposed model on the reasons why older adults are willing to work may be applied also to the motives to engage in bridge employment. Nakai and colleagues (2011) grouped mature job seekers into three clusters: *satisficers*, those who continued working primarily for economic and family reasons (basically males and married individuals); *free agents*, those who seek employment for personal satisfaction, learning opportunities and growth (more females and unmarried individuals); and *maximizers*, those who seek employment for a wide range of reasons (a larger proportion of females and poorly qualified individuals).

The decision to prolong working life may be further encouraged by interventions and programs aimed at ameliorating working conditions, particularly promoting greater opportunities to aged workers with respect to involvement in new organizational forms, training and learning new things at work (Villosio *et al.* 2008) and improving organizational perceptions of and attitudes to older workers and retirement (Zaniboni *et al.* 2010; Zappalà *et al.* 2008). However, other data indicate that the decision to forgo the potential benefits of extending working life gains ground when delayed retirement is perceived as being too long, and the health or enjoyment advantages of retiring earlier are perceived as greater (Bidewell *et al.* 2006; de Wind *et al.* 2013). In this regard, the concept of retirement unquestionably means many different things to different people (Sargent *et al.* 2011; Wang 2007), and older workers face an increasingly diverse range of experiences.

To sum up, data from the extensive surveys carried out in the United States over the last two decades show that more than half of the working population above the age of 60 has switched from a full-time job to one or other form of bridge employment, and this employment activity is likely to continue for several years beyond the age of 65. Only around 40 percent of heads of household definitively retire from their full-time jobs, while approximately half continue working part-time for a variable period and around a quarter of such retirees re-enter the labor market after retirement. Partial retirement is not common before the age of 62. However, it increases significantly among those aged between 62 and 67 and then tails off gradually. Even so, the presence of workers aged over 70 in different forms of bridge employment is becoming ever more usual (Bureau of Labor Statistics 2011). The experience of fluid, flexible employment over the course of a person's working life (in contrast to a static career within a single organization) may increase the desire to continue working until late in life and at the same time expand the range of flexible employment systems available to older workers (Alley and Crimmins 2007), benefiting both individuals and organizations, not to mention social security and benefits systems.

Bridge employment benefits

The use of bridge employment strategies and alternatives in different countries worldwide over the last two decades has generated important benefits for both individuals and organizations, including improvements in the quality of psychosocial life and life satisfaction in the period before and after retirement (Kim and Feldman 2000; Topa *et al.* 2009); enhanced job-related well-being and health as a result of the reduction in stress and workload resulting from a switch from full-time working to a job with shorter hours and less responsibility (Bennett *et al.* 2005); reduction of serious illness and functional limitations and improvements in the mental health of older workers (Jex *et al.* 2007; Zhan *et al.* 2009); enhanced autonomy and financial security and well-being in the period after retirement (Munnel and Sass 2008; Topa *et al.* 2011), especially when the retiree has dependent family members (Kim and Feldman 2000); decreases in the experience of age discrimination among older workers, as a result of flexible working arrangements made between them and organizations to the benefit of both parties (Beehr and Bowling 2002; Feldman 2007; Schalk 2010); and the development of flexible working arrangements that allow organizations to retain (and even attract) experienced, skilled workers who have reached the retirement age (Greller and Stroh 2003; Rau and Adams 2005). Lastly, while general evidence for the effects of gradual retirement on productivity remains scarce, the qualitative data suggest that older workers who remain in the labor force are typically well-motivated, highly skilled and productive (Kantarci and van Soest 2008).

A further benefit of bridge employment is to keep older workers of the baby-boomer generation active and productive in the labor force, thereby preventing negative outcomes and dysfunctions in terms of social security contributions and the risks for benefits systems that could arise in the event of mass retirement of large numbers of workers in a very short period (Alley and Crimmins 2007; Pengcharoen and Shultz 2010; Wang *et al.* 2008). Furthermore, bridge employment has the advantage at the beginning of the retirement transition process of ensuring the continuity of lifestyles and patterns (i.e., the balance between work, family life and leisure), preventing the sharp breaks and changes typical of conventional retirement and underpinning positive psychological outcomes associated with personal and social identity, perceptions of personal realization, role performance, entrepreneurial behaviors, etc. (Wang and Shultz 2010). These considerations have been accompanied in recent years by an increasing tendency for organizations to treat bridge employment as an important facet of human resources policy designed specifically for workers above the age of 50 (Rau and Adams 2005). In this regard, future research will be enormously important to facilitate the development by organizations of more effective recruitment strategies and practices designed to attract retired workers to bridge employment jobs through flexible, contingent arrangements that suit both parties, to the benefit of society as a whole (Wang and Shultz 2010).

These changes in retirement patterns have been called a 'new paradigm' (Clark and Mitchell 2005) and a 'redefinition' of retirement (Ulrich and Brott

Introduction and overview 11

2005), and they have been defined as the 'de-institutionalization' or 'individualization' of retirement (Moen and Altobelli 2007). They have also gained an increasing presence and importance in the lives of older workers in the United States, Canada, the United Kingdom, the countries of northern Europe, Australia and Japan. Experiences of this kind in countries like Spain, France and Italy, as well as the nations of central and southern Europe, remain relatively few, however, and bridge employment is still far from being the norm in retirement processes (Börsch-Supan *et al.* 2005; Topa *et al.* 2009, 2014). So, it will be relevant to understand the motivational determinants and goals related to work of later adulthood (de Lange *et al.* 2010), and identify the person characteristics, local work conditions and socio-cultural and economic conditions related to 'to-work goals', 'at-work goals' and 'to-retire goals' among older workers (Kanfer *et al.* 2013).

Workers' expectations and ability to plan ahead and decide the terms of their continued participation in work-life are of enormous importance to the expansion and generalization of gradual transitions between working life and full retirement. In this light, the existence of institutional, structural and legal restrictions and obstacles may have a significant inhibiting effect on bridge employment experiences in different countries (Raymo *et al.* 2010), with the consequent loss of potential benefits for workers, organizations and society in general.

Overview of the book

Our goal as editors has been to present the varieties of bridge employment experiences in different contexts. Thus, we have decided to offer an analysis organized through a geographical arrangement. Part I presents an overview of bridge employment in eight European countries, combining those with more experience in their implementation and development and those where the concept is still emerging. Part II presents an overview of bridge employment in North America by analyzing the situation in the United States and Canada, two of the countries with more experience in the use of modalities designed to extend working life. Part III offers an approach to bridge employment in the Asia-Pacific region, with two chapters on Australia and Japan, both countries that also have long experience in the implementation of these policies and practices. By doing so we pursue an open insight to enable readers to compare the diversity of situations and experiences about bridge employment and flexible transitions from work to retirement around the world.

The chapter by Kène Henkens and Hanna van Solinge analyzes the extent to which older adults in the Netherlands continue to participate actively in the labor market after they have retired, and what factors determine this engagement in paid work after retirement or bridge employment. Their analysis is based on data from the NIDI (Netherlands Interdisciplinary Demographic Institute) Work and Retirement Panel, an ongoing longitudinal survey of older workers (aged 50 and over) in the Netherlands and their partners that started in 2001. In summary, the authors show that, first, bridge employment is widespread among broad layers of

12 C.-M. *Alcover* et al.

retired employees and comes in many shapes and sizes. The second characteristic of bridge employment is the high degree of flexibility. Third, whereas bridge employment is most widespread among the better educated and among people in good health, it is by no means the sole preserve of these categories of employees. Finally, results shows that only a small minority took up bridge employment mainly for financial reasons. The authors conclude that the increasing numbers of people working during retirement years suggests that we are on the eve of a fundamental change of the way work and retirement are organized in old age, linked to a broader development where education, work and leisure are increasingly parallel careers instead of successive stages in the life course.

Meanwhile, Kerstin Isaksson, Gunn Johansson and Sofie Palm begin their chapter noting that Sweden and countries in the north of Europe generally have clearly higher rates employed in all age groups than the south of Europe. Their research aims to identify explanations of the specific employment patterns for older workers in the north of Europe and especially for older women using earlier research and national investigations. Earlier studies have shown a complex pattern of explanations based on societal factors, cultural values and norms, working conditions and individual preferences. They note that there is a need for theories to clarify the relationship between different antecedents leading to a decision to continue working or to retire. Interview data about retirement planning are also used as part of this chapter to shed some light on possible theoretical explanations at the individual level of Swedish older employees. The authors conclude that laws and cultural norms in Sweden are more supportive of later retirement than in many other countries generally. Legal changes made about ten years ago aimed to increase flexibility and postpone retirement and these seem to have been effective to some degree. Further obstacles appear to be workload and the working conditions of older employees with differences apparent between men and women. Finally, they present some recommendations for organizations by identifying some key elements in successful age management in the Swedish context.

Donatienne Desmette and Patricia Vendramin begin their chapter with evidence that, regarding the employment rate of the 55–64 population, it is well-known that, due to persistent early retirement policies, Belgium remains far below the level of 50 percent fixed by the Stockholm and Barcelona targets. Moreover, the activity rate of people aged 55–64 is quite close to the employment rate, and full (early) retirement or unemployment rather than bridge employment constitutes the prevalent reality for most people aged 55 and over. Building on this basis, the authors describe the Belgian contextual factors that frame workers' decisions regarding work and retirement. Government policies and programs related to (bridge) employment and pensions as well as socioeconomic trends of the aging workforce are analyzed. Next they examine, according to the multidimensional view of aging, how preferences and actual patterns of employment among older workers are related to organizational age, lifespan characteristics and psychosocial age. The authors conclude that the main reasons for the intention of working less or retiring earlier are tiredness, a need

Introduction and overview 13

for more time for the family or deteriorating health. Moreover, the results show that bridge employment, rather than full early retirement, was significantly predicted by perceived lower quality of life. They recognize that current part-time policies for older workers that have been implemented in Belgium should thus be reinforced rather than restricted. Nevertheless, alternative routes could also be considered with the aim of improving both older workers' quality of life and active aging issues in the Belgian context.

Traveling to the east-central region of Europe, Piotr Zientara offers an overview of bridging employment experiences in Poland, an EU Member State characterized by a very low employment rate of seniors and a deficit-laden (and, on current trends, unsustainable) pension system. In doing so, the study, drawing on findings from interviews conducted with 13 retirees, explores Poland-specific labor-market realities and highlights difficulties with ensuring that older people move flexibly from work to retirement. In particular, the chapter makes a case for prolonging the working lives of Poles and, at the same time, emphasizes the need for more flexible workplace arrangements so as to ensure more gradual transitions from work to retirement. The author hopes that, by shedding light on the experience of a post-communist country, his chapter will deepen our understanding of the processes at hand and stimulate further research.

Concerning a country in Southern Europe, the chapter by Carlos-María Alcover and Gabriela Topa begins by outlining the current salient features of Spain's socio-demographic context, in particular the marked aging of the population and the foreseeable rise in the dependency rate in the coming years, as well as the immediate impact of these trends on the labor market and retirement and pension systems. They then go on to look at the conditioning factors that affect work-life extension policies and practices, and the obstacles in the way of their adoption. In the third instance, they provide data on early and compulsory retirement in Spain in recent years, and a description of the legal alternatives available to those wishing to continue working, such as partial or flexible retirement. Finally, they sketch the current state of work-life extension in Spain, illustrating the scant possibilities available and experiences of voluntary working after retirement. The chapter ends with some conclusions and recommendations on the future of bridge employment and postponing retirement practices in the Spanish context.

Next, Emma Parry and Dianne Bown Wilson's chapter about bridge employment in the United Kingdom draws specifically on two pieces of research in order to examine people's experiences and attitudes toward careers and work as they approach and pass the state pension age: first, interviews and survey research conducted within five UK organizations looking at the career transitions made by older workers, including the drivers, barriers and support needed for these; and second, interviews with older workers from two UK financial services organizations, examining their motivation for career progression and the factors shaping this. Their chapter examines the results of these studies within the framework of the literature and secondary research in the United Kingdom in order to build a picture of bridge employment within the United Kingdom and

14   C.-M. Alcover et al.

how older workers' actual experiences and motivations relate to this concept. The chapter concludes by examining the implications of this research for the relevance of bridge employment within the UK context.

In their chapter, Marco Depolo and Franco Fraccaroli begin by remarking that in Italy, where a reform of the retirement system has just been approved, the raising of workers' average age is felt to be so urgent that the European Commission stated that Italian workers are soon to be the oldest workers in Europe because of the brand new reforms that oblige employees to exit later from the labor market. However, bridge employment has limited diffusion in Italy. Among the factors detailed are the normative feature, the characteristics of the labor market and the cultural aspect. The Italian labor market has been considered a 'jobs-for-life' one, with a smooth transition to retirement. In fact it may be noticed that a significant share of the working population experienced irregular patterns of labor market activity that consequently had a negative effect on their wages and pensions. In recent years this has been due also to collective dismissals and early retirement practices in large-firms, but it may worsen in the future. The chapter presents some case studies, underlining the specific success factor of the firms that experimented with forms of bridge employment and the factors that are potentially useful in different contexts. They conclude by remarking on the implications of two elements typical of the present Italian situation, i.e., the aging of active population and the modifications in the structure of the labor market due to the financial crisis (first of all, reduction of secure jobs, together with the increase of short-term jobs). The chapter ends by offering future prospects for bridge employment in Italy and their implications for organizations and workers.

The next chapter deals with the German context, which represents the strongest economy in Europe. Jürgen Deller and Leena Pundt begin by offering an outlook on the demographic situation in Germany and, specifically, on older workers. In past decades the situation of older workers in the German labor market has been characterized by a pattern of externalization through extensive early retirement. However, due to the financial and economic situation in Germany and the European Union, the pattern of integration and employability has now become focused on keeping workers in paid labor until the official retirement age in organizations. Next, the chapter introduces and discusses partial retirement policies and practices. It then quantifies the extent of work retirement in Germany followed by qualitative findings to better understand individual perspectives on work in retirement including prerequisites for post-retirement activities. A case study describes the business case of a pioneer company managed by and staffed with retirees that serves a traditional enterprise. The chapter concludes by recommending actions for organizations, society and politics as well as identifying relevant fields of research on flexible transitions to retirement in Germany.

Part II is dedicated to bridge employment in the North American context. The chapter by Mo Wang, Lee Thomas Penn, Agustina Bertone and Slaviana Stefanova focuses on aspects of bridge employment particular to the population of

Introduction and overview 15

the United States, the country with the most clearly defined models and most experience in the implementation of bridge employment practices. With the average age of the US population rising, individuals are increasingly continuing to work into retirement in the form of bridge employment. To begin this chapter, they present an overview of the types of bridge employment, followed by the prevalence and trends of bridge employment in the United States. Overall, the population of the United States is getting older and continuing to work past retirement age. They also suggest that not only is the number of individuals engaging in bridge employment increasing, but these individuals are also becoming more diverse. They then examine the antecedents of bridge employment for retirees from the United States, developing a new taxonomy of motives for bridge employment. In this taxonomy they differentiate three types of factors: *micro-level antecedents* (age, education, health, personality, cognitions about bridge employment, and individual motives as a proximal antecedent of bridge employment), *meso-level antecedents* (work environment and family) and *macro-level antecedents* (labor market and the economy and cultural norms). Next, they postulate a number of outcomes of bridge employment: financial well-being, physical health, psychological well-being, family outcomes and community and organizational impact. They end the chapter with an overview of future research directions on bridge employment and remarking that there is a lack of thorough research on demographic diversity and bridge employment.

Meanwhile, in her chapter on bridge employment in Canada, Tania Saba presents the major individual, organizational and governmental considerations in envisaging end-of-career from the perspective of introducing a viable strategy for active aging. First, she traces the history of how end-of-career management has been viewed in Quebec and Canada. She continues by presenting the underlying principles and motives behind end-of-career behaviors. Next she examines various end-of-career trajectories and describes the types of bridge jobs taken up by retiring Canadian workers and the frequency of this practice. The chapter ends with recommendations for the future, explaining the importance for employers, governments and older workers to link up their efforts in order to be able to assess the advantages and risks associated with bridge employment, thus promoting the employability of older workers and fostering active aging in the Canada context.

Finally, Part III is dedicated to bridge employment in the Asian-Pacific region. From Australia, Philip Taylor, Christopher McLoughlin and Catherine Earl begin their chapter by noting that bridge employment has increasingly become an area of interest but has usually been considered from the perspective of the employee. However, very little has been done to explore employer interest, willingness and benefits in the implementation of transition roles that promote bridge employment options, such as: flexible options, gradual and/or phased retirement work options and alternate bridge employment/jobs. The chapter is based on the 'Working Late' study conducted in Australia in 2010, which included a telephone survey of almost 600 employers in the State of Queensland. The employers consisted of private/for profit and public/government/not-for-profit medium and large organizations from

16   C.-M. Alcover et al.

all employment sectors, resulting in findings with state and national representativeness and generalizability. Despite bridge employment options being heavily promoted and endorsed by government and advocacy groups, the findings showed relatively weak interest in formal gradualist approaches to retirement compared with other potential approaches to workforce aging that are being widely applied. Private-sector employers showed less interest than public/not-for-profit employers and less than larger employers. They conclude that bridge employment is likely to be restricted to certain privileged segments of the labor force, offering 'gradualism' to some groups of workers while others will expect to work on full-time until such time as they exit entirely either due to illness or full retirement or some combination of the two. Finally, the authors compare the present situation with earlier conceptions of the retirement transition and offer perspectives on the implications for successful transitions into old age in Australia.

In their chapter on bridge jobs in Japan, Chikako Usui, Richard A. Colignon and Dan Rosen begin by noting that bridge jobs are increasingly relevant because Japan is one of the most rapidly aging societies in the world with one of the highest life expectancies and lowest birth rates, resulting in a shrinking population. Japan's stagnant economy and high unemployment rates have raised serious concerns about its ability to produce the output necessary to support the baby-boomer cohorts reaching retirement age. Further exacerbating the issue, the Japanese labor force is expected to shrink rather than to expand. One way to solve the problem is to keep healthy older workers in the labor force longer and reduce the burden on public pensions, health care and long-term care costs. To implement these policies, the Japanese government has reformed public pensions, raised the age of entitlement to full pension benefits to 65 and guided companies to retain workers at least until age 65. Starting April 1, 2013, corporations are required by law to provide bridge jobs until 65 or until workers become eligible for full pensions. The chapter examines how this new legislation affects companies of different sizes and different types of workers. The authors conclude that, although Japan has adopted measures of this type in preparation for baby boomers reaching the mandatory corporate retirement age of 60, the prolonged recession during the past two 'lost decades' has heightened worries about its ability to produce the output necessary to support the baby-boomer population. Demographic trends and economic performance have eroded the capacity to support life-long employment. These pressures have strained the key political relationship between government and large corporations.

In the concluding chapter, the editors weave the common themes from across the chapters in order to summarize the complex overview presented above. We identify commonalities and differences in bridge employment patterns through the experiences implemented in the countries included in this handbook. Next, we deal with conceptual issues and practical outcomes of bridge employment patterns in the different socio-economic realities and organizational and work contexts of the countries represented in this book. Finally, we offer an overview of future research and practical implications of bridge employment for the coming years.

Introduction and overview 17

Concluding remarks

Analysis of the multiple issues related to *age, work and retirement* is one of the major challenges facing social research today and it will remain so for some years to come (Alley and Crimmins 2007; Ekerdt 2010; Ilmarinen 2006; Kanfer *et al.* 2013; Shultz and Adams 2007; Truxillo and Fraccaroli 2013; Wang and Shultz 2010), in search of proposals for new strategies and systems to prolong activity in the workplace beyond the normal age of early or mandatory retirement and in pursuit of benefits for both workers and organizations, and for society as a whole (Alcover and Crego 2008; Cahill *et al.* 2013; Clayton 2010; Peiró *et al.* 2013; van der Heijden *et al.* 2008), particularly in times of economic recession (Beck 2013). This book offers a wide-ranging overview of international experiences, lessons learned, challenges and the future outlook for bridge employment, one of the most versatile and effective of the policies and practices so far designed to extend working life.

As described in the above overview, the chapters of this book provide a comprehensive summary of the literature on bridge employment and bring together experiences from all over the world, identifying opportunities, barriers and gaps in our existing knowledge and practice, and offering recommendations to address the issues and cope with future challenges in aging and work, and aging and careers. Each of the chapters also makes substantive and contextualized suggestions for public policy and organizational decision-makers to consider as they confront the potential problems and benefits inherent in late retirement practices. The authors' objective is to provide an overview of progress so far for the first time in the international literature and a roadmap to facilitate the implementation of bridge employment as a part of policies and practices designed to prolong working life, a priority challenge for workers, organizations and societies in the coming decades. We hope this book will be useful to a wide range of readers with an interest in the new concept of retirement and the alternatives available for the prolongation of working life associated with bridge employment. We also trust that its contents will be helpful for both researchers and practitioners in the fields of organizational behavior, labor market analysis, human resource management, career development and career counseling, occupational health, older workers' well-being and public policy administration. In short, we would like this book to be a *bridge* linking researchers, practitioners, workers, business, counselors, policy-makers and older people all over the world.

References

Alcover, C.M. and Crego, A. (2008) 'Modalidades de retiro laboral en Europa: Bienestar psicológico y factores psicosociales asociados' [Varieties of work retirement in Europe: Psychological well-being and associated psychosocial factors], *Revista de Psicología del Trabajo y de las Organizaciones*, 24: 277–82.

Alcover, C.M., Crego, A., Guglielmi, D. and Chiesa, R. (2012) 'Comparison between the Spanish and Italian early work retirement models: A cluster analysis approach', *Personnel Review*, 41: 380–403.

18 C.-M. Alcover et al.

Alley, D. and Crimmins, E. (2007) 'The demography of aging and work', in K.S. Shultz and G.A. Adams (eds.), *Aging and Work in the 21st Century*, Mahwah, NJ: Lawrence Erlbaum.

Armstrong-Stassen, M. and Staats, S. (2012) 'Gender differences in how retirees perceive factors influencing unretirement', *International Journal of Aging and Human Development*, 75: 45–69.

Beck, V. (2013) 'Employers' use of older workers in the recession', *Employee Relations*, 35: 257–71.

Beehr, T.A. and Bennett, M.M. (2007) 'Examining retirement from a multi-level perspective', in K.S. Shultz and G.A. Adams (eds.), *Aging and Work in the 21st Century*, Mahwah, NJ: Lawrence Erlbaum.

Beehr, T.A. and Bowling, N.A. (2002) 'Career issues facing older workers', in D.C. Feldman (ed.), *Work Careers: A Developmental Perspective*, San Francisco: Jossey-Bass.

Bender, K.A. (2012) 'An analysis of well-being in retirement: The role of pensions, health, and "voluntariness" of retirement', *Journal of Socio-Economics*, 41: 424–33.

Bennett, M.M., Beehr, T.A. and Lepisto, L.R. (2005) 'Working after retirement: predictors of bridge employment', paper presented at the annual meeting of the Society for Industrial and Organizational Psychology, Los Angeles, CA, April.

Bidewell, J., Griffin, B. and Hesketh, B. (2006) 'Timing of retirement: Including a delay discounting perspective in retirement models', *Journal of Vocational Behavior*, 68: 368–87.

Börsch-Supan, A. and Jürges, H. (eds.) (2005) *The Survey of Health, Aging, and Retirement in Europe: Methodology*, Mannheim: Mannheim Research Institute for the Economics of Aging.

Börsch-Supan, A., Brugiavini, A. and Croda, E. (2009) 'The role of institutions and health in European patterns of work and retirement', *Journal of European Social Policy*, 19: 341–58.

Börsch-Supan, A., Brugiavini, A., Jürges, H., Mackenbach, J., Siegrist, J. and Weber, G. (eds.) (2005) *Health, Aging and Retirement in Europe: First Results from the Survey of Health, Aging and Retirement in Europe*, Mannheim: Mannheim Research Institute for the Economics of Aging.

Bredgaard, T. and Tros, F. (2006) *Alternatives to Early Retirement? Flexibility and Security for Older Workers in the Netherlands, Denmark, Germany and Belgium*, ILP Innovating Labour Market Policies: Transitional Labour Markets and Flexicurity, Amsterdam, November 30–December 1, 2006. Online. Available at: www.resqre-search.org/uploaded_files/publications/bredgaard2.pdf (accessed August 30, 2013).

Bureau of Labor Statistics (2011) *Number of Jobs Held, Labor Marker Activity, and Earnings Growth among Younger Baby Boomers: Recent Results from a Longitudinal Survey*, Washington, DC: U.S. Department of Labor.

Cahill, K.E., Giandrea, M.D. and Quinn, J.F. (2005) *Are Traditional Retirements a Thing of the Past? New Evidence on Retirement Patterns and Bridge Jobs*, Bureau of Labor Statistics Working Papers, no. 384, Washington, DC: U.S. Department of Labor.

Cahill, K.E., Giandrea, M.D. and Quinn, J.F. (2006a) 'Retirement patterns from career employment', *The Gerontologist*, 46: 514–23.

Cahill, K.E., Giandrea, M.D. and Quinn, J.F. (2006b) *A Micro-level Analysis of Recent Increases in Labor Force Participation among Older Men*, Bureau of Labor Statistics Working Papers, no. 400, Washington, DC: U.S. Department of Labor.

Cahill, K.E., Giandrea, M.D. and Quinn, J.F. (2011) 'Reentering the labor force after retirement', *Monthly Labor Review*, June: 34–42.

Introduction and overview 19

Cahill, K.E., Giandrea, M.D. and Quinn, J.F. (2013) 'Bridge employment', in M. Wang (ed.), *The Oxford Handbook of Retirement*, Oxford: Oxford University Press.

Calvo, E., Haverstick, K. and Sass, S.A. (2009) 'Gradual retirement, sense of control, and retirees' happiness', *Research on Aging*, 31: 112–35.

Clark, R.L. and Mitchell, O.S. (eds.) (2005) *Reinventing the Retirement Paradigm*, New York: Oxford University Press.

Clayton, P.M. (2010) 'Working on: Choice or necessity?', in European Centre for the Development of Vocational Training (CEDEFOP), *Working and Aging: Emerging Theories and Empirical Perspectives*, Luxembourg: Publications Office of the European Union.

Davis, M.A. (2003) 'Factors related to bridge employment participation among private sector early retirees', *Journal of Vocational Behavior*, 63: 55–71.

de Lange, A.H., van Yperen, N.W., van der Heijden, B.I.J.M. and Bal, P.M. (2010) 'Dominant achievement goals of older workers and their relationship with motivation-related outcomes', *Journal of Vocational Behavior*, 77: 118–25.

Dendinger, V.M., Adams, G.A. and Jacobson, J.D. (2005) 'Reasons for working and their relationship to retirement attitudes, job satisfaction and occupational self-efficacy of bridge employees', *International Journal of Aging and Human Development*, 61: 21–35.

de Preter, H., van Looy, D., Mortelmans, D. and Denaeghel, K. (2013) 'Retirement timing in Europe: The influence of individual work and life factors', *Social Science Journal*, 50: 145–51.

de Wind, A., Geuskens, G.A., Reeuwijk, K.G., Westerman, M.J., Ybema, J.F., Burdorf, A., Bongers, P.M. and van der Beek, A.J. (2013) 'Pathways through which health influences early retirement: A qualitative study', *BMC Public Health*, 13: 292. Online. Available at: www.biomedcentral.com/1471-2458/13/292 (accessed August 30, 2013).

Doeringer, P.B. (1990) 'Economic security, labor market flexibility, and bridges to retirement', in P.B. Doeringer (ed.), *Bridges to Retirement*, Ithaca, NY: Cornell University ILR Press.

Dorn, D. and Sousa-Poza, A. (2007) *'Voluntary' and 'Involuntary' Early Retirement: An International Analysis*, IZA Discussion Paper no. 2714, Bonn: Forschungsinstitut zur Zukunft der Arbeit.

Ekerdt, D.J. (2010) 'Frontiers of research on work and retirement', *Journal of Gerontology, Social Sciences*, 65B: 69–80.

Elder, G. and Johnson, M. (2003) 'The life course and aging: Challenges, lessons and new directions', in R.R. Settersten (ed.), *Invitation to the Life Course*, New York: Baywood Publishing.

Engelhardt, H. (2012) 'Late careers in Europe: Effects of individual and institutional factors', *European Sociological Review*, 28: 550–63.

Everingham, C., Warner-Smith, P. and Byles, J. (2007) 'Transforming retirement: Rethinking models of retirement to accommodate the experience of women', *Women's Studies International Forum*, 30: 512–22.

Feldman, D.C. (1994) 'The decision to retire early: A review and conceptualization', *Academy of Management Review*, 19: 285–311.

Feldman, D.C. (2007) 'Career mobility and career stability among older workers', in K.S. Shultz and G.A. Adams (eds.), *Aging and Work in the 21st Century*, Mahwah, NJ: Lawrence Erlbaum.

Feldman, D.C. and Kim, S. (2000) 'Bridge employment during retirement: A field study

20 *C.-M. Alcover* et al.

of individual and organizational experiences with post-retirement employment', *Human Resource Planning*, 23: 14–26.

Giandrea, M.D., Cahill, K.E. and Quinn, J.F. (2008) *Self-employment Transitions among Older American Workers with Career Jobs*, Bureau of Labor Statistics Working Papers, no. 418, Washington, DC: U.S. Department of Labor.

Giandrea, M.D., Cahill, K.E. and Quinn, J.F. (2009) 'Bridge jobs: A comparison across cohorts', *Research on Aging*, 31: 549–76.

Gobeski, K.T. and Beehr, T.A. (2009) 'How retirees work: Predictors of different types of bridge employment', *Journal of Organizational Behavior*, 30: 401–25.

Greller, M.M. and Stroh, L.K. (2003) 'Extending work lives: Are current approaches tools or talismans?', in G.A. Adams and T.A. Beehr (eds.), *Retirement: Reasons, Processes, and Results*, New York: Springer.

Griffin, B., Hesketh, B. and Loh, V. (2012) 'The influence of subjective life expectancy on retirement transition and planning: A longitudinal study', *Journal of Vocational Behavior*, 81: 129–37.

Gruber, J. and Wise, D.A. (2005) *Social Security Programs and Retirement around the World: Fiscal Implications*, Working Paper 11290, Cambridge, MA: NBER.

Henretta, J.C. (2001) 'Work and retirement', in R.H. Binstock and L.K. George (eds.), *Handbook of Aging and Social Sciences*, San Diego, CA: Academic Press.

Henretta, J.C. (2003) 'The life course perspective in work and retirement', in R.R. Settersten (ed.), *Invitation to the Life Course*, New York: Baywood Publishing.

Hershey, D.A. and Henkens, K. (in press) 'Impact of different types of retirement transitions on perceived satisfaction with life', *The Gerontologist*, advanced access. Online. Available at: http://gerontologist.oxfordjournals.org/content/early/2013/02/18/geront. gnt006.abstract (accessed July 17, 2013).

Ilmarinen, J. (2006) *Towards a Longer Worklife: Aging and the Quality of Work Life in the European Union*, Helsinki: Finnish Institute of Occupational Health.

Ilmarinen, J. (2009a) 'Work ability: A comprehensive concept for occupational health research and prevention – Editorial', *Scandinavian Journal of Work, Environment & Health*, 35: 1–5.

Ilmarinen, J. (2009b) 'Aging and work: An international perspective', in S.J. Czaja and J. Sharit (eds.), *Aging and Work: Issues and Implications in a Changing Landscape*, Baltimore, MD: Johns Hopkins University Press.

Jex, S.M., Wang, M. and Zarubin, A. (2007) 'Aging and occupational health', in K.S. Shultz and G.A. Adams (eds.), *Aging and Work in the 21st Century*, Mahwah, NJ: Erlbaum.

Kanfer, R., Beier, M.E. and Ackerman, P.L. (2013) 'Goals and motivation related to work in later adulthood: An organizing framework', *European Journal of Work and Organizational*, 22: 253–64.

Kantarci, T. and van Soest, A. (2008) 'Gradual retirement: Preferences and limitations', *De Economist*, 156: 113–44.

Kim, H. and DeVaney, S.A. (2005) 'The selection of partial or full retirement by older workers', *Journal of Family and Economic Issues*, 26: 371–94.

Kim, S. and Feldman, D.C. (1998) 'Healthy, wealthy, or wise: Predicting actual acceptances of early retirement incentives at three points in time', *Personnel Psychology*, 51: 623–42.

Kim, S. and Feldman, D.C. (2000) 'Working in retirement: The antecedents of bridge employment and its consequences for quality of life in retirement', *Academy of Management Journal*, 43: 1195–210.

Komp, K., van Tilburg, T. and van Groenou, M.B. (2010) 'Paid work between age 60 and 70 years in Europe: A matter of socio-economic status?, *International Journal of Aging and Later Life*, 5: 45–75.

Kooij, D.T.A.M., De Lange, A.H., Jansen, P.G.W., Kanfer, R. and Dikkers, J.S.E. (2011) 'Age and work-related motives: Results of a meta-analysis', *Journal of Organizational Behavior*, 32: 197–225.

Lee, M.D., Martin, B., Sargent, L., Zikic, J., Vough, H. and Bataille, C. (2011) *Late Career and Retirement Trends among Baby Boomer Managers*, Montreal: Desautels Faculty of Management, McGill University.

Lim, V.K.G. and Feldman, D. (2003) 'The impact of time structure and time usage on willingness to retire and accept bridge employment', *International Journal of Human Resource Management*, 14: 1178–91.

Marshall, V.W., Clarke, P.J. and Ballantyne, P.J. (2001) 'Instability in the retirement transition', *Research on Aging*, 23: 379–409.

Moen, P. and Altobelli, J. (2007) 'Strategic selection as a retirement project: Will Americans develop hybrid arrangements?', in J.B. James and P. Wink (eds.), *Annual Review of Gerontology and Geriatrics, The Crown of Life: Dynamics of the Early Postretirement Period*, vol. 26, New York: Springer.

Munnell, A.H. and Sass, S.A. (2008) *Working Longer: The Solution to the Retirement Income Challenge*, Washington, DC: Brookings Institution Press.

Nakai, Y., Chang, B., Snell, A.F. and Fluckinger, C.D. (2011) 'Profiles of mature job seekers: Connecting needs and desires to work characteristics', *Journal of Organizational Behavior*, 32: 155–72.

Noone, J.H., O'Loughlin, K. and Kendig, H. (2013) 'Australian baby boomers retiring "early": Understanding the benefits of retirement preparation for involuntary and voluntary retirees', *Journal of Aging Studies*, 27: 207–17.

Peiró, J.M., Tordera, N. and Potočnic, K. (2013) 'Retirement practices in different countries', in M. Wang (ed.) *The Oxford Handbook of Retirement*, Oxford: Oxford University Press.

Pengcharoen, C. and Shultz, K.S. (2010) 'The influences on bridge employments decisions', *International Journal of Manpower*, 31: 322–36.

Peterson, C.L. and Murphy, G. (2010) 'Transition from the labor market: Older workers and retirement', *International Journal of Health Services*, 40: 609–27.

Phillipson, C. (2002) *Transitions from Work to Retirement: Developing a New Social Contract*, Bristol: The Policy Press.

Phillipson, C. and Smith, A. (2005) *Extending Working Life: A Review of the Research Literature*, Research Report No. 299, Leeds: Corporate Document Services, Department for Work and Pensions. Online. Available at: www.keele.ac.uk/csg/downloads/researchreports/Extending%20working%20life.pdf (accessed July 25, 2013).

Pleau, R.L. (2010) 'Gender differences in postretirement employment', *Research on Aging*, 32: 267–303.

Pleau, R.L. and Shauman, K. (2013) 'Trends and correlates of post-retirement employment, 1977–2009', *Human Relations*, 66: 113–41.

Quinn, J.F. (2010) 'Work, retirement, and the encore career: Elders and the future of the American workforce', *Generations: Journal of the American Society on Aging*, fall: 45–55.

Rau, B.L. and Adams, G.A. (2005) 'Attracting retirees to apply: Desired organizational characteristics of bridge employment', *Journal of Organizational Behavior*, 26: 649–60.

22 *C.-M. Alcover* et al.

Raymo, J.M., Liang, J., Kobayashi, E., Sugihara, Y. and Fukaya, T. (2009) 'Work, health, and family at older ages in Japan', *Research on Aging*, 31: 180–206.

Raymo, J.M., Liang, J., Sugisawa, H., Kobayashi, E. and Sugihara, Y. (2004) 'Work at older ages in Japan: Variation by gender and employment status', *Journal of Gerontology: Psychological Sciences and Social Sciences*, 59B: S154–63.

Raymo, J.M., Warren, J.R., Sweeney, M.M., Hauser, R.M. and Ho, J.-H. (2010) 'Later-life employment preferences and outcomes: The role of midlife work experiences', *Research on Aging*, 32: 419–66.

Ruhm, C.J. (1990) 'Career jobs, bridge employment, and retirement', in P.B. Doeringer (ed.), *Bridges to Retirement*, Ithaca, NY: Cornell University ILR Press.

Ruhm, C.J. (1994) 'Bridge employment and job stopping: Evidence from the Harris/Commonwealth Fund Survey', *Journal of Aging and Social Policy*, 6: 73–99.

Saba, T. and Guerin, G. (2005) 'Extending employment beyond retirement age: The case of health care managers in Quebec', *Public Personnel Management*, 34: 195–213.

Sargent, L.D., Bataille, C.D., Vough, H.C. and Lee, M.D. (2011) 'Metaphors for retirement: Unshackled from schedules', *Journal of Vocational Behavior*, 79: 315–24.

Schalk, R. (2010) 'Matching individual and organization needs to enable longer working lives', in European Centre for the Development of Vocational Training (CEDEFOP), *Working and Aging: Emerging Theories and Empirical Perspectives*, Luxembourg: Publications Office of the European Union.

Schalk, R. *et al.* (2010) 'Moving European research on work and aging forward: Overview and agenda', *European Journal of Work and Organizational Psychology*, 19: 76–101.

Shacklock, K. and Brunetto, Y. (2011) 'A model of older workers' intentions to continue working', *Personnel Review*, 40: 252–74.

Shimizutani, S. (2011) 'A new anatomy of the retirement process in Japan', *Japan and the World Economy*, 23: 141–52.

Shultz, K.S. (2003a) 'Bridge employment: Work after retirement', in G.A. Adams and T.A. Beehr (eds.), *Retirement: Reasons, Processes, and Results*, New York: Springer.

Shultz, K.S. (2003b) 'Work related attitudes of naval officers before and after retirement', *International Journal of Aging and Human Development*, 57: 259–74.

Shultz, K.S. and Adams, G.A. (2007) 'In search of a unifying paradigm for understanding aging and work in the 21st century', in K.S. Shultz and G.A. Adams (eds.), *Aging and Work in the 21st Century*, Mahwah, NJ: Lawrence Erlbaum.

Shultz, K.S. and Wang, M. (2011) 'Psychological perspectives on the changing nature of retirement', *American Psychologist*, 66: 170–9.

Šimová, Z. (2010) 'To work or not to work: Motivation for work after reaching retirement age', in European Centre for the Development of Vocational Training (CEDEFOP), *Working and Aging: Emerging Theories and Empirical Perspectives*, Luxembourg: Publications Office of the European Union.

Szinovacz, M.E. (2003) 'Contexts and pathways: Retirement as institution, process, and experience', in G.E. Adams and T.A. Beehr (eds.), *Retirement: Reasons, Processes, and Outcomes*, New York: Springer.

Taylor, M.A. and Geldhauser, H.A. (2007) 'Low-income older workers', in K.S. Shultz and G.A. Adams (eds.), *Aging and Work in the 21st Century*, Mahwah, NJ: Lawrence Erlbaum.

Topa, G., Alcover, C.M., Moriano, J.A. and Depolo, M. (2014) 'Bridge employment quality and its impact in retirement: A structural equation model with SHARE panel data', *Economic and Industrial Democracy*, 35.

Topa, G., Depolo, M., Moriano, J.A. and Morales, J.F. (2009) 'Empleo puente y bienestar personal de los jubilados: Un modelo de ecuaciones estructurales con una muestra europea probabilística' [Bridge employment and retirees' personal well-being: A structural equation model with a European probabilistic sample], *Psicothema*, 21: 280–7.

Topa, G., Moriano, J.A., Depolo, M., Alcover, C.M. and Moreno, A. (2011) 'Retirement and wealth relationships: Meta-analysis and SEM', *Research on Aging*, 33: 501–28.

Truxillo, D.M. and Fraccaroli, F. (2013) 'Research themes on age and work: Introduction to the Special Issue', *European Journal of Work and Organizational Psychology*, 22: 249–52.

Ulrich, L.B. and Brott, P.E. (2005) 'Older workers and bridge employment: Redefining retirement', *Journal of Employment Counseling*, 42: 159–70.

United Nations (2011) *World Population Prospects: The 2010 Revision, Highlights and Advanced Tables*, Working Paper no. ESA/WP 220, New York: UN, Department of Economic and Social Affairs, Population Division.

van der Heijden, B.I.J.M., Schalk, R. and van Veldhoven, M.J.P.M. (2008) 'Aging and careers: European research on long-term career development and early retirement', *Career Development International*, 13: 85–94.

Vickerstaff, S. (2007) 'What do older workers want? Gradual retirement?', *Social & Public Policy Review*, 1: 1–13.

Villosio, C., Di Pierro, D., Giordanengo, A., Pasqua, P. and Richiardi, M. (2008) *Working Conditions of an Aging Workforce*, Dublin: European Foundation for the Improvement of Living and Working Conditions.

von Bonsdorff, M.E., Shultz, K.E., Leskinen, E. and Tansky, J. (2009) 'The choice between retirement and bridge employment: A continuity theory and life course perspective', *International Journal of Aging and Human Development*, 69: 79–100.

von Nordheim, F. (2004) 'Responding well to the challenge of an ageing and shrinking workforce: European Union policies in support of member state efforts to retain, reinforce and re-integrate older workers in employment', *Social Policy and Society*, 3: 145–53.

Wang, M. (2007) 'Profiling retirees in the retirement transition and adjustment process: Examining the longitudinal change patterns of retirees' psychological well-being', *Journal of Applied Psychology*, 92: 455–74.

Wang, M. (2013) 'Retirement: An introduction and overview of the Handbook', in M. Wang (ed.), *The Oxford Handbook of Retirement*, Oxford: Oxford University Press.

Wang, M. and Shultz, K.S. (2010) 'Employee retirement: A review and recommendations for future investigation', *Journal of Management*, 36: 172–206.

Wang, M., Adams, G.A., Beehr, T.A. and Shultz, K.S. (2009) 'Career issues at the end of one's career: Bridge employment and retirement', in S.G. Baugh and S.E. Sullivan (eds.), *Maintaining Focus, Energy, and Options over the Life Span*, Charlotte, NC: Information Age Publishing.

Wang, M., Henkens, K. and van Solinge, H. (2011) 'Retirement adjustment: A review of theoretical and empirical advancements', *American Psychologist*, 66: 204–13.

Wang, M., Olson, D.A. and Shultz, K.S. (2012) *Mid and Late Career Issues: An Integrative Perspective*, London: Routledge.

Wang, M., Zhan, Y., Liu, S. and Shultz, K.S. (2008) 'Antecedents of bridge employment: A longitudinal investigation', *Journal of Applied Psychology*, 93: 818–30.

Weckerle, J.R. and Shultz, K.S. (1999) 'Influences on the bridge employment decision among older U.S.A. workers', *Journal of Occupational and Organizational Psychology*, 72: 317–30.

24 *C.-M. Alcover* et al.

Zaniboni, S., Sarchielli, G. and Fraccaroli, F. (2010) 'How are psychosocial factors related to retirement intentions?', *International Journal of Manpower*, 31: 271–85.

Zappalà, S., Depolo, M., Fraccaroli, F., Guglielmi, D. and Sarchielli, G. (2008) 'Postponing job retirement? Psychosocial influences on the preference for early or late retirement', *Career Development International*, 13: 150–67.

Zhan, Y., Wang, M., Liu, S. and Shultz, K.S. (2009) 'Bridge employment and retirees' health: A longitudinal investigation', *Journal of Occupational Health Psychology*, 14: 374–89.

Zhan, Y., Wang, M. and Yao, X. (2013) 'Domain specific effects of commitment on bridge employment decisions: The moderating role of economic stress', *European Journal of Work and Organizational Psychology*, 22: 362–75.

Zissimopoulos, J.M. and Karoly, L.A. (2009) 'Labor-force dynamics at older ages: Movements into self-employment for workers and non-workers', *Research on Aging*, 31: 89–111.

Part I

Bridge employment in Europe

2 Bridge employment in the Netherlands

Who, what and why?

Kène Henkens and Hanna van Solinge

Extending working lives was one of the key objectives of the so-called Lisbon strategy in 2000 and still is an integral part of the European Employment Strategy. It has also been seen by successive Dutch cabinets as part of the answer to the aging of the labor market and the challenge of keeping the social welfare state affordable. The prolongation of working life after retirement is one example of how this policy objective can be realized. For society at large, the willingness of experienced older adults to work beyond retirement age provides a valuable resource. The key to capitalizing on this resource is to understand older workers' work-retirement decisions. In this chapter, the focus is on the Netherlands. We will examine the extent to which older adults in the Netherlands continue to participate actively in the labor market after they have retired, and what factors determine this engagement in paid work after retirement.

A growing number of older adults engage in some form of transitional employment between their career employment and complete labor-force withdrawal. Cahill *et al.* (2006), for example, found that about 60 percent of older workers in the United States moved first to some form of 'bridge employment' instead of directly out of the workforce. Exact definitions of bridge employment tend to vary across studies. Wang *et al.* (2008), for example, define bridge employment as employment (either stable or temporary) after *full-time* employment ends and before permanent retirement begins. We define bridge employment as working for pay, either as an employee or self-employed, and for at least one hour a week, after retirement from the main career job. There are similarities with part-time or phased retirement in that bridge employment is often part-time. The main difference is that bridge employment is generally in new jobs with a new employer or in a new occupation or industry (Cahill *et al.* 2006). As a rule, bridge employees in the Netherlands are eligible for any form of regular retirement income.

The structure of this chapter is as follows. We will start with a section on the institutional context of retirement in the Netherlands. This is highly relevant, since this context shapes the opportunities and constraints people face in making choices regarding work and retirement. The second section deals with the process of retirement, and more particularly with the question of how common it is in the Netherlands to re-enter the labor market after retirement. To what extent

28　*K. Henkens and H. van Solinge*

does retirement mean that people actually withdraw from the labor market? The third focuses on *who* decides to embark on a new career after retirement. We will examine specifically whether particular socio-economic categories are over-represented among those who do and whether this is in any way related to the nature of the retirement process. It may well be, for example, that workers who were forced to take early retirement for whatever reason are more inclined to extend their working lives than those who did so voluntarily. In the fourth section, we will address what bridge employment actually entails. Do pensioners opt for part-time jobs with a short working week that are closely related to the work they used to do, or is there little connection with their former job? Do older adults use this opportunity to give a new direction to their career? In the fifth section, we will seek to discover what drives people to continue to participate in the labor market after they retire. We will focus on the reasons post-retirement workers themselves give for continuing to work. This may indicate whether bridge employment is driven primarily by financial or extrinsic motives, or whether intrinsic factors, such as the nature of the job, play a more important role.

This chapter is based on data from the NIDI Work and Retirement Panel, an ongoing longitudinal survey of older workers (50 years and over) in the Netherlands and their partners that started in 2001. Respondents were followed over a period of ten years and were questioned in 2001, 2006 and 2011 (see Appendix 2.1 for more information on the data). The longitudinal character of this study provides the opportunity to follow older workers in the transition to retirement and study participation in bridge employment after leaving the career job.

Retirement in the Netherlands: the changing institutional context

In the Netherlands, state pensions for the over-65s (AOW) were introduced in 1957. Under the AOW, every resident of the Netherlands was entitled to a basic pension upon reaching the age of 65. The age criterion of 65 years was in line with the age limit of the disability legislation. People were not obliged to stop working; the benefits were provided on the basis of a pay-as-you-go system. Whereas the AOW was designed as a basic pension, the elderly could not live on the pension alone. As a result, as many as 20 percent of men over the age of 65 were still active in the labor market in 1960. The pension benefit was raised to the subsistence level in 1965. In 1985 the right to a state pension was individualized, also giving married women who had not participated in the labor force the right to an AOW benefit (Smolenaars 2000).

More often than not, workers did not remain in work until the official retirement age of 65 years. Many older workers withdrew from the labor market prematurely due to personal circumstances (e.g., poor health) or external circumstances, such as business close-downs. Until the mid-1970s, the period between early retirement and the moment at which people were entitled to a state pension was generally tided over with the aid of disability or unemployment

Bridge employment in the Netherlands 29

benefits, which served as de facto early retirement schemes. When the Dutch economy slipped into a recession following the 1973 oil crisis, unemployment rose rapidly, in particular among young people. The trade unions introduced the idea of improving the employment opportunities of young people by stimulating the early retirement of older workers. The idea was that this would serve two objectives: voluntary early retirement would allow older workers, who were no longer able to meet the changing requirements of their jobs, to make way for young job-seekers. The first experiments with voluntary early retirement (VUT) were carried out in 1976 in the education sector and construction industry. Soon after the experiments had begun, it became clear that the early retirement arrangements could not be reversed easily, since expectations had been raised. During subsequent collective bargaining negotiations, early retirement schemes were included as a standard term of employment by almost all branches of industry (Van Koningsveld and Van Ginneken 1988). The first schemes offered 63- and 64-year-olds the possibility of leaving the workforce before actual retirement age. About one-quarter of the eligible employees seized the opportunity to retire early (Huizinga 1977). This proportion has increased steadily over the years, however, and the age at which people are able to withdraw from the labor force has dropped. In the 1990s, more than 300 different early retirement schemes existed in the Netherlands (SZW 1995). These schemes were characterized by quite favorable financial conditions and relatively little variation between companies and organizations, both in the public and in the private sectors (Van Dalen and Henkens 2002). Most Dutch firms used a fixed early retirement age (usually around 60), after which the employees were able to leave the labor force. Replacement rates were generally around 80 percent of the gross wage. Early retirement benefits bridged the period between the cessation of work and entitlement to a state and supplementary pension. Payment of pension contributions and other social insurance contributions continued during the early retirement period, leaving the pension to which retirees were entitled at age 65 largely unaffected. The system was based on pay-as-you-go financing.

From the mid-1990s, most existing VUT schemes were changed into flexible early retirement (FER) arrangements because the system was becoming unaffordable due to the high participation rate combined with the financing method. At the same time, the trend toward ever earlier retirement inevitably had to be reversed in order to ensure a sufficient supply of labor in the future. The FER system was collective and participation compulsory. Pension entitlements were earned on an individual basis, however. Early retirement benefits were directly related to the individual employee's employment history and the contributions paid. The shorter the 'pension career', the lower the early retirement benefits. The FER system was based on a standard early retirement age (usually around 62, which is 1–2 years later than in the VUT schemes) but offered employees flexibility in choosing the age at which they wished to retire and – through additional savings – the level of benefits to be received. Employees with a complete pension history (based on 40 years of contributions) who left the labor force at this standard early retirement age received between 70 and 80 percent of their gross wages. Shorter or broken histories implied lower benefits. Employees were further entitled to stop earlier or later than this standard early retirement age, in which case the benefits were lower or higher respectively. These changes led to higher labor participation among 50- to 64-year-olds and a slight increase in the average age at retirement (Corpeleijn 2005; Siermann and Dirven 2005).

From January 1, 2006, the possibilities of retiring before the age of 65 have been greatly reduced for employees born after January 1, 1950. Pension schemes are no longer allowed to include a bridging pension and pension rights have to be based on a retirement age of 65 years. Tax deductibility of early retirement arrangements was also abolished with effect from January 1, 2006. These changes mark the end of collective early retirement schemes.

In 2012 new legislation was approved by both houses of parliament: the age at which people are eligible for a public pension will be increased gradually to age 67 by 2023 and will be linked to the development of the life expectancy after 2023.

The process of retirement and bridge employment

Traditionally, retirement has been thought of as an abrupt and complete discontinuation of paid employment in later life. Retirement today, however, can be characterized as a process that can take multiple forms (Beehr and Bennett 2007). Many older adults engage in some form of paid employment between their career employment and complete labor-force withdrawal. Dutch national statistics reveal that working for pay after retirement has gained importance in the Netherlands. Van Dalen *et al.* (2009), using data from the Labor Force Survey (LFS) for the period 2002–2007, show that in 2007 23 percent of Dutch older adults receiving some form of retirement pension were active in paid labor for at least one hour a week. Five years earlier, in 2002, this was only 16 percent. These national statistics provide only limited insight into the determinants of bridge employment as well as dynamics with regard to post-retirement work. In the remaining of this chapter, we will present data from the NIDI Work and Retirement Panel, an ongoing longitudinal study on work and retirement behavior. The longitudinal character of this study provides the opportunity to follow older workers in the transition to retirement and study participation in bridge employment after leaving the career job.

Bridge employment over the life course

Figure 2.1 provides a picture of the process of retirement of this cohort of older workers born between 1936 and 1951 and the role of bridge employment in this respect. The figure shows – for all participants that participated in all study waves – the relationship to the labor market in 2011. The figures have been broken down by age. The youngest participants were 60 years old in 2011. Whereas a majority of this youngest cohort still worked in their career job in

Bridge employment in the Netherlands 31

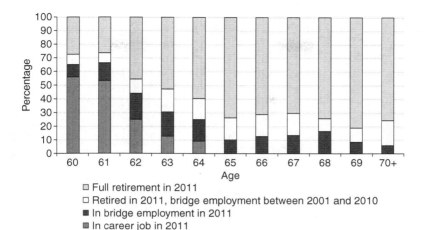

Figure 2.1 Relationship to the labor market in 2011 by age (N = 1,528).

2011 (dark grey bars at the bottom), this percentage is seen to drop rapidly for older cohorts. This has to do with the fact that the majority of the participants in the study had access to relatively generous early retirement schemes from age 61–62 onwards. Less than one in ten 64-year-old participants had *not* made use of the possibility to retire early and were still in their career job. As shown by the black and white sections of the bars in the figure, retirement does not necessarily mean the cessation of paid work. The black section refers to those who transitioned to bridge employment and still had a job at the time of the survey in 2011; the white section refers to those who had a bridge job after retirement but have since dropped out of the workforce. The upper section of the bars gives the percentage of older workers who did not engage in any form of paid work after retirement.

The figure provides an insight into the retirement process of this generation of older workers. Interestingly, many of those who took up a bridge job retired from their career job long before they reached official retirement age (65 years). Figure 2.1 also shows that the degree to which people extended their working lives differs considerably. For some, bridge employment constitutes a 'short-term experience' in their transition to full-time retirement, whereas for others bridge employment is a more substantial period of their post-retirement life. Roughly one-third of the 63-year-old participants, for example, was engaged in bridge employment after retirement, but no less than half of them stopped working altogether before or at the age of 63. Others, however, continued working for some length of time and the state pension age of 65 was hardly an obstacle for them to remain active in the workforce. In 2011 more than 10 percent of the 65- to 69-year-olds participated in some form of bridge employment.

32   K. Henkens and H. van Solinge

Finding a bridge job: not everyone is successful

The manner in which older workers make the transition to bridge employment differs considerably. Whereas some choose to retire – whether early or not – with the specific aim of starting a second career or taking up bridge employment, others may not come up with the idea of doing so until they have actually stopped working for a while. In the latter case, they may have regretted their decision to retire as they came to realize that they missed certain aspects of their working lives. Alternatively, it may take a while before older workers find new employment. In the 2011 survey, we asked those respondents who had found a bridge job for more detailed information on the nature of the process of finding new employment opportunities. Whereas four out of ten older workers who had opted for bridge employment said the transition had been virtually seamless, most re-entrants had first taken time out. Almost a quarter embarked on a new job after at least a year without work. Our study did not offer the opportunity to look into the reasons for this time-out, but it may well have been the result of obstacles encountered in the labor market and difficulties in finding a new job. This is also borne out by the fact that – aside from those who did start anew – there is a category of elderly who did not succeed in finding new paid employment, despite their efforts to do so. Seven percent of all retired employees made an effort to find bridge employment but didn't succeed. Table 2.1 shows employees' interest in finding paid work after retirement, broken down by birth cohort. Each cohort spans two years. Although we need to be cautious when interpreting the results for the youngest and oldest cohorts, the figures suggest that the younger cohorts are more interested in post-retirement work than the older cohorts. We see, for example, that a large majority (70 percent) of the 1942–1943 cohort made no effort at all to find a job, and that only one-quarter of this cohort re-entered the labor market. Looking at the 1948–1949 cohort, we see that almost 40 percent started anew and that another 9 percent tried to find bridge employment, but to no avail. Another interesting finding is the large percentage

Table 2.1 Interest in finding work after retirement, by cohort (N = 1,310 retired employees)

	Successful in finding work: bridge employees (%)	Interested in bridge job: not successful in finding work (%)	Not interested in bridge job (%)	Total (%)	Number
1936–1941	19	4	77	100	110
1942–1943	26	4	70	100	200
1944–1945	25	5	70	100	257
1946–1947	33	8	59	100	391
1948–1949	39	9	52	100	296
1950–1951	39	24	37	100	83
Total	31	7	62	100	1,310

of people in the youngest cohort (born in 1950–1951) – almost one-quarter of those who retired early – who went in search of work but didn't succeed. When comparing those who went in search of a job but didn't find one with those who did succeed in doing so, we see that women, divorced and single people, the less-educated and people who lost their jobs involuntarily due to restructuring were more highly represented among the former group.

Older workers in bridge employment: who are they?

The previous section has shown that post-career transitions into bridge employment are increasingly common in the Netherlands. In this section we will have a closer look at these bridge employees. We will examine the extent to which the socio-demographic characteristics of older workers who opted for bridge employment differ from those of people who withdraw from the labor force entirely. Special attention will be given to human capital and related factors such as education and health. Older adults' household situation will also be addressed. In the second part of this section, we will examine the relationship between bridge employment and characteristics of the retirement process. In previous studies on the same data (Van Solinge and Henkens 2007), we found that involuntary retirement and retirement at a relatively young age were widely reported in the period between 1995 and 2006. Here we will look into the question of whether voluntariness and timing of retirement are related to successful re-entry into the workforce.

Characteristics of people who opted for bridge employment

Human capital is a key factor in explaining labor-force choices and opportunities. In general, chances in the labor market are greater for individuals that have greater access to human capital (Becker 2009). The amount of human capital in terms of education and experience may also influence the degree to which re-entering the workforce after retirement is an attractive option as well as the older adult's chances of finding work (Ruhm 1990).

Figure 2.2 shows the percentage of older workers who re-entered the labor force after retirement, broken down by educational attainment and sex. What immediately comes to the fore in this figure is that men appear to be more work-oriented following retirement than women. This difference was particularly marked among those with lower and medium levels of education. Whereas the percentage of women with a lower or medium level of education who worked beyond retirement stood at 15, the percentage of men was twice as high. The difference between more highly educated men (42 percent of re-entrants into the labor market) and women (33 percent of re-entrants) was not as large. Figure 2.2 also shows that working beyond retirement is by no means the sole preserve of the higher levels of education, at least in the case of men; it was also widespread among men with at most a lower vocational education.

Another important factor that has been found to have a strong influence on the probability of finding a job and the ability to work is health (Crimmins *et al.*

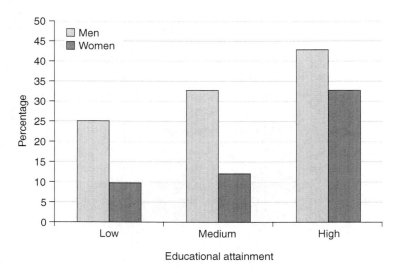

Figure 2.2 Probability of taking up bridge employment by level of education and sex (N = 1,310 retired employees).

1999). People who have health problems are more likely to withdraw from the labor market and are expected to be less inclined – and able – to re-enter the labor market after early retirement, even if the job were more flexible and less taxing than the work they used to do (Pond *et al.* 2010).

Figure 2.3 shows the relationship between health status (as perceived by the older adults themselves) in 2001 and bridge employment after retirement. Although we can say in general that healthy seniors are more likely to re-enter the workforce than those who are in poorer health, more than one in five older adults who were in poor or bad health participated in bridge employment. It may well be that bridge employment offers this group of older workers the possibility to extend their working lives precisely because the employment conditions can be more easily adapted to their health impairments. The pattern shown in Figure 2.3 is very similar to the pattern we see when we take into consideration the perceived state of health in 2006 and 2011 rather than in 2001. Here, too, we see that many people who perceive their health as being poor continue working beyond retirement (not shown in figure).

There is wide evidence that decisions relating to early retirement are also strongly influenced by non-work-related factors. Particularly the partner seems important in this respect (Denaeghel *et al.* 2011; Smith and Moen 1998). Partners often discourage older workers from extending their working lives and even encourage them to retire early (Henkens and Van Solinge 2002). Kim and Feldman (2000) have studied the role of the partner in the bridge employment decision. They argued that one of the main discontinuities associated with full retirement is the lack of social interaction with others. For married older

Bridge employment in the Netherlands 35

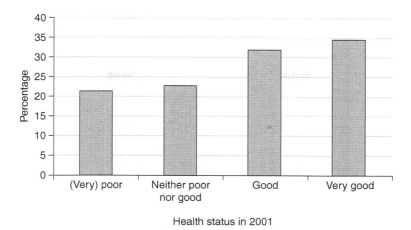

Figure 2.3 Probability of taking up bridge employment by health status (N=1,310 retired employees).

workers, social interaction with the spouse can at least partially substitute for continued interaction with colleagues; for unmarried workers bridge employment is likely to be more critical in maintaining social contacts with others. Older workers without a partner may therefore be more likely to continue in bridge employment. One might therefore expect bridge employment to be far more widespread among unmarried persons, because of the opportunities for social integration offered by a job, or out of financial necessity (which would be particularly relevant to the divorced), yet the contrary appeared to be the case (at least for men). Figure 2.4 shows that bridge employment was much more

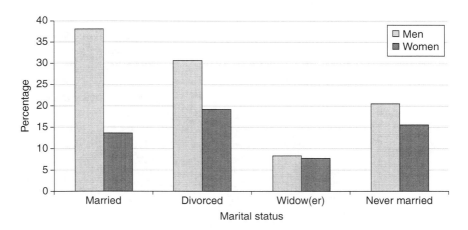

Figure 2.4 Probability of taking up bridge employment by sex and marital status (N=1,310 retired employees).

36   K. Henkens and H. van Solinge

common among married men than among all the other categories distinguished. This pattern was not found among women: bridge employment was most common among women who were divorced.

Characteristics of the retirement process: timing and degree of choice

For many employees, retirement will be voluntary in the sense that they have been preparing for this transition for many years (Adams and Rau 2011). A substantial number of employees are, however, 'forced' to leave the labor force long before the mandatory retirement age (Dorn and Sousa-Poza 2010; Szinovacz and Davey 2005). As a result, for many employees retirement will take place much earlier in their life course than they had initially planned. The feeling that they have no control over the transition into retirement, or that retirement has taken place 'too early', is expected to encourage employees to engage in bridge employment. Whether they actually succeed in finding work depends in part on their chances in the labor market. And whereas these chances tend to be slim for people over the age of 50 (Dennis and Thomas 2007; Taylor *et al.* 2010), this may vary considerably from one individual to the next. In this section we will examine the degree to which three factors influence the probability of entering bridge employment. We will first examine the age at which people leave their career job and whether or not this was a voluntary decision. Another factor we will address is the influence of how older workers perceive their own labor-market opportunities.

Given today's debate about extending working life, one might almost forget that retirement well before the age of 60 used to be no exception in the Netherlands (see also Appendix 2.1). Almost 30 percent of the participants in the study retired at age 58 or younger; 46 percent at age 60 or younger. Almost half of the 'very young retirees' (age 58 or younger) opted for bridge employment. Among those who retired substantially later (at age 62 or older), just over 20 percent re-entered the labor market (Figure 2.5). Among women, the age at retirement had little effect on whether or not they entered bridge employment. This can probably be explained by the fact that women – among whom withdrawing from the labor force at any age tends to be a far more common phenomenon – may be less exposed to prevailing norms about the most appropriate age to retire (Byles *et al.* 2013). Men who retire at a much earlier age than is commonly the case appear to be particularly susceptible to this pressure and this may be one of the reasons why many go in search of a bridge job (Settersten and Hagestad 1996). Another factor to bear in mind is that married women are more likely to have a partner who is already retired (Hurd 1990), because on average women are two years younger than their partners.

Earlier research by Van Solinge and Henkens (2005, 2008) has shown that difficulty adjusting after retirement was strongest in the event of a forced exit from the labor market. The well-being of older workers was found to be seriously affected by the lack of control they felt over this important transition in life. As bridge employment could alleviate the negative effects of involuntary

Bridge employment in the Netherlands 37

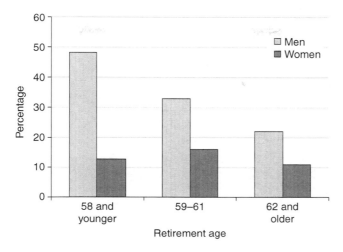

Figure 2.5 Probability of entering bridge employment by sex and age at retirement (N=1,310 retired employees).

retirement, we would expect to find a particularly large number of bridge employees among this category of workers. Figure 2.6, however, shows that this is only partially the case. The figure breaks down the percentage of people in bridge employment by the various reasons for involuntary retirement. If we compare these percentages with the percentage of bridge employees among

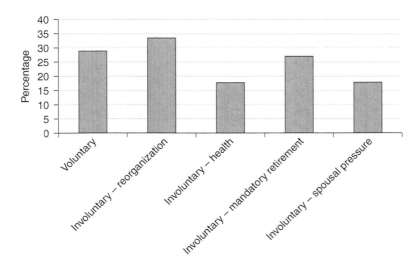

Figure 2.6 Probability of entering bridge employment by reasons for involuntary retirement (N=1,310 retired employees).

38   K. Henkens and H. van Solinge

those who took retirement voluntarily, the conclusion is clear: individuals who were forced to leave for organizational reasons (e.g., restructuring) or because they had reached mandatory retirement age were far more likely to re-enter the labor market than those who retired involuntarily because of health problems or because their partners pressured them to do so. Interestingly, though, no fewer than 17 percent of older workers who left their career jobs for health reasons moved to a bridge job after retirement.

Bridge employment: a world of variety

In the previous sections we saw that bridge employment is not becoming a more common phenomenon in the Netherlands. This section will look into the diversity in bridge jobs. Whereas some workers who retire embark on a second full-time career, others in bridge employment work highly flexible hours and only when it suits them. In addressing this diversity, we will examine different aspects of the job, such as the nature of employment, the type of work and earnings. We will also look at the quality of the job as perceived by persons engaged in bridge employment and compare this with the perceived quality in their former career jobs. We focus on flexibility, workload and job challenge.

Our first conclusion relating to the nature of bridge employment in the Netherlands is that it is mostly part-time. More than 80 percent of the respondents had a full-time job prior to retirement. In contrast, and as is shown in Table 2.2, no more than 12 percent worked full-time in their bridge job. More than half worked 16 hours a week or fewer after retirement and around 30 percent worked at most eight hours a week. The average number of hours per week worked in bridge employment was 17. These short working weeks put the importance of the phenomenon of bridge employment into perspective. Whereas people do not sever their connection to the labor market entirely, the time spent in paid work tends to be much shorter than the extra leisure time people get when they retire. In that sense, a bridge job tends to be something most people do 'on the side'.

Their weaker ties with the labor market are also reflected in the type of employment contracts most of them have. Almost half of the bridge employees have a zero-hour contract or work on a standby basis. One in five are employed under a temporary contract. No more than one in three have a contract for an indefinite period of time. People who work full-time and those who retired at a relatively young age (at age 58 or younger) are most likely to have a permanent contract.

The fact that bridge employment tends to be more flexible is also reflected in employment type. Table 2.2 shows that more than a quarter opted for self-employment or freelance work. Note, in this respect, that the research population consisted only of people who used to be in salaried employment. These figures confirm the trend that self-employment at older ages has gained considerable momentum in recent years in the Netherlands (Van Solinge and Henkens 2010). Just over half of all employees who opted for salaried bridge employment found a job with a new employer. Some 12 percent returned to their former employers

Table 2.2 Characteristics of bridge employment

	Percentage	Total
Type of bridge job		
Wage and salaried work:		
• at old employer	12	48
• other employer/employment agency	50	201
Self-employed	26	107
Combination self-employed/wage and salaried work	8	34
Unknown	3	14
Total	100	404
Number of working hours		
1–8	31	124
8–16	25	103
17–24	22	87
25–35	10	40
36 or more	12	50
Total	100	404
Average number of working hours	17.1	404
Type of activities		
More or less the same as in career job	40	138
Completely different work	40	137
Unknown	20	67
Total	100	342
Earnings		
Less than in career job (on an hourly basis)	50	87
More or less the same	17	30
More than in career job (on an hourly basis)	11	19
Unknown	22	38
Total	100	174
Type of contract		
Permanent contract	25	43
Temporary contract	14	25
Zero-hour contract/standby basis	33	57
Not applicable: self-employed	28	49
Total	100	174

– under different employment conditions – and 8 percent combined salaried employment with freelance work.

When studying bridge employment due attention must be given to remuneration. Research among employers has clearly shown that there is felt to be a discrepancy between the earnings and productivity of older workers. They are said to be relatively expensive, which does no good for their position in the labor market (Conen *et al.* 2011). The concept of demotion plays an important role in policy discussions about how to improve the attractiveness of older workers for employers. Demotion – that is to say, wage reduction – could make employing older workers a more attractive option. In practice, however, demotion is very uncommon in most career jobs. But it is less so following retirement, as becomes clear from Table 2.2. Based on the figures for the remuneration of bridge jobs, we can say that de facto almost half of all bridge employees had been demoted. They earn – in terms of hourly wages – less than they did in their former jobs. A mere 11 percent earn more. This might indicate that people in bridge employment are more inclined to accept a lower salary because they also receive income from an early retirement or pension benefit.

A comparison of the type of work prior to and after retirement did show, however, that many workers who extended their working lives made a switch – 40 percent found a job in a completely different field. The more highly educated individuals with higher-grade jobs were more likely to possess job-specific human capital and those who entered bridge employment tended to do so in the same field (Figure 2.7). In many cases they opted for self-employment. The less-educated were found to be more inclined to make a career switch (e.g., taking on a job as a postman, courier, chauffeur, handyman, salesperson). Self-employment was far less widespread among the less-educated.

The flexible nature of the work carried out by bridge employees offers employers the possibility of using the services and experience of the early retired when it suits them. But how do these older workers view their own situation? Do they consider their labor market position to be a problem? One way of looking into this is to compare their level of satisfaction with the bridge job with that of their former career job. As shown in Figure 2.8, people in bridge employment

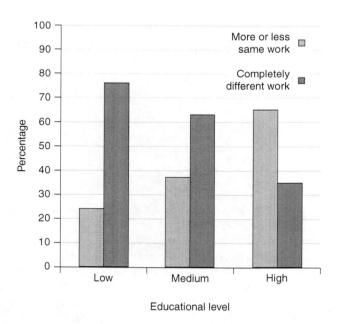

Figure 2.7 Bridge employees by level of education and type of bridge employment (N=318 people who are or used to be in bridge employment).

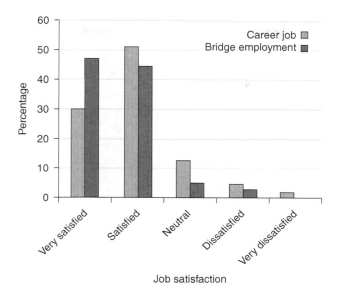

Figure 2.8 Job satisfaction in old and new job (N=141 people active in bridge employment in 2011).

appear to be satisfied with their work. Almost half of all re-entrants are very satisfied with the work they do now, with no more than 30 percent being very satisfied with their former job.

For those re-entrants who were still active in the labor force in 2011 we were able to further compare the quality of their career job in 2001 with that of their bridge job. We made a distinction between aspects relating to the degree to which the work was felt to cause strain (physically demanding and workload) and the degree to which the work gave them satisfaction and offered opportunities for personal development (job challenge) and flexibility. The comparison showed that, whereas bridge jobs were felt to be far less stressful, this did not always mean that these jobs offered less of a challenge. The workload in particular was felt to be much lower. More than one-third of all re-entrants said that at times the workload in their career jobs had been so high that it created tensions at work (Table 2.3). No more than 10 percent of them had a similarly high workload in their bridge jobs. Just over 10 percent derived little or no challenge from their post-retirement work. The quality aspects of the job differed depending on the level of education. The less-educated felt their work to be considerably more taxing and stressful than re-entrants with a higher level of education. Additionally, the better educated found more challenge in their work than the less-educated.

In terms of flexibility we found that employees had ample opportunity to combine their work with other activities, even in their career jobs. More than 80

42   *K. Henkens and H. van Solinge*

Table 2.3 Perceived quality of the work in career job and bridge job, in percentages (N = 141 people active in bridge employment in 2011)

	Career job 2001	Bridge job 2011
'My work is physically demanding'		
Agree/totally agree	15	12
Neutral	18	13
Disagree/totally disagree	67	75
Total	100	100
'At times the workload is so high that it creates tension'		
Totally agree	5	1
Agree	28	9
Neutral	18	19
Disagree	35	52
Totally disagree	13	19
Total	100	100
'My work is characterized by many challenging tasks'		
Totally agree	13	15
Agree	49	42
Neutral	23	31
Disagree	11	10
Totally disagree	5	3
Total	100	100
Are you able to:		
Take a day off	85	95
Start work later or leave earlier	85	79
Work from home/do telework	47	56
Take unpaid leave	36	81
Go on holiday	81	96

percent were free to take a day off as they pleased, start work later or leave earlier, and to go on holiday. Possibilities to work from home were somewhat more limited, yet still an option for most. Interestingly, flexibility was considerable in their former jobs and it scarcely increased in bridge employment. Post-retirement work was found to be far more flexible only in terms of the possibility of taking unpaid leave, with more than 80 percent being allowed to take such leave. These figures shed further light on the conclusion of earlier research that greater flexibility was an important precondition for working beyond retirement (e.g. Patrickson 2003; Phillipson 2004; Van Loo *et al.* 2006). Our figures suggest that this relates in particular to the freedom for bridge employees to interrupt the continuity of their work as they please by taking unpaid leave.

What drives bridge employment?

In this section we will deal in more detail with the question of what drives people to continue working beyond regular or early retirement. We will look into this question from two perspectives. Our first approach entails presenting the

Bridge employment in the Netherlands 43

results of a multivariate regression analysis in which we analyze bridge employment based on a variety of factors. Our second approach to gaining a better insight into what drives people to start afresh after retirement entails examining the reasons that people in bridge employment themselves give for doing so. This information can shed more light on the question of whether their decision is driven primarily by financial or extrinsic factors or whether intrinsic factors such as the nature of the job play a more important role.

Bridge employment: a multivariate analysis

The decision to re-enter the workforce – in bridge employment – after retirement is the result of a decision-making process that is influenced both by the employee's individual characteristics and by the context in which retirement took place. Individual characteristics that play a role are sex, marital status, level of education and health. These factors represent the respondents' socio-demographic position and their human capital. Characteristics of the retirement process that could influence the decision of whether or not to re-enter the labor market are: the age at retirement as well as whether their retirement was voluntary or involuntary. The previous sections examined whether each of these individual factors are related to bridge employment. In this section we will analyze the relationship between the various factors in an effort to determine the relative importance of each of them in the decision whether or not to extend one's working life. In addition to the factors mentioned, we will explicitly examine the role of financial factors such as the older worker's financial position (in terms of their accumulated wealth) and whether or not they have a pension shortfall.

The results of the logit analysis used to explain bridge employment decisions are presented in Table 2.4. So-called marginal effects are presented. A marginal effect of x percent means that an individual with that specific characteristic will – under otherwise similar circumstances – have a higher likelihood of x percentage-points on average of entering bridge employment. The marginal effect for men is 0.176. This means that compared with women, men have a 17.6 percentage-point higher likelihood of working beyond retirement.

By and large, the results of the analysis in Table 2.4 are in line with the results presented earlier. A factor that plays a role in addition to sex (see above) is marital status. We see that divorced and single older workers are less inclined to work beyond retirement than married people. We also see that, whereas bridge employment is not found exclusively among the more highly educated, level of education was an important factor. Compared with older workers with a medium level of education, the better educated had a 12.1 percentage-point higher probability of entering bridge employment and the less-educated had a 7.2 percentage-point lower probability. Another factor that was found to increase the likelihood of successfully moving to bridge employment was self-perceived good health. Contrary to our expectations, factors relating to the older workers' financial position did not have a significant effect on bridge employment. One might expect older workers with a pension shortfall to be more inclined to extend their

44 K. Henkens and H. van Solinge

Table 2.4 Results of the logit regression explaining bridge employment decisions among older workers in the Netherlands, marginal effects and standard errors (N=1,296 retired employees)

	Probability of entering bridge employment after (early) retirement	
	Marginal effects	*SD*
Individual characteristics		
Gender		
Female	–	–
Male	0.176 ***	0.028
Marital status		
Married	–	–
Widowed	–0.020	0.049
Divorced	–0.192 **	0.061
Never married	–0.124 **	0.043
Educational attainment		
Low	–0.072 *	0.037
Medium	–	–
High	0.121 ***	0.031
Perceived health	0.055 **	0.016
Accumulated wealth	0.000	0.008
Perceived pension shortage		
No	–	–
Yes/may be	0.012	0.029
Retirement context		
Age at retirement (%)		
Younger than 55	0.214 ***	0.053
56–57	0.122 **	0.044
58–59	0.045	0.039
60–61	–	–
62 and older	–0.108 **	0.033
Voluntariness of retirement		
Voluntary	–	–
Involuntary – organizational reasons	–0.009	0.036
Involuntary – health reasons	–0.066	0.050
Involuntary – other reasons	0.102	0.057
Chi^2	169.53	
Df	16	
Log Likelihood	–711.261	
Pseudo R^2	10.7%	
Sample Size	1.296	

Notes
*Significant at $p < 0.05$; ** Significant at $p < 0.01$; *** Significant at $p < 0.001$

Bridge employment in the Netherlands   45

working lives. Note, in this connection, that a majority (53 percent) did not report a pension shortfall. Nor did their accumulated capital – a more general indicator of an employee's financial position – show any significant correlation with bridge employment. Here, capital wealth was defined as their total net worth (including a home, minus mortgage and other debts) in 2001.

The results show that the time of retirement was an important factor in determining bridge employment, as the lower the retirement age, the greater the likelihood of an individual re-entering the labor market. The probability of transitioning to bridge employment was therefore smaller for those who retired after the age of 60–61 years (the reference group), the age at which most people in these birth cohorts took early retirement. Involuntary retirement was not found to encourage older workers to re-enter the workplace. This would seem to make sense for older workers who retire for health reasons, but not so much so for those who take early retirement because of a restructuring.

Reasons for working beyond retirement age

A different approach to finding out what drives older workers' decisions to continue working beyond retirement is to ask the people in bridge jobs themselves what their reasons for doing so were. Whereas the drawback of this approach is that the respondents may give socially desirable answers, the advantage is that the reasons may tie in better with the respondents' own experiences. In the survey we made a distinction between four major reasons for entering bridge employment and respondents were asked to indicate which reason was most important in their particular case. The reasons distinguished were: for the money, social contacts, like working, and working as a means to dispelling the boredom that comes with too much leisure time. Figure 2.9 presents the answers, broken down by level of education.

The figure clearly shows that intrinsic reasons ('like working') were mentioned most in all levels of education.[1] Financial reasons came in second place, being the most important reason for continuing to work for about one in five people in bridge employment. A need for social contact and too much leisure time was the decisive factor for no more than a small minority. These findings paint a picture of bridge employment as being driven mainly by positive intrinsic reasons for working beyond retirement. This notion is further strengthened when we compare people in paid employment and the self-employed (not shown in figure). No less than two-thirds of the self-employed indicated that they worked primarily because they enjoyed doing so. Earlier, we saw that over 20 percent of the older workers who were in poor or bad health transitioned to bridge employment despite their state of health. Financial reasons were far more important among this group than among healthy older workers; 43 percent of older workers in poor to bad health continued working because of the money; among those in very good health no more than 12 percent said money was the most important reason.

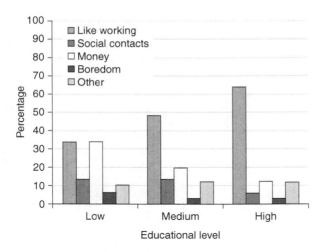

Figure 2.9 Bridge employees by level of education and reasons for working beyond retirement age (N=350 people who are or used to be in bridge employment).

Summary and conclusions

With the imminent retirement of the baby-boomer generation, increasing attention is being paid by employers and policy-makers to strategies that could encourage older workers to extend their working lives (Schlosser *et al.* 2012). Bridge employment may be a forceful instrument in postponing the age at which workers finally leave the labor market (Wang and Shultz 2010). The key to capitalizing on this resource is to understand older workers' work-retirement decisions.

The purpose of the current chapter was to determine what factors contribute to the propensity to engage in paid work after retirement among older adults in the Netherlands. The chapter is based on data from the NIDI Work and Retirement Panel, an ongoing longitudinal survey of older workers in the Netherlands and their partners that started in 2001. We examined a subset of 1,300 respondents aged 50 and over at baseline who were in a career job at the time of the first interview and retired from this career job in the period between 2001 and 2011. In this chapter we have described this process in more detail and have sought to find an answer to the questions of how these re-entrants can be characterized, what type of work they do and what their main reasons are for starting a new career after retirement. We will here summarize our most important findings.

Bridge employment is widespread among broad layers of retired employees and comes in many shapes and sizes. Roughly one-third of all retired employees re-enter the labor market after retirement. In some cases bridge employment serves only as a brief transition to full retirement. For others, however, ties with the labor market are strengthened and extend beyond the age of 65. Bridge jobs differ not only in the number of years worked, but also in terms of the average number of hours worked a week, with part-time jobs and a very short working week being most common. No more than 12 percent work more or less full-time and a majority work at most two days a week.

The second characteristic of bridge employment is the high degree of flexibility. No less than a quarter are self-employed or work freelance and only a small minority of those in paid employment have a permanent contract of employment. A majority of bridge employees earn an hourly wage below that received in their career job. Bridge employment is therefore de facto a demotion, a career step that is still considered a taboo but which apparently is not felt to be a problem in practice as long as it is voluntary. It may well be that bridge employees do not consider this to be a drawback because they receive a pension in addition to their income from work. It would appear that bridge employment offers employers the possibility of matching pay to productivity. It remains to be seen, however, whether people who work beyond retirement age will still be prepared to work for a lower wage in the future, when pensions will not be as handsome as they are now.

The research results show that whereas bridge employment is most widespread among the better educated and among people in good health, it is by no means the sole preserve of these categories of employees. The less-educated were also widely found to extend their working lives beyond retirement, but – much more so than the more highly educated – they tend to embark on a completely different line of work after retirement. Nor were health problems found to stand in the way of re-entry into the workplace. This may possibly be explained by the relatively strong intrinsic motivation of people in bridge employment, many of whom indicated that they enjoyed their work and that this was the most important reason why they chose to continue to participate in the labor market. Only a small minority took up bridge employment mainly for financial reasons.

The increasing numbers of people working during retirement years suggests that we are on the eve of a fundamental change in the way work and retirement are organized in old age. This change is linked to a broader development where education, work and leisure are increasingly parallel careers instead of successive stages in the life course. Studying these life course trajectories, their antecedents and consequences will provide an important area for further research in an aging labor market.

Appendix 2.1: data

This chapter is based on data from the NIDI Work and Retirement Panel. This is a multi-actor panel study, where older workers and their spouses have been followed for a period of ten years. The first wave of this longitudinal study was carried out in 2001. In the private sector, in three large Dutch multinational companies (Unilever, IBM, VendexKBB), and in the public sector (civil service) data were collected in collaboration with the HRM departments. The companies

48 *K. Henkens and H. van Solinge*

provided the random sample as well as financial background information (such as salary, replacement rate). The mailing was carried out by the companies, under the supervision of the researchers. A random sample of employees aged 50 and over working in the different operating companies of these multinationals (for the civil service, different ministries) received an envelope with the company's logo, including a questionnaire for themselves and a separate questionnaire for their married or unmarried partner, if present. The questionnaire included questions with respect to the older workers' financial, work, health and family situation, as well as their work-retirement plans. The data show a large variability with respect to different occupational settings and individual characteristics. Response rates in this first wave were 63 percent for workers and 95 percent for their spouses.

In 2006–2007 a follow-up survey was conducted (Wave 2), in which all surviving Wave 1 participants were re-surveyed, once again by mail questionnaire. The Wave 2 survey asked respondents about changes in employment status, including retirement and retirement plans and behavior, since Wave 1. A total of 2,240 questionnaires were sent to surviving Wave 1 participants. Some 1,678 surveys were returned, providing complete or virtually complete data. Wave 2 response rates, following two reminder notices, were 75 percent for older workers and 97 percent for partners.

In 2011, all surviving respondents were re-interviewed, again by way of a mail questionnaire. A total of 1,636 questionnaires were sent to surviving Wave 2 participants; 1,276 surveys were returned, providing complete or virtually complete data (response rate 78 percent). The respondents and their partners were between the ages of 60 and 75 at this third wave of data-collection. The Wave 3 survey asked respondents about changes in employment status, including retirement, since Wave 2. We collected detailed information on characteristics of bridge jobs (objective characteristics as well as perceived quality of the jobs in terms of perceived stress, autonomy, job challenge), and information on health and psychological well-being. Information regarding events and behavior between Waves 1, 2 and 3 were collected using the anchored retrospective approach (Bumpass and Raley 2006). For this particular study, we examined a subset of 1,304 respondents who were in a career job at the time of the first interview and retired from this career job in the period between 2001 and 2011.

Note

1 Among the less-educated intrinsic and financial reasons are equally important and both come in first place.

References

Adams, G.A. and Rau, B.L. (2011) 'Putting off tomorrow to do what you want today: Planning for retirement', *American Psychologist*, 66: 180–92.

Becker, G.S. (2009) *Human Capital: A Theoretical and Empirical Analysis, with Special Reference to Education*, Chicago: University of Chicago Press.

Beehr, T.A. and Bennett, M.M. (2007) 'Examining retirement from a multi-level perspective', in K.S. Shultz and G.A. Adams (eds.), *Aging and Work in the 21st Century*, Mahwah, NJ: Lawrence Erlbaum Associates.

Bumpass, L.L. and Raley, R.K. (2006) 'Measuring divorce and separation: Issues and comparability of estimates across data sources', in S. Hofferth and L. Casper (eds.), *Measurement issues in family research*, Mahwah, NJ: Laurence Erlbaum Associates.

Byles, J., Tavener, M., Robinson, I., Parkinson, L., Smith, P.W., Stevenson, D., Leigh, L. and Curryer, C. (2013) 'Transforming retirement: New definitions of life after work', *Journal of Women and Aging*, 25: 24–44.

Cahill, K.E., Giandrea, M.D. and Quinn, J.F. (2006) 'Retirement patterns from career employment', *Gerontologist*, 46: 514–23.

Conen, W.S., Henkens, K. and Schippers, J.J. (2011) 'Are employers changing their behavior toward older workers? An analysis of employers' surveys 2000–2009', *Journal of Aging & Social Policy*, 23: 1–18.

Corpeleijn, A. (2005) 'Stoppen met werken rond 60e jaar verminderd' [Labor force exit around age 60 has declined], *CBS Webmagazine*, November 9, 2005. Online. Available at: www.cbs.nl/nl-NL/menu/themas/dossiers/levensloop/publicaties/artikelen/archief/2005/2005-1770-wm.htm (accessed June 4, 2013).

Crimmins, E.M., Reynolds, S.L. and Saito, Y. (1999) 'Trends in health and ability to work among the older working-age population', *Journal of Gerontology Series B: Psychological Sciences and Social Sciences*, 54: S31–S40.

Denaeghel, K., Mortelmans, D. and Borghgraef, A. (2011) 'Spousal influence on the retirement decisions of single-earner and dual-earner couples', *Advances in Life Course Research*, 16: 112–23.

Dennis, H. and Thomas, K. (2007) 'Ageism in the workplace', *Generations*, 31: 84–9.

Dorn, D. and Sousa-Poza, A. (2010) ' "Voluntary" and "involuntary" early retirement: An international analysis', *Applied Economics*, 42: 427–38.

Henkens, K. and Van Solinge, H. (2002) 'Spousal influence on the decision to retire', *International Journal of Sociology*, 32: 55–73.

Huizinga, W.P. (1977) 'Hoe zit het met de experimenten vervroegd uittreden?' [What do we learn from experiments with early retirement?], *Sociaal Maandblad Arbeid*, 32: 569–77.

Hurd, M.D. (1990) 'The joint retirement decision of husbands and wives', in D.A. Wise (ed.), *Issues in the Economics of Aging*, Chicago: University of Chicago Press.

Kim, S. and Feldman, D.C. (2000) 'Working in retirement: The antecedents of bridge employment and its consequences for quality of life in retirement', *Academy of Management Journal*, 43: 1195–210.

Patrickson, M. (2003) 'Human resource management and the ageing workforce', in R. Weisner and B. Millet (eds.), *Human Resource Management: Challenges and Future Directions*, Brisbane: Wiley.

Phillipson, C. (2004) 'Work and retirement transitions: Changing sociological and social policy contexts', *Social Policy and Society*, 3: 155–62.

Pond, R., Stephens, C. and Alpass, F. (2010) 'How health affects retirement decisions: Three pathways taken by middle-older aged New Zealanders', *Ageing and Society*, 30: 527–45.

Ruhm, C.J. (1990) 'Bridge jobs and partial retirement', *Journal of Labor Economics*, 8: 482–501.

Schlosser, F., Zinni, D. and Armstrong-Stassen, M. (2012) 'Intention to unretire: HR and the boomerang effect', *Career Development International*, 17: 149–67.

50   K. Henkens and H. van Solinge

Settersten, R.A. and Hagestad, G.O. (1996) 'What the latest? II. Cultural age deadlines for educational and work transitions', *The Gerontologist*, 36: 602–13.

Siermann, C. and Dirven, H.J. (2005) 'Uitstroom van ouderen uit de werkzame beroepsbevolking' [Exit of older workers from the labor force], *CBS Sociaal-economische trends, 3e kwartaal 2005*: 32–6.

Smith, D.B. and Moen, P. (1998) 'Spousal influence on retirement: His, her and their perception', *Journal of Marriage and the Family*, 60: 734–44.

Smolenaars, E. (2000) *De macht van het getal: Honderd jaar pensioen- en ouderenbeweging* [*The power of numbers: pensioners unions and their lobby*], Amsterdam/ Utrecht: Stichting Beheer IISG/ANBO.

Szinovacz, M.E. and Davey, A. (2005) 'Predictors of perceptions of involuntary retirement', *The Gerontologist*, 45: 36–47.

SZW (1995) *CAO-afspraken 1994. Een onderzoek naar de resultaten van CAO-onderhandelingen over het contractjaar 1994* [*Contractual Wage Agreements 1994: A Report on the Results of Collective Wage Agreements for the Contract Year 1994*], The Hague: Ministry of Social Affairs and Employment.

Taylor, P.E., Brooke, L. and di Biase, T. (2010) 'European employer policies concerning career management and learning from a life-span perspective', in G. Naegele (ed.), *Soziale Lebenslauf Politik*, Wiesbaden: VS Verlag.

Van Dalen, H. and Henkens, K. (2002) 'Early retirement reform: Can it and will it work?', *Ageing & Society*, 22: 209–31.

Van Dalen, H.P., Henkens, K., Lokhorst, B. and Schippers, J.J. (2009) *Herintreding van vroeggepensioneerden* [*Re-entry in the labor market of early retirees*], The Hague: Raad voor Werk en Inkomen.

Van Koningsveld, D.B.J. and Van Ginneken, P.J. (1988) *VUT, nu en straks* [*Early retirement: Now and in the future*], Assen: Van Gorcum/Stichting Management Studies.

Van Loo, J., De Grip, A. and Montziaan, R. (2006) *Active aging bij overheid en onderwijs: vernieuwend omgaan met vergrijzing* [*Active Aging in the Civil Service and Educational Sector*], Maastricht: ROA/ABP.

Van Solinge, H. and Henkens, K. (2005) 'Couples' adjustment to retirement: A multi-actor panel study', *Journal of Gerontology: Social Sciences*, 60B: S11–S20.

Van Solinge, H. and Henkens, K. (2007) 'Involuntary retirement: The role of restrictive circumstances, timing and social embeddedness', *Journal of Gerontology: Social Science*, 62B: 295–303.

Van Solinge, H. and Henkens, K. (2008) 'Adjustment to and satisfaction with retirement: Two of a kind?' *Psychology and Aging*, 23: 422–34.

Van Solinge, H. and Henkens, K. (2010) 'Ondernemerschap steeds vaker alternatief voor pensioen' [Self-employment increasingly common among retirees], *Pensioenmagazine*, 15: 18–22.

Wang, M. and Shultz, K.S. (2010) 'Employee retirement: A review and recommendations for future investigation', *Journal of Management*, 36: 172–206.

Wang, M., Zhan, Y., Liu, S. and Shultz, K.S. (2008) 'Antecedents of bridge employment: A longitudinal investigation', *Journal of Applied Psychology*, 93: 818–30.

3 Bridge employment, a Swedish perspective

Kerstin Isaksson, Gunn Johansson and Sofie Palm

The proportion of individuals in Sweden above the age of 60 still actively working is relatively high in the European context. Recent employment statistics show that the general employment rate (ages 16–64) in Sweden is about 74 percent, which is clearly above the mean for the European Union (64 percent; Eurostat Employment Statistics, August 2012). Similar numbers can be observed for other countries in the North-Western part of Europe. For the age group above 55 years, however, Sweden has the highest proportion working: slightly above 70 percent in the oldest age group (60–65) are still working compared to the mean for EU-27, which is 47 percent. Similarly high levels for older workers can also be found in Norway and Iceland. Differences between the north and south of Europe are relatively small for men but for women, the north of Europe generally has clearly higher rates employed in all age groups than the south.

Changing policies in most European countries, such as increasing the lowest age for retirement, were shown to relate to increased bridge employment among men (Brunello and Langella 2012). However, this effect was only found in the northern European countries. In the southern countries the same policy change seemed instead to lead to longer tenure in the career job. Availability of temporary and part-time jobs in the north seems to be one of the differences between south and north that could partly explain the different patterns. Generally, gradual retirement is unusual across Europe compared to the United States and Japan. This could be attributed to policy differences but also to societal norms about the proper age for retirement. Thus, it seems highly relevant to compare different parts of Europe with regard to the importance of societal factors and welfare systems and their interaction with psychological factors as influencers of exit from the labor market for older workers.

This chapter will aim to identify explanations for these specific employment patterns for older workers in the north of Europe and especially for older women, using earlier research and national investigations. Earlier studies have shown a complex pattern of explanations based on societal factors, cultural values and norms, working conditions and individual preferences. There is a need for theories to clarify the relationship between different antecedents leading to a decision to continue working or to retire. Interview data about retirement planning

52 K. Isaksson et al.

will also be used as part of this chapter to shed some light on possible theoretical explanations at the individual level of Swedish older employees.

Retirement and bridge employment in Sweden

The general mandatory retirement age in Sweden has been 65 since the 1970s. Pensions in Sweden come from several sources. If you have worked and lived in Sweden, you will get a national retirement pension based on your taxed income during your working years. If you have never worked or worked for only a few years there is a basic guaranteed pension for all citizens above 65, but this pension is quite low. A majority of Swedes have additional occupational pensions paid by their employer and based on different collective agreements for blue-collar and white-collar workers. Also this occupational pension is based on years of service and salary up to a certain level. On top of this, individuals may also have private pension schemes or savings.

This means that the Swedish pension is strongly based on years of service and income during these years with generally higher levels for those who worked for many years and have higher salaries. Since the benefit is so closely tied to the size of income over the life course, a lower income due to, for example, part-time work or housework has a strong negative effect on the size of your pension. Obviously, this situation is more common among women with a history of child care and part-time employment than among men in Sweden, as shown by a recent investigation (Ds 2011:42). Among women, 25 percent belong to the category with a low financial standard as compared to 20 percent among men. As a result, older women, especially those living alone, belong to the category of low-income retirees with a relatively low standard of living (Ds 2011:42) and, thus, are in need of extra income.

Bridge employment in Sweden

Bridge employment is here defined in line with EU 2012 as part-time or temporary employment as part of a gradual transition from full-time work to full-time retirement. There are two main types described in the literature: career bridge employment (in the same industry or field as the previous career job) and bridge employment in a different field (see, e.g., Wang *et al.* 2008). There is a range of possible reasons for this form of gradual retirement and its increasing popularity during recent decades. Again, with reference to statistics from the European Union, it is obvious that the rate of these two ways of postponing retirement varies as an effect of both welfare system and labor market regulation in different countries. Such structural differences appear to have a profound effect both on the timing of retirement and on the willingness to use some form of bridge employment in the transition to full-time retirement.

The relatively generous social insurance system that provides all retirees with a basic pension is probably a factor behind the relatively low level of bridge employment in Sweden. Table 3.1 shows the change in employment rates from

Bridge employment, a Swedish perspective 53

Table 3.1 The Swedish labor market 1987–2010 for ages 55–74 divided by age and gender

	1990		2000		2010	
	55–64 years	*65–74 years*	*55–64 years*	*65–74 years*	*55–64 years*	*65–74 years*
Employment rate	70.5	8.5	69.4	10.3	74.6	12.1
Men	75.5	12.3	72.8	15.1	79.2	16.7
Women	65.7	5.1	65.9	6.1	69.9	7.7

1990 to 2010 for men and women aged 55–64 and 65–74 (table adapted from SOU 2012:28).

Over the three decades, the table shows an increasing trend of working after the age of 65 for both men and women. Still the difference between men and women remains with about a 10 percent difference between men and women in the 55–64 year group and twice as many men working compared to women in the older group. A closer look at 66-year-olds shows that the proportion with some income from paid work increased from 19 to 36 percent between 1997 and 2009 (Ds 2011:42). At age 71 the rate had decreased to 21 percent. A closer look at those who continued working after age 65 revealed that most of them had an academic education and reported that they continued working because their work was interesting and stimulating. The proportion of men aged 66 who continued working was 34 percent compared to 27 percent of women; in higher ages this gap between men and women remained at about 10 percent (Pensions-myndigheten 2012). Those who continued working after general retirement age in Sweden were mostly those who already had a career and probably also a relatively high salary and pension. Thus, it seems that women with lower incomes and clearly in need of working to get a higher pension were not reached by these policy changes. Horizontal labor market segregation is strong in Sweden with women most often employed in human services work in the public sector, where we also find relatively high levels of stress and problems with the psychosocial work environment and sickness absence (SOU 2012:28).

During the last decade some legislative changes in Sweden seem to have increased work flexibility and changed the patterns of working in old age. One example is that the right to remain employed was set at 67 instead of 65 years in 2003. Previously, the *actual* age for retirement was substantially lower than 65. During the recession at the beginning of the 1990s the mean retirement age in Sweden was as low as 58. For 2011, however, statistics show a clear increase to 63.3 years. Again the benefits offered by social insurance seem to have influenced the choices made by senior workers regarding the timing of retirement. Furthermore, in Sweden there is eligibility for part-time retirement starting at 61 years and an increasing proportion of employed individuals now use this opportunity to reduce working hours. During the recent decade, and as a result of

54   *K. Isaksson* et al.

legislative changes, working patterns have become increasingly flexible among older workers, both in terms of an increasing proportion of senior workers bridging the gap between full-time work and retirement with part-time work after the age of 65 and by reducing their working hours before the age of 65 with part-time retirement.

The policy and regulative changes made in Sweden appear to have had a positive effect in the expected direction. The obvious reason is that the private household economy and the size of the expected pension are critical both for planning and for deciding whether to continue working or not. Earlier research mostly focused on the retirement *decision*, i.e., when older workers were leaving work for retirement. During the last decades, however, research has expanded to include also retirement planning, a process starting years before the actual exit occurs (e.g., Feldman and Beehr 2011; Topa *et al*. 2009).

Antecedents and consequences of bridge employment

Looking at the individual explanations for bridge employment, good health and lower income appear to be primary decisive factors reported in several American studies (Kim and Feldman 2000; Zhan *et al*. 2009). Results have been fairly consistent over the years and across countries about the antecedents of decisions to continue working or to retire (Topa *et al*. 2009; Pinquart and Schindler 2007; Isaksson and Johansson 2000, 2003). A more recent Swedish study of a representative sample concerning factors affecting the decision to continue working after the age of 65 in Sweden (Soidre 2005) described positive attitudes toward work as critical for plans to continue working. These attitudes were affected by the perception of the present working conditions. Moreover, there was a gender-specific pattern of push and pull factors. For women, but not for men, bad working conditions tended to push them into retirement. For men, a socially rewarding job seemed to make them want to stay working after 65.

Three main categories of antecedents of bridge employment are described by Wang *et al*. (2008) in their longitudinal study: *individual attributes* (younger, higher education, good health); *job-related psychological variables* (job satisfaction, low level of stress); and *less planning for retirement*. The interaction between factors in all three categories leads to a large variation both between countries related to cultural norms, social insurance and welfare systems, and on the individual level. With increasing participation of women in paid work there seems to be a stronger emphasis of household- and family-related factors in the planning of retirement and the decisions to retire.

Among these factors, the job-related ones, which describe the situation in the workplace, are of particular interest since they can be adjusted to address the special needs of older employees. The decision to continue working has been reported to be strongly related to job satisfaction (see, e.g., Wang *et al*. 2008). For this reason it seems pertinent to take a closer look at the working conditions of older employees. The association between age and job satisfaction is generally U-shaped, indicating that the young and the old are more satisfied than the middle-aged (Peeters and Emerick 2008). This is an interesting fact that should send positive signals to policy-makers. As can be expected, job satisfaction negatively predicts retirement planning (Topa *et al.* 2009), i.e., satisfied workers are less inclined to plan their exit. For this reason it is reasonable to expect that those who like their jobs in general would be willing to work a bit longer. The meta-analysis by Topa *et al.* (2009) showed that job satisfaction was a very poor predictor of the retirement decision. This clearly shows that determinants of the decision are part of a different process than the planning of retirement. The planning of retirement seems to be very much affected by conditions in the workplace. When the time for retirement approaches, however, the decision to retire will be decided by factors out of the individual's control, such as the family situation, health and availability of bridge employment.

The consequences of bridge employment for the individual seem to be generally positive. Examples given are higher levels of satisfaction both for employees and also later when people are retired, including the financial situation. Perhaps even more important is the positive health condition of retirees reported after bridge employment (Kim and Feldman 2000). A study by Zhan *et al.* (2009) confirmed these results, showing better mental health among employees engaged in bridge employment as compared to full-time retirees. The most positive outcomes were found among those engaged in career bridge employment as compared to those who had switched to different types of jobs. This was explained in terms of the stress related to starting a new job in a new workplace. Continued work with the same employer could be easier in terms of social relations and support.

Preferences of the older worker

The decision to retire or to continue working has been the focus of research for several decades, during which the health and well-being of the working population developed in a positive direction. The psychological process involved is interesting and in some ways similar to the processes related to other forms of exit from the labor force. Simply, this means that influence and voluntary changes generally are perceived as more positive than the opposite. The development of social insurance systems in Western countries has improved possibilities for the individual to exert influence over the planning and timing of retirement, as has the increase in different forms of extra retirement benefits sometimes offered by employers as part of a downsizing scheme. Our own research during the 1990s on Swedish insurance employees showed that individual preferences were indeed critical as predictors of well-being after exit (Isaksson and Johansson 2000). Other critical factors influencing the decision were also individual, such as health and financial situation, but also the social situation in the family. Reviews of research on retirement decisions have further emphasized the interplay between these factors.

Recent research confirms that individual preferences also play a critical role in the planning of retirement. The perception of an entitlement to work after formal retirement was described as overwhelmingly positive in a recent study by Buyens *et al.* (2009). Being forced to work by legislation or other reasons, on the other hand, was perceived as negative by as many as 90 percent of senior workers.

A recent government investigation in Sweden (SOU 2012:28) presented results from the Swedish Pensions Agency comparing ratings by men and women aged 55+ about their reasons and plans for retirement at a certain age. Figure 3.1 shows some of the results.

Figure 3.1 shows that the most common reason for retirement, given by over 60 percent of both men and women, was the opportunity to pursue leisure activities, followed by individual retirement planning and plans to leave at a certain age. These responses were more common among women than men. There was also a higher proportion of women than men reporting that their working conditions were a reason to retire. Difficulties in finding a new (bridge) job was another reason, given by about 35 percent. Plans to leave at a certain age (which would probably be 65) were very common and could be seen as a strong cultural norm in Sweden.

Barriers to bridge employment

Ageism and cultural stereotypes

As stated above, there is evidence indicating that individual and context-related factors influence the planning of retirement and the actual decision to retire. Our own research indicates that continued working was part of gradual retirement plans for a sizable proportion of senior workers in a Swedish insurance company. However, difficulties in finding suitable bridge employment proved to be a barrier that resulted in full-time retirement earlier than would have been preferred for the former employees (Isaksson and Johansson 2000). The Swedish

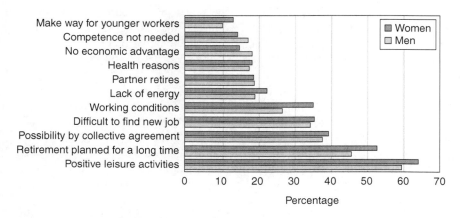

Figure 3.1 Reasons for retirement (source: adapted from SOU 2012: 28).

Bridge employment, a Swedish perspective 57

government investigation mentioned above concludes that age discrimination in the labor market is extensive in Sweden and results in even stronger effects for employees than ethnic discrimination (SOU 2012:28). Based on Swedish studies, the report concludes that ageism is one of the most important barriers to prolonged working in old age. It is a definite barrier for senior employees wanting to change jobs and to find new employment after a period of unemployment. There are widespread negative attitudes against older workers, which most probably result in fewer opportunities for job interviews. A study by Kadefors and Johansson Hanse (2012) found that employers often reported perceived competence-related barriers (e.g., difficulties in adapting and learning) as obstacles for unemployed older employees.

Unwillingness by organizations to arrange courses and education for older employees mirrors the negative attitudes and stereotypes about older workers. As part of such stereotypical attitudes, the aging workforce is seen as less productive and flexible and unable to learn. This often results in layoffs of older employees as part of downsizing in large organizations. In line with the norm that older workers should leave to make way for younger generations, this form of downsizing often provokes relatively less protest from unions and employees. Stereotypes and negative attitudes also seem to have a negative effect on older workers, which could result in reduced willingness to continue working as part of a self-fulfilling prophecy (Buyens *et al.* 2009).

Taylor and Walker (1994) concluded that age discrimination does not exist only as individual prejudice. Ageism is also the product of culturally embedded norms, policies and methods in organizations. Attitudes toward older employees form part of the organizational culture as the view of older employees is shaped by norms, values and beliefs among managers and co-workers. To change these conditions is a long and complex process but increasing participation of older employees in the workplace could be an effective preventive measure with long-term positive effects.

Several empirical studies support the notion that there is a lack of age-relevant management practices in today's organizations. Although age discrimination is prohibited by law, it is still very common in Sweden and in other countries (Wood *et al.* 2008). A recent Finnish study revealed large differences between business sectors regarding age management. The general conclusion was that older individuals were employed only when it was considered strategically sound by the company. The study described the service sector, in which younger employees were preferentially hired because the target customers were expected also to be young (Pärnänen 2012). A study from the Norwegian hospitality industry (Furunes and Mykletun 2007) indicated negative attitudes and underlying prejudice among managers toward older workers that could lead to failure for diversity management efforts.

The study by Buyens *et al.* (2009) also investigated organizational policies aimed at keeping older employees in the organization and how these policies were implemented. They investigated different beliefs, needs and preferences among older employees regarding the shaping of the end of their careers. In a questionnaire, senior workers evaluated a list of 17 HRM practices and the degree to which each practice would motivate them to work longer. Results showed that as many as 46.8 percent responded that opportunities for a longer vacation most likely would be a motivating factor and would increase their own willingness to continue working. Continued education and flexible working hours were other highly rated factors. One conclusion was that all measures taken by the organization should be adjusted to individual needs and preferences.

In summary, it seems that several of the most important antecedents to bridge employment are beyond the control of the individual worker: government policies and regulations, norms and attitudes against older workers, HR policies and practices in the organization and availability of bridge employment. The final decision about retirement or continued working however, rests with the individual. If negative values prevail and employers are less inclined to make flexible arrangements for older employees, then full-time retirement could be perceived as a more attractive option. A closer look at working conditions could give some ideas about changes that could instead make them prefer working.

Working condition

The Swedish government investigation cited above (SOU 2012:28) asked about psychosocial working conditions in order to identify reasons for early exit as compared to regular retirement or continued working beyond this age. Figure 3.2 shows some working conditions that affect the decision to retire before 65, at 65 or later among older workers in Sweden.

Among the most important reasons to stay on were good social relationships in the workplace and autonomy. Good relations with superiors were also rated highly together with getting appreciation for the work done. Furthermore, the

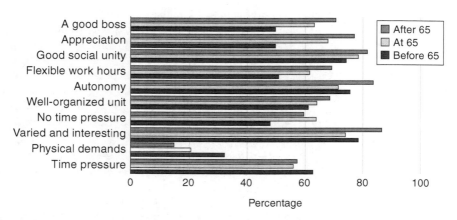

Figure 3.2 Working conditions related to planned retirement before 65, at 65 or after 65 (source: adapted from SOU 2012: 28).

Bridge employment, a Swedish perspective 59

results showed that varied and interesting work was mentioned by more than 80 percent as a factor that could make them continue working beyond the regular retirement age of 65.

Among the conditions most typically reported in other studies as having a negative impact on the willingness to continue working are work-related stress and high workload (Wang *et al.* 2008). A Swedish longitudinal study by Isaksson and Johansson (2003) reported that perceived role overload together with age were related to early exit. Wang *et al.* (2008) reported that *low* level of work-related stress and job satisfaction increased the chances that an individual would engage in bridge employment. A positive social climate in the workplace was reported by Bal *et al.* (2012) as a factor related to increased willingness to continue beyond retirement. Figure 3.2 also clearly indicated that a high workload was a critical factor affecting the decision to retire. More than 60 percent report that a high workload would make them want to leave before 65 years. There also seem to be interesting gender differences affecting the intentions to continue working. According to a longitudinal Finnish study, women seem to be somewhat more affected by work-related psychological factors compared to male workers, who were more affected by health issues in their intentions to retire or to continue working (von Bonsdorff *et al.* 2009).

In summary, improvement of the psychosocial working conditions seems to be important in keeping senior workers in employment. Furthermore, there seems to be a high level of agreement and evidence from research as to the direction of changes needed. A special look at women and their psychosocial working conditions, most often in the public sector, also seems to be warranted. In terms of theoretical explanations, however, the picture is less clear.

Theoretical explanations: motivation to work in old age

Changes in labor-market participation in late career and willingness to take on bridge employment has been explained by three individual level theories: continuity theory, role theory and life course theory. The first, *continuity theory*, claims that the general pattern of adaptation during the process of leaving work for retirement is characterized by individual strivings for continuity. The typical pattern of social relations before retirement tends to continue in a similar way across the lifespan and also during retirement (Atchley 1989). *Role theory* emphasizes the role of the worker and retirement is seen as a transition to a new role that could be difficult in some cases. The fact that a high level of work involvement is often reported as an antecedent of bridge employment could be explained both by continuity theory and by role theory. In the latter case the transition to retirement and the new role could be worrying for older workers if work is an important part of their identity. Whereas role theory and continuity theory are relevant and have empirical support, these theories still largely fail to consider contextual factors. The interaction of individual and contextual factors is partly explained by *life course theory*, which articulates the interdependence of individual life spheres. The ample evidence of the significance of social support from family and friends and of joint planning by couples is an indication of the relevance of this theory. With women entering the workforce in increasing numbers, a life course perspective seems increasingly relevant. An example is to investigate how the interaction between paid and unpaid work affects both general well-being and plans and decisions regarding working (Payne and Doyal 2010). As indicated above, however, the range of context-related factors is very extensive. The large variation in trajectories from work to retirement could be seen as an indication that no single theory can be expected to explain the full complexity in this process.

Several authors have described retirement in line with life course theory as a process with several phases. Feldman and Beehr (2011), in an overview of the field, suggested that the critical factors most often reported differ slightly in importance depending on the phase the individual is at in the process from work to retirement. The first phase was labeled 'Imagining the future' and includes the individual's first considerations and emerging plans for the exit process. In the Swedish context, and probably elsewhere, this phase would primarily involve a financial plan and it would vary between individuals due to the expected pension income. Furthermore, social and cultural norms about the proper age to retire would be influential. Older employees with low incomes or those who discover that they will have a relatively low pension may feel forced to continue working, since in the Swedish system every additional year of working in old age will lead to increased pension. This would imply close consideration of what life during retirement will be like as compared to working life in terms of economy, preferences, activities, social relations etc.

The second phase suggested by Feldman and Beehr (2011) is called 'Assessing the past: deciding the time to let go'; this is where contextual factors such as legislation and availability of bridge employment would be more closely investigated. Finally, the third and last stage in the process suggested is the 'actual retirement' when the step is taken and employees exit from work to retirement.

Topa and her colleagues (2009) used meta-analysis to test the phase approach and investigated whether *retirement planning* and *retirement decision* could be shown to have different antecedents and consequences. Their results generally supported the stage theory. Results showed that poor health, negative working conditions and household economy predicted retirement planning but not the decision to retire. Work involvement was not significantly related to planning but strongly negatively related to the decision, so that poor job involvement predicted earlier retirement. This would mean that a strong work identity would show its effect when the decision comes closer and the time frame is set. Since older men generally seem to have a higher level of work involvement than women, this could be another reason why men more often than women can be found in bridge employment.

To work or not? A question of self-determination

It is quite obvious that external motivation such as financial situation has a critical role for individuals and affects whether they actually perceive that they have

Bridge employment, a Swedish perspective 61

a choice to retire at their preferred age or to continue working. A second external factor is the availability of a bridge job either in the same or in a different field. The Swedish labor market allows opportunities for individuals to continue in their career job because labor legislation is relatively strict and protects older workers with long tenure. The guiding principle in layoffs is called 'last one in – first one out'. There is a cultural norm, however, supporting a trend toward leaving at the mandatory retirement age often motivated by arguments about leaving to allow young workers to enter. Organizations have been slow in adapting age-related management practices allowing workers flexibility to adapt to age-related requirements. Finally, the strong age-related segregation in the labor market complicates the situation and the perceived options. There is always the risk that an individual won't get a new job. Nevertheless, if it is possible to work as a bridge to retirement, the intrinsic motivation to work in terms of individual satisfaction will be of crucial importance.

Despite the relative lack of age-related support from management, older workers in Sweden seem to find ways to achieve flexibility and reduce workload in order to continue working in old age. This trend is clearly shown by the increasing numbers of older workers accepting part-time pensions documented by current investigations (SOU 2012:28). Besides the theories already discussed above, it seems relevant to also include individual motivation theories to explain this development.

In a recent review, Kooij and colleagues (2011) examined the relationship between age and intrinsic and extrinsic motives. Meta-analytic results showed a significant positive relationship between age and intrinsic motives, and a significant negative relationship between age and strength of social and security motives. With a focus on intrinsic motivation the self-determination theory by Deci and Ryan (2000) is relevant in this context. This theory describes a continuum of self-determination ranging from *lack of motivation* on one end, over *extrinsic motivation* which is partly externally controlled, to *intrinsic motivation* on the other end with the highest level of self-determination (by the individual preferences). Human beings are seen as active and growth-oriented agents. According to Deci and Ryan (2000), an understanding of human motivation requires consideration of innate psychological needs for competence, autonomy and relatedness. Satisfaction of these three needs can be obtained in many ways but the idea here is to use the theory as a guide to better understanding the decisions underlying bridge employment. It is reasonable to assume that in the context of society and culture where bridge employment is available, satisfaction of the basic needs through work would make workers want to remain in the labor market.

The next part of this chapter will present results from an interview study of Swedish white-collar workers aged 60 and over. The aim was to investigate work experience, motivation and retirement planning in a sample of nine older white-collar workers still employed in different occupations. Respondents were men and women aged between 60 and 68 who were in work that was mentally rather than physically demanding. They responded to questions about positive

62   *K. Isaksson* et al.

and negative factors related to working in old age and about their plans for retirement or continued working.

Empirical study

Extrinsic motivation

Although the respondents mostly described intrinsic motivating factors, extrinsic factors were also mentioned by almost everyone. The respondents talked about the importance of the financial situation, both as a motivating factor to continue working and in relation to their plans for retirement. There were large differences between individuals, however, regarding the role played by household economy. One man described how the size of his pension was totally critical for his decision about the time for exit. Getting annual updates about the savings made for his pension, he had decided that he would only work as long as it would take for him to secure a reasonable level of living, and then he would leave. Others described the economy as the least important factor for their plans to continue working or not, and some were in between. As one respondent stated: 'The economy is not the most important, instead it is that I have a good general situation [at work]. That's worth much more.'

Everyone seemed to realize that their income would be lower during retirement. Still, they wanted their pension to be as high as possible with sufficient resources for different activities in their life when retired. Most of them realized that they would have to adapt to a different and slightly lower income, as in one typical response: 'But of course, I will have to lower my standard of living. I'll definitely have to do that. But I'm prepared for that. I'll manage.' Contrary to our expectations, no gender differences were found in the responses. Instead, men and women seemed to have similar opinions. This is an interesting result in itself and perhaps typical for Northern Europe. A few respondents had found an independent external adviser to discuss future retirement and were really satisfied with the outcome and the advice they had received.

Intrinsic motivation

Most of the older workers reported several intrinsic factors as the most motivating for continued working in old age. Contributing and helping colleagues was the most common suggestion and described both as rewarding for themselves and as a contribution to workplace efficiency. This was also described either in terms of 'meaningful work' and to 'feel that your work is needed' or as a need for autonomy and independence at work, as in this example: 'This is exactly what I mean, to feel that you're really needed in your organization. That's what it's like here and yes, it really, *really* motivates me and especially since it's on my own terms.' Continued working could also be motivated by the chance to get more flexibility and variety in an individual's daily activities and avoid the risk of being bored. Furthermore, respondents explained that it would be motivating

Bridge employment, a Swedish perspective 63

to be able to learn and develop their own skills also as a senior worker with challenging and interesting new tasks, as in the following:

> That's why I decided to go for this new thing that was completely different compared to my earlier job. Thus, it is immensely stimulating to do something new and learn new stuff when you become older. It is more of a challenge then.

A very common topic in the interviews was the social relationships with colleagues in the workplace. This was described as, for example, being part of a social fellowship, and the social exchange at work was described as critical for motivation. In addition to the social contacts in work, which could give feedback and appreciation, good and stimulating discussions with colleagues at work were also mentioned.

Bridge employment

The majority of respondents answered that they would consider bridge employment before full-time retirement. As many as six of the nine suggested working part-time in one way or another after mandatory retirement as their preferred course of action. Three replied that part-time wasn't an option at the moment and that they would prefer full-time work for a shorter period as a bridge to retirement. Working part-time was generally seen as a way to decrease working gradually and make the transition between full-time work and full-time retirement more smoothly.

The type of bridge employment suggested by interviewees was almost exclusively to continue in their present job. The respondents had several suggestions as to what their employer could do to make them more motivated to work longer. A popular suggestion was to act as some kind of mentor for younger colleagues on a part-time basis, to help them in their career. That would be a positive way to transfer knowledge to younger generations, perhaps reduce youth unemployment and, at the same time, facilitate the adaptation to retirement for themselves.

One of the respondents presented the idea that employers should review the work tasks of their older workers in order to be able to adapt them to individual needs. As a senior in the organization an individual may prefer not to exert the same energy as before or to be on the 'front line'. In these cases employers should aim to meet individual preferences and find other relevant work. Other tasks could be offered, such as planning, education, supporting younger colleagues, or even tasks that you generally would not have time to do such as filing and transfer of knowledge. This suggestion would require employers to undertake interviews with all the older workers about their preferences and skills in order to find out how best to use them in the organization. One participant stated that under such conditions she could work for any amount of time. She said:

> You should have a dedicated person in the organization to investigate this and say 'now look what we could use her to instead of offering her a

64   *K. Isaksson* et al.

contract for early retirement'. If I would be boss I would do it like that instead of just giving her the money for early retirement. I would try to find a win–win situation. You would only have to work 80 percent or even 70 percent. I would definitely do that if I owned the company.

Another interviewee was on a similar track and agreed that if he had work tasks and compensation in line with his preferences he would be interested in working after the age of 65. With the tasks that he had today, however, he did not want to continue much longer.

Three of the respondents did not believe that their employer could do much to make them motivated to continue working. They claimed that retirement was more dependent on their health, if an individual felt well, and on other individual factors beyond the control of employers. One of them said:

[T]hey have tried to make me stay and motivate me, told me that I'm indispensible and other nice things. But no, neither money nor anything else could persuade me to do it. It's my own decision and my own preferences that will rule ... I want this time [as retired].

There were, however, also respondents who admitted that financial benefits would certainly motivate them to continue working longer than they planned today: 'yes, that would be money, salary [laughs]. No I wouldn't really say that perhaps, but I see nothing else.'

Finally, the interviewer asked whether the respondents had a dialogue with their employer about their preferences for retirement and which options the employer would offer at the end of their career. Four of the respondents had already had such a discussion about retirement and three out of the four had initiated this conversation themselves. Two of them saw this as a good idea with an early dialogue. One of them said:

It's not a bad thing really if you started this process a bit earlier ... then in the end it depends on whether they want you to stay or not. I mean that it depends on the job you have. Some of us have experience that is needed and in that case it would be good to start the discussion early so that you haven't already decided that you want to retire at [for instance] 63. If you already had these ideas and almost made up your mind about it, then it could be difficult to have workers accept something different. If you have already started to plan together with your wife then you would probably like to leave.

This quotation also highlights the importance of the family plans and the fact that couples plan retirement together.

Table 3.2 shows a summary of factors mentioned by the participants as motivating for continued working in old age.

Table 3.2, listing the pros and cons of continued working, may give the impression that negative factors toward working in old age were more commonly

Table 3.2 Summary of factors influencing the motivation to continue working in old age (N = 9, number of responses in brackets)

Decreased motivation	Increased motivation
Competence of older employees is not taken care of (3)	Improve my economy (9)
Health decline (3)	Social contacts (5)
Nobody knows how long you'll live (2)	Flexible working conditions (6)
Want to spend time with grandchildren (2)	The company needs me (4)
Want to spend time with partner (2)	Continue my own development (4)
Prefer to decide myself how to spend my time (2)	Working is fun (2)
I've been working for such a long time already	I have work tasks that suit me well (2)
There are other things in life (than work)	Partner/friends are younger and not yet retired
Too much work related travelling	My job is an important part of my identity
Illness of partner	

suggested, but this was not the case. Instead there was more variation in negative factors and there was a higher level of agreement among respondents as to which factors would increase motivation.

Finally, one of the respondents summarized his ideas about older workers and the transition to retirement in the following way:

> These ten years between 65 and 75, you have to think about what these ten years should be like. Is it golf in Mallorca that is the only option or some other form of structure? It's a joint responsibility [in society] in a way, if I should be honest, and this is important.

This empirical study of Swedish older employees made in 2012 is clearly in line with other similar studies showing that flexibility and individual adaptation is indeed critical for the work motivation of older employees. Intrinsic factors, such as getting feedback on performance and sharing knowledge and experience with younger colleagues are most often suggested. The practical measures suggested to improve age-related management include flexible working hours, involving seniors as mentors for younger employees and an early dialogue with employees about their plans for retirement. The ultimate goal would be to improve individual flexibility at the end of the career.

Concluding discussion

The general aim of this chapter was to discuss research evidence that could inform us about the possible reasons behind the typical Swedish (and Nordic) pattern of working in older age. This pattern includes relatively large proportions of older employees, aged 55 and over, still active in the work force. Second, the older work force consists of both men and women. A last typical feature of the Swedish labor market for older employees is the relatively low level of bridge employment which mostly consists of career bridge employment with reduced working hours.

First of all, our interview data clearly suggested that the preferred type of bridge employment in Sweden would be career bridge employment, i.e., to continue in your career job often with a reduction of working hours and sometimes with different tasks than before. A bridge between full-time work and full-time retirement in Sweden can be achieved either by collective agreements allowing employees to collect a part-time pension from the age of 61, while working in their regular job or by allowing continued working until the age of 67. The interviews also indicated that the rationale behind this response can be found in difficulties for older workers to find a new job when they were dismissed or wanted to change their line of work.

For the past ten years, each individual in Sweden has received an annual estimation, 'the orange envelope', showing his or her expected pension. This occurs from the moment an individual enters the workforce. These estimations clearly show that almost everyone will have a reduced income from a pension compared to work but also that an individual's pension increases with increasing years in the workforce. All workers are encouraged to make financial plans for their retirement, including private savings and insurance on top of the general benefits. This has increased general awareness in the population about the economic aspect of retirement. The closer a person gets to retirement the more accurate estimations will probably be. This, in turn, will lead to financial planning probably becoming more salient to the individual. There was an agreement among respondents in the interviews about the importance of financial incentives and the size of the pension. The fact that the state provides a guaranteed pension for everyone guarantees basic security. Against this background it is perhaps not unexpected that intrinsic factors and individual flexibility and adjustment were more often suggested by the respondents as reasons to continue working.

The basic psychological needs suggested by self-determination theory (Deci and Ryan 2000) were all mentioned by interviewees. The need for social belonging and social relationships were described in several interviews as highly motivating. Belonging to a team and meeting colleagues with similar interests were clearly important. The need for knowledge and skill development at the end of an individual's career and also the opposite – the negative reactions if a person was not allowed further development – were common topics. If retirement would mean the end to personal development and to 'put your brain on a shelf' it could even appear as worrying and fearful for individuals. The need for autonomy as a senior worker, finally, was described as the wish to do things their own way, use their experience and skills and decide about their tasks and working hours.

The empirical study showed no gender differences in motivating factors or retirement plans as expected. We expected that women would worry more about their economy during retirement but no such indications were found in this small sample. This could perhaps be explained by the fact that the sample was very homogeneous and that respondents were white-collar workers with relatively similar career situations. Clearly the interview study has a limited research value and can only be used as a descriptive illustration showing how some Swedish workers express their opinions about the topic.

Older workers in Sweden

Laws and cultural norms in Sweden are more supportive of later retirement than in many other countries generally. Retirement is at the age of 65, which has been stable for a relatively long time. Legal changes made about ten years ago aimed to increase flexibility and postpone retirement and these seem to have been effective to some degree. Further obstacles appear to be workload and the working conditions of older employees, with differences apparent between men and women. These need further investigation. Women seem to be more likely to have problems with workload and psychosocial working conditions than men. This is shown both in higher levels of sickness absence and in lower levels of bridge employment. Similar to many other countries, there is a lack of examples of successful age management in organizations, perhaps because of cultural norms and stereotypes and negative attitudes toward older workers. These factors also seem to lead to discrimination against older workers in recruiting.

A range of policy initiatives have recently been introduced by the Swedish government, mostly aimed at increasing flexibility and financial incentives to prolong working life and postpone retirement. Low-income groups could, for example, get a tax reduction if they work after the regular pension age. Advice for policy-makers would be to focus on changing the organization's cultural norms leading to older workers leaving their job to make way for younger generations. Second, employers should support age-related management and OHS initiatives for older workers in order to maintain their workability with an increased awareness of existing gender differences. Bal *et al.* (2012) investigated motivation of older employees and used the concept of 'I-deals' (Rousseau 2005). This concept describes idiosyncratic, non-standardized deals negotiated between employers and individual workers. For organizations, investigating how older employees could best contribute and at the same time being prepared to adjust to individual needs and preferences seems to be one of the key elements in successful age management.

References

Atchley, R. (1989) 'A continuity theory of normal ageing', *The Gerontologist*, 29: 183–90.

Bal, P.M., De Jong, S.B., Jansen P.G.W. and Bakker, A.B. (2012) 'Motivating employees to work beyond retirement: A multi-level study of the role of I-deals and unit climate', *Journal of Management Studies*, 49: 306–31.

Brunello, G. and Langella, M. (2012) 'Bridge jobs in Europe', Forschungsinstitut zur Zukunft der Arbeit, Bonn: IZA DP No. 6938.

68   *K. Isaksson* et al.

Buyens, D., Van Dijk, H., Dewilde, T. and De Vos, A. (2009) 'The aging workforce: Perceptions of career ending', *Journal of Managerial Psychology*, 24: 201–17.

Deci, E.L. and Ryan, R.M. (2000) 'The "what" and "why" of goal pursuits: Human needs and the self determination of behavior', *Psychological Inquiry*, 11: 227–68.

Ds 2011:42 (2011) *Efter 65 – inte bara pension?* [*After 65, not just pension?*]. Online. Available at: www.regeringen.se/sb/d/14009/a/182549.

Eurostat (2012) *Employment Statistics*. Online. Available at: http://epp.eurostat.ec.europa. eu/statistics_explained/index.php?title=Employment_statisticsandprintable=yes (accessed March 7, 2013).

Feldman, D. and Beehr, T. (2011) 'A three-phase model of retirement decision making', *American Psychologist*, 66: 193–203.

Fraccaroli, F. and Depolo, M. (2009) 'Careers and ageing at work', in N. Chmiel (ed.), *An Introduction to Work and Organizational Psychology*, Oxford: Blackwell.

Furunes, T. and Mykletun, R. (2007) 'Why diversity management fails: Metaphor analyses unveil manager attitudes', *Hospitality Management*, 26: 974–90.

Isaksson, K. and Johansson, G. (2000) 'Adaptation to work and early retirement following downsizing: Long-term effects and gender differences', *Journal of Occupational and Organizational Psychology*, 73: 241–56.

Isaksson, K. and Johansson, G. (2003) 'Managing older employees after downsizing', *Scandinavian Journal of Management*, 19: 1–15.

Kadefors, R. and Johansson Hanse, J. (2012) 'Employers' attitudes toward older workers and obstacles and opportunities for the older unemployed to reenter working life', *Nordic Journal of Working Life*, 2: 29–47.

Kim, S. and Feldman, D.C. (2000) 'Working in retirement: The antecedents of bridge employment and its consequences for quality of life in retirement', *Academy of Management Journal*, 43: 1195–210.

Kooji, D.T.A.M., De Lange, A.H., Jansen, P.G.W., Kanfer, R. and Dikkers, J.S.E. (2011) 'Age and work-related motives: Result of a meta-analysis', *Journal of Organizational Behavior*, 32: 197–225.

Pärnänen, A. (2012) 'Does age matter in HR decision making?', *Nordic Journal of Working Life Studies*, 2: 67–88.

Payne, S. and Doyal, L. (2010) 'Older women, work and health', *Occupational Medicine*, 60: 172–7.

Peeters, M. and Emerick, H. (2008) 'An introduction to the work and well-being of older workers: From managing threats to creating opportunities', *Journal of Managerial Psychology*, 23: 353–63.

Pensionsmyndigheten [Swedish Pensions Agency] (2012) *Skäl att gå i pension eller inte* [*Reasons to Retire or Not*]. Report from Pensionsmyndigheten 2012:1.

Pinquart, M. and Schindler, I. (2007) 'Changes in life satisfaction in the transition to retirement: A latent class approach', *Psychology and Ageing*, 22: 442–55.

Rousseau, D.M. (2005) *I-DEALS: Idiosyncratic deals employees bargain for themselves*, New York: M.E. Sharpe.

Soidre, T. (2005) 'Retirement-age preferences of women and men aged 55–64 in Sweden', *Ageing and Society*, 25: 943–63.

SOU 2012:28 (2012) *Längre liv, längre arbetsliv* [Longer Life, Longer Worklife] (in italics). Government Report to the Pension-Age Investigation.

Taylor, P. and Walker, A. (1994) 'The ageing workforce: Employers' attitudes towards older people', *Work Employment and Society*, 8: 569–91.

Topa, G., Moriano, J.A., Depolo, M., Alcover, C.M. and Morales, J.F. (2009) 'Antecedents and consequences of retirement planning and decision-making: A meta-analysis and model', *Journal of Vocational Behavior*, 75: 38–55.

von Bonsdorff, M., Huhtanen, P., Tuomi, K. and Seitsamo, J. (2009) 'Predictors of employees' early retirement intentions: An 11 year longitudinal study', *Occupational Medicine*, 60: 94–100.

Wang, M., Zhan, Y., Liu, S. and Shultz, K.S. (2008) 'Antecedents of bridge employment: A longitudinal investigation', *Journal of Applied Psychology*, 93: 818–30.

Wood, G., Wilkinson, A. and Harcourt, M. (2008) 'Age discrimination and working life: Perspectives and contestations – a review of the contemporary literature', *International Journal of Management Reviews*, 10: 425–42.

Zhan, Y., Wang, M., Liu, S. and Schultz, K.S. (2009) 'Bridge employment and retirees' health: a longitudinal investigation', *Journal of Occupational Health Psychology*, 14: 374–89.

4 Bridge employment in Belgium

Between an early retirement culture and a concern for work sustainability

Donatienne Desmette and Patricia Vendramin

Introduction to the Belgian issue

Among aging Western countries, Belgium seems a somewhat specific case regarding the employment rate of older workers. Indeed, it is well known that, mainly because of persistent public policies of early withdrawal from the workforce, Belgium remains far below the level of 50 percent fixed by the Barcelona targets for people aged 55–64. In 2011, 37.3 percent of those aged 55–59 and 21 percent of those aged 60–64 were still working while the official retirement age was 65. Beyond this age, retirees are exposed to serious cuts in their pension income if they combine paid work with a pension income, and work is an exception: less than 2 percent of people aged 65+ still had some professional activity (Higher Council for Employment [HCE] 2012). In other words, full and early withdrawal constitutes a salient reality for a majority of older Belgian workers, even if achieved by quite diverse means.

In this context, bridge employment, defined as transitional participation in the labor force of older workers who are leaving their jobs and moving toward full retirement (e.g., Schultz 2003), seems rather restricted. Moreover, under pressure from both the Organization for Economic Cooperation and Development (OECD) and the European Community (EC), federal Belgian authorities have developed strategies in order to improve the activity rate of older individuals.[1] Public policies have firstly been aimed at restricting early withdrawal opportunities. More recent age-related employment policies tend to combine measures aimed at increasing the attractiveness and the sustainability of working life for older workers. Some of these policies take the form of bridge employment as part-time jobs. However, in contrast to past part-time end-of-career jobs that were routes for gradually leaving the labor market, recent part-time measures are primarily aimed at supporting active aging (Fusulier *et al.* 2009; Vandenbroucke and vander Hallen 2002). Other policies aim at encouraging age diversity in the workplace. Marginally, retirees' rights to work have also been enhanced (HCE 2012) and have gained space on the political agenda.[2] Obviously, the current concern in Belgium is to know how to lead individuals to work longer. Related to this, we may ask what the most relevant factors are in the perspective of active aging in employment in the Belgian landscape and what promises age policies could hold in a context where (full) early retirement is still considered as legitimate.

The literature on (early) retirement and, more recently, on bridge employment identifies macro- (i.e., historic and normative influences), meso- (i.e., work- and organization-related aspects) and/or micro- (i.e., related to the individuals) factors predicting why people decide to partly or fully withdraw from the workforce (Beehr and Bennett 2007; Feldman and Beehr 2011; Topa *et al.* 2009; Wang and Schultz 2010). In particular, Sterns and Miklos (1995) propose that, besides chronological age which is a somewhat inconsistent predictor, four other age dimensions should be considered. Functional age – a performance-based definition of age – includes health aspects that have been shown to be significantly related to the decision to fully retire, poor health being a push factor (e.g., Topa *et al.* 2009). Organizational age refers to tenure and related aspects such as job demands. Roles that can cause pain, night or shift schedules, time pressure, recognition of lack of experience, risks of skills obsolescence, frequent organizational changes and restricted access to training are significant reasons for older workers to withdraw (Bertrand *et al.* 2010b; Blekesaune and Solem 2005; Delay and Huyez-Levrat 2006; Schreurs *et al.* 2011). As a matter of fact, we will see that in Belgium health and working conditions play a significant role in the attitude of older workers regarding the prospect of working until the retirement age. Based on the idea that behavioral changes occur throughout the course of life due to the joint influences of individual and contextual factors (e.g., Baltes and Baltes 1990; Gielnik *et al.* 2012), the lifespan approach proposed by Sterns and Miklos (1995) invites us to look at the influence of work–life balance (e.g., care duties for elderly or disabled; personal growth motives) on the retirement process (Guillemard 2003; Raymo and Sweeney 2006). This issue appears as especially important in Belgium in relation to working-time reduction schemes that have been specifically created for workers aged 50 or 55+. Finally, psychosocial age refers both to personal perceptions workers have of themselves in terms of age and to social perceptions about older workers in the organization. The rising concern about age diversity puts forward the issue of intergenerational relationships at work and their role in older workers' attitudes (Méda and Vendramin 2010, 2013; Vendramin 2010a, 2010b) which appear particularly relevant in the Belgian context. Indeed, the issue of ageism (i.e., the stigmatization of and discrimination against people because they are or are perceived to be old; Butler 1969; Bytheway 2005) could be of particular importance in Belgium where 6.3 percent of workers aged over 50 experience age discrimination in the workplace (compared to 4.9 percent in average for the EU-27; Vendramin *et al.* 2012).

In relation to this and on the basis of empirical data collected in Belgian samples through the European Working Condition Survey (Vandenbrande *et al.* 2012; Vendramin *et al.* 2012) and the studies of Desmette and colleagues (e.g., Desmette and Gaillard 2008), this chapter analyzes factors that underlie older workers' attitudes toward work and retirement in the framework of an active aging perspective in Belgium.

Measures to curtail the early retirement culture

In Belgium, the 'on-time' age for retiring is 65, for both men and women.[3] However, full and definitive withdrawal earlier than this has been allowed for older workers via three main routes: early retirement (i.e., withdrawal from the labor market before the age of being entitled to 'on-time' retirement; Schreurs *et al.* 2011), unemployment without a job-seeking obligation and retirement.[4] In fact, as soon as they were 55 years old, early retirees and unemployed people were considered to be out of the labor market, so the perspective of bridge employment was not on the agenda. All workers were eligible to retire at 60 rather than 65 with career requirements (the equivalent of 35 years working). Since 2000, early withdrawal routes have been limited: conditions for access to early retirement have been made more restrictive and the minimum age for being considered as a non-job-seeker unemployed/retiree has been raised to 58. Moreover, in the near future (by 2016), the minimum age to be eligible for retirement will be raised from 60 to 62 with a requirement to have had 40 rather than 35 years of employment. Incentives have also been provided to workers to increase the attractiveness of employment (e.g., since 2000, a bonus of pension benefits was introduced for those who continue their activity beyond the age of 62) (HCE 2012).

In fact, the age for effective retirement has increased over recent years: while the mean age for retiring was 56.8 in 2000, it reached 61.6 in 2008 (European Commission 2012). Indeed, early retirement has become less frequent. However, during the same period, the number of unemployed non-job-seekers increased, especially among those aged 50–54. As a whole, in 2011, 9 percent of workers aged 50–54, 21 percent of those aged 55–59 and 60 percent of the 60–64 age group still benefited from some kind of early withdrawal routes. Moreover, 8 percent of those aged 50–65 were invalid in 2011 and shifted from retirement statistics to disability statistics (HCE 2012). In other words, in Belgium, the decrease in early retirement has been shown to be related to a shift toward other types of withdrawal and the activity rate of older Belgian workers still remains among the lowest in the European Union. Therefore, understanding how older workers perceive the sustainability of their job seems of prime relevance in the perspective of active aging.

Older workers and the prospect of working until the age of 60

The European Working Conditions Survey (EWCS), 2010 wave, conducted by the European Foundation for the Improvement of Working and Living Conditions (Eurofound) enables us to draw a profile of aging Belgian workers.[5] In comparison to younger age categories, workers aged over 50 are represented more highly in the public sector, particularly women: 39 percent of women and 28 percent of men aged over 50 work in this sector. Older workers are more likely to have an indefinite contract (to a similar extent for men and women). They are represented more highly in large organizations (41 percent of men and 33 percent of women work in companies employing more than 100 people). Some 18 percent of workers aged over 50 (mainly men) are self-employed (11

Bridge employment in Belgium 73

percent for those below 35 and 16 percent for the median age category), and 52 percent of women and 17 percent of men aged over 50 work part-time (the average for EU-27 is, respectively, 42 and 12 percent).

Perceived sustainability can be approached with a specific question from the EWCS – 'Do you think you will be able to do the same job you are doing now when you are 60 years old?' – with three possible answers ('Yes, I think so', 'No, I don't think so', or 'I wouldn't want to'). The answers of the Belgian workers over 50 are, respectively, 65 percent ('think so'), 22 percent ('don't think so') and 13 percent ('wouldn't want to'). Respondents' judgments of capacity ('I think/don't think I would be able' to do the same job until 60) were analyzed.[6] The percentage of those who think they would be able to do the same job at the age of 60 is below the European average, which is 70 percent for EU-27, and is also quite below most neighboring countries: the Netherlands (89 percent), the United Kingdom (84 percent) and Germany (80 percent), but with the exception of France, which registered 54 percent.

The distribution of answers by sex indicates that women are less likely than men to consider that they would be able to do their current job when they are 60 years old (a difference of 5.5 percentage points). The type of occupation appears to be an important factor in job sustainability. Positive answers are more frequent among clerical support workers, technicians and associate professionals, managers and professionals, who stand above the average for positive answers. Conversely, only a minority of service and sales workers (48 percent) or craft and related trades workers (47 percent) think they will be able to do the same job when 60. The score for elementary occupations is particularly low (37 percent); in this occupational category, those who do not think they would be able get the higher score (38 percent). In almost all occupations, men are more likely than women to think they will be able to do the same job when 60. Statistical analysis of the relationship between the perceived sustainability of the job and working hours (full-time vs. part-time) does not give conclusive results.

Besides the 50+ age category, it is interesting to look at how the perceived sustainability of work evolves with age (Figure 4.1). The distribution by age categories indicates clearly that positive answers increase with age and negative answers decrease. However, this result does not necessarily mean that the jobs of older workers are more sustainable than those of younger workers. Indeed, the meaning of this question would not be the same depending on the workers' age: at the age of 30, it refers to career and mobility, while at 50 it refers to the capacity to stay in a position taking into account the characteristics of the job (physical and mental difficulty, interest).

Specifically, a shift occurs around the forties, in the 40–44 age category for men (minus 7 percentage points) and the 45–49 age category for women, for whom the decrease in perceived work sustainability is stronger (minus 13 percentage points). For both sexes, the percentage of positive answers increases after the age of 50, raising the hypothesis of a withdrawal from the labor market or a change in the workplace for those who gave a negative answer five or ten years previously.

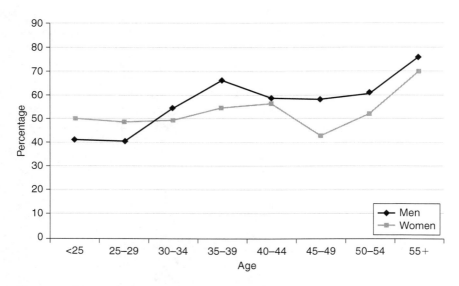

Figure 4.1 Do you think you will be able to do the same job you are doing now when you are 60 years old? All employees who answered: 'Yes, I think so' (source: Eurofound, EWCS 2010).

What makes work sustainable for older workers in Belgium?

The issue of work sustainability has been present in social science research, at the international level, for about ten years, in order to take into account the simultaneous – and partly contradictory – development of working conditions on the one side, and of the demography of active population ('structural aging') on the other. A handbook on sustainable work systems, initiated by Swedish researchers with contributions from various countries, opened the discussion in this field in 2002 (Docherty *et al.* 2002). The authors contrast 'sustainable' work systems with 'intensive' ones. They analyze the extent of the latter, and their negative effects in the long run on workers' well-being, and in terms of the quality of goods and services. In this chapter, we have adopted the rather wide characterization used by Vendramin and colleagues (2012) in a recent report on sustainable work and the aging workforce. The authors consider as 'sustainable' a system where work is adapted to the functional properties of the human organism (bio-compatibility) and to their evolution with age, thus enabling efficient work strategies to be designed (ergo-compatibility), and allowing self-fulfillment in family and social areas, and the possibility of controlling the course of one's life (socio-compatibility). This conceptualization of work sustainability is particularly relevant as regards functional and organizational age as well as the lifespan perspective proposed by Sterns and Miklos (1995).

In this perspective, in the following section, we examine specifically which factors related to working conditions, health and work–life balance are perceived by older workers as compatible with the perspective of working longer.[7] This section is based on a recent report that analyzed the data concerning Belgium from the EWCS 2010 (Vendramin and Valenduc 2012).

Perceived sustainability of work is approached through the three dimensions that appear as the most relevant for older workers according to the data from the EWCS 2010: the quality of work, health and the opportunity to reconcile work and private life.

The quality of work

Most authors consider job quality to be a multi-dimensional concept (Muñoz de Bustillo *et al*. 2009; Holman and McClelland 2011). Brown *et al*. (2007) give priority to work content, working conditions and employment conditions (in a broad meaning, including wages) while Eurofound (2002) also adds work–life balance. The Laeken indicators of job quality combine a set of ten dimensions covering the labor market, working conditions and social policies (Davoine *et al*. 2008). In addition to working conditions, the ILO concept of 'decent work', in accordance with its worldwide scope, pays more attention to labor rights, social protection and social justice (Ghai 2003).

In their report on quality of work in Belgium based on the data from the EWCS 2010, Vandenbrande and colleagues (2012) propose 22 indicators to measure the quality of work distributed into four main dimensions: job content, working conditions, employment conditions and social relations. On the basis of these 22 indicators, Table 4.1 compares the scores for workers in the 50+ age category (Vendramin and Valenduc 2012).

Regarding dimensions related to job content, 'emotional pressure' (i.e., strain related to working with people and emotion management at work), 'repetitive tasks' (i.e., jobs involving short tasks) and 'time pressure' (i.e., high-speed work, external control of pace and lack of time to get the job done) are scored higher by those who think they won't be able to do the same job when they are 60 years old. 'Task autonomy' (e.g., control of the methods and the speed to perform the task) and the autonomy related to working time (i.e., the autonomy in working-time arrangements as well as well as having people under supervision) also have an impact on the assessment of the sustainability of the job but in a positive direction.

As regards working conditions, the main variation in the averages concerns the 'risks' indicator. This summarizes the scores on questions dealing with a variety of exposures for employees at work (musculo-skeletal disorders, bio-chemical and ambient risks such as high or low temperatures). The average is significantly higher for those who do not think they will be able to do the same job when they are 60 than for those who think they will still be able to do so.

In the group of indicators concerning employment conditions, the most significant variation concerns the sub-dimension 'career opportunities'. Perceptions that 'their job doesn't offer good prospects for career advancement' are stronger among older workers who do not perceive their job as sustainable.

The 'social relations' sub-dimension (e.g., being involved in decisions, getting feedback and social support) shows positive relationships for all

76 D. Desmette and P. Vendramin

Table 4.1 Sub-dimensions of job quality (able to do the same job when 60 years old). All employees in the 50+ age category

	Mean	Yes, I think so	No, I don't think so	Sig.
Job content				
Autonomous team work	0.35	0.34	0.36	
Emotional pressure	0.49	0.47	0.52	***
Repetitive tasks	0.37	0.34	0.40	***
Speed pressure	0.35	0.32	0.39	***
Task autonomy	0.70	0.72	0.68	**
Task complexity	0.70	0.70	0.71	
Working time autonomy	0.38	0.42	0.35	***
Working conditions				
Risks	0.19	0.15	0.24	***
Dealing with people	0.57	0.60	0.55	***
Fixed workplace	0.40	0.38	0.43	*
Employment conditions				
Career opportunities	0.49	0.54	0.44	***
Contract	0.86	0.88	0.86	**
Earnings	0.29	0.29	0.28	*
Full-time work	0.70	0.72	0.69	**
Training	0.41	0.42	0.41	
Unusual working hours	0.30	0.28	0.32	***
Working-time flexibility	0.30	0.29	0.33	***
Social relations				
Say	0.50	0.54	0.47	***
Supportive management	0.80	0.83	0.77	***
Social support	0.68	0.71	0.66	***
Violence and harassment	0.11	0.07	0.16	***
Voice	0.63	0.65	0.60	**

Source: Vendramin and Valenduc, 2012.

Notes
*$p < 0.05$; **$p < 0.01$; ***$p < 0.001$.

indicators with the assessment of job sustainability. Most of the indicators concerning social relations seem to have more impact on a negative evaluation of the sustainability of a job in the case of women. This is also the case for 'career opportunities', 'unusual working hours', 'working-time flexibility' and 'emotional pressure'. In contrast, repetitive tasks are an important reason for men to assess a job as not sustainable.

Health

The EWCS data provide information on the perceived positive and negative effects of quality of work through a set of more individual indicators, notably regarding health, which appears to be crucial in explaining the perception of job sustainability.

Positive evaluations on 'general health', 'physical health' (backache, muscular pain in the upper body, muscular pain in the lower body) and 'psychological health' (depression or anxiety, fatigue and insomnia) are at the highest levels for those who think their current job is sustainable (see Table 4.2). Another question asks employees if their work impacts positively, negatively or has no impact on their health. Obviously, when work is perceived as a risk for health, older workers are more likely to consider they will be unable to do their current job when they are 60.

Figure 4.2 shows the answers of men and women who reported that their work affected their health 'mainly negatively' for all ages. It is interesting to note that for both men and women the proportion of people reporting a negative influence grows from 30 to 50 years of age, especially between the ages of 40 and 50, but thereafter this proportion decreases (see Figure 4.1). Again, we can suppose that the negative influence of work on health could contribute either to

Table 4.2 Health and sustainability (able to do the same job when 60 years old). All employees in the 50+ age category

	Mean	Yes, I think so	No, I don't think so	Sig.
Work-related health risk	0.40	0.33	0.50	***
General health	0.78	0.81	0.73	***
Physical health	0.61	0.69	0.50	***
Psychological health	0.78	0.83	0.72	***

Source: Vendramin and Valenduc, 2012.

Notes
***$p < 0.001$.

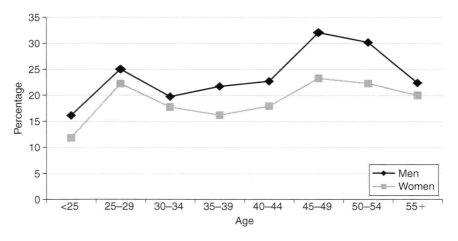

Figure 4.2 Does your work affect your health? All employees. Answer: 'Yes, mainly negatively' (source: Eurofound, EWCS 2010).

78 D. Desmette and P. Vendramin

older workers' withdrawal from the labor market (selection bias) or to a change of job when approaching 50.

To sum up, congruently with past research that has shown the role of autonomy in preventing early retirement (e.g., Elovainio *et al.* 2005; Zappalà *et al.* 2008) and in line with the lifespan psychology approach (e.g., Gielnik *et al.* 2012), Belgian data from the EWCS underline that both autonomy in the task and career-development opportunities are especially likely to support work sustainability for workers aged over 50 (see also Bertrand *et al.* 2010b; Claes and Van Loo 2011 for congruent data about Belgian samples). Impaired health has also been shown to significantly affect work sustainability. In fact, these factors are probably among the best addressed by age policies in Belgium. However, characteristics of the Belgian workforce as well as other Belgian data from the EWCS lead us to highlight, beyond quality of job and health, factors related to bridge employment and the conciliation between the work and private life issue.

Working time and the issue of work–life balance

Part-time working is widespread in the Belgian workforce: in 2011, 24.7 percent of workers aged 15–64 worked part-time (9.2 percent for men and 43.3 percent for women; Labour Force Survey 2011). As for older workers, 52 percent of women and 17 percent of men aged 50+ work part-time (the average for EU-27 is, respectively, 42 and 12 percent). In fact, in a range of sectors (e.g., health, education and public administration), due to the high level of unionization in Belgium, particularly among older workers, several collective agreements have created popular working-time reduction schemes specifically for workers aged 50 or 55+. Moreover, under some conditions, workers aged 50+ who do not want to or can no longer work full-time may reduce their working time through part-time early retirement or a specific 'break-time-end-of-career' device without time limitations (in contrast to 'break-time' devices for all other workers that are restricted to a maximum of five years). The use of these age-related part-time measures (which can be likened to '*career bridge employment*', i.e., bridge employment in the same industry or field; Schultz 2003) increased between 2000 and 2011: in 2000, 1.6 percent of those aged 50–64 used a measure of part-time whatever the type, against 6.2 percent in 2011 (HCE 2012).

In fact, studies show that aging workers in Belgium often wish to reduce their working hours (e.g., Bertrand *et al.* 2010a). The examination of two questions about working time in the EWCS gives a picture of desired working hours by Belgian workers ('Provided you could make a free choice regarding your working hours and taking into account the need to earn a living, how many hours per week would you prefer to work at present?') vs. real working hours ('How many hours per week are you really working?'). In response to the question about the number of hours per week they would ideally prefer to work, 65 percent of men and 31 percent of women said they would prefer a full-time job. In other words, 35 percent of men and 69 percent of women expressed their preference for part-time but through different routes. Men wished to have small reductions in their working hours and would prefer to work between three-quarter time and full-time. Among women, the preferences showed more significant reductions: they would prefer to work between 18 and 32 hours a week (from half-time to four-fifths time). Therefore, part-time policies should be reinforced rather than alleviated for older workers. Indeed, helping older workers to better conciliate work and private commitments appears as a route to active aging.

The issue of work–life balance is explicitly addressed by two questions from the EWCS. The first one asks about the extent to which working hours fit well or poorly with family or social commitments outside work. The other asks whether it is more or less easy to take an hour or two off during working time to deal with personal concerns. The EWCS 2010 data show that, while situations seem rather similar for all age groups in Belgium (14 percent of the workers aged 50+, 16 percent of the middle-aged category and 16 percent of the younger workers consider that work does not fit well with personal or family commitments), older workers have somewhat better opportunities than the other groups to balance their working time with personal or family commitments or needs: 70 percent of older workers, 64 percent of the middle-aged group and 61 percent of the younger age group declare that they can balance work and private life quite easily. However, EWCS data show that Belgian respondents for whom the working hours do not fit well with the other commitments are much less likely to think they will be able to do the same job when 60 years old (35 percent vs. 54 percent for the average of all employees). Obviously, in the Belgian context, it seems relevant to put bridge employment on the political agenda.

However, whatever the quality of working conditions and work–life conciliation facilities, work environment can remain inhospitable for older workers. In Belgium, because early retirement is still widespread, stereotypes about older workers may associate them with withdrawal attitudes (Guillemard 2007). Related to these negative perceptions, older workers may experience discrimination across the full spectrum of human resource management (Finkelstein and Farrell 2007; Posthuma and Campion 2009). Recent employment policies call for a better integration of intergenerational relationships in human resource policies (Delay et al. 2010).

Age diversity in the workplace

Stereotypes about older workers' motivation to work appear as broadly negative in Belgian organizations (e.g., Gaillard and Desmette 2007; Malchaire et al. 2006) and older individuals are a 'group at risk' in the matter of employment (e.g., the likelihood of not being invited to a hiring interview is 7 to 8 percentage points higher for applicants over the age of 45 than for younger applicants, according to the Center for Equal Opportunities and Opposition to Racism 2012). Recent public policies have implemented three routes to increase age diversity in companies (CCT 104; HCE 2012): incentives and constraints for

80   *D. Desmette and P. Vendramin*

employers (e.g., reductions in employers' contributions when they hire a worker aged over 50 and greater obligations to fund outplacement resources for workers aged over 45); equal opportunities policies relating to age (e.g., organizations are encouraged to establish an annual plan for the employment of workers aged over 45); and measures for improving the image of older workers (e.g., non-discriminatory campaigns in the media).

In this framework, two aspects are relevant: the first one concerns the role played by ageism in older workers' attitudes regarding retirement and the second one questions the potential of age diversity practices for reducing ageism in Belgium. In the light of social identity theory (Tajfel and Turner 1979) and stereotype threat theory (Steele and Aronson 1995), we may suppose that early retirement intentions and other withdrawal attitudes are strategies that older workers can adopt to cope with identity threat related to ageism. Indeed, age prejudice can be experienced as a stressor by workers (e.g., Iweins *et al.* 2012a) and retirement could be an avoidance reaction to ageism in the workplace. In other words, ageism could act as a 'push factor' as soon as a worker self-identifies as an 'older worker'.

In a set of studies conducted in Belgium, the relationship between age-related social identity and intentions to retire early has been analyzed. The data showed repeatedly that self-identifying as an older worker (i.e., recognizing oneself to be a member of the group of workers aged over 45 or 50, depending on the study) positively predicts intentions of retiring early. In other words, controlling for individual variables (e.g. gender, health, wealth) and working conditions (physical workload and job control), the more workers identify themselves with the group of older workers, the more they wish to retire as soon as possible (e.g., Desmette and Gaillard 2008; Gaillard and Desmette 2008a). Interestingly, full retirement but not bridge employment (i.e., reducing working hours) was predicted by self-categorization as an older worker (Desmette and Gaillard 2008). On the contrary, the more older workers perceived an imbalance between work and private roles (from work to private life), the more they were willing to reduce the hours they work (the relationship with early retirement was not significant). Additional analyses including a measure of perceived quality of life (Leplège *et al.* 2000) in the multiple regression supported the hypothesis of differentiated processes for early retirement on the one hand and bridge employment on the other hand: perceived quality of life significantly predicted bridge employment intentions ($\beta=-0.209$, t $(351)=-3.447$, $p=0.001$) but not early retirement intentions ($\beta=-0.077$, t $(351)=-1.283$, *ns*). In other words, congruently with EWCS data, bridge employment seems to fill a need to recover when well-being is impaired. Early retirement would instead be a strategy to fully disengage from a domain where an age-identity threat exists.

In two other studies conducted in Belgium, Gaillard and Desmette (2010) confronted older workers with a bogus newspaper-type article presenting either positive or negative stereotypes about older workers' professional ability in order to test age stereotype threat effects. The authors showed that older workers' early retirement intentions were higher when negative rather than when positive age-related stereotypes were activated. Interestingly, participants in a control condition (no age stereotype activated) appeared to be as willing to retire early as those who were explicitly confronted with negative age-related stereotypes. In other words, making salient their age (in all conditions, participants had to indicate their age at the beginning of the questionnaire) was enough to implicitly activate negative stereotypes related to older workers and induce stereotype threat effects (see also Gaillard and Desmette 2008b for similar effects of age categorization on older workers' cognitive performance).

To sum up, self-categorizing as an older worker is still experienced as associated with negative stereotypes and age prejudice (see also Bertrand *et al.* 2010b). Consequently, when the context makes salient the identity of 'older worker', older individuals are more likely to disengage from work. In this respect, organizations should be attentive to contextual cues that trigger the negative processes related to age identity not only because of the 'push effect' for older workers but because organizations, depending on the way they manage age diversity, contribute either to reinforce or to decrease ageism.

In Belgium, several policies supporting the employment of older workers (e.g., age-related part-time measures and improvements in the workplace for workers aged over 45 only) may be viewed as preferential treatment (or affirmative action), that is, policies that are specifically devoted to target groups (Crosby *et al.* 2003). However, research has consistently shown that affirmative action based on gender or race can have detrimental effects on the perceived competence of beneficiaries (e.g., Crosby *et al.* 2003; Heilman and Welle 2006). Similar effects of preferential treatment have recently been shown regarding age in Belgian organizations.

Iweins *et al.* (2012b) have experimentally shown that when Belgian younger workers suspected that a new older colleague benefited from preferential treatment related to age when hired, they perceived the group of older workers as a whole as less competent. They were also more likely to feel greater contempt and to behave more negatively toward them. Moreover, in another study carried out in a hospital in Belgium, the more the younger workers perceived their organization to have adapted working conditions specifically to their older colleagues, the more they denied the competence of all the older workers. In other words, like other kinds of preferential treatment, specific measures devoted to older workers are likely to increase ageism in the workplace. Therefore, organizations are confronted with the challenge of developing differentiated treatment to manage functional limitations due to aging, but without activating the deleterious effects of preferential treatment. One promising route might be the management of age diversity (Delay *et al.* 2010). Indeed, Belgian younger workers who have positive contact with older colleagues and/or perceived that their organization recognizes and values each age group in the workplace have been shown to be less prejudiced toward older workers as a whole due to, among others, feelings of higher procedural justice (Iweins *et al.* 2013).

82   *D. Desmette and P. Vendramin*

Concluding comments: the routes toward bridge employment in Belgium

The main concern in Belgium is the sustainability of the current social security system in ensuring pension benefits: this concerns both the aging of the population and the low activity rate of older workers. So the perspective of bridge employment, defined as transitional labor-force participation, mostly concerns measures of active aging in employment, aimed at preventing older workers from retiring earlier rather than helping them to prepare to retire. In other words, bridge employment exists as an employment measure rather than a transition to full retirement – at least from the point of view of public policies. Indeed, because of a long history of an early retirement culture, the desires and the needs of the individuals themselves can be different, impacting therefore the potential efficacy of an active aging policy.

What are the implications of the Belgian context for the analysis? The literature considers that, despite common roots, bridge employment, early retirement, and 'on-time' retirement are partly predicted by specific factors (e.g., Wang *et al.* 2008). In particular, compared to 'on-time' retirement, early retirement would be perceived as involuntary and negative by older workers (Wang and Schultz 2010). In comparison, regarding the retirement decision process in Belgium, should we conclude that early retirement is rather a matter of voluntary and positive choice due to the pull factors associated with a prevalent early retirement culture? Obviously not. In fact, being able to stay in one's job until the last stages of a standard career seems to be less likely in Belgium than in the neighboring countries. In other words, early retirement can also result from a forced choice due to perceived negative working conditions that act as push factors in the decision to retire early. Therefore, to be effective, strategies aimed at reducing early exit must be associated with measures supporting work sustainability for older workers. If not, older workers could withdraw from the workforce through alternative exit routes (e.g., through disability schemes).

However, until recently, as a consequence of past 'age management by exclusion', many Belgian organizations had no explicit and systematic age strategy but instead resorted to ad hoc practices when problems surfaced (Bredgaard and Troos 2006; Claes and Heymans 2008). From this chapter, on the basis of empirical data collected in Belgian samples, we can suggest some promising routes with regard to active aging policies in the area of work.

Specific attention to working conditions

The EWCS data (Vandenbrande *et al.* 2012; Vendramin *et al.* 2012) point to several dimensions of poor job quality and, in particular, time pressure, physical risks and restricted autonomy in the task that contribute to low levels of work sustainability for older workers. In this perspective, the 'ergonomics of ageing' (e.g., Volkoff and Pueyo 2008) as an emerging concern especially in Belgium appears of prime interest for encouraging those aged over 50 to work longer.

Related to this issue, understanding the relationships between age and health constitutes another crucial perspective, particularly the long-term risks associated with past working conditions (Molinié *et al.* 2012) as well as the influence of health status (chronic diseases, functional disabilities, declining capacities, etc.) on early retirement (when health is perceived as impaired by work, work sustainability is lower). Moreover, the fact that the mid- and late forties seem to be a period of doubt for Belgian workers highlights two issues. On the one hand, related to the EWCS that has shown that career development opportunities contribute supporting work sustainability for workers aged 50+ (see also Bertrand *et al.* 2010b; Claes and van Loo 2011), human resource managers should pay more attention to offering career prospects that correspond to the needs and motives of their older employees until the last stages of the career. On the other hand, because of normative reminders such as specific age policies, individuals start to think of themselves as 'older workers' and become concerned with psychosocial age (e.g., Guillemard 2007). Because ageism contributes to early retirement, age diversity should be not just implemented but actively managed in organizations.

The challenges of age diversity management

Communicating explicit positive information about older workers as a group, which is a strategy currently implemented by the Belgian federal government, seems a successful strategy to reduce older workers' early retirement from work (Gaillard and Desmette 2010). To this end, organizations should be attentive to valuing positive contact between generations. Indeed, while age diversity has sometimes been shown to be a cause of conflict (Kunze *et al.* 2011), Iweins and colleagues (2013) have revealed that age diversity rather than exclusion can contribute to reduce ageism at work when it is experienced through positive intergenerational relationships and a multi-age organizational perspective. An erroneous conclusion from these findings would be that any age categorization has to be avoided, especially when it can be associated with preferential treatment of older workers because of its deleterious effects regarding ageism (Iweins *et al.* 2012b). Indeed, the ergonomics of aging – or more broadly the management of aging – requires some differentiated treatment on the basis of age in order to support work sustainability during the last stages of a career (e.g., Volkoff and Pueyo 2008). The issue for human resource management is to know how to implement differentiated treatment without activating the deleterious effects related to preferential treatment. Combining the ergonomics of aging with strategies valuing all age groups because they contribute to feelings of justice (Iweins *et al.* 2013) seems a promising route.

Toward new working time patterns

Research demonstrates that the wish to leave the labor market early is due to a desire for free time and the need to find a way of reconciling occupational and

84 *D. Desmette and P. Vendramin*

private obligations. How to reconcile working time and non-working time is important for all workers, but there are different characteristics at different ages. In particular, the desire to reduce working time is significant for aging workers. The main reasons for the intention of working less or retiring earlier are tiredness, a need for more time for the family or deteriorating health (Vendramin and Valenduc 2012). Moreover, our data showed that bridge employment (i.e., reduction in working hours), rather than full early retirement, was significantly predicted by perceived lower quality of life. Therefore, it seems reasonable to suppose that for those who need to recover, reducing working hours would be especially relevant in making work more sustainable. Current part-time policies for older workers that have been implemented in Belgium should thus be reinforced rather than restricted. Nevertheless, alternative routes could also be considered with the aim of improving both older workers' quality of life and active aging issues. Flexibility in the work schedule looks a promising route in order to help older workers reconcile work and private needs. Finally, improving the work–life balance during the working life can contribute to easing the transition and the adjustment to successful retirement (Adams and Rau 2011).

The limits of the conclusions rely on the empirical basis that mainly consists of active older workers. As a matter of fact, most research on older workers only addresses 'labor market survivors', neglecting those who have become unemployed or have been dismissed at an earlier stage of their career, through company restructuring or plant closure, thereby introducing a selection bias within the targeted population. This is also why we paid some attention to those in their forties in the analysis of the EWCS data. Moreover, this chapter did not address whether retirees should be engaged in paid or voluntary work. In Belgium, specific policies to allow more blurred boundaries between retirement and work have only emerged through particular opportunities allowing retirees to work. Until now, however, they have been fairly marginal.

Notes

1 Employment policies are a federal matter. The regional governments (of the Regions of Brussels, Flanders and Wallonia) can choose specifically to reinforce some of the federal policies.
2 Since 2012, civil servants have been authorized to remain in their jobs after the retirement age of 65. Since 2013, retirees aged 65+ who have had 42 years of career may have a paid job without a negative impact on their pension income. For those younger than 65 or who have less than 42 years of employment, restrictions remain but they have been reduced. In 2001, 22,714 people aged 65+ were engaged in paid work, against 38,816 in 2011. The number of employees among retirees has increased from 5,000 to 12,000. The number of self-employed aged 65+ is, meanwhile, nearly 27,000 (data from the federal public service for economy).
3 'On-time' retirement is mandatory in Belgium. The retirement age was 60 for women until 1997 but increased to 65 in 2009. This has led to a slight increase in all categories of early withdrawal for 60–64-year-olds.
4 Early retirement was implemented in the context of the economic crisis of the 1970s as a socially acceptable way to cut back on staff (Bredgaard and Troos 2006). Since then, however, early retirement has been made accessible to every older worker whatever the

economic context, as long as a collective agreement allows it in the organization. In fact, because of the high level of unionization, particularly among older workers, early retirement schemes have been very popular in Belgium. The age at which early retirement can be taken is 60, but in case of collective redundancies or collective agreements, it has been allowed at 52 or even 50. Unemployment without a job-seeking obligation was created in 1985 for workers aged 55+ who were fired in sectors without a collective agreement allowing early retirement.
5 Since its launch in 1990, the EWCS has provided an overview of working conditions in Europe. In the 2010 survey (fifth wave), Belgium decided to finance a bigger national sample resulting in a target sample size of 4,000 units whose 722 employees were aged 50 and over (no self-employed were included in the present analyses).
6 Judgments of willingness to do the same job appeared inconsistent in the database and were removed from the analyses.
7 In the data analysis, 'older workers' refers to the 50+ age category.

References

Adams, G.A. and Rau, B.L. (2011) 'Putting off tomorrow to do what you want today: Planning for retirement', *American Psychologist*, 66: 180–92.

Baltes, P.B. and Baltes, M.M. (1990) 'Psychological perspectives on successful aging: The model of selective optimisation with compensation', in P.B. Baltes and M.M. Baltes (eds.), *Successful Aging: Perspectives from the Behavioural Sciences*, Cambridge: Cambridge University Press.

Beehr, T.A. and Bennett, M.M. (2007) 'Examining retirement from a multi-level perspective', in K.S. Shultz and G.A. Adams (eds.), *Aging and Work in the 21st Century*, Mahwah, NJ: Lawrence Erlbaum.

Bertrand, F., Lemaire, C., Barbier, M. and Hansez, H. (2010a) 'Le maintien dans l'emploi des travailleurs âgés dans trois entreprises belges' [Maintaining older workers in employment, the case of three Belgian companies], *Relations industrielles/Industrial Relations*, 65: 400–23.

Bertrand, F., Peters, S., Pérée, F. and Hansez, I. (2010b) 'Facteurs d'insatisfaction incitant au départ et intention de quitter le travail: Analyse comparative des groupes d'âges' [Dissatisfaction factors encouraging exit and intention to leave work: A comparative analysis of age groups], *Le Travail humain/Human Work*, 73: 213–37.

Blekesaune M. and Solem P.E. (2005) 'Working conditions and early retirement: A prospective study of retirement behavior', *Research on Aging*, 27: 3–30.

Bredgaard, T. and Troos, F. (2006) 'Alternatives to early retirement? Flexibility and security for older workers in the Netherlands, Denmark, Germany and Belgium', paper for the ILP Innovating Labour Market Policies: Transitional Labour Markets and Flexicurity, Amsterdam, November 30–December 1, 2006. Online. Available at: www.resqresearch.org/uploaded_files/publications/bredgaard2.pdf (accessed April 4, 2013).

Brown, A., Charlwood, A., Forde, C. and Spencer, D. (2007) 'Job quality and the economics of New Labour: a critical appraisal using subjective survey data', *Cambridge Journal of Economics*, 31: 941–71.

Butler, R.N. (1969) 'Age-ism: Another form of bigotry', *The Gerontologist*, 9: 243–6.

Bytheway, B. (2005) 'Ageism and age categorization', *Journal of Social Issues*, 61: 361–74.

Center for Equal Opportunities and Opposition to Racism (2012) *Report on Diversity: Employment*, Brussels: Author.

Claes, R. and Heymans, M. (2008) 'HR professionals' views on work motivation and

86   D. Desmette and P. Vendramin

retention of older workers: a focus group study', *Career Development International*, 13: 95–111.

Claes, R. and Van Loo, K. (2011) 'Relationships of proactive behaviour with job-related affective well-being and anticipated retirement age: An exploration among older employees in Belgium', *European Journal of Ageing*, 8: 233–41.

Convention Collective de Travail 104 [Collective Agreement for Work 104] (2012) *National Council for Work*. Online. Available at: www.febetra.be/uploads/arbeiders/F12-065f% 20CCT.pdf (accessed February 12, 2013).

Crosby F.J., Iyer A., Clayton S. and Downing R.A. (2003) 'Affirmative action: Psychological data and the policy debates', *American Psychologist*, 58: 93–115.

Davoine, L., Erhel, C. and Guergoat-Larivière, M. (2008) *A Taxonomy of European Labour Markets Using Quality Indicators*, final report for the European Commission (DG Employment), Paris: Centre d'Études de l'Emploi no. 45.

Delay, B. and Huyez-Levrat, G. (2006) 'Le transfert d'expérience est-il possible dans les rapports intergénérationnels?' [Is the transfer of experience possible within intergenerational relationships?], *Sociologies pratiques/Practical sociologies*, 12: 37–49.

Delay, B., Méda, D. and Bureau, M.-C. (2010) 'How socio-organisational systems support competition or synergies among age groups?', in P. Vendramin (ed.), *Generations at Work and Social Cohesion in Europe*, Brussels: P.I.E. Peter Lang, 'Work and Society'.

Desmette, D. and Gaillard, M. (2008) 'When a "worker" becomes an "older worker": The effects of age-related social identity on attitudes towards retirement and work', *Career Development International*, 13: 168–85.

Docherty, P., Forslin, J. and Shani, A.B. (2002) *Creating Sustainable Work Systems: Emerging Perspectives and Practice*, London: Routledge.

Elovainio, M., Forma, P., Kivimaki, M., Sinervo, T., Sutinen, R. and Laine, M. (2005) 'Job demands and job control as correlated of early retirement thoughts in Finnish social and health care employees', *Work & Stress*, 19: 84–92.

Eurofound (2002) *Quality of work and employment in Europe: Issues and challenges*, Foundation Paper 2002/1, Dublin: European Foundation for the Improvement of Living and Working Conditions.

European Commission (2012) *Employment and social developments in Europe, 2011*, Luxembourg: Publications Office of the European Union.

Feldman, D.C. and Beehr, T.A. (2011) 'A three-phase model of retirement decision making', *American Psychologist*, 66: 193–203.

Finkelstein, L.M. and Farrell, S.K. (2007) 'An expanded view of age bias in the workplace', in K.S. Schultz and G.A. Adams (eds.), *Aging and Work in the 21st Century*, Mahwah, NJ: Lawrence Erlbaum.

Fusulier, B., Moulaert, T., Tremblay, D.-G. and Larivière, M. (2009) *Travailler plus longtemps? L'aménagement des fins de carrière en Belgique et au Québec* [*Working Longer? Ends of Career in Belgium and Quebec*], Research Report 2009–1, Montreal-Louvain-la-Neuve: ARUC. Online. Available at: http://benhur.teluq.uquebec.ca/SPIP/aruc/IMG/pdf_NR09-01-ARUC.pdf (accessed March 3, 2013).

Gaillard, M. and Desmette, D. (2007) 'Les attitudes professionnelles des travailleurs âgés' [Attitudes of older workers regarding work], in G. Herman (ed.), *Travail, chômage et stigmatisation; une analyse psychosociale* [*Work, Unemployment and Stigma: A Psychosocial Analysis*], Brussels: De Boeck.

Gaillard, M. and Desmette, D. (2008a) 'Intergroup predictors of older workers' attitudes towards work and early exit', *European Journal of Work and Organizational Psychology*, 17: 450–81.

Gaillard, M. and Desmette, D. (2008b) 'Can age-related identity salience disrupt older workers' cognitive test performance? The moderating role of work-specific regulatory focus', in M. Gaillard, *Lorsque l'âge se fait menace: Une approche psychosociale du vieillissement au travail* [*When Age Is Threatening: A Psychosocial Approach to Ageing at Work*], Unpublished thesis, Université catholique de Louvain.

Gaillard, M. and Desmette, D. (2010) '(In)validating stereotypes about older workers influences their intentions to retire early and to learn and develop', *Basic and Applied Social Psychology*, 32: 86–95.

Ghai, D. (2003) 'Decent work: Concept and indicators', *International Labour Review*, 142: 121–58.

Gielnik, M.M., Zacher, H. and Frese, M. (2012) 'Focus on opportunities as a mediator of the relationship between business owners' age and venture growth', *Journal of Business Venturing*, 27: 127–42.

Guillemard, A.-M. (2003) *L'âge de l'emploi: les sociétés à l'épreuve du vieillissement* [*The Age of Employment: Societies Facing Ageing*], Paris: Armand Colin.

Guillemard, A.-M. (2007) 'Pourquoi l'âge est-il en France le premier facteur de discrimination dans l'emploi?' [Why is age, in France, the main discriminating factor in employment?], *Retraite et société/Retirement and society*, 2/51: 11–25.

Heilman, M.E. and Welle, B. (2006) 'Disadvantaged by diversity? The effects of diversity goals on competence perceptions', *Journal of Applied Social Psychology*, 36: 1291–319.

Hess, T.M., Auman, C., Colcombe, S.J. and Rahhal, T.A. (2003) 'The impact of stereotype threat on age differences in memory performance', *Journal of Gerontology: Psychological Sciences*, 58B: P3–P11.

Higher Council for Employment (2012) *Report 2012*. Online. Available at: www.emploi.belgique.be/publication (accessed April 21, 2013).

Holman, D. and McClelland, C. (2011) *Job Quality in Growing and Declining Economic Sectors of the EU*, WALQING working paper 2011.3, Deliverable 4 of the WALQING project, SSH-CT-2009-244597, Manchester.

Iweins, C., Desmette, D. and Yzerbyt, V. (2012a) 'La perception de discrimination liée à l'âge: L'influence du contact intergénérationnel et de la gestion de la diversité des âges' [The perception of age prejudice: The influence of intergenerational contact and age diversity management], in C. Iweins de Wavrans, *Pour sortir de l'âgisme au travail: Analyse du rôle du contexte social et organisationnel* [*To Exit from Ageism at Work: Analysis of the Role of Social and Organizational Context*], Unpublished thesis, Université catholique de Louvain.

Iweins, C., Desmette, D. and Yzerbyt, V. (2012b) 'Ageism at work: What happens to workers who benefit from preferential treatment?', *Psychologica Belgica*, 52: 327–49.

Iweins, C., Desmette, D., Yzerbyt, V. and Stinglhamber, F. (2013) 'Ageism at work: The impact of intergenerational contact and organizational multi-age perspective', *European Journal of Work and Organizational Psychology*, Online first publication, DOI:1 0.1080/1359432X.2012.748656.

Kanfer, R. and Ackerman, P.L. (2004) 'Aging, adult development, and work motivation', *Academy of Management Review*, 29: 440–58.

Kunze, F., Boehm, S. and Bruch, H. (2011) 'Age diversity, age discrimination climate and performance consequences: A cross organizational study', *Journal of Organizational Behavior*, 32: 264–90.

Labour Force Survey (LFS) (2011) Eurostat.

Leplège, A., Réveillère, C., Ecosse, E., Caria, A. and Rivière, H. (2000) 'Propriétés

88 D. Desmette and P. Vendramin

psychométriques d'un nouvel instrument d'évaluation de la qualité de vie, le WHO-QUOL-26, à partir d'une population de malades neuro-musculaires' [Psychometric properties of an instrument for assessing quality of life, WHOQUOL-26, from a population of neuromuscular patients], *Encéphale*, 26: 13–22.

Malchaire, J., Burnay, N., Braeckman, L. and Lingier, S. (2006) *Réponses aux stéréotypes concernant le travailleur âgé [Answers to stereotypes about older worker]*, Brussels: Service public fédéral Emploi, Travail et Concertation sociale.

Méda, D. and Vendramin, P. (2010) 'Les générations entretiennent-elles un rapport différent au travail? [Do generations have a different relationship to work?], *SociologieS: Théories et recherches*. Online. Available at: http://sociologies.revues.org/index3349. html (accessed February 2, 2013).

Méda, D. and Vendramin, P. (2013) *Réinventer le travail [Reinventing Work]*, Paris: PUF.

Molinié, A.-F., Gaudart, C. and Pueyo V. (2012) *La vie professionnelle: Age, experience et santé à l'épreuve des conditions de travail [Working Life: Age, Experience and Health Facing Working Conditions]*, Toulouse: Octarès.

Muñoz de Bustillo, R., Fernandez-Macias, E. and Anton, J., (2009) *Indicators of Job Quality in the European Union*, Study for the Directorate General for Internal Policies, Policy Department A: Economic and Scientific Policy, IP/A/EMPL/ST/2008–2009, Brussels: European Parliament.

Pettigrew, T.F. and Tropp, L.R. (2006) 'A meta-analytic test of intergroup contact theory', *Interpersonal Relations and Group Processes*, 90: 751–83.

Posthuma, R.A. and Campion, M.A. (2009) 'Age stereotypes in the workplace: Common stereotypes, moderators, and future research directions', *Journal of Management*, 35: 158–88.

Purdie-Vaughns, V., Steele, C.M., Davies, P.G., Ditlman, R. and Crosby, J.R. (2008) 'Social identity contingencies: How diversity cues signal threat or safety for African Americans in mainstream institutions', *Journal of Personality and Social Psychology*, 94: 615–30.

Raymo, J.M. and Sweeney, M.M. (2006) 'Work–family conflict and retirement preference', *Journal of Gerontology: Social Sciences*, 61B: S161–S169.

Schreurs, B., De Cuyper, N., Van Emmerik, I.J.H., Notelaers, G. and De Witte, H. (2011) 'Job demands and resources and their associations with early retirement intentions through recovery need and work enjoyment', *Journal of Industrial Psychology/SA Tydskrif vir Bedryfsielkunde*, 37(2). Online. Available at: www.sajip.co.za/index.php/sajip/article/view/859.

Schultz, K.S. (2003) 'Bridge employment: Work after retirement', in G.A. Adams and T.A. Beehr (eds.), *Retirement: Reasons, Processes, and Results*, New York: Springer.

Steele, C.M. and Aronson, J. (1995) 'Stereotype threat and the intellectual test performance of African Americans', *Journal of Personality and Social psychology*, 69: 789–811.

Sterns, H.L. and Miklos, S.M. (1995) 'The aging worker in a changing environment: Organizational and individual issues', *Journal of Vocational Behavior*, 47: 248–68.

Tajfel, H. and Turner, J.C. (1979) 'An integrative theory of intergroup conflict', in W. Austin and S. Worche (eds.), *The Social Psychology of Intergroup Relations*, Pacific Grove, CA: Brooks/Cole.

Topa, G., Moriano, J.A., Depolo, M., Alcover, C.M. and Morales, J.F. (2009) 'Antecedents and consequences of retirement planning and decision-making: A meta-analysis', *Journal of Vocational Behavior*, 75: 38–55.

Vandenbrande, T., Vandekerckhove, T., Vendramin, P., Valenduc, G., Huys, R., Van Hootegem, G., Hansez, I., Vanroelen, C., Puig-Barrachina, V., Bosmans, K. and De

Witte, H. (2012) *La qualité du travail et de l'emploi en Belgique [Quality of Work and Employment in Belgium]*, Report for the SPF Emploi, travail et concertation sociale, Brussels.

Vandenbroucke, G. and vander Hallen, P. (2002) 'Active strategies for older workers in Belgium', in M. Jepsen, D. Foden and M. Hutsebaut (eds.), *Active Strategies for Older Workers in the European Union*, Brussels: European Trade Union Institute.

Vendramin, P. (ed.) (2010a) *Generations at Work and Social Cohesion in Europe*, Brussels: PIE Peter Lang, 'Work & Society', no. 68.

Vendramin, P. (2010b) 'Connivences et dissonances entre générations au travail' [Collusion and dissonances between generations at work], in G. Hamel, C. Pugeault-Cicchelli, O. Galland and V. Cicchelli (eds.), *La jeunesse n'est plus ce qu'elle était [Youth Is Not What It Was]*, Rennes: PUR.

Vendramin, P. and Valenduc, G. (2012) 'Older workers and work sustainability', in T. Vandenbrande, T. Vandekerckhove, P. Vendramin, G. Valenduc, R. Huys, G. Van Hootegem, I. Hansez, C. Vanroelen, V. Puig-Barrachina, K. Bosmans and H. De Witte (eds.), *La qualité du travail et de l'emploi en Belgique [Quality of Work and Employment in Belgium]*, Report for the SPF Emploi, travail et concertation sociale, Brussels.

Vendramin, P., Valenduc, G., Volkoff, S., Molinié, A.-F., Léonard, É. and Ajzen, M. (2012) *Sustainable Work and the Ageing Workforce*, Report ef1266, Dublin: Eurofound.

Volkoff, S. and Pueyo (2008) *The Quality of Working Life: Challenge for the Future – Aging at Work and the Health Challenges it Raises*, Brussels: Prevent, 116–119.

Volkoff, S., Touranchet, A. and Derriennic, F. (1998) 'The statistical study of the links between age, work and health', in J.-C. Arquié, D. Paumès and S. Volkoff (eds.), *Working with Age*, London: Taylor & Francis.

Wang, M. and Shultz, K.S. (2010) 'Employee retirement: A review and recommendations for future investigation', *Journal of Management*, 36: 172–206.

Wang, M., Zhan, Y., Liu, S. and Schultz, K.S. (2008) 'Antecedents of bridge employment: A longitudinal investigation', *Journal of Applied Psychology*, 93: 818–30.

Wolsko, C., Park, B. and Judd, C.M. (2006) 'Considering the tower of Babel: Correlates of assimilation and multiculturalism among ethnic minority and majority groups in the United States', *Social Justice Research*, 19: 277–306.

Zappalà, S., Depolo, M., Fraccaroli, F. and Guglielmi, D. (2008) 'Postponing job retirement? Psychosocial influences in the performance for early or late retirement', *Career Development International*, 13: 150–67.

5 Flexible transitions from work to retirement

Evidence from Poland

Piotr Zientara

Introduction

It is now widely acknowledged that the average life expectancy is on the rise all over the developed world (Neuman 2011). In this context, it is worthwhile to note that by 2025 the median age in Europe will be 44 and 21 percent of its population will be 65 (Wooldridge 2008). This stands in stark contrast to the demographic situation in Africa and Asia, where the median age is, respectively, 20 and 30 (*The Economist* 2011b). The implication is that both Europe and Japan (and, to a lesser degree, the United States) are having to cope with the problem of population aging (*The Economist* 2011a; European Commission 2005; Ilmarinen 2005; OECD 2006). Of course, increasing life expectancy per se is not – and should not be regarded as – an unequivocally unfavorable phenomenon; on the contrary, from a certain point of view, it bears witness to civilizational advancement in general and exceptional progress in medicine and health care in particular (Zientara 2008b).

Yet the aging of the population, if accompanied by specific labor-market trends and other economic developments, poses a veritable challenge to developed-country policy-makers. For instance, a constantly declining labor-force participation of older people – only approximately two-fifths of 55-to-64-year-olds are still working in Western Europe (Eurostat 2013) – puts a question mark over the sustainability of national pension and health care systems (*The Economist* 2008; European Commission 2004; European Commission 2005; European Commission 2006; OECD 2006). In times of soaring public debts and sizable budget deficits, the pension-related burden is likely to hamper economic growth in the long term, at the same time making it harder to overcome the crisis in the short run. Given that slow growth translates into lower government revenues, mounting expenditure on health care and pensions in the industrialized economies could conceivably usher in an era of permanent (and probably unsustainable) indebtedness and prolonged stagnation as higher taxes choke enterprise.

Arguably, this predicament has taken on particular gravity in the European Union and Japan. The following passage from *The Economist* (2011a: 32) illustrates the point very well:

Evidence from Poland 91

The elderly share of Japan's population is already the highest in the world. By 2050 the country will have almost as many dependents as working-age adults, and half the population will be over 52. This will make Japan the oldest society the world has ever known. Europe faces similar trends, less acutely. It has roughly half as many dependant children and retired people as working-age adults now. By 2050 it will have three dependants for every four adults, so will shoulder a larger burden of ageing, which even sustained increases in fertility would fail to reverse for decades. This will cause disturbing policy implications in the provision of pensions and health care, which rely on continuing healthy tax revenues from the working population.

Poland – a former communist country and a new EU Member State – is no exception in this regard. Its demography is unfavorable (an aging population and a falling fertility rate foreshadow a high dependency ratio) and its pension system unsustainable (every year it generates huge deficits and is propped up with billions of zlotys from the central budget). Equally importantly, the labor market is considered to be comparatively inflexible – with the value of employment protection legislation (EPL) equaling 2.1 (OECD 2013) – and bears all the hallmarks of an insider–outsider duality (Gawrońska-Nowak and Skorupińska 2006; Rymsza 2005; Zientara 2008a). This, together with generous early-retirement arrangements, is thought to lie behind a very low employment rate of older people. It does not help that Poland fares badly in business-friendliness and competitiveness rankings (World Bank 2013; World Economic Forum 2013), which stifles private enterprise and thus indirectly hinders new job creation (Siemianowicz 2006; Zientara 2009a).

Given all this, it should come as no surprise that many Poles see retirement – and thus an exit from the labor market – as a way to escape employment insecurity or joblessness (see also European Commission 2004; Zientara 2008b). It follows that urgent action of a holistic character ought to be taken with a view to reversing these negative tendencies. The most obvious thing to do would be to extend the working lives of Polish citizens. In fact, in 2012 the coalition government announced plans to raise, albeit gradually, the pensionable age of men and women to 67. For a variety of socio-psychological reasons, the *de jure* obligation to continue one's worklife is bound to be highly problematic for many an older employee (Zientara 2008a). Symptomatically, according to public-opinion polls, most Poles oppose the reform. For instance, in a survey conducted in 2012 by TNS OBOP, 80 percent of respondents came out against the plan (Polskie Radio 2013). More specifically, only 7 percent of respondents declared themselves in favor of raising the retirement age for men to 67, and only 3 percent for women (other surveys reveal similar attitudes).

In the light of these findings, it seems that Poles not only exhibit clear unwillingness to work longer, but also tend to downplay the consequences (for the country's public finances) of a low labor-force participation of seniors. One of the ways to change that thinking might be to make their transition from work to retirement less abrupt and more gradual. This is because the actual possibility of

92   P. Zientara

a gradual transition – helped, among other things, by the availability of flexible workplace arrangements – can encourage some individuals to postpone a *definitive* exit from the labor market (Armstrong-Stassen 2008; Davis 2003; Doeringer 1990; Hirsch 2005; Lissenburgh and Smeaton 2003; Spiegel and Schultz 2003; Villosio *et al.* 2008). Besides, there is evidence that an abrupt passage from work to inactivity (also as a result of being pensioned off) tends to negatively affect retirement satisfaction (Barnes *et al.* 2002; Bender 2004; Blundell *et al.* 2003; Charles 2002; Elder and Rudolph 1999; Neuman 2011).

The present chapter, while making the case for a longer worklife (see also Dychtwald *et al.* 2004), focuses on the issue of transition from work to retirement in Poland, an ex-communist country that is characterized by serious structural weaknesses and unfavorable socio-demographic trends. Crucially, the study, drawing on semi-structured interviews with a group of Polish retirees, explores the nitty-gritty of this process on the basis of concrete real-life examples. Its structure is as follows. The next section offers an historical background by briefly discussing the functioning of communism – with a special emphasis being placed on its impact on corporate modus operandi and personnel management – as well as the nature of the systemic transformation. The main idea is to place the issues under consideration into a wider context so as to facilitate more profound understanding and hence more meaningful discussion. We then provide an overview of Poland's demography and labor-market statistics together with a concise description of its pension system. The following part focuses on main theories and notions bearing upon the transition from work to retirement. Subsequently, we discuss findings from the interviews. The conclusion examines the results in light of the previous research, summarizes the argument and lays out further research directions.

Historical background

The functioning and practical implications of the communist system

As is well known, communism, ideologically embedded in Marxist thought (Balibar 1995; Forman 1972; Hyman 1971), was imposed on Central and Eastern European countries (CEE) by the USSR after the Second World War (Davis 2005; Tischner 1992). The forced change had profound political and economic consequences. Above all, the state was conflated with the Socialist/Communist Party, which, claiming to represent the proletariat, controlled all aspects of public life. This was done through a complex mechanism that – engrained in the apparatus of state – used a perverse combination of carrot (employment and career prospects) and stick (censorship and secret-police invigilation and, *in extremis*, persecution and imprisonment) (Tischner 1992). It is true that non-communist parties and non-governmental organizations existed, but the fact remains that they were independent in name only: their existence was supposed to demonstrate that basic human rights were respected in the Soviet bloc. Thus, notwithstanding a democratic facade, the system was in fact a dictatorship that

Evidence from Poland 93

smothered pluralism, independent thinking and grass-roots activism (Balcerowicz 1988; Tischner 1992; Zientara 2009a).

Even the private life of citizens was subject to Party meddling. Every member of a communist society, be it a student, a clergyman or a university lecturer, was expected both to toe the Party's line and to accept the superiority of communism and collectivism over capitalism and individualism (Davis 2005; Tischner 1992). To further that end, the authorities implemented a program of intensive indoctrination grounded in Marxist-Leninist ideology in schools, factories and offices as well as carried out a smear campaign depicting the West as a hotbed of imperialism and demoralization. Needless to say, such values as uniformity, conformity and obedience were championed (Zientara 2009a).

The suppression of political pluralism and civil freedom was accompanied by the replacement of the market forces with a command-and-control (or a centrally planned) economy (Balcerowicz 2003). This was done through sweeping nationalization (without adequate compensation) and bureaucratic expansion. State ownership of the means of production and development of heavy industry were seen as the chief drivers of societal progress (Balcerowicz 1995). Unsurprisingly, ubiquitous red tape – on top of the elimination of private ownership – literally throttled individual (and corporate) entrepreneurship (Balcerowicz 1995; Siemianowicz 2006; Zientara 2009a). In practice, communist central planners came up with grandiose and unachievable five-year plans and ordered state-owned enterprises to implement them (whatever the cost). These entities were administered in a top-down fashion by Party-nominated managers, who executed instructions passed 'from on high' (Dobosz-Bourne and Jankowicz 2006; Koubek and Brewster 1995). In other words, the *raison d'être* of these pseudo-managers was to execute bureaucrats' instructions rather than to act autonomously with the aim of improving organizational performance. Furthermore, since they were accountable not to shareholders but to central planners at special sectoral management units (called in Polish *zjednoczenia*), their main objective was to become well connected as this guaranteed access to unavailable or hard-to-get materials.

The impact of communism on the workplace reality and the HR function

As might be intuitively expected, one-party rule and a highly centralized model of socio-economic development had significant implications for the workplace reality. Indeed, there is little doubt that the HR function under communism was both ideologically skewed and badly underdeveloped. In retrospect, it is fair to say that the way workers were managed resembled a totally politicized and one-dimensional variant of old-style personnel management (Fey *et al.* 1999; Jankowicz 1998; Tung and Havlovic 1996). As the state and the Party were conflated, personnel departments were run by Party-vetted functionaries, who had greater interest in the propagation of the communist ideology than in the development of workers' potential and its integration into the corporate strategy. Worse, personnel

94   *P. Zientara*

departments used to keep detailed records on the performance and personal lives of workers (especially those who were not Party members), which were regularly passed on to the secret police (Soulsby and Clark 1998; Tung and Havlovic 1996). This not only fostered mistrust, but also undermined a sense of togetherness and hence weakened organizational *esprit de corps*.

The freedom-restricting nature of the communist system had a particularly negative effect on employee treatment, organizational participation (together with employee voice) and workplace autonomy – three HRM aspects seen to play an increasingly important role in modern managerial thinking (see, e.g., Boxall and Purcell 2008; Budd 2004; Dundon *et al*. 2004; Marchington and Wilkinson 2005; Strauss 2006). Communist-era managers – who, to reiterate, functioned in an environment unsupportive of disobedience – tended to behave in a similar fashion toward their subordinates and, consequently, were inclined to adopt an undemocratic management style (Maczynski 1994; Martin 2006). Moreover, as democracy was a sham at the politico-institutional level, employee voice at the enterprise level was asphyxiated, too. Likewise, any form of participation (empowerment) was ruled out since it could erode – if not directly challenge – the power of Party-vetted management (Fey *et al*. 1999; Jankowicz 1998). In other words, empowering workers, to follow the communists' line of argument, risked undermining the domination of the Party and thence the foundations of the entire system. The irony in all this was that, at least according to orthodox Marxism (Hyman 1971) and official propaganda, it was workers themselves who were meant to manage their factories (which de facto implied absolute empowerment). For similar control-related reasons, workplace autonomy was frowned upon.

But there was far more to it than that. Considering that pay did not reflect – in keeping with Leninism-inspired collectivism and egalitarianism – individual work effort, there was considerable wage compression. Besides, since improving one's skills had no actual impact on wage increases or promotion prospects, employees tended to play down the usefulness of training, which was, anyway, provided for the sake of central planners' statistics (Koubek and Brewster 1995). Crucially, as promotion and career were conditional upon Party membership (or connections), in-house meritocracy and procedural justice were a fiction. This, alongside a centralized mechanism of employment allocation (whereby one had to accept a post assigned to him or her by ministerial bureaucrats), enfeebled organizational commitment and diminished job satisfaction (Zientara and Kuczyński 2009). Accordingly, communist-era workers used to shirk, and were dissatisfied with their jobs and uncommitted to their companies. Yet such attitudes and behaviors hardly mattered since poor performance and lack of commitment were seldom punished; under communism – in stark contrast to capitalism – unemployment officially did not exist so dismissals were extremely rare. For the same reason, state-owned enterprises created new jobs so as to please central planners (who were loath to see joblessness materialize) rather than to address their concrete HR requirements.

The course and consequences of the systemic transformation

The collapse of the Berlin Wall in 1989 and the disintegration of the Soviet Union two years later triggered a difficult transition from communism and central planning to capitalism and multi-party democracy (Balcerowicz *et al.* 1997; Tittenbrun 1992). This entailed embedding freedom of speech and political pluralism in the constitutions of CEE countries and holding genuinely free parliamentary elections. Simultaneously, efforts were made to establish a proper legal-cum-institutional framework so as to protect property rights and to guarantee contract enforcement. It soon turned out that the introduction of the free-market economy – with its emphasis upon efficiency, productivity and competitiveness – laid bare the wastefulness and ineffectiveness of communism. As we know, the centrally planned economy was based on state-owned enterprises that, being a byword for mismanagement and technological retardation, were unable (in most cases) to function independently and successfully in a new socio-economic reality.

Hence privatization – or the de facto reversal of nationalization – came to be seen as one of the crucial components of the reforms brought in across the region (Balcerowicz 1995; Egorov 1996; Uhlenbruck and De Castro 2000). The 1990s, therefore, saw the sales of 'unprecedented levels of former state-owned property' (Egorov 1996: 90). What the Eastern European governments intended to achieve was to divest themselves of loss-making entities and subsequently turn them around under new (usually foreign) ownership. In the short term, these privatization programs were meant to lay the foundations of a healthy capitalist system and to improve public finances (thanks to the savings resulting from the decrease in subsidies and to the proceeds from sales). In the longer run, they were supposed to better overall economic performance and, by extension, to boost growth. However, due to numerous privatization-related irregularities and abuses, the entire process came in for heavy criticism (Dharwadkar *et al.* 2000; Egorov 1996; Filatotchev *et al.* 1999; Lavigne 1999). Although blatant mistakes and fraudulent acts were committed in all CEE countries, it was in Russia that things went particularly wrong (Filatotchev *et al.* 1999). The following excerpt from *The Economist* drives the point home:

> In the 1990s privatization in Russia was meant to be a way to wipe clean the vestiges of the Soviet economy and to create a new class of property owners. It had some success but, by creating a class of very rich oligarchs, it both weakened the state and planted seeds of resentment among ordinary Russia.
>
> (*The Economist* 2013: 28)

Regardless of the actual merit of the critique (discussion of which goes beyond the present chapter's scope), the fact remains that the privatization programs had a lasting effect on Eastern European economies in general and managerial thinking in particular. For one thing, privatization-induced rationalization immediately highlighted the problem of over-employment, thereby exposing the

96 P. Zientara

inefficiency of the old system's personnel policy. The substantial layoffs that ensued only bore this truth out in a painful manner. Yet these redundancies were part of the inevitable restructuring process and, at the same time, a hangover from the times when unemployment officially did not exist. For another, the introduction of modern HRM policies at newly privatized companies (as well as in foreign-owned greenfield-investment entities) came as a shock to many an employee. Especially older workers found themselves at a loss in a diametrically different work environment. In the event, shirking, absenteeism and weak organizational commitment were no longer tolerated while individual performance began to be meticulously assessed (Zientara and Kuczyński 2009). Even more importantly, some Western managers started to expect their Polish subordinates to be creative, innovative and non-conformist; in other words, at issue were the qualities that had been suppressed by years of communist indoctrination.

As a result, older Poles came to be regarded as unemployable. Having worked all their lives in mismanaged state-owned enterprises, they were stereotypically perceived as incompetent, uncreative and indolent (see also Tittenbrun 1992). In sum, in the eyes of many new-era employers, they literally embodied the socialist work ethic, which rendered them unsuitable for a capitalist workplace (Sztompka 2002). As old habits die hard, their argument ran, it seemed more sensible to employ young people, whose attitude toward work had not been distorted by the communist ideology and inadequate workplace practices (in this sense, not at all paradoxically, a job-seeker's lack of professional experience was his or her greatest asset). Rather than trying to root out older employees' undesirable habits or to modify their occupational mentality, most bosses simply decided to inculcate capitalist norms and values in the young generation. Consequently, older people found themselves at a clear disadvantage and, feeling discriminated against, despaired of finding employment (Zientara 2008b). Their anxiety was amplified by the brutal reality of Polish joblessness: an insidious combination of very low unemployment benefits, little understanding of the functioning of the capitalist labor market and no effective assistance from job center officials usually turned a spell of unemployment into a particularly traumatic experience.

This, in turn, led many workers in their early fifties to take advantage of generous early-retirement arrangements, which, in effect, allowed them to exit the labor market. Thus they saw early retirement as a way to escape job insecurity or unemployment. And, crucially, this practice has continued ever since (even though the authorities have recently introduced some modest changes that make it harder for certain professional groups to retire early). Such is the background against which we will explore the question of transition from work to retirement in Poland. Yet, before we move on, let us first examine the country's demography, labor-market statistics and pensions-related data.

Aging of the Polish population: basic data and statistics

Poland's demography as well as labor-market trends and statistics

As mentioned in the Introduction, not only is Poland's economy characterized by worrying demographic trends and labor-market developments, but it is also plagued by a number of serious structural weaknesses. Above all, to reiterate, the country fares comparatively badly in ease-of-doing-business and competitiveness rankings (though, over the past decade, modest progress has been made in this respect). Specifically, it occupies 55th position in the World Bank (2013) ranking and 45th in the global competitiveness index compiled by the World Economic Forum (2013). Besides, Poland is ranked 26th out of 36 countries on the Summary Innovation Index and 22nd out of the 27 EU Member States (PRO INNO Europe 2011), which implies that the economy is neither remarkably innovative nor technologically advanced. Likewise, the Polish labor market, regulated by the labor code that dates back to 1974, is relatively inflexible: the strictness of employment protection legislation (for regular open-ended contracts) is 2.1 (OECD 2013). This, arguably, is not conducive to (badly needed) new job creation.

Tellingly, in February 2013 the nationwide unemployment rate stood at 14.4 percent, but in some regions it exceeded 18 percent (Central Statistical Office 2013a). In this context, there needs to be a recognition that in December 2012 the number of the unemployed aged 55 or above stood at 267,000, or 12.5 percent of all the jobless (Central Statistical Office 2013c). Compared with the previous year, that number increased by 6.4 percent. And it is the high unemployment rate of seniors that is the thrust of the government's program called 'Solidarity of Generations 50 Plus'. Its chief purpose is to facilitate the employment of jobless individuals aged over 50 by, among other things, exempting employers who hire such people from paying (high) social security contributions (this echoes our earlier comment on the low employability of communist-era seniors at the beginning of the transformation; it emerges that, after more than two decades, older people are still regarded as 'unattractive', which prices them out of legal employment, and thence necessitates government support in the form of exemptions).

Furthermore, according to the Central Statistical Office's (2013b) predictions, the average life expectancy in Poland is set to rise from 74.5 years in 2012 (with 70.4 for men and 78.8 for women) to 77.8 in 2015 (74.6 and 81.2) and to 80 in 2030 (77.6 and 83.3). In 2012 those aged 60 or over constituted almost 21 percent of the country's entire population. Now, on average, Polish men aged 60 can expect to live another 18.3 years, while the figure for women is 23.5. It is estimated that the number of those aged 60 or over will systematically increase: from 8.7 million in 2015 to 10.3 million in 2025 and to 10.6 million five years later (Central Statistical Office 2013b). This trend will be accompanied by such adverse phenomena as skill erosion and, critically, a low fertility rate. In the event, official estimates suggest that between 2010 and 2020 Poland's fertility

98   *P. Zientara*

rate will not exceed 1.2 (Central Statistical Office 2013b). That is far lower than 2.1 – the so-called replacement rate – which is 'usually taken to be the level at which the population eventually stops growing' (*The Economist* 2011a: 30). All this foreshadows a high dependency ratio (which implies an increasingly heavy fiscal burden for the country's working population).

Still in a similar vein, in 2011 the average duration of working life in Poland stood at 31.8 years. The country's working-age population amounted to 24.6 million while that of post-working age was 6.4 million (Eurostat 2013). In the same year its overall employment rate stood at 50.6 percent (58.6 percent for men and 43.4 percent for women). Tellingly, the employment rate of workers aged 55–64 was, at 34 percent, 12 percentage points below the EU-27 average (Eurostat 2013) and hence one of the lowest in the whole Community (more specifically, the employment rate of older men stood at 45.3 percent while that of women was 24.2 percent). Compared with such Scandinavian countries as Iceland (79.8 percent), Sweden (70.5 percent) or Norway (68.6 percent), Poland does not fare well in this respect.

Poland's pension system and retirement-related data

It is essential to point out here that the number of Polish employees allowed to retire in their fifties, albeit falling slightly of late, is very high. The important thing to realize is that the official retirement age for women is 60 and for men 65. Yet, in practice, the former retire at 56, while the latter retire two years later (Central Statistical Office 2013b). This is predominantly due to relatively easy access to the aforesaid early-retirement schemes. In fact, a number of professional groups (such as policemen, railwaymen and miners) can retire *shockingly* early. For example, policemen can stop working after 15 years of service, and miners after 25 years of work down the pit (and irrespective of age). Thus, in certain circumstances, a policeman who starts his or her professional career upon graduating from high (secondary) school at the age of 19 can become a retiree at 34 (with his or her pension amounting to 40 percent of the final salary). And there is ample anecdotal evidence that most policemen who decide to retire at an early age choose to work as sleuths or security advisers in the private sector (often without a formal employment contract; then they receive a pension and, under the table, an untaxed salary).

Besides, those who work in health-impairing conditions (in such industries as steel-making and construction) are entitled to early retirement. Due to this regulation, some workers can retire, depending on their post and branch of industry, at the age of 40 (women) and 45 (men). There also exist two types of pre-retirement payments: a so-called pre-retirement benefit and a pre-retirement allowance. The former can be claimed by a person within five years of retirement who has been laid off as a result of company liquidation or insolvency and has an appropriate amount of service (for women, 20 years and men, 25 years). The latter can be claimed by a person who is entitled to unemployment benefit and has pension-entitling job tenure (as above). To recapitulate, even though in

Evidence from Poland 99

other OECD countries the age at which people actually retire is well below the official retirement age (OECD 2006), in Poland this phenomenon has assumed perturbing proportions.

All this matters in view of the perilous condition of the Polish pension system. Revamped in the late 1990s, it is made up of three components: (1) a pay-as-you-go scheme (run by the Social-Security Institution, or ZUS); (2) a mandatory individual-defined contribution account; and (3) an optional individual account (taking the form of a private pension fund) (Góra 2003). As we have already indicated, every year ZUS – which is, in principle, financed from the social security contribution paid jointly by the employer and the employee – has a huge hole in its finances. And this is despite the fact that most pensions are meager: an average monthly pension, at almost 1,990 zlotys gross (as of January 2013), was almost half as much as an average monthly salary, at about 3,700 zlotys gross (ZUS 2013). It follows that most Polish pensioners, in stark contrast to their German or Swedish counterparts, can hardly get by (low pensions are a hangover from the communist times: today's pensioners spent part of their lives working unproductively in a system that, rather than generating wealth, impoverished society and brought the economy to the brink of bankruptcy). As a result, ZUS is directly subsidized from the central budget (or de facto by the taxpayer) in order for it to pay its pension bill. In 2013, for instance, it is set to receive 65.7 billion zlotys (*Forbes* 2013). It is fair to say, therefore, that ZUS's obligations are bound to weigh heavily on Poland's public finances (Zientara 2008b). Indeed, in the worse-case scenario (a combination of severe recession and soaring unemployment), its accumulated deficit might reach €239 billion by 2017 (*Forbes* 2013).

Bearing in mind Poland's sizable budget deficit, such a huge shortfall calls into question the sustainability of the entire system and, at the same time, gives urgency to the issue of reform. That would mean, as has been suggested throughout the chapter, prolonging the working life of all Polish citizens. And indeed, as we already know, plans are afoot to raise the pensionable age for both sexes to 67, although the change is meant to be gradual – the full transition is due to be completed by 2040 – and is likely to be fiercely opposed by trade unions (let us note that a number of European countries, with Norway and Germany to the fore, have already fixed the retirement age at 67 for men and women). They argue that an obligation to retire at the age of 67, in the words of Piotr Duda, leader of the Solidarity trade union, 'condemns Poles to work till death' (onet.pl 2013).

Even though such demagogical slogans evidently jar with the constant increase in the average life expectancy (Central Statistical Office 2013b), they seem to appeal to the general public. This is because, not coincidentally, they reflect popular views. As transpires from the TSN OBOP survey referred to in the introduction, the vast majority of Poles (80 percent, to repeat) oppose the government's plans. This result is heavy with implications. In fact, the findings suggest that Poles must be truly dissatisfied with their jobs. It seems that the prospect of working longer really displeases and irritates – if not terrifies – most of

100 P. Zientara

them. But this also speaks volumes about the quality of jobs offered in Poland and, by extension, about the way employees are managed (of which more below). Still, irrespective of whether there is a causal link between the quality of HRM in Poland-based companies and the job satisfaction of Poles (see also Zientara and Kuczyński 2009), it is undeniable that the entire issue of retirement (with its multiple policy implications and socio-economic consequences) deserves special consideration and requires decision-makers to come up with holistic and well-thought-out solutions.

In this sense, the question of transition from work to retirement comes to the fore. This is because, as argued earlier, the way it is handled can not only affect retirement satisfaction, but also an individual's decision to stop working. There is evidence that having the option of moving gradually (flexibly) from work to retirement tends to enhance one's retirement satisfaction and, crucially, can encourage some individuals to put off a definitive exit from the labor market (see also Armstrong-Stassen 2008; Hirsch 2005; Lissenburgh and Smeaton 2003; Quick and Moen 1998; Spiegel and Schultz 2003; Villosio *et al*. 2008), which is what, to reiterate, the Polish economy urgently needs. And *à rebours*, an abrupt and/or forced passage from work to retirement typically decreases retirement satisfaction and can lead to other undesirable outcomes (Bender 2004; Charles 2002; Elder and Rudolph 1999). This problematics is the focus of the next section.

Transition from work to retirement: mechanisms and implications

Decision-making in the transition from work to retirement

There is little doubt that making a decision on whether or when to retire is one of the most important moments in the life of an older employee (Armstrong-Stassen 2008; Bender 2004). At this juncture, let us quote Neuman (2011: 982), who states that

> a basic model of retirement predicts that individuals retire when the expected utility from continuing to work falls below the expected utility from retiring. According to this model, anything that reduces the expected utility from working will increase the likelihood of retirement even though the expected utility from retiring has remained unchanged. At the same time, being 'pushed' into retirement through reductions in the expected utility of working may make retirement relatively less satisfying than if the individual had been 'pulled' into retirement by increases in the expected utility of retiring.

That bears directly upon the question of decision-making in the transition from work to retirement. This process is thought to be underpinned by the choice–control dichotomy (Arthur 2003), which holds that decision-making in the transition from work to retirement hinges on the degree of choice and control one

Evidence from Poland 101

exerts over fundamental aspects of his or her life. This mechanism is largely conditioned by two factors: an individual's health and financial situation. It follows that if a worker's health has deteriorated, thereby making him unable to continue working, he has no choice and, as a rule, decides to leave the labor market. The same goes for the financial standing: if an individual is fully aware that his pension will condemn him to (relative) poverty (or will just cause him to have difficulties making ends meet), he tends to perceive himself as having little choice and, accordingly, is inclined to remain at work (Barnes *et al.* 2004). The implication is that the better health and pension-related prospects a senior enjoys, the more control he or she has over his or her life.

In the light of these considerations, it is legitimate to assume that exerting control over the key aspects of life allows one to *consciously* choose when (and how) to retire (even such things as having children at college can make people delay retirement; Weber Handwerker 2011). In this context, Wiatrowski (2001) notes that nowadays seniors are faced with an increasingly broad choice of retirement ages (see also Gendell 1998). This is partly due to the paradigmatic changes that have taken place over the last few decades. In a knowledge-based economy, which favors mental activity over manual labor, age-induced health deterioration has less of an impact on seniors' 'work ability' (although excessive stress, associated with white-collar occupations, can sometimes wear employees out more rapidly than physical work). This notion is defined as the balance between one's work requirements and personal characteristics (see also Armstrong-Stassen 2008; Hirsch 2005; Ilmarinen 2005; Lissenburgh and Smeaton 2003; Loretto and White 2006; Villosio *et al.* 2008). The loss of the balance usually leads to the collapse of the 'work ability model' (Villosio *et al.* 2008: 13), which, in turn, prompts a (definitive) labor-market exit. In other words, when older people find themselves unable to maintain their 'work ability', they tend to leave the labor market as soon as possible.

One of the most important ways of helping seniors preserve the balance is to provide them with adequate ('tailor-made') training and learning opportunities. It is hardly in dispute that, given the intrinsic nature of a knowledge-based economy, access to training and further skill development is instrumental in extending the working life (OECD 2004). Even though, by and large, all age groups benefit from learning in terms of employability enhancement, it is older workers – often (stereotypically) perceived as less IT competent than their younger colleagues – that are particularly well-positioned to gain from continuing to acquire new knowledge and to update their skills (Phillipson and Smith 2005). McNair (2005), therefore, makes the case for recognizing older people's specific learning requirements while the OECD emphasizes the importance of 'promoting a culture of lifelong learning' (OECD 2004: 116).

It is also advisable to encourage seniors to embark on a healthy lifestyle (which combines wholesome eating habits and regular medical check-ups with moderate exercise). Being fit is central to maintaining one's 'work ability', even though nowadays the physical and cognitive changes that potentially make it hard (or impossible) for older individuals to execute workplace tasks occur later

102   *P. Zientara*

in life than three or four decades ago (Dychtwald *et al.* 2004; Ilmarinen 2005; Warr 1996). That, too, goes some way toward explaining why more and more seniors decide to return to work after retirement (Armstrong-Stassen 2008; Herz 1995). However, post-retirement employment is more prevalent in the United States than in Europe, where, with the notable exception of northern countries, people still tend to retire early and rarely return to work (OECD 2006).

Retirement satisfaction

The combination of increasing life expectancy and decreasing retirement age means that, in effect, a growing number of people 'spend more time in retirement than ... their counterparts in past generations' (Neuman 2011: 981), which highlights the significance of retirement satisfaction. Given that in the West an average retiree is likely to remain professionally inactive for at least 15 years, it should come as no surprise that recent years have seen a resurgence of interest in post-employment realities. This, in turn, has led to the proliferation of research into the predictors of retirement satisfaction or retirement quality (see, inter alia, Barnes *et al.* 2002; Bender 2004; Blundell *et al.* 2003; Charles 2002; Elder and Rudolph 1999; Neuman 2011; Smith and Moen 2004). There is evidence, for instance, that those who were pleased with their last (pre-retirement) job and who enjoyed good health also exhibited high levels of retirement satisfaction (Bender 2004; Quick and Moen 1998). By contrast, people who were pensioned off or experienced health problems or reported low income were found to be less satisfied with their retirement (Quick and Moen 1998).

Significantly, it is argued that ceasing to work *abruptly* – rather than gradually – can have a negative effect on retirement satisfaction (Armstrong-Stassen 2008; Bender 2004; Charles 2002; Elder and Rudolph 1999; Fouquereau *et al.* 2005; Neuman 2011; Smith and Moen 2004). This is largely because people who have been professionally active prior to retirement suddenly find themselves with plenty of free time and little idea of what to do with it – an uncomfortable situation that produces a variety of undesirable outcomes. Thus some retirees fall prey to physical inertia and/or intellectual sluggishness. Not coincidentally, in 2005 *The Economist* suggested that one should 'never retire' as 'it rots the brain' (*The Economist* 2005: 14). Others feel unneeded and frustrated (Zientara 2009b). Equally importantly, lack of continued social interaction – resulting from fewer face-to-face contacts with colleagues – risks reinforcing a sense of loneliness and alienation (experienced especially acutely by singletons). As a result, some pensioners are likely to suffer from depression. The title of a paper by Charles (2002), 'Is Retirement Depressing?', evocatively highlights this point. All this underscores the importance of ensuring a more gradual (flexible) transition from work to retirement.

Indeed, there is evidence that moving gradually from work to inactivity can not only minimize the negative consequences of retirement, but also encourage people to postpone an exit from the labor market (Armstrong-Stassen 2008; Doeringer 1990; Lissenburgh and Smeaton 2003). This is usually achieved through flexible workplace arrangements, such as part-time employment (in developed economies prevailing in the service sector) and the virtualization of work ('telework' or 'untethered work'), which refers to performing one's tasks from home or any other place thanks to IT-based connectivity (Johns and Gratton 2013). Such practices allow would-be retirees to progressively get used – in accordance with their individual qualities and preferences – to a less heavy workload and decreased physical presence in the office. At the same time, they enable them to feel busy (albeit to a lesser extent than before) and to stay in touch with their colleagues (of course, thanks to IT, it is also possible to do so without leaving one's home; nonetheless, face-to-face contacts trump online relationships).

Arguably, what is principally needed for the introduction of such arrangements is an organizational culture that, drawing on age-management concepts, values older employees. Given that experience (alongside strong organizational commitment, industriousness and reliability) is seniors' greatest asset (Zientara 2009b) and that successful innovation generation is conditioned by tacit-knowledge exchange (Peltokorpi *et al.* 2007), a failure to retain those aged over 60 may prove to be self-defeating, thereby eroding, *ceteris paribus*, a firm's competitive advantage (Frank *et al.* 2004; Magd 2003). It follows that ensuring a gradual transition from work to retirement is set to produce win–win outcomes, being actually in the interest of both companies and senior employees.

Unfortunately, as will be demonstrated in the following section, for many Polish citizens, moving from work to retirement is not a gradual process in which personal characteristics and predispositions take center stage. Rather, being underpinned by a sense of fatigue or fear of unemployment, the transition is abrupt (which de facto rules out post-retirement employment) and has more to do with external circumstances than individual preferences. This is partly due to labor-market rigidities in general and the 'unfriendliness' of the labor code toward flexible working arrangements (with 'untethered work' to the fore) in particular. High overall joblessness, covert ageism and an underdeveloped service sector (in Poland agriculture and manufacturing still account for more than 50 percent of employment) play their part, too (Zientara 2009b). All this, coupled with low pensions (ZUS 2013) and the nation's overall poor health (Symonides *et al.* 2010), makes it naive to expect most Poles to be particularly satisfied with their retirement. The next section, while showing what moving from work to retirement looks like in practice, explores these issues in the context of empirical example.

The experience of moving from work to retirement in Poland

Method

Since the choice of a research method should reflect the purpose and nature of a study (Yin 2003), we carried out semi-structured interviews (Kvale 1996). This is because they offer 'high validity of the linguistic and social categories used by

104   *P. Zientara*

protagonists in order to make sense of their situation' (Mueller *et al.* 2003: 79). Generally, interviewing, regarded as especially suitable for an exploratory study (Saunders *et al.* 1997), is an effective tool for gaining access to – and investigating – opinions, views and perceptions (Kvale 1996). Specifically, we came up with a set of specific questions (in Polish) bearing upon the issues under consideration. They were derived from the literature on the subject. In particular, we drew on the work by Armstrong-Stassen (2008), Quick and Moen (1998), Fouquereau *et al.* (2005) and Neuman (2011). Sample items of the questions are as follows: 'Were you satisfied with your job near the end of your professional career?', 'Would you describe your passage from work to retirement as abrupt or gradual?', 'Why did you decide to retire?', 'Did you want to continue working, but for some reasons you had to quit?', 'Did you take into account such factors as the financial situation or health while deciding to retire?', 'Did your employer do anything to ensure flexible working arrangements?' and 'What do you think of the government's proposal to increase the pensionable age to 67 for both sexes?'.

We then asked by email HR managers from six Pomerania-based companies (in the north of Poland) to contact, on our behalf, their recently retired employees and to invite them to be interviewed. The businesses in question were representative of the local economic base: a provider of financial services, a cosmetics producer, a bank, an upmarket hotel, an insurance corporation and a high-end furniture manufacturer. Subsequently, the HR managers provided us with the email addresses of those employees who agreed to be interviewed (on condition of anonymity). We then contacted them and arranged interviews. Altogether, we talked to 13 retired individuals (ten men and three women). They were all aged over 55 and had retired at least six months earlier (so, when they were being interviewed, they had been pensioners for at least six months). In this context, it is important to note that, while carrying out interviews (in the first half of 2012), we allowed our interlocutors to express themselves freely (which de facto determined the course of the conversation), treating the pre-set questions as prompts or pretexts for exploring the nuanced specificity of individual experience.

Discussion of the findings

As transpires from Table 5.1, having reached their pensionable age, none of the interviewees wanted to continue working. All of them admitted to being stressed and/or worn-out or just bored at the end of their professional careers. One of the interlocutors, who used to work in the hotel, even described himself as being 'totally burnt-out'.

Thus, in a way, they were all looking forward to retirement. The following utterance by a former (female) mid-ranking employee of the bank eloquently captures this state of mind:

> As time passed by, I realized that coming to work every morning really tires me: same faces, same chores, same documents ... And I felt that this

Table 5.1 Findings from the interviews

Retiree (R)	Aspect									
	Felt worn-out or bored	Accepted flexible workplace arrangements (including part-time work and telework from home)	Reckoned his or her job involved too much strain or experienced deteriorating health	Worries about future financial situation	Described his or her movement from work to retirement as gradual	Is happy as a retiree	Considers post-retirement employment	Approves of reformist plans	Feared dismissal before reaching the pensionable age	Does things he or she could not do before retiring
R1	+	−	+	−	−	+	−	+	+	+
R2	+	−	+	−	−	+	−	+	+	+
R3	+	−	+	−	−	+	−	+	?	+
R4	+	−	+	−	−	+	−	+	+	+
R5	+	−	+	?	−	+	−	+	+	+
R6	+	+	−	−	+	+	−	−	+	+
R7	+	+	+	−	+	+	−	+	?	+
R8	+	−	+	−	−	+	−	+	?	+
R9	+	−	+	−	−	+	−	−	?	+
R10	+	−	+	?	−	+	?	+	+	+
R11	+	−	+	+	−	−	?	+	+	+
R12	+	−	−	−	−	+	−	−	+	+
R13	+	−	+	?	−	+	?	−	+	+

Sources: Interviews conducted by the author.

Notes
+ = yes; − = no; ? = maybe.

106   P. Zientara

routine, this monotony somehow killed the joy of working and of meeting others. I simply did not feel like getting up in the morning. Besides, I had – and still have – problems with my health ... well, actually, some complications with my thyroid ... So at a certain time I realized that what I really wanted was to retire. And I did so as soon as I could.

She went on to say that she did not try out flexible workplace arrangements (although her employer had asked her to consider part-time employment). Likewise, the aforesaid hotel employee said that he had also been encouraged to work part-time, but he turned down this offer. And he added that being employed at an upscale hospitality establishment entails working seven days a week at unsocial hours, which puts a lot of strain on an older individual, even if he or she does not work full-time (in fact, both he and the bank employee seemed to be dissatisfied with their pre-retirement jobs). Another interviewee (previously working for a furniture manufacturer), while admitting to enjoying his last job, noted that his fast-deteriorating health simply did not allow him to continue working. Again, even though his employer wanted him to work part-time, he ruled this out. Indeed, 11 individuals reckoned that their last job involved too much strain or that they experienced health problems.

Altogether, only two retirees acknowledged having taken advantage of flexible workplace practices ('telework') and, not coincidentally, it was they who described their transition from work to retirement as gradual. Let us quote one of them (a woman previously employed in the cosmetics manufacturer):

Yes, I accepted the possibility of telework or working from home – it was rather convenient as I did not have to get up early and waste time in traffic jams. Of course, the character of my job made it possible. I know very well that there are many occupations which simply require people to be present in the office.... Well, but after a few months I decided to give it up, anyway ... I was very tired. You know, even if you work from home, you've got to meet deadlines, and this generates stress. And I simply didn't want to experience this feeling any more.

Others simply stopped working without any sort of intermediate stage facilitated by the availability of flexible arrangements (thus their passage from professional activity into retirement can be seen as abrupt). What all the interviewees highlighted, however, was the fact that, although they enjoyed a relatively high degree of job security, they feared dismissal (and, by implication, unemployment). In point of fact, nine of them acknowledged feeling terrified by the prospect of being fired before reaching the official pensionable age (it should be noted, however, that Polish workers are specially protected from dismissal during the last four years before retirement). They appeared well aware that – considering high unemployment, the incidence of ageism and the unfavorable characteristics of Poland's labor market – they stood little chance of finding new employment or feared that applying for a job at their age would constitute a humiliating experience. A former senior bank manager summed up these thoughts in the following way:

> Although I've got years of experience and know banking backwards, the very thought that I would have to apply for a job and go through a multi-stage recruitment process made me sick. And, you know, despite all the talk about equal opportunities, anti-discriminatory practices and all that jazz, ageism is still prevalent in Polish workplaces. Thank God, I wasn't fired and didn't have to go through this hell.

Given that, as we already know, Polish pensions are low, it is surprising that 12 interlocutors declared themselves happy as retirees (thereby exhibiting high levels of retirement satisfaction) and all said that they were doing things for which they had had no time before. Only one person (the worker at the furniture manufacturer) was not happy as a retiree (hence was dissatisfied with retirement). Perhaps not accidentally, he was the only person who expressed worries about his future financial situation (considering what he had done before retirement, one can presume that he had the lowest pension of all the interviewees). In this context, we may note in passing that the vast majority of interviewees also said that they had nothing against helping to mind their grandchildren. That could be related to the prevalence among older Poles of the traditional vision of the family, whereby grandparents help their children rather than to spend their time traveling or theater-going. Unsurprisingly, ten ruled out post-retirement employment (though three actually were willing to consider returning to work).

What is also worth emphasizing is the fact that four interviewees came out against the government's plans to raise the pensionable age for both sexes to 67, but the rest approved – albeit not without certain reservations – of the reform. Let us cite in this context a retiree from a financial service provider, who said that:

> Of course, I'm in favor of the reform ... without it, Poland will undoubtedly go bust! It's inevitable, you know. Moreover, we've got to realize that in 30 years' time, people will be much fitter and will enjoy better health than today's pensioners, and almost everybody will be IT literate. This generation will be totally different from ours and they'll be able to work longer.

But a few divergent opinions were aired, too. One pensioner, for instance, remarked that he 'can't imagine manual workers retiring at 67'. And he wryly pointed out that, compared with other Western European countries, Poland's average life expectancy is relatively short, so 'many Polish retirees will have little time enjoying themselves after decades of hard work'. This, admittedly, echoes the Solidarity leader's catchy statement that Poles will have to 'work till death' if, or when, the reform is eventually carried through. Yet the overall result – four people against and nine in favor – may be seen as surprising, considering that in most public-opinion polls, including the one we have referred to in the introductory part, the vast majority of respondents opposed the reformist plans.

108   P. Zientara

It is true that our sample is not representative, but the fact remains that support for the reform might actually be greater than the polls suggest among those in white-collar occupations and/or with university degrees. This constitutes an encouraging sign for the government and, for all the misgivings, bodes well, however cautiously, for the effective implementation of the change.

Conclusions

In the light of the above evidence, it is justified to assert that a gradual (flexible) transition from work to retirement is still rare in Poland. In fact, only two retirees admitted that they had gradually moved from professional activity into retirement. This was facilitated by the availability of flexible workplace arrangements. Yet there needs to be a recognition that most interlocutors acknowledged that flexible practices were in place in their workplaces (by the way, it is heartening to find out that, despite regulatory hostility to labor-market flexibility, Polish employers are increasingly willing to offer such solutions). Interestingly, other findings do not always confirm the results of earlier research (carried out in the West). So how do our findings relate to the insights from the literature reviewed in the theoretical part of the chapter?

Above all, in line with previous work, poor health proved to be an important predictor of (early and/or definitive) exit from the labor market (Arthur 2003; Barnes *et al.* 2004; Ilmarinen 2005). What is also striking in this context is the prevalent sensation of weariness and boredom – all the interlocutors described themselves as worn-out or stressed (which is hardly conducive to good form). From a certain point of view, this might be interpreted as a symptom of the sub-standard quality of HRM in Poland-based firms (although much rests on individual factors, such as one's lifestyle, etc.). Likewise, the fact that some pensioners – as we inferred, since we did not ask about it directly – seemed to have been dissatisfied with their pre-retirement jobs may bear out the presupposition that HRM in Poland still leaves much to be desired (which merits a follow-up study in its own right). On the other hand, health problems were not found to be associated with low retirement satisfaction. This is not in keeping with the conclusions drawn by Quick and Moen (1998), who found that those who experienced health problems (or reported low income) were less satisfied with their retirement.

As regards income, the situation – due to the specificity of Poland's socio-economic reality – is much more complicated. Indeed, the person who expressed worries about his financial situation (and who must have had a comparatively low pension) was not particularly pleased with his retirement. The rest declared themselves happy and satisfied, even though an average pension in Poland is quite low. In the light of what has been said about seniors' poor standing in the labor market, it is legitimate to claim that Polish older employees are faced – to a far greater extent than their Western European counterparts – with an unenviable dilemma: either retirement and relatively low but *secure* income or, in case of dismissal, an extremely ungenerous unemployment benefit (approximately one-third of an average pension) and bleak prospects for any job. Unsurprisingly, most go for the former. Of course, one might convincingly argue that the pensions of almost all the interviewees were (probably) high by Polish standards, so the fact that they were satisfied with their retirement was not that unusual and, in a sense, confirmed previous results.

Also worth emphasizing is the interlocutors' general reluctance to consider post-retirement employment. This finding is at odds with the evidence from the West, where a growing number of people actually return to work (Armstrong-Stassen 2008; Herz 1995). This might be due to the above-mentioned feeling of tiredness and boredom (which, in effect, discourages them from returning to work) and/or the apparent satisfaction with their pension-related income (which – albeit not very high, but secure – guarantees an acceptable standard of living). The willingness to help their children (by, for example, minding grandchildren) may play a part, too (as a return to professional activity, even on a part-time basis, might compromise this intent). One way or another, Poles will have to come to terms with the necessity of working longer. Given the European Commission's insistence on extending worklife in general and EU countries' tendency to raise the retirement age in particular, it is in Poland's interest to promote post-retirement employment.

Admittedly, the major limitation of this study is its small sample: indeed, 13 interviewees is not a large number (although the interviewees represented Pomerania's local economy base). Another problem is related to the way data were collected: the interview is a self-reported method, which suggests that, while interpreting and generalizing the results, some caution is in order. This is because the interlocutors – for a number of individual socio-psychological reasons – might not have been wholly sincere. That said, we strongly believe that the interviews were not marked by insincerity.

Thus it is hoped that the entire chapter offers important insights into the nitty-gritty of transition from work to retirement in an ex-communist country that is in the process of catching up with more affluent economies in Western Europe. Of course, further work building on the quantitative research framework is required to confirm and advance the chapter's findings. One might, therefore, carry out a questionnaire survey among older workers or recent retirees, which – by gleaning data from a larger number of people – would make the findings more representative and hence generalizable. Another follow-up study might focus on the attitudes of employers or policy-makers toward workplace arrangements facilitating a gradual transition from work to retirement. Given the developed world's demographics and public finances, this problem is likely to remain the focus of public policy interest and managerial thought for years to come. And Poland, which has not yet managed to completely shake off the communist legacy, is unlikely to be an exception in this respect.

110   *P. Zientara*

References

Armstrong-Stassen, M. (2008) 'Organisational practices and the post-retirement employment experience of older workers', *Human Resource Management Journal*, 18: 36–53.

Arthur, S. (2003) *Money, Choice and Control*, Bristol/York: Policy Press/Joseph Rowntree Foundation.

Balcerowicz, L. (1988) *The Soviet Type of Economic System and Innovativeness*, Warsaw: SGPIS.

Balcerowicz, L. (1995) *Freedom and Development: The Free-market Economics*, Kraków: Znak.

Balcerowicz, L. (2003) *Toward the Limited State*, Washington, DC: World Bank.

Balcerowicz, L., Błaszczyk, B. and Dąbrowski, M. (1997) 'The Polish way to the market economy 1989–1995', in S. Parker, J.D. Sachs and W.T. Woo (eds.), *Economies in Transition*, Cambridge, MA: MIT Press.

Balibar, E. (1995) *The Philosophy of Marx*, London: Verso.

Barnes, H., Parry, J. and Lakey, J. (2002) *Forging a New Future: The Experiences and Expectations of People Leaving Paid Work over 50*, Bristol: Policy Press.

Barnes, H., Parry, J. and Taylor, R. (2004) *Working after State Pension Age: Qualitative Research*, Department for Work and Pensions Research Report 208, London: DWP.

Bender, K.A. (2004) *The Well-being of Retirees: Evidence Using Subjective Data*, Center for Retirement Research, Working Paper 2004, 24.

Blundell, R., Lessof, C. and Nazroo, J. (2003) *Health, Wealth and Lifestyles of the Older Population in England: The 2002 English Longitudinal Study of Ageing*, London: Institute for Fiscal Studies.

Boxall, P. and Purcell, J. (2008) *Strategy and Human Resource Management*, New York: Palgrave Macmillan.

Budd, J.W. (2004) *Employment with a Human Face: Balancing Efficiency, Equity, and Voice*, Ithaca, NY: Cornell University Press.

Central Statistical Office (2013a) *A Monthly Report on Unemployment in Poland in February 2013*, Warsaw: Central Statistical Office. Online. Available at: www.stat.gov.pl/gus/5840_1446_PLK_HTML.htm (accessed March 27, 2013).

Central Statistical Office (2013b) *Population Forecast in 2003–2030*, Warsaw: Central Statistical Office. Online. Available at: www.stat.gov.pl/cps/rde/xbcr/gus/prognoza_ludnosci_ogolem.xls (accessed March 26, 2013).

Central Statistical Office (2013c) *Registered Unemployment in 2012*, Warsaw: Central Statistical Office. Online. Available at: www.stat.gov.pl/gus/5840_676_PLK_HTML.htm (accessed March 31, 2013).

Charles, K.K. (2002) 'Is retirement depressing? Labor force inactivity and psychological well being in later life', National Bureau of Economic Research, Working Paper 9033.

Davis, F. (2003) 'Factors related to bridge employment participation among private sector early retirees', *Journal of Vocational Behavior*, 63: 55–71.

Davis, N. (2005) *God's Playground*, New York: Columbia University Press.

Dharwadkar, R., George, G. and Brandes, P. (2000) 'Privatization in emerging economies: An agency theory perspective', *Academy of Management Review*, 25: 650–69.

Dobosz-Bourne, D. and Jankowicz, A.D. (2006) 'Reframing resistance to change: Experience from General Motors Poland', *International Journal of Human Resource Management*, 17: 2021–34.

Doeringer, P.B. (1990) *Bridges to Retirement: Older Workers in a Changing Labor Market*, Ithaca, NY: ILR Press.

Evidence from Poland 111

Dundon, T., Wilkinson, A., Marchington, M. and Ackers, P. (2004) 'The meanings and purpose of employee voice', *International Journal of Human Resource Management*, 15: 1149–70.

Dychtwald, K., Erickson, T. and Morison, B. (2004) 'It is time to retire retirement', *Harvard Business Review*, 82: 48–58.

Economist, The (2005) 'Gerontocapitalism', 8458: 14.

Economist, The (2008) 'Work in progress', 8571: 37.

Economist, The (2011a) 'A tale of three islands', 8756: 29–32.

Economist, The (2011b) 'The sun shines bright', 8762: 68–70.

Economist, The (2013) 'To privatise or not to privatise', 8819: 28.

Egorov, V. (1996) 'Privatization and labor relations in the countries of eastern Europe', *Industrial Relations Journal*, 27: 89–100.

Elder, H.W. and Rudolph, P.M. (1999) 'Does retirement planning affect the level of retirement satisfaction?', *Financial Services Review*, 8: 117–27.

European Commission (2004) 'Increasing the employment of older workers and delaying the exit from the labor market', COM(2004) 146, Brussels.

European Commission (2005) 'Confronting demographic change: A new solidarity between the generations', COM(2005) 94, Brussels.

European Commission (2006) *Ageing and Employment: Identification of Good Practice to Increase Job Opportunities and Maintain Older Workers in Employment*, Brussels: Directorate General for Employment, Social Affairs and Equal Opportunities.

Eurostat (2013) *Employment and Unemployment*. Online. Available at: http://epp.eurostat.ec.europa.eu/portal/page/portal/employment_unemployment_lfs/data/database (accessed March 26, 2013).

Fey, C., Engström, P. and Björkman, B. (1999) 'Effective human resource management practices for foreign firms in Russia', *Organizational Dynamics*, Autumn: 69–79.

Filatotchev, I., Wright, M. and Bleaney, M. (1999) 'Privatization, insider control and managerial entrenchment in Russia', *Economics of Transition*, 7: 481–504.

Forbes (2013) 'Budget will pay even 65.7 billion zlotys to pensions in 2013'. Online. Available at: www.forbes.pl/artykuly/sekcje/wydarzenia/budzet-doplaci-nawet-65-7-mld-zl-do-emerytur-w-2013,20973,1 (accessed April 1, 2013).

Forman, J.D. (1972) *Communism from Marx's Manifesto to 20th Century Reality*, New York: Watts.

Fouquereau, E., Fernandez, A., Fonseca, A.M., Paul, M.C. and Uotinen, V. (2005) 'Perceptions of and satisfaction with retirement: A comparison of six European Union countries', *Psychology and Aging*, 20: 524–8.

Frank, F.D., Finnegan, R.P. and Taylor, C.R. (2004) 'The race for talent: Retaining and engaging workers in the 21st century', *Human Resource Planning*, 23: 12–25.

Gawrońska-Nowak, B. and Skorupińska, K. (2006) 'Labor-market flexibility and the character of institutions in European countries', *Gospodarka Narodowa*, 3: 23–40.

Gendell, M. (1998) 'Trends in retirement age in four countries, 1965–95', *Monthly Labor Review*, 121: 20–30.

Góra, M. (2003) *System Emerytalny*, Warsaw: Polskie Wydawnictwo Naukowe.

Herz, D.E. (1995) 'Work after early retirement: An increasing trend among men', *Monthly Labor Review*, 118: 13–20.

Hirsch, D. (2005) *Sustaining Working Lives: A Framework for Policy and Practice*, York: Joseph Rowntree Foundation.

Hyman, R. (1971) *Marxism and the Sociology of Trade Unionism*, London: Pluto Press.

Ilmarinen, J. (2005) *Towards a Longer Worklife! Ageing and the Quality of Worklife in*

112   *P. Zientara*

the European Union, Helsinki: Ministry of Social Affairs and Health, Finnish Institute of Occupational Health.

Jankowicz, A.D. (1998) 'Issues in human resource management in Central Europe', *Personnel Review*, 27: 169–76.

Johns, T. and Gratton, L. (2013) 'The third wave of virtual work', *Harvard Business Review*, January–February: 66–73.

Koubek, J. and Brewster, C. (1995) 'Human resource management in turbulent times: HRM in the Czech Republic', *International Journal of Human Resource*, 6: 223–38.

Kvale, S. (1996) *Interviews*, London: Sage.

Lavigne, M. (1999) *The Economics of Transition: From Socialist Economy to Market Economy*, New York: St. Martin's Press.

Lissenburgh, S. and Smeaton, D. (2003) *Employment Transitions of Older Workers: The Role of Flexible Employment in Maintaining Labor Market Participation and Promoting Job Quality*, Bristol/York: Policy Press/Joseph Rowntree Foundation.

Loretto, W. and White, P. (2006) 'Employers' attitudes, practices and policies towards older workers', *Human Resource Management Journal*, 16: 313–30.

McNair, S. (2005) 'The age of choice: A new agenda for learning and work', in A. Tuckett and A. McAulay (eds.), *Demography and Older Learners*, Leicester: NIACE.

Maczynski, J. (1994) 'Culture and leadership styles: A comparison of Polish, Austrian and US managers', *Polish Psychological Bulletin*, 28: 255–67.

Magd, H. (2003) 'Management attitudes and perceptions of older workers in hospitality management', *International Journal of Contemporary Hospitality Management*, 15: 393–401.

Marchington, M. and Wilkinson, A. (2005) 'Direct participation and involvement', in S. Bach (ed.), *Managing Human Resources*, Oxford: Blackwell.

Martin, R. (2006) 'Segmented employment relations: Post-socialist managerial capitalism and employment relations in Central and Eastern Europe', *International Journal of Human Resource Management*, 17: 1353–65.

Mueller, F., Sillence, J., Harvey, C. and Howorth, C. (2003) 'A rounded picture is what we need: Rhetorical strategies, arguments and the negotiation of change in a UK hospital trust', *Organization Studies*, 25: 75–93.

Neuman, K. (2011) 'Is there another union premium? The effect of union membership on retirement satisfaction', *Industrial and Labor Relations Review*, 64: 981–99.

OECD (2004) *Ageing and Employment Policies: United Kingdom*, Paris: OECD.

OECD (2006) *Live Longer, Work Longer*, Paris: OECD.

OECD (2013) *StatExtracts*. Online. Available at: http://stats.oecd.org/Index.aspx? QueryId=19465 (accessed March 27, 2013).

onet.pl (2013) *Duda: The Pension Bill Condemns Poles to Work till Death*. Online. Available at: http://wiadomosci.onet.pl/emerytury,5140992,temat.html (accessed April 2, 2013).

Peltokorpi, V., Nonaka, I. and Kodama, M. (2007) 'NTT DoCoMo's launch of I-Mode in the Japanese phone market: A knowledge creation perspective', *Journal of Management Studies*, 44: 50–72.

Phillipson, C. and Smith, A. (2005) *Extending Working Life: A Review of the Research Literature*, Department for Work and Pensions Research Report 299, London: DWP.

Polskie Radio (2013) *TNS OBOP Survey*. Online. Available at: www.polskieradio.pl/5/3/ Artykul/570335,Sondaz-TNS-OBOP-Polacy-nie-chca-dluzej-pracowac (accessed March 28, 2013).

PRO INNO Europe (2011) *Innovation Union Scoreboard 2010*. Online. Available at:

Evidence from Poland 113

www.proinno-europe.eu/inno-metrics/page/innovation-union-scoreboard-2010 (accessed May 26, 2011).

Quick, H.E., and Moen, P. (1998) 'Gender, employment, and retirement quality: A life course approach to the differential experiences of men and women', *Journal of Occupational Health Psychology*, 3: 44–64.

Rymsza, M. (2005) 'In search of balance between labor-market flexibility and social safety: Poland on the road towards flexicurity', in M. Rymsza (ed.), *Flexible Labor Market and Social Safety: Flexicurity à la Polonaise? Social-policy Programme*, Warsaw: Instytut Spraw Publicznych.

Saunders, M., Lewis, P. and Thornhill, A. (1997) *Research Methods for Business Students*, London: Pitman Publishing.

Siemianowicz, J. (2006) 'Transformation, integration and then?', *International Journal of Entrepreneurship and Innovation Management*, 6: 102–9.

Smith, D.B. and Moen, P. (2004) 'Retirement satisfaction for retirees and their spouses: Do gender and the retirement decision making process matter?', *Journal of Family Issues*, 25: 262–85.

Soulsby, A. and Clark, E. (1998) 'Controlling personnel: Management and motive in the transformation of the Czech enterprise', *International Journal of Human Resource Management*, 9: 79–98.

Spiegel, P.E. and Schultz, K.S. (2003) 'The influence of preretirement planning and transferability of skills on naval officers' retirement satisfaction and adjustment', *Military Psychology*, 15: 285–307.

Strauss, G. (2006) 'Worker participation: Some under-considered issues', *Industrial Relations*, 45: 778–803.

Symonides, B., Tyszkiewicz, J., Figurny-Puchalska, E. and Gaciong, Z. (2010) *National Test of the Health of Poles*. Online. Available at: http://slimak.onet.pl/_m/mep/narodowy_test_zdrowia/MedOnet_'Raport_Narodowy_Test_Zdrowia_Polakow.pdf (accessed December 31, 2011).

Sztompka, P. (2002) *Sociology*, Kraków: Znak.

Tischner, J. (1992) *The Ethics of Solidarity: Homo Sovieticus*, Kraków: Znak.

Tittenbrun, J. (1992) *The Collapse of Real Socialism in Poland*, Poznań: Rebis.

Tung, R. and Havlovic, S. (1996) 'Human resource management in transitional economies: The case of Poland and the Czech Republic', *International Journal of Human Resource Management*, 7: 1–19.

Uhlenbruck, K. and De Castro, J. (2000) 'Foreign acquisitions in Central and Eastern Europe: Outcomes of privatization in transitional economies', *Academy of Management Journal*, 43: 381–402.

Villosio, C., Di Pierro, D., Giordanengo, A., Pasqua, P. and Richiardi, M. (2008) *Working Conditions of an Aging Workforce*, Dublin: European Foundation for the Improvement of Living and Working Conditions.

Warr, P. (1996) 'Younger and older workers', in P. Warr (ed.), *Psychology at Work*, London: Penguin.

Weber Handwerker, E. (2011) 'Delaying retirement to pay for college', *Industrial and Labor Relations Review*, 64: 921–48.

Wiatrowski, W.J. (2001) 'Changing retirement age: Ups and downs', *Monthly Labor Review*, 124: 3–12.

Wooldridge, A. (2008) 'After Bush', *The Economist*, 8573: 3–16.

World Bank (2013) *Economy Rankings*. Online. Available at: www.doingbusiness.org/rankings (accessed March 27, 2013).

114 *P. Zientara*

World Economic Forum (2013) *The Global Competitiveness Index 2012–2013 Rankings.* Online. Available at: www3.weforum.org/docs/WEF_GCR_CompetitivenessIndexRanking_2012-13.pdf (accessed March 26, 2013).

Yin, R.K. (2003) *Case Study Research: Design and Methods*, Newbury Park, CA: Sage.

Zientara, P. (2008a) 'A report on the Polish labor market: An insider–outsider system', *Industrial Relations: A Journal of Economy & Society*, 47: 419–29.

Zientara, P. (2008b) 'Employment of older workers in Poland: Issues and policy implications', *Economic Affairs*, 28: 63–8.

Zientara, P. (2009a) 'Creativity, innovation and entrepreneurship in Poland in the post-war period', *International Journal of Decision Sciences, Risk and Management*, 1: 299–325.

Zientara, P. (2009b) 'Employment of older workers in Polish SMEs: Employer attitudes and perceptions, employee motivations and expectations', *Human Resource Development International*, 12: 135–53.

Zientara, P. and Kuczyński, G. (2009) 'HR practices and work-related attitudes in Polish public administration', *Eastern European Economics*, 47: 42–60.

ZUS (2013) *A Monthly Report on Selected ZUS Payments in 2013*. Online. Available at: www.zus.pl/files/INFMIES022013.pdf (accessed April 2, 2013).

6 Bridge employment in Spain

A possible option to postpone retirement

Carlos-María Alcover and Gabriela Topa

This chapter begins by outlining the salient features of Spain's socio-demographic context, in particular the marked aging of the population and the foreseeable rise in the dependency rate in the coming years, as well as the immediate impact of these trends on the labor market and retirement and pension systems. We then go on to look at the conditioning factors that affect work-life extension policies and practices, and the obstacles in the way of their adoption. In the third place, we provide data on early and compulsory retirement in Spain in recent years, and a description of the legal alternatives available to those wishing to continue working, such as partial or flexible retirement. Finally, we sketch the current state of work-life extension in Spain, illustrating the scant possibilities available and experiences of voluntary working after retirement. The chapter ends with some conclusions and our recommendations on the future of bridge employment in Spain.

The socio-demographic context and the labor market in Spain

Demographic trends and population aging

The over-sixties accounted for 11.2 percent of the world's people in 2011, and this figure is expected to reach 22 percent by 2050. Globally, the number of old people (i.e., those above the age of 60) will increase from 784 million in 2001 to more than 2 billion by 2050, and there could be as many as 2.8 billion by 2100 (United Nations 2011). Though this is a worldwide trend, the challenge seems most acute in Europe, where progressive aging has cast doubt on the medium-term affordability of health, social and pension systems (European Commission 2012; *The Economist* 2012). Long-term population aging could hobble productivity in the countries affected, dragging down growth rates. The United States accounted for 23 percent of world GDP in 2011, while China and the Eurozone each represented 17 percent, and Japan and India 7 percent. According to OECD forecasts, the Chinese economy will account for 28 percent of world GDP by 2060, India 18 percent, the United States 17 percent, the Eurozone 9 percent and Japan 3 percent (OECD 2012). Though aging will carry on apace in Asia over this period, it is expected to peak simultaneously in the countries of Eastern and Southern Europe, resulting in a significant fall in per capita GDP.

Forecasts for the next 50 years suggest that the percentage of old people in the EU-27 will increase progressively, and not just in the 65–79 segment, but most especially among those aged over 80. Taken together, both groups could in fact rise to as much as 30 percent of the world's population (Figure 6.1).

Among the countries of the European Union, Spain is particularly affected by progressive aging (Conde-Ruiz and González 2011; Instituto Nacional de Estadística 2010), as the effects of rising life expectancy combine with a falling birth rate and shifts in the migratory flows that normally cushion processes of this kind (Alley and Crimmins 2007).

Assuming the continuation of current trends, Spain's demographic future looks set to feature progressive decline in the decades to 2052 as the population falls to 45 million in 2022, 2.5 percent less than in 2012, and to 42.5 million by 2052, 10.2 percent less than today, and an inversion of the age pyramid if current trends continue unabated, increasing the imbalance between those over and under 40 years of age (Instituto Nacional de Estadística 2012). Figure 6.2 shows the projected age pyramid for the Spanish population over the next four decades.

The fastest absolute and relative growth rates over the coming 40 years will be concentrated among older people. Specifically, the group aged over 64 will grow to more than twice its current size, increasing by 7.2 million people (89 percent) or 37 percent of Spain's total population. In contrast, the population of Spaniards aged between 16 and 64 will fall by 9.9 million (32 percent), and the group aged between 0 and 15 will fall by some 2 million (26 percent) (Instituto Nacional de Estadística 2012).

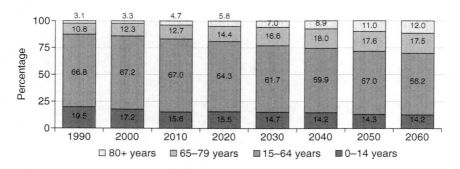

Figure 6.1 Population structure by major age groups, EU-27, 1990–2060 (source: Eurostat (online data codes: demo_pjanind and proj_10c2150p)).

Notes
Excluding French overseas departments in 1990; 2010, provisional; 2020–2060 data are projections (EUROPOP2010 convergence scenario).

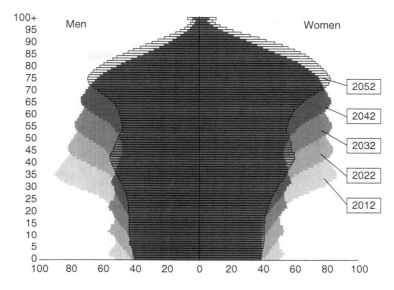

Figure 6.2 Population pyramid forecasts for Spain (source: Instituto Nacional de Estadística).

Evolution of the dependency rate

The dependency rate is calculated as the number of people aged between 15 and 64 for every person aged over 65, and it indicates the burden of dependants carried by potential workers. In 2005, the dependency rate in Spain was 24 dependants for every 100 workers, slightly below the average for Western Europe (Muszyńska and Rau 2012). If current demographic trends and behaviors continue, however, it could rise to as high as 58 percent. This means there would be as many as almost six potentially inactive people (i.e., those younger than 16 or older than 64 years of age) for every ten people of working age in Spain. Furthermore, the country is set to top the world ranking by 2050, ahead of Italy and Japan (Harper 2010) with an estimated dependency rate of more than 76 percent, the highest in Western Europe (Muszyńska and Rau 2012). It is even possible that the rate could reach 99 percent, so there would be almost one dependant for every person of working age (Instituto Nacional de Estadística 2012).

These potential dependency rates could have far-reaching consequences for social security systems, especially conventional pay-as-you-go arrangements like the Spanish one, in which active employees fund pensioners' benefits (United Nations 2011). Like the majority of its European peers (Hershey *et al.* 2010), Spain is one of the countries where public programs tend to be central to the pension system, making up the lion's share of most pensioners' incomes.

The interaction of various factors is expected to double the Spanish dependency rate by the end of the next decade. (1) Infant mortality has fallen to less

118   C.-M. Alcover and G. Topa

than 4 deaths per 1,000 births. (2) Life expectancy has progressively increased. In 2012, it was 81.9 years in Spain, the second highest in the world after Japan, and it will reach 83.3 years for men and as much as 88.1 for women by around 2031 less than two decades from now. At the same time, life expectancy at the age of 65 will increase by 2.9 years for men (to 21.3 years) and 2.6 years for women (to 24.9 years). (3) The migratory balance has turned negative, in the first place because of the decline in the flow of immigrants, who traditionally have a lot of children and significantly boosted the Spain's working-age population in the last two decades of economic boom, and in the second place because of increasing emigration. These factors resulted in a negative migratory balance of 181,479 people in 2012, out of a total population of 46,196,278 people on January 1 of that year (Instituto Nacional de Estadística 2011, 2012).

Labor market, retirement age and pension system

Spain is currently suffering from runaway unemployment, which reached 26.02 percent in the last quarter of 2012 (Instituto Nacional de Estadística 2013), the highest rate in the EU-27 (Eurostat 2012). Joblessness is especially acute among the young, running at a rate of more than 56 percent. The causes of this situation, which is likely to accentuate the inversion of migratory trends still further, can be traced directly to the crisis in the world economy in 2008 and its knock-on effects on the European financial crisis. A weak, shrinking labor market has discouraged immigration and forced ever wider segments of the Spanish population, in particular the young, to seek job opportunities in other European countries and even further afield.

Population aging has a direct impact on the labor market, as rising life expectancy affects not only the legal retirement age and pension systems, but also individual decisions to stay in work longer. For several years now, projections in the United States have relentlessly pointed to the existence of ever fewer workers to support entitlement programs like Social Security and Medicare, and to ever larger cohorts of retirees drawing benefits (Cahill et al. 2011; Lee 2004), prompting concern over financing and discussion of ways to encourage older workers to stay on in the labor force and extend their working lives beyond the compulsory retirement age. This scenario and the associated debate have been mirrored in Canada (Fougère et al. 2005), Japan (Conrad 2008; Peng 2008), the United Kingdom (Clayton 2010; Phillipson and Smith 2005) and other European countries (Börsch-Supan et al. 2005; Ilmarinen 2006).

The recent evolution of these socio-economic and job-related factors in Spain has caused profound concern among workers, trade unions, policy-makers and employers in the last five years, and has opened a pressing debate on the reforms needed to prolong the working lives of older people, reform the system of social security contributions and guarantee the viability of the pension system (Conde-Ruiz and Alonso 2006; Muñoz de Bustillo et al. 2011). Chief among the policies mooted are realignment of the retirement age with the new life cycle of the population (Peláez 2008) and measures to encourage a more flexible transition

Bridge employment in Spain 119

from working life to retirement, in view of the need to hold down rising pension costs and to act on the process of population aging itself. However, the potential policies and practices required face serious obstacles given the characteristics of the Spanish labor market.

Conditioning factors and obstacles to work-life extension in the Spanish labor market

Older workers in the labor market

The participation of workers aged over 55 in the Spanish labor market is below the EU average. In 2005, some 27 percent of women aged between 55 and 64 were in work and 60 percent of men were, compared to average EU-25 rates of 34 percent for women and 52 percent for men. Meanwhile, the overall rate in the 60–64 age bracket was 32 percent, which is actually slightly higher than the EU-25 average (27 percent), but in the 65–69 segment, it was just 4 percent, half the European rate (8 percent) (European Commission 2007). Data for 2010 show that the rate of employment among people aged between 55 and 59 years was 55 percent in Spain, compared to 60 percent for 33 European countries. The rate was 31 percent in the group aged between 60 and 64, which is similar to the European average of 30 percent (European Commission 2012). Other relevant data are the average age at which people leave the labor market (62 years of age in Spain in 2005, one year more than the EU-25 average) and the percentage of health-related inactivity in the group aged between 50 and 64 (23 percent of non-working people in Spain, compared to 16 percent in the EU-25) (European Commission 2007).

The rate of activity among 55- to 64-year-olds in Spain was still some 30 points behind the leading OECD economies in 2010, despite an increase of more than 10 points to around 45 percent since 1995. Furthermore, the activity rate was 84.2 percent in 1970, when Spain was placed behind only Sweden and the United Kingdom in Europe, and behind Japan and Canada among the OECD countries (Conde-Ruiz and Alonso 2006). However, the European Union and the OECD both now predict a sharp increase in the rate of employment among the elderly in Spain to more than 72 percent by 2060 (Doménech and García 2012), although any long-term projections must naturally be treated with caution in such a dynamic context.

As Engelhardt (2012) recently showed using data from the two waves of the Survey of Health, Ageing and Retirement in Europe (SHARE), about 86 percent of the regional variance in labor-market participation and 50 percent of the regional variance in labor-market exit for older males in 11 European nations can be attributed to country-specific factors, such as institutional differences in pension systems and welfare arrangements, employment relation systems, education systems and employment-sustaining active labor-market policies. Similar results were obtained by Börsch-Supan and colleagues (2009) in their analysis of European patterns of work and retirement based on the same sample. The

120   C.-M. Alcover and G. Topa

authors found that institutional differences between countries explain most cross-national divergences in patterns, while differences in health and demographics played only a minor role. Let us now look at the factors with the greatest impact on the Spanish labor market.

Early retirement incentives

The existence of strong organizational pressures to lose employees aged over 55, incentives for early retirement and generous public pension entitlements have created an *early retirement trap*, particularly in Southern and Central Europe (Angelini *et al.* 2009; Engelhardt 2012). At times of economic crisis, and in the face of labor-market contingencies, difficult financial conditions for business and rising unemployment, especially among the young, countries like Spain have allowed and encouraged mass use of early retirement plans over the last two decades, impelling large numbers of workers over the age of 50 to give up work (Alcover *et al.* 2012). As in other European countries (von Nordheim 2003), the spur to leave the labor market before the minimum retirement age has had an impact on various levels of Spanish society, ranging from risks affecting the funding and sustainability of entitlement programs to health and psychosocial welfare. Though the absence of any specific legislation and regulation of early retirement in Spain makes it difficult to establish the exact scope of the phenomenon in terms of the number workers affected and the financial conditions of early retirement plans, recent estimates based on benefits payments to persons aged over 53 suggest that the number of early retirees increased from 166,500 in 2006 to 213,800 in 2009, and 260,000 in 2010 (Jiménez-Martín 2012). These data are in line with international empirical studies, which confirm that early retirement is more prevalent in countries with generous early retirement regulations and incentives (Duval 2003).

Though it can of course be viewed as just another form of retirement, early retirement in fact comprises a wide range of quite different situations, which in turn result in an assortment of individual experiences and outcomes (Schalk *et al.* 2010). In the specific context of Spain, one of the key characteristics of early retirement schemes has been the perception that the process is *involuntary* (Alcover *et al.* 2012; Jociles and Franzé 2008). As Dorn and Sousa-Poza (2007) have argued, the *voluntary* or *involuntary* nature of early retirement is intrinsically subjective, and the key is therefore to examine how the workers affected experience such processes.

The study published by Dorn and Sousa-Poza (2007) shows that 32.5 percent of the early retirement schemes in Spain were perceived by the workers targeted as being *involuntary*, as opposed to 8.8 percent in Denmark, 9.4 percent in the United States and 12.2 percent in Canada. In the 45–69 age group, meanwhile, the ratio of early retirees per worker was 0.328 in Spain, the third highest score in the world behind only Slovenia (0.344) and Hungary (0.342), in contrast to ratios of just 0.062 in Norway, 0.080 in the United States and 0.081 in France. The results of the authors' own surveys of a sample of more than 600 Spanish early retirees reveal that the perception of involuntariness, measured in terms of perceived *employer pressure* as a reason for retirement, was the key push factor, easily trumping motives like *pursuit of own interests, health* or *job stress* (Alcover *et al.* 2012; Alcover and Crego 2005; Fernández *et al.* 2010, 2013). Employer pressure commonly takes the guise of organizational restructuring processes (Van Solinge and Henkens 2007) involving explicit or implicit policies of harassment (changes to working hours, reallocation of tasks, role overload, etc.) intended to create adverse working conditions and discomfit workers, obliging them to accept early retirement plans, albeit unwillingly (Crego and Alcover 2004). Our results are consistent with those derived from other studies carried out in Spain (Artazcoz *et al.* 2010), showing that forced early retirement owing to organizational downsizing reasons is related to poor health indicators, in this case among manual workers.

Early retirement, unemployment and the shadow economy

The strong incentives for unemployed older people to seek early retirement also have significant implications for activity rates. Recent data show that people in work between 60 and 65 years of age tend to retire at around 65, but those in this bracket who are already unemployed display high labor-market exit rates from the age of 60 onwards. The significant unemployment benefits paid at this age subsidize labor market drop-out and in part explain the low rate of re-entry among workers aged over 55, who tend to exhaust their unemployment benefits until they reach the early retirement age (García-Pérez *et al.* 2010). These data also support the evidence for the effect of institutional incentives on individual behavior and decisions.

The prevalence of informal working in the shadow economy is another important feature of the Spanish context. According to recent estimates, the shadow economy accounted for 19.2 percent of Spain's GDP in 2012, which is around the average for the EU-31 but is significantly above the rates in the most developed European and OECD nations, such as Germany where it is 13.5 percent of GDP, the United Kingdom (10.1 percent), Japan (8.8 percent) and the United States (7 percent) (Schneider 2012). Other estimates put Spain's shadow economy at 22.5 percent of GDP, compared to an EU average of 22.1 percent (CEOE 2012). In the absence of official, or wholly reliable, data about the shadow economy and the profiles of those engaging in underground transactions, it has been estimated that a significant number of people who are technically early retirees may in fact be moonlighting in jobs that have no formal existence, contributing to benefit and tax fraud. This means that numerous jobs are not formally recognized, although they certainly exist in the parallel universe of the shadow economy, resulting in a proportional loss of contributions to the social security and pension systems, not to mention a sizable volume of undeclared income taxes, which depresses tax receipts and acts as a drag on the formal economy, where the tax burden must be higher to offset forgone revenues (CEOE 2012). Finally, a larger shadow economy may also depress retirement

122 *C.-M. Alcover and G. Topa*

benefits by lowering the volume of regular social security and pension contributions.

Conclusions: the Spanish labor market and work-life extension

Three very different factors combine in the Spanish labor market to condition, and obstruct, work-life extension, hindering the implementation of effective policies and practices like bridge employment in contrast to developments in other countries over the last two decades. These factors are:

1   Structural: a generous, loosely regulated system allows both private firms and public organizations to launch mass early-retirement processes beginning at ages as low as 50.
2   Psychological and psychosocial: these schemes are perceived and accepted as involuntary, and many of the workers affected assume an attitude of *learned helplessness* (powerlessness, fatalism) in the face of early retirement. At the same time, powerful psychosocial processes construct a social identity for early retirees, in which they are perceived (and perceive themselves) as a class apart, enjoying but also suffering a situation that has both positive and negative features but is in any case irreversible, a kind of limbo that lasts until the age of formal retirement.
3   Legislative and regulatory: the rigid regulation of the labor market, and the social security and pension systems in Spain has so far prevented the development of viable bridge employment formulas that could provide alternatives in the transition between full-time work and final retirement.

The following pages examine the outlook for the future development of effective policy measures to prolong working life in Spain, with particular attention to bridge employment.

Outlook for the development of bridge employment in Spain

Early and compulsory retirement ages and percentages

The general age of compulsory retirement in Spain was 65 until 2012. This age limit was first established in the *Ley de Retiro Obrero* or 'Workers Retirement Act' of 1919, at a time when life expectancy in Spain was 42 years (Peláez 2008) and the vast majority of workers never reached the retirement age. Beginning on January 1, 2013, however, pension entitlements in Spain have been linked both to age and to the cumulative social security contributions made by retirees over the whole of their working lives, and the retirement age has been raised to 67 years, or 65 in the case of those with 38 years and 6 months' contributions. However, the increase in the retirement age from the former 65 years to the current 67 will be applied progressively in increments of one month per year, and it will not become general until 2027.

Bridge employment in Spain 123

Table 6.1 Evolution of the average retirement age in Spain, 2005–2011

CLASS	2005	2006	2007	2008	2009	2010	2011
General System	63.06	62.92	63.06	63.16	63.26	63.43	63.47
Total System	63.61	63.47	63.57	63.65	63.73	63.84	63.87

Source: Elaborated by the authors from Pacto de Toledo (2012b).

These measures are intended to raise the average age of retirement, which has increased only very slowly in comparison to the number of pensioners and rising life expectancy in Spain. Table 6.1 shows the trend for the period 2005–2011.

Spanish social security legislation makes it rigidly incompatible to draw a retirement pension and do paid work. Thus, anyone eligible for a retirement pension who decides to work on, either in a salaried job or as an independent professional, will see their benefits suspended until such time as they finally stop working. This absolute incompatibility explains why suspensions for continued occupational activity affected a mere 3,574 pensions at the close of 2012 (Pacto de Toledo 2012a), an absolutely nugatory figure given the 200,000 pensions awarded in Spain in the same year.

Moreover, the rate of early retirement was high throughout the last decade. According to available data (Pacto de Toledo 2012b), between 60 and 50 percent of retirees in Spain were below 65 years of age in each of the years from 2005 to 2011, and a significant number of these (around 10 percent) were aged 61 or younger.

Figure 6.3 shows the distribution of total new retirement discharges registered in the system in the period 2005–2011, including both self-employed and salaried workers.

As may be observed, the total number of retirement discharges at the age of 65 registered in the social security system is greater than the number of early

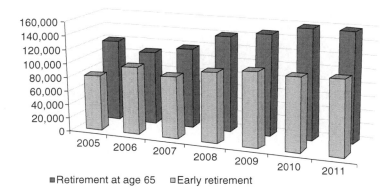

Figure 6.3 Evolution of retirement discharges, 2005–2011, Total System (source: elaborated by the authors from Pacto de Toledo 2012b).

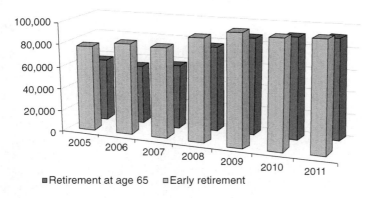

Figure 6.4 Evolution of retirement discharges, 2005–2011, General System (salaried employees, excluding self-employed workers) (source: elaborated by the authors from Pacto de Toledo 2012b).

retirements because of the general rule that self-employed workers are not eligible for early retirement. However, analysis of the General Social Security System, which includes only salaried employees registering for retirement, shows more than 50 percent applying for early retirement (see Figure 6.4), reflecting the strength of the trend in the Spanish labor market.

In short, the data reveal that the majority of Spanish workers who opt to work on are self-employed, and their average retirement age is 65.4 years. This decision is apparently motivated basically by the need to make social security contributions for a longer period in order to match the pensions paid to salaried workers.

Retention and work-life extension measures

The situation of the Spanish labor market in recent years and prevailing employment trends have encouraged the adoption of legislative measures to foster retention of older workers, work-life extension and even labor-market re-entry after retirement.

Though there is no Spanish term for bridge employment in general use, labor legislation allows two alternatives, *partial* and *flexible* retirement, which may be considered analogous to this concept.

Partial retirement

Partial retirement refers to the situation of contracted workers above 60 years of age (63 years in 2027) who voluntarily decide to accept a cut in their working hours and pay in return for drawing a retirement pension in proportion to the salary reduction based on current entitlements. *Partial retirement* is formalized via a part-time contract of employment that may or may not be associated with a relief contract made with an unemployed worker or a worker hired by the firm under a fixed-term temporary contract. The minimum reduction in working hours is 25 percent and the maximum is 75 percent, although this limit may be raised to 85 percent if the associated relief contract is for permanent, full-time employment. Thirty years' effective contributions are required, or 25 years' in the case of the physically or mentally disabled, and eligible employees must have at least six years' service to the employer immediately prior to the date of partial retirement. Another option is *partial retirement* at age 65, or the prevailing ordinary age of retirement, which involves continuation in work under a full- or part-time contract with a reduction of between 25 and 75 percent in working hours. Workers must have a minimum of 15 years' social security contributions to qualify, but there is no requirement either for minimum service with the employer or for any associated relief contract.

The data on *partial retirement* suggest that this option is in fact gaining ground rapidly, as the conditions are not particularly stringent and the application of very short working hours provides access to something like early retirement without any proportional reduction in benefits in the majority of cases. For example, 13,125 of the 25,877 partial retirements recorded in 2011 affected workers aged 60 years who were engaged for an average 18.8 percent of normal hours, but only 211 cases affected workers who had reached 64 years of age (engaged for an average 24.78 percent of hours). The data for the first half of 2012 reflect the same trend, with 12,725 partial retirements and average engagement equal to 20.06 percent of normal working hours (Pacto de Toledo 2012a). In this light, *partial retirement* seems so far to be failing in its principal function, which is to act as a psychosocial mechanism for the transmission of knowledge between generations of workers, facilitating active aging by keeping older people in the labor market on one hand and the uptake of young people in mentoring schemes on the other. Experience shows, however, that the system has been treated merely as a privileged form of early retirement, in which the social security system assumes all of the costs (Pacto de Toledo 2012a).

Flexible retirement

Flexible retirement offers retirees reaching the compulsory retirement age the possibility of combining their pensions with part-time work. This entails a proportional reduction in benefits based on the hours worked by the pensioner in comparison with the hours of a full-time worker doing the same job, defined as a worker in the same firm employed at the same facility under the same kind of contract, and doing the same or similar work. If a firm has no comparable full-time worker, the basis for comparison will be the full-time working hours established per the industry collective bargaining agreement, or in default thereof, the maximum working hours permitted by law. Working hours must be reduced by at least 25 percent with a maximum limit of 75 percent, and the *flexible retirement* arrangements must be formalized in a part-time contract.

126   *C.-M. Alcover and G. Topa*

Flexible retirement is allowed under all Spanish social security systems, except the Special Systems for State Functionaries, the Armed Forces and personnel employed in the Administration of Justice. The retirement pension due is reduced in proportion to the cut in the retiree's working hours compared to a full-time worker doing the same job. Meanwhile, social security contributions paid during the period of post-retirement work and suspension of the retirement pension are applied to increase the benefits the retiree will receive when he/she eventually stops working. The law does not establish any age limit for *flexible retirement*.

These arrangements have struggled to take root in Spain's employment culture, as evidenced by the small number of flexible retirements in the period 2008–2011 – just 2,802 (Pacto de Toledo 2012a). This figure may be considered merely incidental, revealing the negligible incentive provided by this work-life extension formula.

The context of work-life extension in Spain

Despite the limited uptake of the measures described above, public opinion has become increasingly alive to the debate over the extension of working life in recent years. Opinions differ sharply between workers and employers, the political parties and the trade unions.

According to recent data, 36 percent of employers see work-life extension as *highly beneficial*, 50 percent consider it *beneficial* and just 9 percent believe it to be *detrimental*, while 5 percent see it as *inconsequential*. However, those older workers whose continuation remains a matter of interest for employers tend to be highly qualified (92 percent), while medium- and low-skilled workers account for a meager 4 percent each (Doménech and García 2012). These data coincide with the results of SHARE, which clearly show that workforce participation, in terms of paid work, by older Europeans aged between 60 and 70 years is the domain of individuals enjoying already high socio-economic status. Well-educated, wealthy men who have achieved high levels of occupational prestige are particularly likely to engage in paid work, and the same may be said of their female counterparts (Komp *et al.* 2010). In Spain, 18 percent of men and 8 percent of women between the ages of 60 and 70 years are in paid work.

Workers appear markedly less keen on work-life extension than employers, reflecting a key characteristic of Spain's work culture. For example, a recent study (Pérez-Díaz and Rodríguez 2007) showed that 71 percent of Spaniards were against raising the compulsory retirement age in 1996, although this opposition had dropped to 55 percent by 2008. Only 25 percent of active workers over the age of 50 were prepared to contemplate the possibility of retiring after the age of 64, and the majority expressed the wish to retire at 60, although they expected to do so at 63. However, the study's authors found a marked unwillingness to consider the idea of working on, concluding that there was 'deliberate resistance' to work-life extension (Pérez-Díaz and Rodríguez 2007). The preferences of Spanish workers are again clearly expressed in their hostility to proposals to raise the retirement

Bridge employment in Spain   127

age, the least popular option to address the impact of demographic aging on the pension system (Muñoz de Bustillo 2007). This view of retirement in Spanish culture is also reflected in the results of a study involving a sample of men and women aged between 55 and 75, 70 percent of whom claimed to have accepted retirement completely or mostly, compared to only 10 percent who said they could not accept it (Fernández-Ballesteros 2009). As mentioned at the beginning of this chapter, however, perceptions are very different in the case of early retirement, which is widely perceived as involuntary (Alcover *et al.* 2012; Fernández *et al.* 2010, 2013).

Another interesting feature of the Spanish labor market is the tendency for workers aged over 50 to continue working long, full-time hours (43.5 hours per week in the case of men and 35.4 hours for women), portending a brusque switch from work to immediate, full retirement.

In the absence of specific empirical studies of bridge employment among the Spanish population, we may consider the sub-sample for Spain included in the SHARE survey, which has been used in a number of recent publications (Topa *et al.* 2009, 2014). Let us begin by looking at the respondents who were already in receipt of retirement benefits in 2003 (first data-gathering phase) but were also in paid employment. The total sample consisted of 1,190 people, and Spain accounted for 3.5 percent of cases. Correlative analysis of socio-demographic indicators shows that financial well-being, defined in terms of higher retirement incomes, is positively associated among subjects involved in bridge employment with good physical health and negatively associated with deteriorating mental health. Likewise, positive relationships were observed between physical health and length of service in the employer organization. Among psychosocial variables, the existence of family responsibilities (e.g., childcare, caring for the elderly and other domestic tasks) was moderately correlated with life and job satisfaction. Finally, the quality of bridge employment, defined in terms of the rewards obtained by the worker, was positively associated with length of service to the organization and physical health, and negatively associated with depression.

Longitudinal data obtained from the same sample in the following phase of the study (2006) allow a number of further observations. The hours worked in bridge employment in 2004 display negative correlations with measures of physical health and life satisfaction evaluated two years on, but the quality of working life in the bridge job was positively associated with physical health and work-life satisfaction. These data confirm the general trend in the Spanish subsample, which indicates that mere participation in bridge employment as an exit strategy from 'full-time' work is not in itself an indicator of personal well-being. It is also necessary to take into consideration the nature of the job in order to discover its potential to generate desirable personal and organizational outcomes such as life and job satisfaction.

Based on the above data, we may affirm that the Spanish work-life model is defined by the concept of *trajectory*, in which different, sharply contrasting stages are clearly delineated and the notion of a flexible prolongation of working

128   *C.-M. Alcover and G. Topa*

life has little or no place. This conflicts with trends in the majority of developed countries, which have moved toward the extension of working life through alternative employment formulas. One of the main consequences of this development is the replacement of *trajectory* by the concept of *transition* to define the work-life cycle (Elder and Johnson 2003). Above the age of 50, both men and women face a range of work-related, family, personal, economic and leisure events that condition their decisions to stay in the labor market under different conditions from the conventional full-time job, and to prolong their activity beyond the traditional retirement age, substantially altering the linear life course represented by a long period given over to full-time work until the cut-off point of definitive retirement is reached, followed by the passage to a situation of complete and irreversible idleness. As a consequence, retirement tends to come about in gradual steps (Calvo *et al.* 2009) or to take the form of partial retirement (Beehr and Bennett 2007). In short, the lives of people above the age of 50 have become less predictable (Henretta 2003), and variable, complex and contingent *transition* experiences lasting in some cases into an individual's seventies have come to define what was traditionally a well-defined stage in the life course of almost everyone. As Phillipson (2002) has argued, a new social contract is needed to negotiate and regulate these flexible transitions from working life to retirement, allowing institutions, firms and citizens to define fresh terms and conditions to their mutual benefit.

Voluntary work-life extension: the SECOT experience

The lack of a clear legislative framework regulating bridge employment in Spain has prevented many early retirees and pensioners from working on, even where they may have wished to do so. It is mainly for this reason that both individuals and organizations have taken initiatives in pursuit of a range of social and professional goals. The best example in Spain is *Seniors Españoles para la Cooperación Técnica* (SECOT; Spanish Seniors for Technical Cooperation), an independent non-profit association formed in 1989 as an initiative of the business organization *Círculo de Empresarios* with the support of the Spanish Council of Chambers of Commerce and the corporate social responsibility and sustainability consultancy, *Acción Social Empresarial*. SECOT was declared a public interest organization in 1995. SECOT's seniors are mostly early retirees or pensioners, although some of the organization's members still work. These volunteers offer their business know-how and experience to small and medium-sized enterprises (SMEs), young entrepreneurs and voluntary sector entities. SECOT currently has over 1,300 members and 47 branches and offices in numerous Spanish cities.

SECOT's main activities comprise the provision of advice to business start-ups, diagnosis and strategic planning for SMEs and entrepreneurs, participation in international cooperation projects and programs, technical and occupational training aimed at both members and non-members, studies and publications, tutorials, mentoring schemes, organization of seminars on retirement preparation, and the

Bridge employment in Spain 129

creation of think-tanks to address issues related with work-life extension and active aging. In 2011 SECOT provided advisory services to some 2,573 people (1,562 men and 1,011 women) aged between 18 and 35 years (1,324 people), 36 and 45 (888), 46 and 60 (333) and over 60 (28), contributing directly to the creation of 139 businesses and 232 direct jobs. Though this advice was provided mainly to Spanish citizens, the association also helped entrepreneurs from more than 30 different nationalities hoping to start a business in Spain. SECOT has also recently launched an online advisory service and created the *Escuela SECOT de Emprendedores* (ESEMP; School of Entrepreneurship), a business school designed to capitalize on the knowledge and experience of the seniors in the form of training programs for entrepreneurs seeking to start a business project in any field (www.secot.org). It has also taken part in a number of European initiatives including the Grundtvig program and the People project, and it is a member of the Brussels-based Confederation of Senior Expert Services (CESES) formed by 22 seniors' organizations from various EU Member States (www.ceses.net).

SECOT's psychosocial goals are, then, aimed at fostering good physical and mental health among older people by improving their quality of life through professional and intellectual activity in the form of voluntary business and advisory services and the strengthening of intergenerational relations. These activities have direct effects on the psychosocial quality of members' lives, allowing them to feel active and useful both to themselves and to society, obtain positive social feedback from their activities, keep abreast of their professional interests and enjoy physical and mental well-being, taking into account that seniors generally participate into their seventies. In interviews with the authors, various senior members of SECOT described their activities as *secotherapy* to explain the psychosocial benefits produced by their work. They also expressed the opinion that many of the organization's members would opt for bridge employment if the alternative existed in Spain, as they generally perceived the situation of both early and full retirement as an involuntary event.

Conclusions: the future of bridge employment in Spain

The progressive aging of Spain's population, together with the slow and difficult uptake of young people in the labor market and the reversal of the migratory balance, point to a doubling of the dependency rate over the coming decade. Changes to labor legislation will have to be made to sustain the current pension system, backed up by other policies including measures to bring sky-high youth unemployment down to more reasonable levels. In 2013 the Spanish government raised the obligatory retirement age to 67, although implementation will take place progressively over a number of years. Measures of this kind are fiercely opposed by a majority of workers, as the idea that retirement should come as soon as possible is deeply rooted in Spain's work culture. However, some extension of working life must be accepted if a drastic fall in retirement incomes is to be avoided, as various organizations of the self-employed have pointed out in recent years.

130   C.-M. Alcover and G. Topa

We believe that raising the retirement age is not the only measure that can be adopted, and perhaps not even the most effective one, given that not all occupations can be prolonged to the same degree depending on the physical and mental strains involved in the work, and adverse effects on workers' health and well-being. In this light, political leaders and opinion-makers need to look at the options for flexible, voluntary work-life extension negotiated between organizations and their workers, and bridge employment practices fit the bill. After all, the term refers to the continuation of older workers in employment during the transition period between full-time occupation and definitive retirement from the labor market (Feldman and Kim 2001; Shultz 2003).

The data available from other countries over the last 15 years show that the majority of older workers experience at least one transition of this kind between full-time working and full retirement (Cahill *et al.* 2006; Giandrea *et al.* 2007; Weckerle and Shultz 1999). These transitions occur both within the same occupation and in different occupations, and they may take the form either of salaried jobs or of some form of self-employment (Beehr and Bennett 2007). The latter option is the most prevalent as people grow older, as it allows greater freedom to satisfy needs like flexible working hours and personal autonomy, where salaried jobs tend to be more restrictive. This shows that entrepreneurial attitudes and behavior are in no way incompatible with old age (Davis 2003). The option of self-employment as a form of bridge working also has positive consequences for political leaders and employers, as it allows older workers to continue earning and paying social security dues and taxes, while providing organizations with the benefit of their knowledge, skills and experience via contingent agreements (Giandrea *et al.* 2008; Zissimopoulos and Karoly 2009). While motives may differ, the results of a recent meta-analysis suggest that older workers wish to remain in the labor market basically to satisfy intrinsic interests, such as the nature of the work, the satisfaction it provides and the motivation of success, for social reasons and to gain financial security (Kooij *et al.* 2011).

Alternatives for the extension of working life have gained ground in the lives of older workers in the United States, Canada, the United Kingdom, the nations of Northern Europe, Australia and Japan. Experiences of this kind in countries like Spain, France and Italy, as well as the nations of Central and South-Eastern Europe remain relatively few, however, and bridge employment is still far from being the norm in retirement processes (Börsch-Supan *et al.* 2005; Topa *et al.* 2009, 2014). Workers' expectations and ability to plan ahead and decide the terms of their continued participation in work-life are of enormous importance to the expansion and generalization of gradual transitions between working life and full retirement. In this light, the existence of institutional, structural and legal restrictions and obstacles may have a significant inhibiting effect on bridge employment experiences in different countries (Raymo *et al.* 2010), with the consequent loss of potential benefits for workers, organizations and society in general.

We believe the implementation of alternatives for bridge employment would be highly beneficial to achieve the following goals in Spain:

1 to ensure continued labor-market participation by workers who wish voluntarily to prolong their working lives, either for personal or for financial reasons, while they remain capable of working effectively at the required levels;
2 to improve health and general well-being through continued working, and to attain other desirable psychosocial outcomes like the preservation of the individual's social identity and networks, job and life satisfaction, and facilitation of the transition to full retirement;
3 to help organizations retain skilled, experienced employees with high levels of intellectual and social capital, thereby stemming the knowledge drain caused by the mass outflow of older workers from Spanish firms in the last two decades;
4 to bolster policies and practices designed to support active aging and foster a positive image of old people, and to reduce or prevent stereotyping and prejudice associated with old age, and combat increasing age discrimination in the workplace;
5 to secure the viability of current pension and social welfare systems, protecting the model of generational solidarity characteristic of Spanish society in recent decades and helping to maintain the autonomy and dignity of a long-lived population.

In short, the implementation of bridge employment alternatives in Spain, and the incipient reform of the pension system, should seek to reduce early retirement and the expulsion of older people from working life, and help to prolong working life both by raising the obligatory retirement age and removing age limits for people who voluntarily wish to continue working. Measures such as these would surely contribute to improved health and well-being among older citizens in line with the example set by other European countries (Alcover and Crego 2008). However, these measures will also need to be supplemented by additional lifelong-learning programs, as well as a significant expansion of training provision. These policies should not be aimed only at specific groups of unemployed older workers but should consciously target the least skilled (Engelhardt 2012) given that organizations tend to prefer better qualified older workers (Doménech and García 2012), significantly lowering the chances of finding paid work for old people of lower socio-economic status (Komp *et al.* 2010).

As some scholars (e.g., Muñoz de Bustillo 2007) have argued, options to bring forward the age at which young people join the labor market should also be examined, including measures such as the design of effective occupational training programs and short-cycle higher education, in order to extend the working lives of young Spanish people and the total numbers contributing to the social security system.

Finally, bridge employment alternatives are linked to EU directives on workplace health in an aging society, structured around a strategic reorientation combining integration and preventive plans (Morschhäuser and Söchert 2006). Integration seeks to preserve the jobs of older workers, while preventive

132 C.-M. Alcover and G. Topa

approaches also seek to ensure good health and employability over the whole of a worker's active life, regardless of its actual duration. The problems facing Spanish society are certainly great, but ducking the challenge could jeopardize welfare provision for the majority of the population in the coming decades.

References

Alcover, C.M. and Crego, A. (2005) 'Factores implicados en la decisión de retiro laboral temprano: aproximaciones desde el análisis del discurso de una muestra de prejubilados españoles' [Factors implied in early retirement decision: Discourse analysis of a sample of Spanish early retirees], *Revista de Psicología Social Aplicada*, 15: 133–63.

Alcover, C.M. and Crego, A. (2008) 'Modalidades de retiro laboral en Europa: bienestar psicológico y factores psicosociales asociados. Introducción al número especial' [Varieties of work retirement in Europe: Psychological well-being and associated psychosocial factors – Introduction to the special issue], *Revista de Psicología del Trabajo y de las Organizaciones*, 24: 277–82.

Alcover, C.M., Crego, A., Guglielmi, D. and Chiesa, R. (2012) 'Comparison between the Spanish and Italian early work retirement models: A cluster analysis approach', *Personnel Review*, 41: 380–403.

Alley, D. and Crimmins, E. (2007) 'The demography of aging and work', in K.S. Shultz and G.A. Adams (eds.), *Aging and Work in the 21st Century*, Mahwah, NJ: Lawrence Erlbaum.

Angelini, V., Brugiavini, A. and Weber, G. (2009) 'Ageing and unused capacity in Europe: Is there an early retirement trap?', *Economic Policy*, 24: 463–508.

Artazcoz, L., Cortès, I., Borrell, C., Escribà-Agüir, V. and Cascant, L. (2010) 'Gender and social class differences in the association between early retirement and health in Spain', *Women's Health Issues*, 20: 441–7.

Beehr, T.A. and Bennett, M.M. (2007) 'Examining retirement from a multi-level perspective', in K.S. Shultz and G.A. Adams (eds.), *Aging and Work in the 21st Century*, Mahwah, NJ: Lawrence Erlbaum.

Börsch-Supan, A., Brugiavini, A. and Croda, E. (2009) 'The role of institutions and health in European patterns of work and retirement', *Journal of European Social Policy*, 19: 341–58.

Börsch-Supan, A., Brugiavini, A., Jürges, H., Mackenbach, J., Siegrist, J. and Weber, G. (eds.) (2005) *Health, Ageing and Retirement in Europe: First Results from the survey of Health, Ageing and Retirement in Europe*, Mannheim: Mannheim Research Institute for the Economics of Aging. Online. Available at: www.share-project.org/t3/share/uploads/tx_sharepublications/SHARE_FirstResultsBookWave1.pdf (accessed July 27, 2012).

Cahill, K.E., Giandrea, M.D. and Quinn, J.F. (2006) 'Retirement patterns from career employment', *The Gerontologist*, 46: 514–23.

Cahill, K.E., Giandrea, M.D. and Quinn, J.F. (2011) 'Reentering the labor force after retirement', *Monthly Labor Review*, June: 34–42.

Calvo, E., Haverstick, K. and Sass, S.A. (2009) 'Gradual retirement, sense of control, and retirees' happiness', *Research on Aging*, 31: 112–35.

CEOE, Confederación Española de Organizaciones Empresariales (2012) *La economía sumergida en España frente al resto de países desarrollados* [*The Shadow Economy in Spain Compared to Other Developed Countries*]. Online. Available www.cen7dias.es/BOLETINES/356/EconomiaSumergidaEspana.pdf (accessed February 20, 2013).

Bridge employment in Spain 133

Clayton, P.M. (2010) 'Working on: Choice or necessity?', in European Centre for the Development of Vocational Training (CEDEFOP), *Working and Ageing: Emerging Theories and Empirical Perspectives*, Luxembourg: Publications Office of the European Union.

Conde-Ruiz, J.I. and Alonso, J. (2006) 'El sistema de pensiones en España ante el reto del envejecimiento' [The pension system in Spain faced with the challenge of aging], *Presupuesto y Gasto Público*, 44: 51–73.

Conde-Ruiz, J.I. and González, C.I. (2011) *Envejecimiento y ciclo vital* [*Aging and life course*], Apuntes FEDEA, Bienestar 01. Online. Available www.fedea.net/apuntes/apuntes/bienestar/apunte_bienestar01_envejecimiento.pdf (accessed February 20, 2013).

Conrad, H. (2008) 'Human resource management practices and the ageing workforce', in F. Coulmas, H. Conrad, A. Schad-Seifert and G. Vogt (eds.), *The Demographic Challenge: A Handbook about Japan*, Leiden: Brill.

Crego, A. and Alcover, C.M. (2004) 'La experiencia de prejubilación como fenómeno psicosocial: estado de la cuestión y propuesta de un marco teórico para la investigación' [Early retirement experience as psychosocial event: Research status and proposal of a theoretical framework], *Revista de Psicología del Trabajo y de las Organizaciones*, 20: 291–336.

Davis, M.A. (2003) 'Factors related to bridge employment participation among private sector early retirees', *Journal of Vocational Behavior*, 63: 55–71.

Doménech, R. and García, J.R. (2012) 'Prolongación de la vida laboral: retos y oportunidades' [Extending working life: Challenges and opportunities], Universidad Internacional Menéndez Pelayo, *Envejecimiento activo y prolongación de la vida laboral* [*Active Aging and Extension of Working Lives*]. Santander, July 10, 2012. Online. Available at: http://serviciodeestudios.bbva.com/KETD/fbin/mult/120710_Prolongaciondelavidalaboral_tcm346-338524.pdf?ts=1922013 (accessed March 3, 2013).

Dorn, D. and Sousa-Poza, A. (2007) *'Voluntary' and 'Involuntary' Early Retirement: An International Analysis*, IZA Discussion Paper No. 2714, Bonn: Forschungsinstitut zur Zufunft der Arbeit.

Duval, R. (2003) *The Retirement Effects of Old-age Pension and Early Retirement Schemes in OECD Countries*, OECD Economics Department Working Papers No. 24, November 2003. Online. Available at: http://search.oecd.org/officialdocuments/display documentpdf/?doclanguage=en&cote=eco/wkp(2003)24 (accessed March 26, 2013).

Economist, The (2012) *A New Vision for Old Age: Rethinking Health Policy for Europe's Ageing Society, A Report for the Economist Intelligence Unit*, London: The Economist Intelligence Unit Ltd. Online. Available www.managementthinking.eiu.com/sites/default/files/downloads/A%20new%20vision%20for%20old%20age_0.pdf (accessed August 27, 2012).

Elder, G. and Johnson, M. (2003) 'The life course and aging: Challenges, lessons and new directions', in R.R. Settersten (ed.), *Invitation to the Life Course*, New York: Baywood Publishing.

Engelhardt, H. (2012) 'Late careers in Europe: Effects of individual and institutional factors', *European Sociological Review*, 28: 550–63.

European Commission (2007) *Europe's Demographic Future: Facts and Figures on Challenges and Opportunities*, Luxembourg: Publications Office of the European Union.

European Commission (2012) *EEO Review: Employment Policies to Promote Active Ageing 2012*. Luxembourg: Publications Office of the European Union.

134 C.-M. Alcover and G. Topa

Eurostat (2012) *Harmonised unemployment rate*. Online. Available at: http://epp.eurostat. ec.europa.eu/tgm/table.do?tab=table&plugin=1&language=en&pcode=teilm020 (accessed September 10, 2012).

Feldman, D.C. and Kim, S. (2001) 'Bridge employment during retirement: A field study of individual and organizational experiences with post-retirement employment', *Human Resource Planning*, 23: 14–26.

Fernández, J.J., Alcover, C.M. and Crego, A. (2010) 'Percepciones sobre la voluntariedad en el proceso de salida organizacional en una muestra de prejubilados españoles' [Perceptions on the voluntariness in the process of organizational exit in a sample of Spanish early retirees], *Revista de Psicología del Trabajo y de las Organizaciones*, 26: 135–46.

Fernández, J.J., Alcover, C.M. and Crego, A. (2013) 'Psychosocial profiles of early retirees based on experiences during post-working life transition and adjustment to retirement', *Revista de Psicología Social*, 28: 99–112.

Fernández-Ballesteros, R. (2009) 'Jubilación y salud' [Retirement and health], *Humanitas, Humanidades Médicas*, 37: 1–23.

Fougère, M., Harvey, S., Mercenier, J. and Mérette, M. (2005) *Population Ageing and the Effective Age of Retirement in Canada*, HRSDC-IC-SSHRC Skills Research Initiative, Government of Canada, Working Paper 2005 A-03. Online. Available at: www.ic.gc. ca/eic/site/eas-aes.nsf/eng/ra01958.html (accessed October 25, 2012).

García-Pérez, J.I., Jiménez-Martín, S. and Sánchez-Martín, A.R. (2010) *Retirement Incentives, Individual Heterogeneity and Labor Transitions of Employed and Unemployed Workers*, Universitat Pompeu Fabra, Economic Working Papers, 1239. Online. Available at: www.econ.upf.edu/docs/papers/downloads/1239.pdf (accessed February 18, 2013).

Giandrea, M.D., Cahill, K.E. and Quinn, J.F. (2007) *An Update on Bridge Jobs: The HRS War Babies*, Bureau of Labor Statistics Working Papers, no. 407, Washington, DC: U.S. Department of Labor.

Giandrea, M.D., Cahill, K.E. and Quinn, J.F. (2008) *Self-employment Transitions among Older American Workers with Career Jobs*, Bureau of Labor Statistics Working Papers, no. 418, Washington, DC: U.S. Department of Labor.

Harper, S. (2010) *Social Security in an Ageing World: Adapting to Demographic Changes*, Social Policy Highlight 12, Report for the International Social Security Association. Online. Available at: www.ageing.ox.ac.uk/files/2-SPH.pdf (accessed December 9, 2012).

Henretta, J.C. (2003) 'The life course perspective in work and retirement', in R.R. Settersten (ed.), *Invitation to the Life Course*, New York: Baywood Publishing.

Hershey, D.A., Henkens, K. and van Dalen, H.P. (2010) 'What drives retirement income worries in Europe? A multilevel analysis', *European Journal of Ageing*, 7: 301–11.

Ilmarinen, J. (2006) *Towards a Longer Worklife: Ageing and the Quality of Work Life in the European Union*, Helsinki: Finnish Institute of Occupational Health.

Instituto Nacional de Estadística (2010) *Proyección de la población de España a largo plazo 2009–2049* [*Spanish Population Projection in the Long-term 2009–2049*], Madrid: INE, NP 587 January 28, 2010. Online. Available at: www.ine.es/prensa/ np587.pdf (accessed September 10, 2012).

Instituto Nacional de Estadística (2011) *Proyección de la población de España a corto plazo 2011–2021* [*Spanish Population Projection in the Short-term 2011–2021*], Madrid: INE, NP 679 October 7, 2011. Online. Available at: www.ine.es/prensa/np679. pdf (accessed September 11, 2012).

Bridge employment in Spain 135

Instituto Nacional de Estadística (2012) *Proyecciones de Población 2012* [*Population Projections 2012*], Madrid: INE, NP November 19, 2012. Online. Available at: www.ine.es/prensa/np744.pdf (accessed November 20, 2012).

Instituto Nacional de Estadística (2013) *Encuesta de Población Activa (EPA). Cuarto trimestre de 2012* [*Labor Force Survey (LFS): Fourth Quarter of 2012*], Madrid: INE, NP January 24, 2013. Online. Available at: www.ine.es/daco/daco42/daco4211/epa0412.pdf (accessed March 25, 2013).

Jiménez-Martín, S. (2012) 'Propuestas para la reforma de la jubilación anticipada en España' [Proposals for early retirement reform in Spain], *Apuntes FEDEA, Bienestar 08.* Online. Available at: www.fedea.net/apuntes/apuntes/bienestar/apunte_binestar08_prejubilacion.pdf (accessed February 20, 2013).

Jociles, M.I. and Franzé, A. (2008) 'El discurso de la pérdida en las asociaciones *reivindicativas* de prejubilados' [The discourse of loss in early retiress protest associations], *Cuadernos de Relaciones Laborales*, 26: 165–203.

Komp, K., van Tilburg, T. and van Groenou, M.B. (2010) 'Paid work between age 60 and 70 years in Europe: A matter of socio-economic status?', *International Journal of Ageing and Later Life*, 5: 45–75.

Kooij, D.T.A.M., De Lange, A.H., Jansen, P.G.W., Kanfer, R. and Dikkers, J.S.E. (2011) 'Age and work-related motives: Results of a meta-analysis', *Journal of Organizational Behavior*, 32: 197–225.

Lee, R. (2004) 'Quantifying our ignorance: Stochastic forecasts of population and public budgets', *Population and Development Review*, 30: 153–75.

Morschhäuser, M. and Söchert, R. (2006) *Healthy Work in an Ageing Europe: Strategies and Instruments for Prolonging Working Life*, Essen: European Network for Workplace Health Promotion.

Muñoz de Bustillo, R. (ed.) (2007) *Extensión de la vida laboral o inserción temprana de jóvenes. Alternativas al sistema de pensiones* [*Extending Working Life or Young Early Insertion: Alternatives to the Pension System*], Madrid: Ministerio de Trabajo y Asuntos Sociales.

Muñoz de Bustillo, R., Pedraza, P., Antón, J.I. and Rivas, L.A. (2011) 'Working life and retirement pensions in Spain: The simulated impact of a parametric reform', *International Social Security Review*, 64: 73–93.

Muszyńska, M.M. and Rau, R. (2012) 'The old-age healthy dependency ratio in Europe', *Journal of Population Ageing*, 5: 151–62.

OECD (2012) *Looking to 2060: Long-term Global Growth Prospects – A Going for Growth Report*, OECD Economic Policy Papers No. 3, November 2012. Online. Available at: www.oecd-ilibrary.org/docserver/download/5k8zxpjsggf0.pdf?expires=135300 8457&id=id&accname=guest&checksum=1A7F581703D85DFD61F88059F5E98D89 (accessed November 15, 2012).

Pacto de Toledo (2012a) *Informe sobre la compatibilidad de la percepción de la pensión de jubilación y la realización de una actividad* [*Report on the Compatibility of the Perception of Retirement Pension and the Completion of a Work Activity*], Madrid: Ministerio de Empleo y Seguridad Social, Secretaría de Estado de Seguridad Social. Online. Available www.cen7dias.es/BOLETINES/385/informe_compatibilidad_pension_actividad.pdf (accessed February 20, 2013).

Pacto de Toledo (2012b) *Informe sobre la situación de la jubilación anticipada con coeficiente reductor y de la jubilación parcial* [*Report on the Situation of the Early Retirement with Reduction Factor and Partial Retirement*], Madrid: Ministerio de Empleo y Seguridad Social, Secretaría de Estado de Seguridad Social. Online.

136   C.-M. Alcover and G. Topa

Available at: www.cenavarra.es/documentos/ficheros_comunicacion/pactodetoledo.pdf (accessed February 20, 2013).

Peláez, O. (2008) 'Evolución del gasto en pensiones contributivas en España bajo distintos escenarios demográficos (2007–2050)' [Evolution of the Spanish contributory pension expenditure under alternative demographic scenarios (2007–2050)], *Principios: Estudios de Economía Política*, 12: 45–60.

Peng, I. (2008) 'Ageing and the social security system', in F. Coulmas, H. Conrad, A. Schad-Seifert and G. Vogt (eds.), *The Demographic Challenge: A Handbook about Japan*, Leiden: Brill.

Pérez-Díaz, V. and Rodríguez, J.C. (2007) *La generación de la transición: entre el trabajo y la jubilación* [*The Generation of Transition: Between Work and Retirement*], Barcelona: La Caixa, Colección Estudios Económicos 35.

Peterson, C.L. and Murphy, G. (2010) 'Transition from the labor market: Older workers and retirement', *International Journal of Health Services*, 40: 609–27.

Phillipson, C. (2002) *Transitions from Work to Retirement: Developing a New Social Contract*, Bristol: The Policy Press.

Phillipson, C. and Smith, A. (2005) *Extending Working Life: A Review of Research Literature*, Norwich: Department for Work and Pensions, Research Report No. 299. Online. Available at: http://research.dwp.gov.uk/asd/asd5/rports2005-2006/rrep299.pdf (accessed December 9, 2012).

Raymo, J.M., Warren, J.R., Sweeney, M.M., Hauser, R.M. and Ho, J.-H. (2010) 'Later-life employment preferences and outcomes: The role of midlife work experiences', *Research on Aging*, 32: 419–66.

Schalk, R et al. (2010) 'Moving European research on work and ageing forward: Overview and agenda', *European Journal of Work and Organizational Psychology*, 19: 76–101.

Schneider, F. (2012) *Size and Development of the Shadow Economy of 31 European and 5 Other OECD Countries from 2003 to 2012: Some New Facts*, Online. Available www.econ.jku.at/members/Schneider/files/publications/2012/ShadEcEurope31_March%202012.pdf (accessed March 25, 2013).

Shultz, K. (2003) 'Bridge employment: Work after retirement', in G. Adams and T. Beehr (eds.), *Retirement: Reasons, Processes, and Results*, New York: Springer.

Topa, G., Alcover, C.M., Moriano, J.A. and Depolo, M. (2014) 'Antecedents and consequences of bridge employment quality: A structural equation model with SHARE panel data', *Economic and Industrial Democracy*, 35.

Topa, G., Depolo, M., Moriano, J.A. and Morales, J.F. (2009) 'Empleo puente y bienestar personal de los jubilados. Un modelo de ecuaciones estructurales con una muestra europea probabilística' [Bridge employment and retirees' personal well-being: A structural equation model with a European probabilistic simple], *Psicothema*, 21: 280–7.

United Nations (2011) *World Population Prospects: The 2010 Revision, Highlights and Advanced Tables*, Working Paper no. ESA/P/WP.220, New York: UN, Department of Economic and Social Affairs, Population Division.

Van Solinge, H. and Henkens, K. (2007) 'Involuntary retirement: The role of restrictive circumstances, timing, and social embeddedness', *Journal of Gerontology: Social Sciences*, 62B: 295–303.

von Nordheim, F. (2003) 'EU policies in support at Member State efforts to retain, reinforce, and re-integrate older workers in employment', in H. Buck and B. Dworschak (eds.), *Aging and Work in Europe: Strategies at Company Level and Public Policies in*

Selected European Countries, Stuttgart: German Federal Ministry of Education and Research.

Weckerle, J.R. and Shultz, K.S. (1999) 'Influences on the bridge employment decision among older USA workers', *Journal of Occupational and Organizational Psychology*, 72: 317–29.

Zissimopoulos, J.M. and Karoly, L.A. (2009) 'Labor-force dynamics at older ages: Movements into self-employment for workers and non-workers', *Research on Aging*, 31: 89–111.

7 Career transitions at retirement age in the United Kingdom

Bridge employment or continued career progression?

Emma Parry and Dianne Bown Wilson

Over recent years much attention within the United Kingdom has been focused on the work experiences of employees aged 50 and over. This interest has been driven by a number of factors: first, the aging workforce and growing life expectancy of the UK population has led to the need to retain older workers in order to access the skills and experience required by organizations and reduce the strain on social security systems; second, changes in UK legislation have outlawed age discrimination in line with EU Directives and, more recently, abolished employers' ability to set a default retirement age. Consequently people can now continue to work for as long as they are willing and able to do so. On top of this, people themselves are being driven to work longer either for reasons of financial necessity or to meet their desire to remain actively involved in purposeful activity and the social networks that work provides. Within the UK, as across the rest of Europe, this has led to a move away from the trend of early retirement apparent in the 1980s with the result that over the past decade, an increasing number of older people (those aged 65 and over) are remaining in work. This increase is seen in both full-time and part-time employment (ONS 2012), as well as in those returning to work after having retired and stopped work (LV= 2012).

Alongside these changes, some employers have sought to provide alternative working arrangements for those individuals who are reaching the end of their careers – these include reduced working hours or responsibilities, phased or partial retirement and flexible retirement and pension plans. These schemes, often known as 'bridge employment', may be intended for existing employees and/or for older workers who have 'retired' from a career elsewhere. However, although their number is undoubtedly growing (Smeaton *et al.* 2009), determining the prevalence of such schemes is difficult. While some organizations, predominantly large employers such as BT, Sainsbury's, Centrica, B&Q, McDonald's and others, actively promote such schemes as part of 'age-friendly employment practices' and are regarded as role models (TAEN 2012; Smeaton *et al.* 2009), others adopt a less high-profile and more pragmatic route. For example, many employers offer flexible working for all, choosing not to differentiate this as providing bridge employment for older workers. Indeed, to do so would be difficult. As the government's Business Link website advises:

If flexible working is not open to all, then targeting it at older workers would need to be objectively justified. It may be difficult to justify offering flexible working arrangements to older workers, but not to other groups, such as parents of young children.

(Business Link 2012a)

While these 'bridge employment' schemes are generally seen by employers as a means to 'bridge' the transition from a working career into the cessation of work in later life, it is not clear whether this view is shared by older employees themselves. The question is whether such transitions into bridge employment are motivated by a need or desire simply to move into retirement, or are they driven by aspirations for continuing career progression? And which drivers, barriers and supporting factors affect the capacity of older workers to continue making career transitions as they approach retirement?

In this chapter we address these questions within the framework of what is known about bridge employment, based on research conducted within the UK context. In doing so, and in order to examine people's experiences and attitudes toward careers and work as they approach and pass the state pension age, we draw specifically upon two pieces of research. First, we explore interviews and survey research conducted within five UK organizations looking at the career transitions made by older workers, and the drivers, barriers and support associated with these. Second, we use interviews with older workers from two UK financial services organizations, examining their motivation for career progression and the factors shaping this. From these studies, we build a picture of older workers' experiences of bridge employment within the United Kingdom and how their motivations relate to this concept.

'Bridge employment' as a career stage

Bridge employment is generally accepted as being employment that takes place after a person's retirement from a full-time position but before the person's permanent withdrawal from the workforce (Kim and Feldman 2000). 'Retirement' for the majority of workers is a specific career transition marked by the receipt of a pension. At any age, career transitions represent experiences 'which may result in a change of job or profession, or a change in one's orientation to work while continuing in the same job' (Louis 1980: 329). Such changes may be individually or organizationally driven and result from circumstance, compulsion or free choice. In the past, particularly in large organizational settings, work and life transitions occurred in stable orderly sequences linked to traditional hierarchical career structures where employees worked for one or a few employers over the course of their working life. The careers of older workers tended to stop progressing and were generally characterized by decline and withdrawal (Armstrong-Stassen and Schlosser 2008). In essence this pattern continues; for people in their mid-fifties onwards the most common outcomes of any change in working practices are reduced hours and reduced responsibility (McNair *et al.* 2003).

140   *E. Parry and D. Bown Wilson*

Today, however, career paths have become increasingly indistinct. New patterns of work transitions include 'boundaryless' careers (DeFillippi and Arthur 1996) in which careers transcend the boundaries of a single employer or job role, 'protean' careers in which the responsibility for career management rests with the individual (Hall 1976) and 'kaleidoscope' careers (Mainiero and Sullivan 2005) in which roles and relationships are rearranged to create authenticity, balance and challenge in work and personal life. As a result individuals are increasingly driven more by their own desires than by employer practices (Sullivan and Baruch 2009). However, employers still tend to exert considerable influence over their employees' career progression (Baruch 2006).

Regardless of the form of careers the common proposition is that today individuals move through multiple cycles during their career and that changes to career in later life represent another of these cycles (Hall and Mirvis 1995; Mirvis and Hall 1994), albeit that such later-life career transitions may involve and emerge from a changing career identity (Greller and Simpson 1999). Late careers are often more complex than early careers because there is less consistency in how older adults may choose to proceed, such that in later life 'a person may continue a career, start a new career, modify a career, or retire' (Ulrich and Brott 2005: 160). In respect of bridge employment, Ulrich and Brott (2005) reveal that the majority of older workers in their US study remained in the same occupation when they retired but moved into a different role or to a different employer. If they did move out of their previous long-term career they tended to revert to a previous job role or to using skills they had gained throughout their career. Alongside this, a Department for Work and Pensions study into factors affecting the labor-market participation of UK older workers finds that:

> Perceptions of 'what constitutes work' appeared to be entrenched. Respondents had very fixed ideas about the nature of work. Specifically, they viewed it as 'full-time' and 'fixed or permanent', and rarely considered that work could be part-time or flexible and could fit around other interests and commitments.
>
> (Irving *et al.* 2005: 121)

In many studies bridge employment is considered as 'work' of any type that an individual takes after retirement from their previous career or sequence of jobs. Indeed, Ilmakunnas and Ilmakunnas (2006: 3) define bridge jobs as those 'held subsequent to career employment and prior to retirement', thereby, by definition, putting them outside the scope of career progression. Alongside this, numerous investigations (e.g., Davis 2003; Kim and Feldman 2000) have focused objectively on the factors contributing to, or resulting from, bridge employment as a specific type of work. Far fewer researchers have investigated bridge employment in relation to careers, although Moen *et al.* (2001: 6), for example, report that, 'Men with school age children and women with no children are most likely to consider a post-retirement career'. Thus little is known about the subjective aspects of bridge employment and the extent to

Career transitions in the United Kingdom 141

which such transitions may be planned for and regarded by the individuals concerned as career progression.

Motivation for bridge employment

The receipt of a pension may often act as a turning point in an individual's work and career. Motivation for continuing to work past this stage is complex. Labor-market mobility in general is affected by individuals' attitudes to change, employers' attitudes and the influence of the particular industry or sector in which people are employed (Irving *et al.* 2005). Aside from pension eligibility, factors affecting retirement include financial matters, household status, gender differences, life-changing events, health and work status – with personal, social and family-related factors also being highly influential (Irving *et al.* 2005). For numerous people, particularly in the current global recession, financial factors have increasingly come to the fore in encouraging them to work longer. However, this is balanced for many by an equally strong desire to remain in work for reasons such as participation in social relationships and a sense of value and contribution, with a recent UK report suggesting that some 60 percent of wealthy individuals wanted to continue working rather than retire (Barclays Wealth 2010).

Although several studies (e.g., McNair *et al.* 2003; Schultz 2003) show that the majority of older people want to continue to work past retirement, they also demonstrate that older people want different working patterns with increased flexibility. For the majority, flexibility relates to working patterns and hours worked; however, it may extend further than this to encompass flexibility to work on chosen projects, to exercise greater autonomy and to work in a certain way or at a particular pace (Ulrich and Brott 2005).

Other studies (e.g., Irving *et al.* 2005; Ulrich and Brott 2005) consider the extent to which motivation for both retirement and the decision to participate in bridge employment results from a combination of 'push' and 'pull' factors. Variables pushing individuals toward this state include changes in health, caring responsibilities, job role and responsibilities, and work rules and policies; organizational restructuring; and reduced job satisfaction and unmet career expectations. Pull factors include individuals' desire to enjoy quality time and to manage their changing life priorities through having more time and more control over the way they could use time. Davis (2003) also finds that those with entrepreneurial aspirations and/or an awareness of career opportunities either within their existing career industry or a different arena are more likely to consider bridge employment.

Flynn (2010) highlights the importance of autonomy in influencing decisions about when and how to retire, stressing the importance of income, qualifications and job status in addition to the type of work. In his comprehensive study on the work and retirement patterns of older workers he draws attention to the division between the 'haves' who are privileged older workers with high levels of job autonomy, secure pensions and choice over when they retire, and the 'have nots'

142   *E. Parry and D. Bown Wilson*

who are either pushed out of work or forced to continue working due to factors beyond their control. Elaborating on this theme, he concludes emphatically that 'there is not a single "older workforce" which reacts uniformly to programmes meant to encourage longer working life' (2010: 308), underlining the notion that motivation for participation in bridge employment ultimately links to unique configurations of variables at an individual level.

Support and barriers for bridge employment

Aside from motivation, a number of barriers and support variables are likely to have an impact on career transitions, including that into bridge employment. Barriers to labor-market mobility include external factors such as economic restructuring and labor demand and variables that are internal to the individual such as health, caring responsibilities, skills and experience and lack of awareness of rights and opportunities (Smeaton *et al.* 2009; Irving *et al.* 2005). Context and organizational opportunities are fundamental to each of these factors. In terms of context, legislation, industrial relations systems, the labor market and societal attitudes toward older workers are important, while at the organizational level, structure and culture (values and norms), the immediate work environment and policies and practices including training and development and organizational retention policies are significant. In a section entitled 'Providing support for a retiring employee', the UK government's business advice website, Business Link, suggests '[a]llowing them to gradually reduce their working hours for a period of time before their retirement, preferably on full pay. This will give the retiring employee a chance to develop other interests outside work' (Business Link 2012b).

Despite this, a 2012 report by the UK Pensions Policy Institute concludes that although it is clear that there needs to be an appetite from employers if older workers are to be able to remain in work, 'it is not clear if this has yet fed through into employer behaviour and attitudes' (p. 28).

At a fundamental level successful transitions into bridge employment rely equally on employers offering suitable types of work and older workers being both willing and able to undertake it. In respect of this, evidence suggests that older workers are far from equal in terms of the opportunities open to them. For example, Humphrey and colleagues (2003) found that people in professional, administrative and secretarial occupations were most likely to have been offered flexible working whereas only around a quarter of people in skilled trades and plant and machine operatives were offered flexible working as an option. They recognized that in certain occupations, generally professional or public sector occupations, precedents had already been set and employers were increasingly open to flexible working solutions.

Employee confidence in terms of taking on new challenges, willingness to upskill or retrain and to risk rejection by unsuccessfully applying for new jobs or responsibilities are important factors in making the transition into bridge employment. Equally, employer confidence in older workers' capabilities and

Career transitions in the United Kingdom 143

the ability to see beyond ageist stereotypes are key contributing factors. While the majority of employers offer bridge employment as a way to facilitate the retirement of existing employees, some organizations such as B&Q and McDonald's have deliberately designed schemes to attract retired workers and benefit from the qualities they bring.

In order to investigate further the factors affecting older workers' decisions to make a career transition such as that into bridge employment, we will now turn to the results from the first of two studies conducted within the United Kingdom.

Factors affecting career transitions in older workers

The purpose of this study was to investigate the drivers, barriers and support for career changes for different people mapped against their age and life stage. The five UK organizations involved comprised three private-sector companies: a drinks producer and distributor, an energy company and a supermarket chain, and two public-sector organizations: a county council and a National Health Service (NHS) Trust. The study was undertaken in two stages. First, 48 interviews were conducted with male and female employees of the five organizations from a range of industries. Interviewees were divided into three age cohorts – under 30 years of age, 31–50 and over 50. The sample included respondents at a range of organizational levels. The interviews asked individuals to describe their last career transition and to discuss the drivers, barriers and support that were provided/needed. The interviews were recorded and transcribed in full before being analyzed to identify emergent themes under the headings of drivers, barriers and support for career transitions.

Second, a survey was developed based upon the interview results. The survey was administered to employees within four of the five organizations above – the energy company, supermarket chain, county council and NHS Trust. Sampling ensured that the survey was sent to men and women from a range of roles and levels within each organization, and from each of the three age groups stated above. The survey was administered both as an online and paper-based questionnaire via the HR department within each organization. Survey respondents were asked to consider their last career transition, defined as 'any change in your career including changes in organization, role, level or working hours as well as changes to an existing role'. Some 936 survey responses were received, comprising 229 under 30-year-olds, 468 31–50-year-olds and 175 over 50-year-olds. As 54 respondents did not state their age the analysis was based upon 872 respondents.

Overall, people expected to retire at around 61 years old. Just over a third of respondents said they would consider working after retirement age, with flexible working, financial incentives and flexible pension arrangements being identified as the practices that would best enable them to make this choice.

Career transitions were most commonly driven by job satisfaction, the desire to do a good job, gaining experience, the need to be challenged, personal interest in the job and career progression. Older workers were significantly less likely to make a career transition for career progression, to be challenged, for financial reasons, for personal development or training or to gain experience. Older workers were also significantly less likely to attribute their last career transition to luck and circumstance but more likely to link it to organizational restructuring. These differences were supported by our interviewees.

With regard to barriers for career transitions, older workers were significantly less likely to cite financial issues, the current labor market and lack of experience as barriers to career transitions. However, older interviewees were particularly concerned about their lack of skills in technology. For instance, one interviewee explained: 'I would have more opportunities if I were younger. Because it just seems to me you have to be on the ball with computers. Not that I'm not, but I'm not as clued up as the young people here.' A number of older interviewees discussed the impact that their health had on their career choices. It is interesting to note that the difference between age groups with regard to seeing health as a barrier was significant at the 10 percent level, providing some support for this being a bigger issue for older workers. Some interviewees mentioned the impact of major health-related events, while others discussed generally deteriorating health or stamina. For example, one interviewee commented: 'I kind of think if I feel tired now at 51, what will I feel like by the time I am 61?' Interviewees identified a number of barriers relating to the organization or to the role itself. The most common of these was a lack of vacancies within the organization; this was particularly true for more senior roles.

A number of interviewees across age groups had found it difficult to make career transitions because they had not received sufficient support from their line manager, particularly in terms of providing the training or career advice that they had needed. 'When I came [into the department] the manager ... had very little time for his direct reports. I didn't feel personally developed or supported.' Several interviewees felt that a lack of training provided by the organization had acted as a barrier to making career transitions. One interviewee commented that she would have had more opportunities for training if she had been younger. Another commented that she had found it difficult to make a career transition because of a lack of peer support while others suggested that an absence of role models of those who had made similar career transitions had made a move more problematic.

A number of older interviewees suggested that career transitions were more difficult because of their age. In some cases it was felt that the organization they were working for had a particularly 'young' culture and that this would make it difficult for them to find opportunities so that they could progress in their careers. One interviewee suggested: 'Here, if you're not 25 and if you don't have a degree, you're overlooked somewhat despite the fact that we have a policy against age discrimination.' Some other interviewees, however, felt strongly that age had not been an issue in their careers and reported that their skills and experience had been welcomed.

In respect of the support received for their last career transition, older employees were significantly less likely to rate the induction process, training, role models within the organization and a generally supportive organizational culture as effective. The type of support most commonly mentioned was training and development, including induction training, skills or management training, mentoring and developmental secondments. In a number of cases older workers who were finding it difficult to continue in their existing role had been retrained in order to enable them to move into different roles. Interestingly, no interview evidence was found of older workers being provided with less training than younger workers.

A relatively large number of interviewees also mentioned support in the form of flexible working arrangements. Several women with families had undertaken flexible working in order to be able to carry on in an existing position or had moved into new flexible working roles in order to continue with their careers.

It was clear from the interviews that one of the most crucial areas of support in making career transitions was that provided by an individual's line manager. One interviewee explained: 'My line manager has been an incredible support because we do appraisals and one-to-ones [and] ... we're very open and whatever I feel I am not too au fait with, he makes sure I get trained properly.' Several interviewees also described the value of having role models within the organization of those who had made similar transitions or of having sponsors outside their immediate line manager to support and advise them. Interviewees also explained the importance of a generally supportive culture that made them feel that they were able to make career transitions. 'In terms of the organization I think there are lots of opportunities and I've felt very supported throughout my career here.' Interviewees generally found it difficult to explain in detail what it was about the organization that created this generally supportive feeling, although they commonly mentioned the existence of internal opportunities, a willingness to look after people and supportive managers.

Interviews suggested that support from outside the organization was also important, most commonly in the form of personal support from a partner, family or friends. Older workers were, however, significantly less likely than younger workers to see external support mechanisms such as family or friends, external careers information, training or development, or role models as important.

This first study provides some insight into the factors affecting individuals' decisions with regard to career transition, including those into bridge employment. It remains unclear, however, how, if at all, older workers view typical bridge employment offerings such as phased retirement and partial retirement (Wang *et al.* 2009) as qualitatively representing a step to stopping work or as simply another career stage. Our second study was designed to shed some light on this issue.

Conceptualizations of career progression and bridge employment

This study was part of a larger research project focusing on motivation for career progression in older managers. Participants comprised 40 managers who were

146   *E. Parry and D. Bown Wilson*

still employed and were in the process of planning for retirement. They worked for two large private-sector organizations within the financial services industry – a major UK employment sector. Research participants ranged in age from 50 to 63 years. Of the participants, 27 were male and 13 were female. They represented a variety of managerial roles, functions and career experiences in terms of job, role and past inter- and intra-organizational mobility.

Semi-structured interviews were undertaken incorporating the use of a timeline that enabled us to access both how participants made sense of their career in terms of why they had made certain career decisions and what those decisions meant in terms of their career progression, and also their thoughts relating to their career identity. Participants were requested to extend the timeline past retirement to help them focus on what the concept of future career progression might mean for them. Interviews lasted an hour and eight minutes on average. Interviews were recorded, transcribed and analyzed in order to identify emergent themes.

In general participants saw their career as representing a sequence of responses to choices and opportunities that had arisen throughout their working life. The majority indicated that they could see that what had been important to them about their career had now shifted, partly in response to their own attitudes and aspirations but also shaped by changing career contexts. This shift both resulted from and was stimulated by a number of other changes including changing expectations. Beyond this, personal attributes such as increased confidence and autonomy, greater maturity, resilience and wisdom, and changing priorities all contributed strongly to retrospectively shaping the meaning people gave to their career.

Interview responses indicated that individuals had generally outgrown their early career concerns, which had focused on establishing themselves, creating a reputation and achieving 'success' in objective terms, and had gone on to realize that other aspects of life such as contribution and self-realization were now more important to them. People indicated that changing expectations – their own and those of other people – were important to the way they now saw their career. Many of these were seen as being related to becoming an 'older' manager: 'I don't personally expect any more promotion. They only put younger people onto a fast track.' People felt they had developed increased insight into employer practices, other people, the ways of the world and themselves that enabled them to recognize and better understand how things were and what their current and future options might be.

Further aspects that were commonly mentioned related to personal attributes that individuals associated with their taking a different approach to their career and their life in general. These included increased confidence and autonomy, increased maturity, resilience and wisdom and changing priorities. In respect of the latter, individuals described the ways in which they felt that their priorities had changed in relation to their career and what they wanted from life in general. For most this meant that subjective aspects of their career such as meaning, contribution, interest and recognition had now become more important to them than financial remuneration and promotion. This was demonstrated by explanations that related to most of the individuals now being in an improved financial position:

> When you're younger and you're struggling, money makes a difference to how you behave and what you prioritise. There were times when I couldn't afford to be too principled, whereas now I've got no hesitation at all in terms of challenging senior people.

In general, participants indicated that they now saw themselves as strong, active contributors within their organization with a clear sense of purpose. They valued what they had achieved in career terms with many wanting not only to hold on to this but to continue to develop both their career and themselves in later life. For some, their plans for their remaining years of work were focused on extending their existing career identity. However, others indicated that they had made a trade-off in the past between their career and personal fulfillment and now wanted to recognize other aspects of who they were and what mattered in their life through their future work.

Overall, retirement was most commonly conceptualized as a financial milestone associated with the receipt of one or more pensions that would provide the financial freedom to pursue new paths in work and leisure. Subsequent to this, four main conceptualizations of retirement emerged from the coded results, which we labeled 'slow down', 'stick', 'switch' and 'strive'. These concepts were derived from what interviewees said they wanted to do in their next career stage; they were not mutually exclusive categories although individuals tended to identify more strongly with one conceptualization over the others.

Slow down (17 interviewees). This involved reducing work commitments through reduced working hours and/or a less demanding role. It was characterized by part-time or contract work in either the current or a new work type and may include unpaid voluntary work or paid work for a third-sector employer. 'I like coming to work; I get quite a lot out of it but it would be great to be here less, maybe three days; that would give me a chance to do more of the things I want.'

Stick (19 interviewees). This concept focused on career maintenance. Individuals saw themselves as continuing to work in the same occupation or one that utilized their existing specialist skills, either through remaining with their current employer or through an employed/self-employed role elsewhere (sometimes accompanied by a reduction in hours, thereby overlapping with 'slowing down'). 'I would like to use my existing expertise, but I would like to do it in a portfolio of jobs if I possibly could.'

Switch (17 interviewees). Individuals planned to take on a role in a completely different field from their career to date, often in order to achieve unfulfilled ambitions, frequently involving artistic, creative or practical skills. This orientation also overlapped with the previous category, slowing down, i.e., a reduction in hours. 'I wouldn't mind doing something like working in a bookshop or a library; something where I could genuinely be helpful to people.'

148 *E. Parry and D. Bown Wilson*

Strive (5 interviewees). This related to further career advancement and was linked to those who wanted to continue to seek further career challenges and objective advancement and recognition building on existing professional skills and experience. This was often envisaged as being linked to a portfolio of different roles, for example, non-executive director, consultant, interim manager, etc. 'I'm working towards taking on a big trusteeship at age 64 which I would like to do though I have no idea whether I will get it.'

Key to this investigation were individuals' views concerning whether or not they considered that post-retirement work would be a continuation of their career. The majority (28) maintained that it would be a continuation: 'Work might look a bit different than it does now ... my career would continue, but it would be a different aspect of my career.' The remaining individuals (12 interviewees) did not at this time view work post-retirement as a different career stage, merely a continuation of work. The way that they saw this relating to their existing career was most clearly demonstrated in this comment:

> I think it would depend on what it was as to whether I considered it was a continuation of my career. The key would be what skills I was using that I'd taken from my career up to that point. If I was using similar skills then I would see it as an extension. If it was completely different then I'd probably see it as just a job.

Factors affecting individual older managers' conceptualizations of retirement included the expressed or potential attitudes and reactions of their partner and family, employer and work colleagues (current and future), and friends and acquaintances. Some also alluded to their own expectations concerning what they felt would be the 'right' or 'appropriate' thing to do in terms of continuing to work or not, sometimes based on the role models of others: 'My aunt – who I'm very similar to – she's still teaching at 85 plus. And my father is still working at 83, he's very fit. So I'm hoping to follow in their footsteps.'

Social norms also emerged as significant: for example, whether or not an individual's partner would be working, and if and when colleagues and friends stopped work. In terms of organizational influences, notions of what was considered appropriate to do for those who had retired from the organization were influential: for example, many individuals mentioned moving into working in the voluntary sector as being a 'natural' thing to do. Alongside these factors were other observations that demonstrated the influence of individuals' views of what retirement would be like, based on social norms and the experiences of others. For example, numerous comments were made expressing fears about 'doing nothing' in retirement. While individuals saw this option as socially acceptable, it was not one that the majority wanted to adopt: 'Sometimes I do wonder why I work at all, but I'm not ready to stop working. I don't want just to be going out to lunch and going on holidays – I want to do something that is meaningful.'

Ultimately the factors affecting conceptualizations of retirement were individually highly complex. While some factors were more commonly found in

Career transitions in the United Kingdom 149

relation to particular conceptualizations, causal connections definitely could not be established between each conceptualization and the factors that may be related to it.

Summary and conclusions

The findings of both of our studies made it clear that, rather than reducing their commitment, older individuals were as likely as younger colleagues to be motivated for bridge employment by the desire to do a good job, making a difference, interest in the job and job satisfaction. Except in cases of particular financial need, older individuals were significantly less likely to be driven by financial remuneration. Such findings suggest that individuals might not see bridge employment merely as a step to retirement and highlight the need for employers and line managers to consider alternative forms of reward and recognition for older workers as incentives for career change. Employers also need to supply positive feedback and job enrichment for older employees to ensure continuing engagement through providing them with new challenges.

It was clear that personal confidence was an issue for older workers, together with organizational politics, as barriers to career transitions. Confirming earlier studies, health issues, including tiredness and stress, were perceived as important barriers for some older people as were workload and lack of management support. From the interviews in our first study, it appeared that individuals of all ages who received support from their line manager appeared to make career transitions more easily. Part of this may have related to the boost such support gave to their confidence as well as good communication with their manager being a way of better understanding and overcoming organizational politics. In light of these findings employers need to focus on the role of the line manager in employee development while reducing older worker stress through improved personal control and flexible working options. Finally, in relation to support for career transitions, an appraisal system was valued by all age groups, as was peer support.

Although it was clear from the interviews that training and development plays a fundamental role in enabling people to make successful career transitions, our survey showed that, in fact, unlike earlier studies that have highlighted an absence of older worker training and development, this was not the general experience of the individuals in this study. However, returning to the issue of barriers, it may be that increased levels of training in relation to specific skills, especially those relating to the adoption of new technology, may help older people in terms of improved confidence for making transitions and their ongoing performance.

Quality of working life may hold the key to views about the nature of bridge employment and whether or not it is regarded as a career transition. The degree to which an individual identifies with their career is significant – those who in the past have been highly career focused may want to continue to develop either in their career role or through a new career. However, this is to be balanced by

150   *E. Parry and D. Bown Wilson*

the fact that some may want to stop work entirely and may do so if they are financially able. This probably also extends into the amount of control employees have over the type of work they do. Both factors underline that at this stage in their career people are now driven more by their own desires than employer policies, an attitude that extends to their conceptualizations of the nature of bridge employment.

Our second study revealed that while issues such as the ability to keep working and providing for oneself and dependants were important to many individuals, the majority seemed much more concerned about the potential loss of purpose and identity that may accompany retirement, and a strong desire to avoid 'being thrown on the scrapheap'. They were keen to progress beyond their current role in order to avoid such an outcome. This meant, however, that most realized that they would have to align their goals with what was likely to be realistic and achievable in terms of future work opportunities and their own abilities.

For the majority of the sample in our second study a career transition post-retirement was envisaged as either working in the voluntary sector where their existing skill-set would be valued and/or part-time work might be available, or undertaking interim or consultancy work or self-employment. In broad terms, individuals saw retirement as either continuing to work in their current type of job in a more advanced role within their current career path, continuing their current type of work but for a different employer, continuing their career in another occupation, and/or continuing their career in another way, for example, reduced hours. They therefore saw future bridge employment as doing something different in retirement based on a desire for reduced pressure, ongoing meaning and interest, greater self-realization and/or an enriched lifestyle. Although this 'reinventive contribution' has been linked in general to women's careers (O'Neil and Bilimoria 2005), our findings showed that many men also shared a drive to increase significantly their contribution to an organization and/or their community and family through future work post-retirement.

Our studies confirmed that what individuals regard as 'retirement age' depends on health, energy levels, partner situation and a wide variety of other variables. Throughout their careers individuals make career transitions in response to their changing circumstances. In our second study those circumstances acted to affect conceptualizations of bridge employment and retirement itself. For example, a male manager who was financially secure but felt creatively stifled planned to set up a home-based business as a carpenter. A female manager who needed to continue to earn money to boost her post-retirement income but felt frustrated in her role aimed to work part-time in her career occupation for a local employer while developing a horse-grooming business alongside. Both of these ambitions were based on interests that individuals had pursued throughout their lives. Another male manager planned to transfer his existing specialist skills to a working future in the charitable sector as this would provide the income for him and his wife to make frequent visits to their only daughter who lived in America. In this way, future retirement and bridge employment plans were positioned within ongoing frameworks of social and individual identity and social contexts.

What then is the evidence for conceptualizing bridge employment as a new career stage? Overall our studies confirm that factors pertaining to career transitions are complex and interrelated, with age often being used as a proxy explanation for a number of other changes – positive or negative – which may take place in late career (e.g., stagnation in the face of lack of career opportunities or training rather than age-related career plateauing). Certainly the managers we interviewed in our second study did not identify with traditional conceptions of retirement or bridge employment. Their perceptions of and plans for their future working life demonstrated a rich variety of aspirations and pathways, founded on personal ambition, self-realization and control. The findings from both our studies clearly suggest that for many individuals the meaning of retirement is not about a cliff-edged end to working life, but a transition to another career stage in which they see themselves as continuing to develop, contribute and add value. In practice, this transition would be made in response to changing circumstances such as the forthcoming receipt of a pension or a reduction in work-related opportunities, in the same way as other transitions are made in response to changing circumstances earlier in life, for example, having children. This supports the proposition that individuals move through multiple career cycles and that, for many, changes in employment in later life such as a move to bridge employment represent another of these cycles.

References

Armstrong-Stassen, M. and Schlosser, F. (2008) 'Benefits of a supportive development climate for older workers', *Journal of Managerial Psychology*, 23: 419–37.

Barclays Wealth (2010) *The Age Illusion*. Online. Available at: www.barclayswealth. com/insights/volume12.htm (accessed June 1, 2012).

Baruch, Y. (2006) 'Career development in organizations and beyond: Balancing traditional and contemporary viewpoints', *Human Resource Management Review*, 16: 125–38.

Business Link (2012a) *Flexible Working for Older Workers*. Online. Available at: www. businesslink.gov.uk/bdotg/action/detail?itemId=1082250997&type=RESOURCES (accessed June 3, 2012).

Business Link (2012b) Online. Available at: www.businesslink.gov.uk/bdotg/action/detai l?itemId=1073791201&type=RESOURCES (accessed May 8, 2012).

Davis, M. (2003) 'Factors related to bridge employment participation among private sector early retirees', *Journal of Vocational Behavior*, 63: 55–71.

DeFillippi, R.J. and Arthur, M.B. (1996) 'Boundaryless contexts and careers: A competency-based perspective', in M.B. Arthur and D.M. Rousseau (eds.), *The Boundaryless Career: A New Employment Principle for a New Organizational Era*, New York: Oxford University Press.

Employers Forum on Age and Cranfield University (2010) *Change at Any Age*. Online. Available at: www.efa.org.uk/publications.php/646/change-at-any-age-report (accessed June 3, 2012).

Flynn, M. (2010) 'Who would delay retirement? Typologies of older workers', *Personnel Review*, 39: 308–24.

152   E. Parry and D. Bown Wilson

Greller, M.M. and Simpson, P. (1999) 'In search of late career: A review of contemporary social science research applicable to the understanding of late career', *Human Resource Management Review*, 9: 309–47.

Hall, D.T. (1976) *Careers in Organizations*, Glenview, IL: Scott, Foresman.

Hall, D.T. and Mirvis, P.H. (1995) 'The new career contract: Developing the whole person at midlife and beyond', *Journal of Vocational Behavior*, 47: 269–89.

Humphrey, A., Costigan, P., Pickering, K., Stratford, N. and Barnes, M. (2003) *Factors Affecting the Labor Market Participation of Older Workers*, Department for Work and Pensions, Research Report No. 200, London: DWP.

Ilmakunnas, P. and Ilmakunnas, S. (2006) *Gradual Retirement and Lengthening of Working Life*, Discussion Paper no. 121, Helsinki Centre of Economic Research. Online. Available at: https://helda.helsinki.fi/handle/10138/16513/search (accessed June 3, 2012).

Irving, P., Steels, J. and Hall, N. (2005) *Factors Affecting the Labor Market Participation of Older Workers*, Department for Work and Pensions, Research Report No. 281, London: DWP.

Kim, S. and Feldman, D. (2000) 'Working in retirement: The antecedents of bridge employment and its consequences for the quality of life in retirement', *Academy of Management Journal*, 43: 1195–210.

Louis, M.R. (1980) 'Career transitions: varieties and commonalities', *Academy of Management Review*, 5: 329–40.

LV= (2012) *Working Late*. Online. Available at: www.lv.com/adviser/working-with-lv/news_detail/?articleid=2776173 (accessed June 3, 2012).

McNair, S., Flynn, M., Owen, L., Humphreys, C. and Woodfield, S. (2003) *Changing Work in Later Life: A Study of Job Transitions*, Centre for Research into the Older Workforce, University of Surrey.

Mainiero, L.A. and Sullivan, S.E. (2005) 'Kaleidoscope careers: An alternate explanation for the "opt-out" revolution', *The Academy of Management Executive*, 19: 106–23.

Mirvis, P.H. and Hall, D.T. (1994) 'Psychological success and the boundaryless career', *Journal of Organizational Behavior*, 15: 365–80.

Moen, P., Plassman, V. and Sweet, S. (2001) *Cornell Midcareer Paths and Passages Study: Summary 2001*, Ithaca, NY: Bronfenbrenner Life Course Center, Cornell University.

O'Neil, D. and Bilimoria, D. (2005) 'Women's career development phases: Idealism, endurance, and reinvention', *Career Development International*, 10: 168–89.

ONS: Office for National Statistics (2012) *Older Workers in the Labor Market*. Online. Available www.ons.gov.uk/ons/rel/lmac/older-workers-in-the-labor-market/2011/older-people-in-the-labor-market.html#tab-Older-workers-in-the-labor-market (accessed May 8, 2012).

Pensions Policy Institute (2012) *Retirement Income and Assets: The Implications for Retirement Income of Government Policies to Extend Working Lives*. Online. Available at: www.pensionspolicyinstitute.org.uk (accessed May 8, 2012).

Schultz, K.S. (2003) 'Bridge employment: Work after retirement', in G. Adams and T. Beehr (eds.), *Retirement: Reasons, Processes and Results*, New York: Springer Publishing.

Smeaton, D., Vegeris, S. and Sahin-Dikmen, M. (2009) *Older Workers: Employment Preferences, Barriers and Solutions*, Equality and Human Rights Commission/Policy Studies Institute, Research Report 43.

Sullivan, S. and Baruch, Y. (2009) 'Advances in career theory and research: A critical review and agenda for future exploration', *Journal of Management*, 35: 1542–71.

TAEN – The Age and Employment Network (2012) *Three UK Employers Win Global Award for Innovative Older Workforce Practice.* Online. Available at: http://taen.org.uk/media/view/144 (accessed June 3, 2012).

Ulrich, L. and Brott, P. (2005) 'Older workers and bridge employment: Redefining retirement', *Journal of Employment Counseling*, 42: 159–70.

Wang, M., Adams, G., Beehr, T. and Schultz, K.S. (2009) 'Bridge employment and retirement: Issues and opportunities during the latter part of one's career', in S.G. Baugh and S.E. Sullivan (eds.), *Maintaining Focus, Energy and Options over the Career*, Charlotte, NC: Information Age Publishing, Inc.

8 No bridge and no employment?

Problems and challenges for older workers in Italy[1]

Marco Depolo and Franco Fraccaroli

Introduction

This chapter presents some experiences in Italy relative to bridge employment. Although Italy does not at present have specific legislation on the matter, it is possible to identify forms of post-retirement employment managed on informal bases or through individual relations, added to a rather extensive area of irregular work after retirement. Although it is therefore difficult to provide a complete and detailed account of the situation in Italy, the chapter tries to summarize both empirical data describing the Italian situation and the main elements of the social and economic debate about how to cope with the issue of the consequences for older workers, their transitions from work to retirement and its consequences. For a better understanding, a brief summary of demographic data as well data on the national labor market and legislation on retirement is needed.

The demographic picture of Italy

Italy's demographic situation shares features with those of the other European countries (of Southern Europe especially), but with some crucial differences.

The average age of the Italian population is increasing because of constantly extending life expectancy and an extremely low birth rate. In regard to the latter, the ISTAT (Istituto Nazionale di Statistica) (2012a) reports a constant decline of births in the country, especially ones where both parents are Italian (whereas the percentage of births to one or two foreign parents is growing). For example, 15 percent less births were registered in 2011 compared with 2010. The total fertility rate (TFR, the number of children per woman) is 1.39, which is one of the lowest rates in Europe (consider that the TFR required to ensure generational turnover is estimated at 2.1). Although it concerns the whole of Europe, the issue of demographic deficit is particularly salient in Italy. If the current mortality and fertility rates persist, the Italian population will constantly decrease to reach around one-fifth in 2050 unless it is bolstered by substantial migratory inflows (OECD estimate).

The issue of Italy's low birth rate and generational turnover is flanked by the equally important problem, which is also shared by other European countries, of

Challenges for older workers in Italy 155

the aging of the population. In Italy the figures tend to be more extreme than those for other comparable European countries. At the end of 2011, the average age of Italians was 43.7 years: 14 percent of the population were aged 0–14, 65.3 percent were aged 15–64 and 20.6 percent were aged over 65. The overall aging process can be highlighted by the fact that the average years of life already lived (around 43.7) is greater than the average remaining life expectancy (around 40 years). Hence, Italy's population has more of a 'past' than a 'future', and this has significant implications for the capacity of the available 'human capital' to sustain employment levels and future pensions.

The old-age dependency ratio (OADR: the ratio between the projected total number of people aged 65 and over – usually retired people – and the projected number of people of working age – 15–64 years old) is one of the indicators most widely used to determine a population's aging rate and the sustainability of pensions systems. Eurostat data (Eurostat 2013) show that the OADR in Italy is expected to double between 2010 and 2060, from 31 percent to 57 percent. This means that Italy will switch from three people of pensionable age for every ten people of working age (2010) to six people of pensionable age for every ten people of working age in 2060. Although this pattern is more or less in line with EU-27 (26 percent and 53 percent, respectively) and appears less dramatic than in other countries, for instance Latvia (26 percent and 68 percent) or the more comparable Germany (31 percent and 60 percent), Italian figures seem more worrying because of the characteristics of the local situation (labor market and labor regulations), as we are going to briefly discuss in the next sections.

The Italian labor market for older workers

The structural tendencies just outlined are matched by a series of labor-market trends that further accentuate the salience of aging processes and generational imbalances in Italy – with possible effects on the economic sustainability of the pensions system and on the possibility to maintain current employment levels. The most indicative finding in this regard concerns the employment rate for people aged between 55 and 64. The European Commission established a target of 50 percent for 2010, in an attempt to encourage national governments to adopt policies for postponing retirement. Italy has been unable to reach this target, considering that the rate was around 40 percent in 2012.

Three main socio-economic and cultural factors explain this worrying delay. First, gender plays a decisive role. In Italy, labor-market participation by women is significantly below the European standard for all age classes (in 2012 the female employment rate in Italy was 47.2 percent, compared with the EU-27 rate of 58.6 percent; OECD 2013a). If the analysis is restricted to the 55–64 age class, although the female rate has grown by around 10 percentage points in the past ten years, it still stands at around 30 percent (ISTAT 2013b). The second explanatory factor is education. The older Italian population has an education level below the corresponding European average. The lowest-educated Italians who started to work at an extremely young age are more likely to exit early from

156   *M. Depolo and F. Fraccaroli*

the labor market, and this again affects the overall rate to Italy's detriment. The third explanatory factor consists of the early retirement policies adopted in the past 20 years to respond to situations of economic crisis and corporate restructuring (Malpede and Villosio 2009). In more recent years, as a result of the retrenchment of such policies and the introduction of measures to raise the pensionable age, the average effective age of retirement in Italy in the period 2006–2011 was 59.2 years for women and 60.8 for men (OECD 2013b).

Nevertheless, further measures are considered necessary to attenuate the current demographic imbalances. Malpede and Villosio (2009), in fact, warn of a possible labor shortage in the next 15 years due to the exit from the labor market of the baby-boomer generation, with a possible labor-force deficit of around 4–5 million units compared with the levels of the early 2000s.

Already a cause for concern in themselves, these processes are exacerbated by a number of tendencies in Italy's youth labor market. At the beginning of 2013, the youth unemployment rate (15–24-year-olds) reached worrisome levels of around 40 percent owing to the economic crisis that has hit numerous countries of the Eurozone (especially in Southern Europe). But besides these percentages – which, though dramatic, may be the effects of transitory periods of crisis – to be stressed are the data indicative of a more profound crisis in the relationship between young people and work.

Italy holds the European record for the presence of NEETs (not in employment, education and training): that is, inactive and demotivated young people extraneous to processes of work entry and professional development. The European Foundation for the Improvement of Living and Working Conditions (2012) showed that Italy has the worst situation among the comparable EU countries in terms of both quantity of NEETs and social costs. Data (referred to 2011) show that Italian NEETs constitute 20 percent of the 15–24-year-old population (EU 13 percent, Germany 8 percent, France 12 percent), while the social cost paid is equivalent to 2.1 percent of the national GDP (EU 1.2 percent, Germany 0.6 percent, France 1.1 percent). In absolute figures, for Italy it means about two million young NEETs, and a total national cost of €32.6 billion. Added to this is Italy's European record for the percentage of young people (aged 18 to 34) living with their parents: in 2011 the percentage exceeded 50 percent of the total, amounting to seven million individuals (ISTAT 2012b).

These data provide evidence that the labor-market behavior of older workers and processes of transition to retirement in Italy may also be significantly conditioned by trends in the youth labor market and by dynamics of family structure. Discussion of these aspects will be resumed in the conclusion.

The law on retirement in Italy

The main provider of pensions for Italian employees, in both the private and public sectors, has to date been the national social security system. This system has been quite complex and comprised different types of pensions; however, until recently, the main ones were the age-based pension and the seniority-based

Challenges for older workers in Italy   157

pension. Aside from a number of differences not relevant to the purposes of this chapter, the age-based pension was available to workers aged between 55 (female) and 60 (male), provided that they had worked for a minimum number of years (almost 15), while the seniority-based pension was granted to employees who had accumulated at least 35 years of contributions to the social security system, regardless of their age.

Until the first major national reform of the pensions system (in the mid-1990s), the amount of the benefit was calculated on the basis of final average earnings. Although this system was certainly able to guarantee pensioners a standard of living correlated with that of active workers, it engendered a hidden but risky economic process of transfer of resources from the younger generation – paying contributions to the national security system from their salaries – to the older one – receiving pensions much larger than the amount of their contributions, because the pension was calculated on the basis of the salary received in the last working years, with no direct relationship with the amount of the contributions made to the social security system during the working life. No effective evaluation of the budgetary costs was carried out until the mid-1990s, when it was estimated that the system had involved a net transfer to living generations of about 80 percent of GDP (Castellino 1996).

Since the mid-1990s, a series of reforms have modified the Italian pension system. Without entering into the normative and economic details of the legislation that has modified the system, it will suffice here to recall the main features of the current situation. Many psychosocial, cultural and motivational aspects today relevant to understanding the everyday lives of older Italian workers, as well the strategies and plans of enterprises, are the consequences of a few, though crucial, modifications introduced by Italian law.

There have been three main consequences:

1   The age required to receive a pension has increased, and is still increasing.
       In 2013, approximately 42 years of contributions are needed (some years ago 35 were required): persons complying with this requirement but aged under 62 are subject to a large cut in the pension received. The combined effect of the new rules has been a negative incentive to retire (because of the financial loss) and an important extension of working life.
2   The purchasing power of the pensions received by many retirees will be so low that their standard of living will be jeopardized.
       Some 17 million Italian retirees receive a pension from the national social security system. According to the most recent report by the National Bureau of Statistics (ISTAT 2013a), the average 2011 pension was just under €12,000 per year; however, 13 percent of the pensions were less than €6,000 per year, and 44 percent did not reach €12,000 per year. Hence it appears that many elderly people, often living alone and with no other source of income, must cope with rather difficult economic circumstances. It should be borne in mind that ISTAT calculated the absolute poverty threshold in 2011 at €8,000 per year (one person, 60–74 years old).

158   *M. Depolo and F. Fraccaroli*

3   Future generations will not be able to obtain a decent level of income from the public pension system in their older age.

In fact, the situation will be even worse for young people entering (or having recently entered) the labor market because of both the difficult labor market (jobs come later, are more precarious and less well paid) and the shift to a pension system based exclusively on the contributions paid by workers during their working lives. Without the intervention of other factors, the smaller amount of working years, together with lower salaries, will produce a generation of poor retirees unable to maintain any 'normal' standard of living.

As Anxo *et al.* (2012) showed in their research conducted in Denmark, France, Germany, Italy, the Netherlands, Sweden, Poland and the United Kingdom, besides inter-country differences, working longer will produce important (and often unexpected) effects:

> Specific questions will be more acute with the effective postponement of retirement: increasing inequalities between groups of older workers, increasing uncertainty about the age of retirement, the way to keep lower educated workers in their jobs, sustainable working conditions, increasing risks of age discrimination, and impact of care of older relatives.
>
> (Anxo *et al.* 2012: 612)

It is evident that these questions are more critical in the countries hardest hit by the economic crisis. Italy is indubitably one of these countries. It is for this reason that bridge employment is not a topic on the Italian government's agenda, nor is it of interest in the everyday lives of work organizations. Compared with the more severe economic problems summarized above, as well as with the psychosocial consequences for present and future retirees, making the transition from work to retirement easier for older workers and for the organizations in which they work seems to be a minor concern, not a fundamental one.

Nevertheless, a certain number of companies have experimented with new ways to address this problem. While bridge employment is not envisaged by Italian law, some good practices have emerged from attempts to add value to the contribution of older workers. The following part of this chapter will provide an overview of the practices and their outcomes by drawing on a number of cases and studies.

Any bridge, any employment for older workers?

The above description of the demographic situation in Italy highlights several critical issues, both for the labor market in general and for older workers in particular. Put briefly, the economic crisis of the 2000s made Italy suddenly aware of the unintended medium- and long-term consequences of a risky system: the combination of an inflexible labor market and a welfare system of pensions conceived and built in times of more abundant resources.

Challenges for older workers in Italy 159

Retirement from work has been traditionally conceived in Italy as a sudden transition: until the last day of work, the retiree still holds the same job that s/he has always had. The day after retirement, s/he is out of work and enters a new world and a new role. This way of coping with the transition from work to retirement was quite 'normal' (in the statistical sense) until some years ago, when the above-mentioned reforms were made to the Italian retirement system.

When people realized that they were required to work longer for a pension that was sometimes even lower than previously expected, they were suddenly hit by the combined subjective impact of, on the one hand, frustration at having been forced to remain longer in work and, on the other, the difficult task of maintaining their incomes at a sufficiently high level (by compensating for lower pensions with post-retirement work), and this in a labor market with few opportunities for persons older than 50.

Given that the transition from work to retirement is a complex process per se (see Fraccaroli and Depolo 2008), the additional difficulties due to the mandatory increase in the age of retirement makes the situation of older workers even more precarious. At the same time, organizations must cope with the problems caused by this situation. In Italy, as a recent study has shown (Accenture 2012), the increase in the retirement age requires HR units to deal with three main challenges: (1) a larger number of older workers remain longer at work within the company; (2) older workers produce an increase in the average cost of salaries (because of their higher seniority); (3) the natural turnover of personnel is modified because fewer retirements mean fewer new entries.

Smarter companies have started to concern themselves with these problems, which are also apparent in the answers given by managers and employees (aged over 50) in a sample of Italian companies (70 percent with more than 1,000 employees) to a questionnaire administered during the same survey (Accenture 2012). The data are rather interesting because they suggest a composite picture: older workers consider themselves fully able to contribute to the company's performance, but they feel relatively neglected by HR policies.

In more detail, the employees did not feel too old for their jobs, even if they were perceived as stressful because of long working hours. They also thought that age did not matter in their jobs, and they thought that the employer wanted to continue with them. Their skills and knowledge were not outdated and were still crucial for the company's performance, even though their jobs were often not stimulating. They did not believe that younger workers would be more efficient and productive than seniors, but they felt that companies could not offer them interesting career opportunities. However, senior workers were less optimistic when they assessed the ability and the resources of their managers to cope with aging at work in the company: employees felt that management should do more in order to achieve a better match between older workers' characteristics and their jobs or assignments. Finally, the most important area of intervention suggested was the improvement of policies concerning working-time flexibility and pay for older workers.

160 *M. Depolo and F. Fraccaroli*

Case histories

Case 1: ManagerItalia

One of the most recent and interesting initiatives is the so-called 'Interageing, a pact between generations in the company' program launched in 2013 by ManagerItalia (www.manageritalia.it), an association grouping more than 35,000 managers of private and public companies operating in the service industry.

Based on the experience of many individual companies, the program aims to encourage companies to adopt one or more of the following four pillars for action:

1 *The Relay.* On a voluntary basis, a senior worker may switch from a full-time to a part-time contract, thus allowing a younger worker to obtain an apprenticeship contract, either in the same team or elsewhere within the company.
2 *The Variable.* On a voluntary basis, a senior manager may change the mix of the fixed and variable parts of his/her salary, the variable being linked to the results obtained. By reducing fixed costs for the company (the fixed part of the manager's pay), the senior obtains a new contract for a junior worker.
3 *The Tandem Arrangement.* A senior manager is paired with a junior one with similar functional skills and professional ambitions. They jointly manage a project with specific goals to be rewarded by predefined bonuses.
4 *Mentoring.* This is a training plan for couples formed of a junior employee who has shown good potential assisted by a senior employee using his/her ability and experience within an official mentoring relationship.

The 'Interageing' program seeks to help companies achieve a number of positive outcomes: among them, capitalizing on the investment in senior workers' competences; creating new jobs for younger people; and improving the organizational climate, thus providing concrete proof that the company is genuinely interested in adding value to human capital and improving the corporate identity. The program also aims to give benefits to employees: a number of jobs are saved and/or created; senior workers' competences are maintained and valued; career plans are clearer for both senior and junior employees; and opportunities for payment by objectives are created.

Although only the first and the second of the four main measures forming the program can be considered as bridge employment, it appears that the effort is worthwhile. Since Italy has no bridge employment by law, and since the flexibility that bridge employment entails must be found by offering an advantage to both the company and the employee, the idea of a 'pact between generations' seems to be aligned with the spirit of the European Union, recalling the *solidarity between generations* in the title of a well-known report by Eurostat (2012).

Case 2: Azienda Napoletana Mobilità Spa[2]

Azienda Napoletana Mobilità Spa (ANM) is the public bus transport company in the city of Naples. In July 2003, ANM received the SA 8000 standard of international certification for respect for human rights and worker rights, and for its health and safety initiatives in the workplace. In about 25 years, ANM reduced its workforce of around 7,500 employees by half. The large part of employees (around two-thirds) were bus drivers, and many of them (42 percent) were aged over 50.

As a special initiative intended to protect the health of older workers, the company and the unions negotiated an arrangement that allowed older drivers not to work on weekends. The initiative proved successful, as also confirmed by a decrease in the absenteeism rate among the older drivers involved. However, subsequent economic difficulties made it impossible to ensure replacements for older bus drivers using this arrangement, and the program was halted. Despite the forced end of the initiative, ANM continued its efforts to improve the working conditions of older workers: for instance, by introducing a successive-shift timetable and a provision allowing drivers with health problems to work on fixed shifts only. What is interesting is that these programs were in fact open to drivers of all ages, although they benefited older workers in particular.

Once again, this is not a genuine instance of bridge employment policy, although special attention to working conditions that may impair the health of older workers has been translated into specific actions.

Case 3: Unicredit Produzioni Accentrate Spa

Unicredit Produzioni Accentrate (UPA) is an in-house unit of the Unicredit Group resulting from a merger that created one of the biggest Italian banking companies. UPA provides administrative and accounting services to the Group's banks and companies and has more than 2,000 employees in several geographical units. More than half of them are aged over 45, which per se requires special attention by the company.

The kind of services offered by UPA involves activities that often require considerable experience, so that older workers are crucial for the company's performance. When Unicredit had to cope with the above-mentioned merger, UPA was put in charge of a service to the Group that mainly involved an improvement of back-office work, traditionally seen as less valued than front-office work. Given that front-office work was undertaken mainly by recently hired younger workers, the growing importance of back-office tasks (performed mainly by older employees) set up at the new UPA central unit pushed the company to invest in older workers' skills and reputation.

The redeployment of about 1,000 workers as a consequence of the reorganization entailed major investment in training. Both the company and the employees were satisfied with the redeployment. Back-office employees developed strong feelings of loyalty and commitment to the company, as well as greater job satisfaction.

162　*M. Depolo and F. Fraccaroli*

Among its HR activities, UPA created an additional training program exclusively devoted to its older employees (50 years was the minimum enrollment age). This course was designed to help participants develop new skills and work strategies. Its aim was to help older workers deal with continuous change in job demands and adjust to culture changes resulting from the merger of several companies. Since the company presented itself as placing high value on older workers, in accordance with this declared value the training initiative also sought to increase respect for older workers as a component of the corporate culture.

Nor can UPA be presented as a true bridge employment case. However, the action taken by the company at the moment of the merger seems to confirm that concrete interventions in favor of older workers can take multiple forms, even if the job description remains substantially unchanged. Other working conditions can be manipulated to obtain the desired outcome: improvement in the working conditions of employees in the final part of their careers.

Concluding remarks

At the end of this chapter, the reader may now be more aware of why we chose the title 'No bridge and no employment'. Demographic changes and the economic crisis are unfortunately building a difficult future in Italy for all workers. Among them, older workers will have to cope with greater difficulties due to labor-market rigidity and the prolongation of retirement.

Of course, even if younger people are experiencing major problems of labor-market entry, this is not a matter of 'a problem shared is a problem halved'. The focus is on difficulties specific to older workers that require particular responses. Such responses do exist, although the implementation of activities and programs intended to produce positive changes is likely to be hampered by the economic crisis. As an entrepreneur replied to an interview question on the possible concrete actions to be taken to reduce the generational gap for older workers:

> The crisis has created closer attention to the 'cost' factor. In a time of crisis and cost-cutting, a balance must be found among the cost of cutting higher wages [typical of older employees], the need for the company not to lose rare or strategic skills, and the economic difficulties of persons who may lose their only source of income, namely their job at our company.
>
> (Age Management 2012)

Treu (2012) has argued that national policies in favor of older workers at all levels require a mixture of public and private action.

> To be noted is a significant number of public interventions, especially in the more advanced countries, in both the regulatory phase (starting from the rules on retirement) and the implementation of the various active ageing policies (training, employment services and mobility).... Examples of success often concern groups comprising people of different ages that

combine the advantages related to the competences of those various ages. This confirms that cooperation between young people and the elderly in the workplace and enhancement of their diversity may be an asset to the company.

(Treu 2012)

Treu (2012) added that, in this regard, Italy needs innovative practices made largely the responsibility of the main actors: entrepreneurs, management, workers of different ages, starting from older people themselves. Good practices that have proved examples to be followed have always been original adaptations of general principles to the specific conditions of a particular company, or even specific units within it.

Big problems, complex solutions

In more detail, Olini (2012) has proposed an adaptation to the Italian situation of the general principles suggested by the European Union to make senior workers better able to cope with the task of satisfactorily managing the final stage of their careers in such difficult times. The points of the proposed strategy most relevant to our purposes here can be summarized as follows:

1 Support and update skills. Since continuing education in Italy is insufficient for all ages, older workers are more at risk of expulsion from the labor market. Moreover, the risk is even greater for low-skilled employees.
2 Strengthen the culture of learning in the workplace. Job rotation and teamwork by employees with diverse experiences and also different ages are good practices to implement.
3 Maintain work opportunities for seniors. There is prejudice concerning the ability of older workers to adapt to organizational and technological changes, so that it is less likely that they will be offered a job (or kept in their job) without consideration of their real skills.
4 More support for senior jobseekers. Active labor-market policies tend to be less efficient for older people seeking employment.
5 Reduce the gap in the labor cost between younger and older workers. Calculations by Assolombarda (2013) on OECD 2011 data have shown that the so-called tax wedge (i.e., the difference between the net salary received by employees and the total cost of labor) in Italy is among the highest in the world. For instance, on setting the net salary at 100, the total cost of labor rises to 191, comprising every other cost (income tax and social security contributions paid by the employee, plus social security contributions paid by the employer). Moreover, data show that the cost in Italy per employer is among the highest in the European Union, amounting to 46 percent of the net salary. This index is higher only for France (59 percent) and Belgium (52 percent), with Italy occupying one of the first positions in the ranking. Considering that, due to the Italian industrial relations system, seniority is

164 M. Depolo and F. Fraccaroli

the most powerful factor in the salary level (other things being equal), it is evident that older workers are more at risk when downsizing requires cuts to personnel costs.

Further confirmation that Italy should be viewed as a difficult case – because of its current economic crisis – is indirectly provided by SHARE (Survey of Health, Ageing and Retirement in Europe) data. SHARE is a multi-disciplinary and cross-national panel database of micro data on health, socio-economic status and social and family networks of more than 85,000 individuals aged 50 or over (approximately 150,000 interviews) from 19 European countries (plus Israel) (www.share-project.org). From a general point of view, SHARE (2013: 2) states that

> The crisis hit frail older people most. The effect of the crisis on health and well-being is stronger in regions that experienced a larger economic slowdown. Financial distress especially increased in Southern and Eastern Europe. Individuals with low education, low income, poor health and single females were particularly affected. The crisis was associated with a reduced likelihood of retirement: many individuals responded to the economic pressures of the crisis by working longer. In addition, financial assets were liquidated during the crisis when incomes declined. The crisis has negative effects on old-age health. This is particularly pronounced in areas with rising unemployment. In addition, unemployed aged 50 and over exhibit a substantially elevated risk of depression.

With regard to Italy, data on the specific impact of the crisis on retirement behaviors (Meschi *et al.* 2013) show that individuals living in the Mediterranean European countries (namely Italy and Spain) have changed their retirement behavior relatively more than those in other countries, and that this change can be attributed to the effect of the economic crisis.

For these reasons, too, it is difficult to find a consistent exit strategy for Italy similar to those of other countries where bridge employment policies have been implemented. It appears that, apart from the strong governmental intervention on pensions (which has given rise to a longer working time before retirement), no institutional and systematic set of interventions is likely to be found and applied. It seems more likely that partial – or at least one-dimensional – approaches and interventions will be the unwritten rule. Interventions of this kind, in fact, may sometimes produce positive outcomes even without a systematic frame of reference.

This is probably the case of a recent (2013) agreement between the unions and the employers' association in the Italian chemicals industry. As Gandini (2012) has argued, flexicurity in Italy has suffered because of a lack of substantial funding. A change factor may be the decision to create a national fund of about €40 million to allow regional agreements between unions and businesses. The purpose is to incentivize those workers (as well companies) that

Challenges for older workers in Italy 165

in the last three years of their work careers are ready to switch to part-time jobs so that the company can create new full-time apprenticeship contracts for young people. Accordingly, the 'Employability' chapter of the most recent national collective agreement introduces the 'Bridge Project'. Sapelli (2012: 44) comments that this agreement

> creates a pact between generations that not only gives young people the opportunity to work but reduces the workload of the elderly ... this project, within a challenging frame of subsidiarity, highlights the need for legislative action in order to mitigate the impact of the transition from full- to part-time work on the amount of the future pension.

Notes

1 The authors wish to thank Gianluca Maestrello (ManagerItalia) for the documents provided, and the Italian branch of Accenture Ltd for kindly providing a preview of their study 'Lavorare a lungo, lavorare meglio'.
2 This case, as well the following concerning UPA, have been taken from Principi and Lamura (2007).

References

Accenture (2012) *Lavorare a lungo, lavorare meglio [Working Longer, Working Better]*. Unpublished research report.
Age Management (2012) *Modello di intervista per la rilevazione della domanda per la gestione strategica di risorse umane 'aged' [An Interview Format to Describe the Demand for Strategic Management of 'Aged' Human Resources]*. Online. Available www.agemanagement.it/allegati/strumenti/Esempio_output_Intervista.pdf (accessed July 31, 2013).
Anxo, D., Ericson, T. and Jolivet, A. (2012) 'Working longer in European countries: underestimated and unexpected effects', *International Journal of Manpower*, 33: 612–28.
Assolombarda (2013) *Confronto del cuneo fiscale tra i principali paesi OCSE – 2011 [A Comparison of Tax Wedge in OCSE Main Countries]*. Online. Available at: www. assolombarda.it/proposte-di-lettura/analisi-periodiche/confronto-del-cuneo-fiscale-tra-i-principali-paesi-ocse-2011 (accessed July 31, 2013).
Catellino, O. (1996) 'La redistribuzione tra ed entro generazioni nel sistema previdenziale italiano' [Redistribution between and within generations in the Italian pension system], in F.P.S. Kostoris (ed.), *Pensioni e risanamento della finanza pubblica*, Bologna: Il Mulino.
European Foundation for the Improvement of Living and Working Conditions (2012) *NEETs: Young People Not in Employment, Education or Training – Characteristics, Costs and Policy Responses*. Online. Available at: www.eurofound.europa.eu/publications/htmlfiles/ef1254.htm (accessed July 31, 2013).
Eurostat (2012) *Active Ageing and Solidarity between Generations*. Online. Available epp.eurostat.ec.europa.eu/portal/page/portal/product_details/publication?p_product_code=KS-EP-11-001 (accessed July 31, 2013).
Gandini, A. (2012) 'Cambiare lavoro a 63 anni: necessità biografica personale e opportunità sociale' [Changing job at 63: Biographic personal need and social opportunity],

166 M. Depolo and F. Fraccaroli

Newsletter Nuovi Lavori, 109. Online. Available at: www.nuovi-lavori.it/newsletter/article.asp?qid=1287&sid=115 (accessed July 31, 2013).

ISTAT (2012a) *Natalità e fecondità della popolazione residente. Anno 2011 [Birth Rate and Fertility in Resident Population, Year 2011]*, Statistiche Report ISTAT.

ISTAT (2012b) *Terzo rapport sulla coesione sociale*. Online. Available at: www.istat.it/it/archivio/77697 (accessed January 30, 2014).

ISTAT (2013a) *Trattamenti pensionistici e beneficiari [Pension and Beneficial Treatments]*. Online. Available at: www.istat.it/it/archivio/87850 (accessed July 31, 2013).

ISTAT (2013b) *Employment Rate for Italian Population Aged 55–64 Still Far from the European Average*. Online. Available at: http://noi-italia2013en.istat.it/index.php?id=55&user_100ind_pi1%5Bid_pagina%5D=797 (accessed January 30, 2014).

Malpede, C. and Villosio, C. (2009) *Dal lavoro al pensionamento [From Work to Retirement]*, Milan: Franco Angeli.

Meschi E., Pasini G. and Padula M. (2013) 'Economic crisis and pathways to retirement', in A. Börsch-Supan, M. Brandt, H. Litwin and G. Weber (eds.), *Active Ageing and Solidarity between Generations in Europe: First Results from SHARE after the Economic Crisis*, Berlin, Boston: De Gruyter. Online. Available at: www.degruyter.com/view/product/185064 (accessed July 31, 2013).

OECD (2013a) *Quarterly Employment Situation*, News Release, 3rd Quarter 2012. Online. Available at: www.oecd.org/std/labour-stats/employmentsituationthirdquarter-2012oecd.htm.

OECD (2013b) *Pensions at a Glance 2013: Retirement-Income Systems in OECD and G20 Countries*. Online. Available at: www.oecd.org/pensions/pensionsataglance.htm (accessed January 30, 2014).

Olini, G. (2012) 'Differenziali retributivi tra giovani e anziani' [Differences in pay between younger and older workers], *Newsletter Nuovi Lavori*, 109. Online. Available at: www.nuovi-lavori.it/newsletter/article.asp?qid=1285&sid=115 (accessed July 31, 2013).

Principi, A. and Lamura, G. (2007) *Employment and Labor Market Policies for an Ageing Workforce and Initiatives at the Workplace: National Overview Report – Italy*, Eurofound. Online. Available at: www.eurofound.europa.eu/publications/htmlfiles/ef07058.htm (accessed July 31, 2013).

Sapelli, G. (2012) 'L'accordo che non piace più alla Cgil' [The agreement that Cgil does not like anymore], *Il Corriere della Sera*, September 25, 2012: 44.

SHARE (2013) *Book Launch: Active Ageing and Solidarity between Generations in Europe – First Results from SHARE after the Economic Crisis*. Online. Available at: www.share-project.org/fileadmin/press_information/News_and_Events/share_press_en.pdf (accessed July 31, 2013).

Treu, T. (2012) 'Recuperare un ritardo propositivo' [Making up for a delay in proposing], *Newsletter Nuovi Lavori*, 109. Online. Available at: www.nuovi-lavori.it/newsletter/article.asp?qid=1293&sid=115 (accessed July 31, 2013).

9 Flexible transitions from work to retirement in Germany[1]

Jürgen Deller and Leena Pundt

Introduction

Recently the broader German public and actors in the labor market have become more aware of the challenges of demographic change. The current debate started with the gradual increase of the retirement age to 67 in Germany, which was decided on in 2007 and has been the subject of controversy since then. Gradually also the phenomenon of work beyond retirement is being discussed. Following the very first analysis by Deller and Maxin (2009) of German microcensus data for work in retirement, Micheel and Panova (2013) have also used microcensus data to look into two decades of work in retirement. These developments are taking place a few years before the retirement of the first German baby-boomer cohorts and their necessary replacement in the labor market with cohorts that are smaller by hundreds of thousands of individuals per year. As a consequence, we can notice a growing interest in the intentions and behaviors of retiring cohorts regarding work in retirement.

Demographic situation in Germany

From its current level of roughly 16 million, the number of over 65-year-olds in the German population will increase to over 22 million as early as 2030. One inhabitant in three will be 65 or older in 2050 (Bundesinstitut für Bevölkerungsforschung 2008). At the same time, life expectancy is increasing, leading to a further rise in the remaining lifetime after retirement. According to the German statutory pension insurance scheme (Deutsche Rentenversicherung), men draw a pension for an average of 16 years and women for 20.6 years. In 2001, these figures were only 13.8 and 18.9 years, respectively (Deutsche Rentenversicherung 2012). The old-age dependency ratio will double in the next 40 years. While there are currently 33 retirees for every 100 persons of working age, there will be more than 60 per 100 in 2050 (Bundesinstitut für Bevölkerungsforschung 2008). This can be expected to present considerable challenges to the German social welfare system and the existing pay-as-you-go pension system (Moog and Raffelhüschen 2010).

The already existing shortage of skilled workers in some sectors will also continue to spread in all sectors of the economy in the coming years. If the

168 *J. Deller and L. Pundt*

present framework persists, there might already be a shortfall of nearly three million more workers in 2015 (Gramke *et al.* 2009). At the same time, however, many people potentially remain able to contribute to the economy beyond statutory retirement age (Lehr and Kruse 2006) and willing to continue to make use of their productivity. The Federal Institute for Population Research surveyed a representative group of 55- to 64-year-olds in dependent employment, 47.3 percent of whom considered the possibility of continuing in employment beyond their retirement age (Micheel *et al.* 2010). In a survey of partially retired employees at one company, two-thirds of them could have imagined working for longer (Aleksandrowicz *et al.* 2010).

However, in view of different professional groups with different workload demands and individual health conditions, it is necessary to distinguish between the nature and magnitude of continued employment. One indication of these disparities is the current average age of retirement being 60.8, much earlier than the statutory retirement age (Deutsche Rentenversicherung 2012). This may indicate that not all individuals in the German labor market possess the requisite physical and intellectual fitness to work longer, as only a specific group of individuals remain active and productive at retirement age. Nonetheless, a considerable degree of 'silver work' can be observed (Deller and Maxin 2009).

This chapter first introduces and discusses partial retirement policies and practices in Germany. It then quantifies the extent of work in retirement followed by qualitative findings that shed light on individual perspectives on work in retirement including prerequisites for post-retirement activities. A case study describes the business case of a pioneer company managed by and staffed with retirees that serves a traditional globally active enterprise. The chapter concludes by recommending actions for organizations, society and politics as well as identifying relevant fields of research.

Older workers in the German labor market

In the past decades the situation of older workers in the German labor market has been characterized by a pattern of externalization through extensive early retirement (Bangali 2008). It is only recently that growing awareness of the demographic situation has led to a national policy change that is beginning to show consequences in organizations. Now, the pattern of integration and employability (Bangali 2008) has become a focus to keep workers in paid labor until the official retirement age. So far, the labor-market potential of retirees has hardly been addressed officially. Only pioneering organizations are making use of the potential of retirees by offering project-based forms of bridge employment. Correspondingly, the number of working retirees has been unknown until the end of the last decade in official statistics due to a lack of interest in analysis. Only recently has growing interest in the field become noticeable in Germany in both organizations and research; however, not so much in the political sphere.

Pension policy in Germany: Partial Retirement Act

Starting in the 1970s, early retirement was mostly used as a method of restructuring and reorganizing institutions. While retiring early was seen as a social benefit for long working life by many workers and their representatives, it was also intended to provide jobs for young entrants to the labor market. This was based on the idea that young individuals cannot find jobs because of older job incumbents who do not retire. However, recent research across several countries suggests that the main driver for both youth and elder employment is the economy that makes the employment of both age groups rise or decline simultaneously (Gruber *et al.* 2009). Nonetheless, according to the Partial Retirement Act (Altersteilzeitgesetz), extensively used from 1996 to 2009, employees aged 55 and older could reduce their working time by exactly 50 percent on average to work part-time for up to ten years. Employers then paid an extra 20 percent at least of the last full-time gross income (on average 23 percent, in some cases up to 35 percent; Wanger 2009) to compensate for financial losses. They also continued to contribute to social security on a level of at least 80 percent, thus partly securing the pension level. Participation in the scheme allowed individuals access to an early pension at the earliest at the age of 60 (with 65 being the prevalent formal retirement age then). In the case of hiring an unemployed worker or apprentice, the 20 percent step-up plus the additional social security payments were reimbursed by the Federal Employment Agency for contracts signed until 2009 for a maximum of six years. This was the case for about 35 percent of all contracts. Each partial retirement case needed an annual investment of €13,000 (Wanger 2009), making this program one of the most costly of the agency (Brussig *et al.* 2009). The net cost of the program in 2007 alone was an estimated €900 million (Pimpertz and Schäfer 2009).

One original idea behind this law was to gradually phase out individuals from full-time via part-time employment into full retirement in order to alleviate the transition from work into retirement. Proponents understood partial retirement as an appropriate and flexible option to individually transit from employment to retirement and to stay economically active for a longer period of time. Opponents, however, critique the act as stemming from an elapsed epoch to fight unemployment by eliminating older workers early from working life (Brussig *et al.* 2009).

This partial retirement scheme was one of the most extensively used labor-market instruments over the years. Since 2005 at least 500,000 employees (44 percent female; Wanger 2009) are in partial retirement every year, about 20 percent of all individuals aged 55 plus subject to social insurance contribution in 2009 (Brussig *et al.* 2009), the figures being somewhat higher for the older group of age 60 plus (about one in four in 2007; Wanger 2009). The entry per year continued to be about 50,000 cases between 2001 and 2012 (Statistik der Bundesagentur für Arbeit 2013), mostly white-collar employees (Wanger 2009). Despite the original intention to support a gradual phase-out transition from the labor market, the Federal Employment Agency, jointly with the social partners,

170 *J. Deller and L. Pundt*

has interpreted the act to implement the so-called 'block model'. This model splits the duration into two parts of equal length: full-time work followed by a non-work period. The rules of the non-work period prohibit any work, including paid activity for any other employer. Critics argue that, using the block option, workload is not reduced and urgent impulses for a further humanization of work are not given. The only reduction realized would be the length of work strain, however, not the strain itself. Proponents of the block model underline its attractiveness and the necessity to safeguard options for an early withdrawal from the labor market, supporting organizations to reduce their labor force in a socially acceptable way (Brussig *et al.* 2009). However, the part-time policy and transition aspects of this instrument have been put into practice for about every tenth participant of the program only (Wanger 2010b). Therefore, the conceptual idea of gradually reducing work on the way to full retirement has been realized for only a fraction of all participants. Authors like Brussig and Wübbeke (2009) understand the option to offer a form of bridge employment; however, partial retirement – despite the growing retirement age – still tends to lead to earlier receipt of pension than regular work that is subject to social insurance contributions (Wanger 2010a). The norm in Germany for several decades was and still is to *not* bridge into retirement by gradually working part-time to allow for a smooth transition. As indicated before, nine out of ten participants in the partial retirement program do *not* reduce work time. They drop out earlier instead. After a first unsuccessful attempt to introduce a gliding transition to retirement in the late 1980s and early 1990s (Naegele and Krämer 2002; Wanger 2010b), Germany today still does not have a formal culture of bridging from full-time employment to full retirement.

Germany's new pension policy and labor-market reforms

Changing this prevalent culture and pattern requires a major shift in policy and practice. Following a better understanding of the challenges of the demographic shift, including the impacts of a low birth rate, longer life expectancy and securing the future of pensions in Germany's pay-as-you-go system, the externalization pattern is now in a process of change to a pattern of integration. The new pension policy orientation is mainly characterized by the dominance of contribution rate stability at the expense of supply levels. In addition to the pension policy changes various labor-market reforms make early exit from the labor force more difficult. Eliminating public financial support for the partial retirement scheme makes outsourcing of older employees more expensive. Though this reform is young, it has shown a rapid and significant effect. Since younger cohorts also will not be able to replace retiring cohorts in the labor market in the coming years, one of the political aims is now to better integrate older workers into the labor market by improving and extending working life. Therefore, government, employers and individuals are more and more interested to keep up employability for a longer period of time laying the foundations for a longer productive working life. Policies for this are being developed now. The pension age is being gradually raised from 65 to 67 until the cohort of 1964 retire in the year 2029. However, this approach neither focuses on retirees yet, nor does it facilitate aspects of flexible transition to retirement.

Working beyond retirement age

Working beyond retirement age is not on the agenda for many individuals, most employers and politicians. Given this background, it is not too surprising that Germany does not have much experience with flexible, gradually phased out employment as the concept of bridge employment understands it, for example, to keep individuals in the workforce longer. Little is known so far about the realities of work in retirement in Germany. Only a few scientific studies have been published, and only a few organizations have developed policies for working with retirees.

Bridge employment in Germany

Extent of bridge employment in Germany

Since the population of traditional working age is shrinking, attractive framework conditions may be helpful for recruiting workers of all ages including retirees. Work should be offered in an attractive and suitable form to all population groups. In this chapter we address the phenomenon of bridge employment in Germany, called 'silver work' by us. This broader semantic label offers a wider space of meaning, including individuals who continue to work only after a temporal intermission. As a rule, the legal termination of work in Germany is based on collective agreements between employer associations and unions that refer to numerical age. Should employers that are bound to collective agreements want to opt to continue employment beyond retirement, employee protection against dismissal will continue to be valid. This protection on the other hand makes it very difficult to terminate a regular full- or part-time work contract. Therefore, employers are very reluctant to continue regular employment in the same job with the same company. In practice, this legal situation prevents bridge employment with the former employers in the same job for most individuals. As a consequence employees in industries regulated by collective agreements terminate work at the age supported by the respective collective agreement. As long as collective agreements remain unchanged, any continuation needs a different legal form not governed by collective agreements, such as freelancing or working for an organization or part of an organization not subject to collective agreements. However, this legal situation does not offer the level of protection guaranteed by collective agreements. It becomes obvious that the actual legal situation is not supporting bridge employment. The other reason for using the term 'silver work' is – in some cases – the temporal intermission after retirement before retirees start to think about continuing to work. Therefore, the concept of silver work also includes the initiation of work in retirement after the initial

172   J. Deller and L. Pundt

experience of retirement, leaving a gap in the bridge from employment into full retirement. The term 'silver work' bridges this gap.

Micheel and Panova (2013) argue that the employment behavior of the age group from 65 years is rarely considered in detail, because it is usually in retirement. Therefore, not much is known about work in retirement in Germany. Gradual or phased transition in retirement may be the norm elsewhere. However, these retirement patterns have not played a major role in policies in Germany to date. To the contrary, the widely applied concept of partial retirement (see above) as a rule meant for most an early exit from the workforce before reaching retirement age. This has been very popular during the last two decades. However, in contrast to official policies, work in retirement exists in Germany as well. And numbers seem to be growing. Gradually, organizations, companies and researchers have become increasingly aware of the phenomenon. It is only in the last five years, though, that research on work in retirement has started to gain momentum.

In order to illustrate the phenomenon of silver work, we first try to quantify the extent of officially recorded post-retirement work in Germany describing approaches based on different data sets. We then present explorative results of an empirical qualitative study, indicating the concrete situation and prerequisites for post-retirement activities in Germany. This section is concluded by a case study presenting a pioneer company offering project-based jobs to retirees.

Although bridge employment is a widespread phenomenon in North America (Wang *et al.* 2008), very few figures were available until recently on active retirees' labor-market participation in Germany. Official data are not available (Naegele *et al.* 2012). Participation can be measured in different ways using administrative (e.g., from employment agencies, pension funds, social security organizations and tax offices) or survey data (Eurofound 2012). To determine the extent of post-retirement work in Germany, different approaches have been realized. These include using data from a microcensus, the German Federal Employment Agency, the German Ageing Survey (Deutscher Alters-Survey – DEAS), the German Socio-Economic Panel (SOEP), the Organization for Economic Co-operation and Development (OECD) and recipients of statutory pension payments. These sources are characterized by different objectives and ways to collect data. Thus, reported results always reflect these objectives and different approaches to estimate the number of working retirees lead to differing results.

First, we would like to look at numbers of persons in paid employment as they are regularly collected in the microcensus by the Germany Federal Statistical Office. As Micheel and Panova (2013) argue, the employment behavior of the age group from 65 years is rarely considered in detail, since it is usually in retirement. Although the Federal Statistical Office has collected this information for many years, data for the group aged 65 and older were reported for the first time for 2007 (Deller and Maxin 2009). Figure 9.1 shows the number of persons in paid employment after retirement age for 2007 (for data on labor-market participation by age for single years between the ages of 65 and 80, see Deller and

Transitions from work to retirement in Germany 173

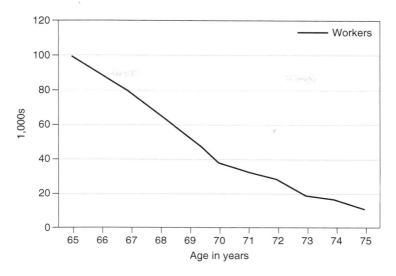

Figure 9.1 Persons in paid employment, 2007, aged 65 to 75 (absolute figures in 1,000s) (source: Maxin and Deller 2010. Copyright CPoS).

Maxin 2009). As anticipated, an ongoing reduction in the number of persons by age in paid employment can be observed. Whereas at the age of 65, 100,000 persons in paid employment are reported nationally, 11,000 individuals are still in paid employment at the age of 75. Furthermore, paid employment is still found in the even older cohorts on a case-by-case basis. Here, however, more precise observations can likely be made only after data from a new census are available, given that in the microcensus the number of cases in the 75-plus age group has shrunk to a size that does not allow for extrapolation.

Of particular interest are the self-employed. They form the largest professional group among those in retirement age, their share clearly growing with increasing age (see Figure 9.2). Roughly 55,000 self-employed persons are in the age group of 70–74 alone. At the same time, professional activity on the part of civil servants in the same age group can no longer be observed. This suggests that pensioners in this group seek other forms of employment based on the existing restrictions on post-retirement work, possibly in self-employment.

Looking at the percentage of self-employed and of assistant family members among persons in paid employment (Figure 9.2), a relative increase with rising age can be observed for both groups. The self-employed account for only 12.4 percent of persons in paid employment aged 50 to 54, but for almost half of those aged 75 to 79 (47.7 percent). If one adds the assistant family members helping the self-employed, this combined group accounts for 65.9 percent of all persons in paid employment in the highest age group.

174 *J. Deller and L. Pundt*

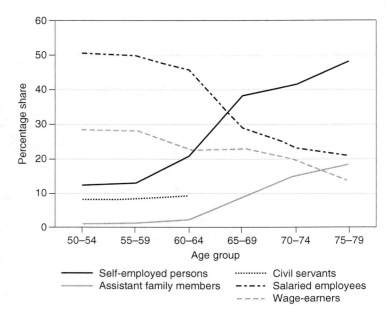

Figure 9.2 Percentage of all professional groups among persons in paid employment of the respective age group in 2007 (source: Maxin and Deller 2010. Copyright CPoS).

According to the 2010 microcensus, a total of 668,000 employed persons were 65 years or older (Micheel and Panova 2013). A different source of information is the German Federal Employment Agency reporting the situation in December 2012. Their data are precise as they reflect the nationwide enumerated number of work contracts of employees aged 65 and over for two groups, regular employees and minimally remunerated (up to €400 per month) individuals. The first group is subject to social security contributions and amounts to 174,810 employees (Bundesagentur für Arbeit 2013b), the second one to 798,320 individuals (Bundesagentur für Arbeit 2013a). In these numbers, the group of self-employed individuals and their assistant family members is not reflected. However, based on the findings of Deller and Maxin (2009) and other sources (cf. Brenke 2013) we assume that up to half of those working post-retirement age in Germany are self-employed and their assistant family members. Without going into detail regarding the overlap between employees and self-employed, we have reason to believe that the overall number of individuals working in pension age in Germany easily exceeds a million.

Looking further into this issue it becomes obvious that in the meantime the employment of retirees and especially certain groups is noticeable in Germany. However, since official data are missing (Naegele *et al.* 2012) there is no consensus on the degree of silver work in Germany. Depending on different sources, reported employment rates vary. Based on Eurostat, Eurofound (2012) estimate the employment rate among 65- to 69-year-olds in Germany to be 10 percent in 2011. Brussig (2010) found slightly higher numbers for highly qualified retirees as well as for retired males in West Germany (as opposed to East Germany) based on microcensus data. He discovered an employment rate between 10 and 15 percent for 2007. The rates are lower for medium qualified retirees and about half for low qualified individuals. An even higher labor-force participation rate of about 20 percent is reported by Hochfellner and Burkert (2013) based on recipients of statutory pension payments.

How has the labor-market participation of individuals of pension age developed over time? Looking into this development, Eurofound (2012) estimate an increase of 3.5 percentage points from 2005 to 10 percent in 2011 in the employment rate among 65- to 69-year-olds in Germany. According to Micheel and Panova (2013), numbers more than doubled between 1991 and 2010. At the same time the number of individuals in this age group increased by only 42 percent. This supports the notion of substantial changes of employment behavior in retirement age. The demographic development thus contributes only a partial explanation for the increasing employment in this age group. Micheel and Panova (2013) report details on participation changes of 65- to 69-year-olds using index numbers based on microcensus data, The authors differentiate employees by education groups at different times, with 1996 used for each education group as a basis for comparison (see Figures 9.3 and 9.4). While the number of men with low education working in retirement has decreased in 2010 compared to 1996, the numbers in the respective female group increased by 20 percent. However, in the medium and high education

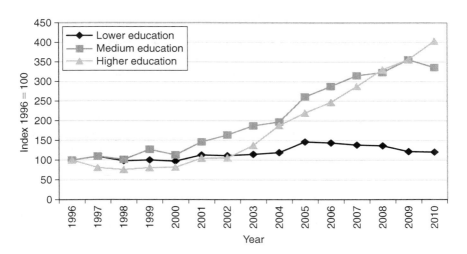

Figure 9.3 Development of gainful employment of women aged 65–69, according to education groups, 1996–2010 (source: German microcensus 2010, data and figures received from R. Panova, May 2013; translation by the authors).

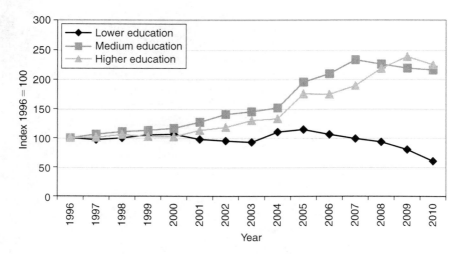

Figure 9.4 Development of gainful employment of men aged 65–69, according to education groups, 1996–2010 (source: German microcensus 2010, data and figures received from R. Panova, May 2013; translation by the authors).

groups the same pattern applies to both men and women, albeit at different levels: rates have increased for both sexes. Whereas the figures for men have about doubled, those for women have tripled (medium education) and even quadrupled (higher education). The labor market for individuals in retirement age shows substantial development for those who are better educated, not for those with low education. However, it may be this group that will have higher financial needs prompting their continuing to work after retirement based on reductions in pensions due to actuarial cuts (Naegele *et al.* 2012).

Scherger *et al.* (2012) based their analyses of the development of labor-market participation on the third wave of the DEAS conducted in 2008. They also used calculations from earlier waves as well as OECD data and the SOEP. The authors limit their observations to individuals of legal retirement age or over (65 for men and women). According to OECD data, more men than women are in paid employment in Germany. The data support an increase in numbers with a steep rise for men in 2011 in the 65–74 age group. Also Scherger *et al.* (2012) argue that this dynamic development cannot be explained by the rather stable poverty rates.

Scherger and colleagues (2012) also report valuable findings on specific aspects of work in retirement, such as employment and pension receipt by age and sex (see Table 9.1). They distinguish four groups: no pension, working; pension, working; no pension, not working; pension, not working. While almost every tenth (9.9 percent) man aged 65 and older is working in pension age, about every twentieth woman (4.91 percent) reports doing so.

Table 9.1 Employment and pension receipt by age and gender

	Men				All	Women				All	Total
	Age					*Age*					
	65–69	*70–74*	*75–79*	*80–85*		*65–69*	*70–74*	*75–79*	*80–85*		
No pension, working	1.80	(0.52)	(0.98)	(0.00)	1.03	1.31	(0.28)	(0.00)	(0.54)	0.59	0.79
Pension, working	13.00	9.13	4.70	(1.28)	8.87	7.92	5.46	2.16	(1.62)	4.92	6.72
No pension, not working	2.20	1.26	(0.59)	4.10	1.88	12.25	11.14	13.63	18.34	13.21	8.04
Pension, not working	83.00	89.08	93.74	94.62	88.23	78.52	83.12	84.21	79.50	81.28	84.45

Source: German Aging Survey, Wave 3 (2008), own calculations with respondents aged 65–85, unweighted. Unweighted N = 2,767 (1,518 men, 1,249 women); values in brackets indicate an unweighted N of below 5.

Notes
Employment and pension receipt by age and gender (from Scherger *et al.* 2012: 37, kindly supported by Emmy Noether Research Group, University of Bremen, Germany, Center for Social Policy Research).

178 *J. Deller and L. Pundt*

Overall, the estimates of the numbers of individuals working after retirement differ quite dramatically across the methods applied. However, the number of workers after retirement seems to be growing in Germany.

Quantitative findings on bridge employment in Germany

In very recent years, several authors report empirical results from quantitative studies. Based on a detailed description of empirical findings, Scherger *et al.* (2012) report that post-retirement workers are in better health and, on average, younger than other retirees. The better their own health is rated, both objectively and subjectively, the higher is the proportion of those working. This is supported by the findings of Naegele *et al.* (2012), who argue that paid work after retirement is overrepresented among younger retirees (between 65 and 70), former self-employed, male retirees, restricted lines of business and retirees with a comparatively good state of health. The level of educational qualification correlates positively with work in retirement while receiving a pension for men and women. With university education the likelihood of paid employment in retirement is almost twice the average. Also the desire to continue work in retirement is more frequent among individuals who have a high professional status (Micheel *et al.* 2010). In their representative survey of 1,500 men and women almost half of the sample (47.2 percent of respondents aged 55–64) considered the possibility of working beyond retirement age. The authors also report a negative correlation between disposable household income and the willingness to remain in employment in retirement. This is supported by Scherger *et al.* (2012): higher-level managers and professionals as well as small employers and the self-employed are more likely to be in paid employment than all others, while lower-level sales and service, lower-level technical workers as well as routine job classes before retirement show the smallest incidence of post-retirement work. At the same time, 'the richest in terms of house-hold income are more likely to be in paid employment' (Scherger *et al.* 2012: 46). In the group of those working while receiving a pension 3.3 percent of the recipients of the lowest compared to 13 percent of the highest net equivalent household income quintile report employment. People with a partner in employment are more likely to be in employment in retirement age as well, even if they receive a pension. Lower lifetime earnings, however, do not lead to higher employment after retirement.

Scherger and colleagues (2012) also report characteristics of the post-retirement jobs. Three out of four (76.5 percent) individuals work less than 30 hours per week while receiving a pension, while the others work more hours. The part-time findings are supported by Hochfellner and Burkert (2013) who found mostly part-time work and Brenke (2013) who reports two-thirds in part-time employment. Also Brussig (2010) points to a considerable amount of part-time employment at the end of working life: about half of those retirees drawing a pension work up to 15 hours per week on average. Part-time work and flexible working schedules are typical and, as Naegele *et al.* (2012) put it, one prime requisite for paid work after retirement.

According to Scherger *et al.* (2012), prevalent economic sectors are retail and wholesale (18 percent) and manufacturing (14.4 percent). The most prominent reason for working is enjoyment (72.2 percent), followed by only *non*-financial reasons (68 percent). Contact with others (45.6 percent) and wanting to continue doing something useful (45.5 percent) apply to almost every second working pensioner. One out of nine pensioners (11 percent) gave the financial situation as the *only* reason for working, while one out of three (32 percent) named several reasons, with the financial situation being one of them. Deller and Maxin (2010) found very similar reasons in their qualitative study. Table 9.2 also gives an overview of the reasons for working differentiated by previous occupational class of pensioner. Non-financial reasons are dominant in all classes. However, similar to the findings of Scherger *et al.* (2012), Naegele *et al.* (2012) report more financial necessities among the low-skilled pensioners while intrinsic motivations are found among the high skilled to a greater extent. Among the first group they state empirical evidence for pure existential need.

Furthermore, life satisfaction of working pensioners overall is highest for those who work for other than financial reasons (70.1 percent report an additive index life satisfaction of 8–10 points ranging from 0–10 points) and lowest for those who mention the current financial situation (53.9 percent report 8–10 points). Brenke (2013) also looked at satisfaction, finding higher overall life satisfaction in working compared to non-working retirees. Working retirees were also more satisfied with their own and their household income situation as well as with their health.

Qualitative findings on bridge employment in Germany

In the following sections we present results of a comprehensive study on the life realities of paid and unpaid working retirees in Germany (for more details, see Deller *et al.* 2009; Deller and Maxin 2008; Maxin and Deller 2010). We started to research the phenomenon of work in retirement in Germany in a qualitative-interpretative approach to first understand the phenomenon and lay the groundwork for later quantitative research. We agree with Scherger *et al.* (2012) who recently demanded evidence from such an approach since quantitative data alone cannot be the basis for studying the meaning of work beyond retirement in Germany. The goal was to arrive at a differentiated depiction of the life reality of this specific group of individuals.

Target group

We developed open-ended questions, the answers to which were largely left to the respondents themselves in terms of their length and content. Selected aspects were explored on the basis of existing theories with the aid of quantitatively anchored scales. Our sample consisted of silver workers, officially retired persons who continue to engage in one or several paid or unpaid activities. The reasons for, and framework of, these activities formed the focus of the explorative survey. For details on the questionnaire, see Maxin and Deller (2010).

Table 9.2 Reasons for working

	Large employers, higher managers/ professionals	Lower managers/ professionals, higher supervisory/ technicians	Intermediate occupations	Small employers and self-employed (non-agric., agric.)	Lower supervisors and technicians	Lower sales and service/ lower technical	Routine	All
My current financial situation	9.88	24.19	(24.19)	42.87	55.83	73.46	9.88	32.03
Only financial situation (derived)	(3.30)	(11.70)	(24.19)	(14.58)	(0.00)	(10.25)	(15.23)	11.01
I enjoy working	72.53	72.09	55.13	79.16	93.54	76.70	61.58	72.20
Contact with other people is important to me	45.98	35.25	37.66	46.41	50.94	59.26	57.40	45.63
I want to continue doing something useful	49.22	38.15	30.91	51.21	68.75	46.96	41.97	45.51
Only *non*-financial reasons (derived)	90.12	75.81	75.81	57.13	44.17	26.54	61.79	67.97

Source: German Aging Survey, Wave 3 (2008), own calculations with respondents aged 65–85, weighted. Unweighted N=178; values in brackets indicate an unweighted N of below 5.

Notes
Reasons for working (Scherger *et al.* 2012: 58, kindly supported by Emmy Noether Research Group, University of Bremen, Germany, Center for Social Policy Research).

Transitions from work to retirement in Germany   181

Sample characteristics

A total of 146 retirees in paid or voluntary work aged 60 to 85 (M=67, SD=4.2) were surveyed in telephone interviews lasting an average of 60 minutes. Some 31 percent of the sample were women and 69 percent men. Almost 60 percent of the interviewees held a university degree. The sample hence has an above-average level of education. Because of the qualitative nature of the data material, it was not possible to make an unambiguous distinction between paid and unpaid work. The respondents worked an average of 52.3 hours per week in their former professional positions (SD=12.8). These numbers refer to the actual working hours, and ranged from 10 to 85 hours per week. Four out of five respondents (80.3 percent) had worked more than 40 hours per week. For post-retirement activities, the working hours ranged between one and 60 hours per week, averaging out at 18.3 hours (SD=12.3), which corresponds to roughly one-third of the former hours per week. One-third of respondents (30.5 percent) worked for more than 20 hours per week in retirement.

The activity currently carried out was established largely as a result of contacts from previous working life, through both external enquiries and following own initiative and active searches.

The selected results in the question areas described, namely transition into retirement as well as reasons and framework for post-retirement work, are presented in the following sections. These results provide an overview of relevant areas for an initial understanding of the reality of active retirees in Germany. Further results are presented in Maxin and Deller (2010).

Results: transition to retirement

More than half of the respondents had entered retirement with positive feelings. Only 11.8 percent spoke of negative feelings in the transition into retirement. Four out of ten respondents stated that it had been stipulated by company regulations. More than one-quarter of the respondents cited internal company reasons such as job cuts or even insolvency of the company as the reason for retirement. Only 12.7 percent mentioned health-related reasons leading to the termination of regular work. Looking back, the vast majority of the respondents would once again decide for the selected time of transition into retirement. Not all respondents retired of their own accord, but largely after a fulfilled working life and with positive feelings.

One-quarter of the silver workers affirmed that post-retirement activity had been established on the basis of the previous work or contacts from working life (see Table 9.3 for details).

It should be taken into account here that multiple attributions were possible and that an individual's attributions could occur in various categories. When asked whether they had gained greater freedom in retirement, respondents reported considerably more freedom in retrospect: 79.7 percent responded positively to the question. Almost two-thirds of them referred to gaining greater

182   *J. Deller and L. Pundt*

Table 9.3 Development of post-retirement activities

Category	Occurrences (%)
From previous work, contact from job	24.1
External enquiry (passive)	23.6
Own initiative, active search	19.7
Continuation, intensification of work or hobbies	15.8
Contacts, network (not from old work)	7.4
Same old work, different scale	2.5
Follow-on work was already decided on during working life	2.5
Others	4.4

Source: Maxin and Deller (2010), copyright CPoS.

Note
Open-ended question: 'How did you find your present work?' Multiple responses were possible. Content-analytical categorized fields. Krippendorff's $\alpha = 0.69$. N = 142. 203 occurrences. Occurrences stated as percentages.

freedom as being indispensable. More than half of the skills used in post-retirement work were identical to those used in their former work. The largest share of the respondents reported a flowing transition between leisure and work. For example:

> First of all, I get up a little bit later.... I do not make any appointments before 10 am.... That is to say that I am away twice a week, otherwise I am at home. Go in for something together with my wife or with the grandchildren.

One-third rigorously distinguished between the two areas. By contrast, one-fifth did not distinguish between work and leisure at all.

Results: reasons and framework

The main reasons for taking up post-retirement activities are shown to be the areas of helping, the desire to pass on knowledge, wishing to remain active, own development and contact with others. In two open-ended questions, a main general question was first asked about the reasons for post-retirement activities, and later in the course of the interview about aspects of post-retirement work that are particularly important to the respondent. The results of the two questions suggest that the category of wishing to help others and pass on knowledge is central. In the unstructured statements on the reasons for continuing in activities, it accounts for one-eighth of the occurrences, and for almost one-third in the answers on importance. It is salient across both question areas in the category, indicating that it is a major element in the motivation for continuing to work. Another such element is contact with others, which is linked with post-retirement activities, with one-sixth of occurrences regarding importance. A further fundamental component of the

Transitions from work to retirement in Germany   183

motivation for continuing activities is personal development and the desire to remain active, with more than one-third of occurrences regarding the reasons. Recognition and appreciation experienced through post-retirement activities are similarly frequent in both areas, indicating that they are a further essential component of the motivation to engage in activities in retirement. Financial matters also appear within both the reasons for employment and the important aspects of activity in retirement, albeit with a comparatively small number of occurrences. The topic of remuneration was named in the responses to both open-ended questions. Enjoyment and interest in the work were mentioned comparatively frequently among the reasons for post-retirement activities, but do not appear at all among important aspects of post-retirement work (see Table 9.4 for details).

In the overview of the open-ended questions on the ideal framework of post-retirement activities obtained by content analysis (Table 9.5), the design of a specific personnel policy for older people, and in general on the areas with the greatest need for action for firms with regard to the employment of elderly people, age-tailored working conditions and the consideration of specific needs, as well as recognition and appreciation, are shown to be promoted with different intensities. The salience of these categories is a clear indication that they are major structural elements in job design after retirement. These aspects are fundamental components of the design of post-retirement activities.

A large share of the occurrences stresses intergenerational exchange and passing on of knowledge as a major component, although the only statements quantified here were answers to questions on the specific contents of a personnel policy for elderly employees and on locating the greatest need for action for organizations. Here, silver workers gave their personal retrospective accounts of

Table 9.4 Reasons for post-retirement activities

Reasons and importance	Reasons[1] in percent	Importance[2] in percent
Helping, wanting to pass on knowledge	12.3	30.5
Contact with others	7.6	16.7
Wanting to remain active, personal development	36.0	10.3
Own demand, performance	–	10.3
Recognition, appreciation	9.3	9.8
Fulfillment, well-being	–	8.9
Financial reasons	6.4	2.5
Enjoyment, interest	18.6	–
Other	6.8	5.4
Other contexts	3.0	5.4

Source: Maxin and Deller (2010), copyright CPoS.

Note

Content-analytical categorized fields. Information as a percentage of the occurrences. Open-ended questions: 1 'What reasons do you have for working in retirement?' (N = 139; 236 occurrences; Krippendorff's $\alpha = 0.78$); 2 'What is particularly important to you in your work?' (N = 141; 203 occurrences; Krippendorff's $\alpha = 0.87$).

184   *J. Deller and L. Pundt*

Table 9.5 Framework for post-retirement activities

Organizational framework	Ideal in retirement[1]	Personnel policy for the elderly[2]	Need for firms to take action[3]
Flexible working hours	29.1	12.8	–
Advisory, freelance work	11.8	–	–
Self-determination, freedom to make decisions	9.8	–	–
Working conditions tailored to age, consideration of needs	7.2	18.3	11.9
Providing a structure	5.6	–	–
Providing a meaning and a goal	5.2	–	–
Financial recognition, special remuneration arrangements	4.9	–	2.0
Offering self-realization	4.6	–	–
Facilitating social contact	4.2	–	–
No permanent job or employment	4.2	–	–
Remaining active	3.6	–	–
Recognition and appreciation	2.3	8.5	23.8
Full-time, permanent post	2.0	–	–
Using experience and know-how, exchange between young and old	–	15.2	29.1
Active involvement in the company	–	15.9	18.5
Involvement in further and advanced training	–	5.5	5.3
Specific services for elderly workers	–	10.4	–
Offering possibilities for flexible retirement	–	7.9	–
No special treatment	–	4.2	2.0
Changing state regulations	–	–	3.3
Other	5.6	1.2	4.0

Source: Maxin and Deller (2010), copyright CPoS.

Notes

Content-analytical categorized fields. Information as a percentage of the occurrences. Open-ended questions:

1 'What should be the ideal conditions for work in retirement?' (N = 141; 306 occurrences; despite a reduction in the complexity of the data it was not possible to calculate Krippendorff's α without combining the categories further, with the loss of content which this would have entailed.)

2 'What should a specific personnel policy for elderly workers be like?' (N = 111; 164 occurrences; Krippendorff's α = 0.67.)

3 'Where do you consider there to be the greatest need to act for firms with regard to the employment of elderly people?' (N = 120; 151 occurrences; Krippendorff's α = 0.71.)

the work situation prior to retirement. For post-retirement activities, it becomes clear that advisory, self-employed work is the goal, in which self-determination and freedom to take decisions are fundamental. Aspects that were named across several question areas assume particular prevalence in the perception of the respondents. Financial remuneration of the contributions made by silver workers is named for both the desired framework and the identified need for action. Even when, overall, a relatively small number of occurrences focus on this aspect, it is

Transitions from work to retirement in Germany   185

nonetheless worth noting that it turns up unprompted and independently in two question areas. The financial resources available to respondents appear to be an influencing element here. Moreover, a need for action on the part of the employing organization in providing financial recognition was identified. Furthermore, remuneration is frequently regarded as constituting recognition of the contribution that has been made. From silver workers' perspective, the responsibility is definitely on companies at this juncture: the financial recognition of work in retirement does not always appear to be managed satisfactorily. Working retirees would also like organizations to involve them more in basic and further training and quite clearly consider the companies to be responsible for this: one out of 20 occurrences in the question areas on specific personnel policy for the elderly and on the greater need to act on the part of firms, respectively, call for including the elderly in further and advanced training. Some respondents called for equal treatment of all age groups in two question areas in unprompted statements. The two latter aspects, each occurring across different question areas, correspond with one another in terms of content. Treating elderly workers *normally*, that is, equally vis-à-vis workers of all age groups also encompasses inclusion in further and advanced training.

Bridge employment in German organizations

In Germany initial practical bridge employment models have been developed relating to the use of the professional skills offered by skilled retirees. These models are currently exclusively concerned with the imparting of expert knowledge and skills. Organizations complying with the concept of the Senior Expert Service (SES), Bosch Management Support GmbH (BMS) or Erfahrung Deutschland GmbH (ED) place retirees in voluntary (SES) or paid work either within a company (BMS) or without taking former company affiliations into consideration (ED). The existence of these organizations demonstrates that, when suitable frameworks and appropriate skills are available, employment in retirement can be interesting for both individuals and organizations. As a pioneer for large-scale bridge employment in Germany, the Bosch group started Bosch Management Services, a company for retirees managed by retirees in 1999. The following case study describes this organization.

Case study: Bosch Management Support GmbH

Robert Bosch GmbH is a privately owned German multinational engineering and electronics company based in the Stuttgart area. With more than 350 subsidiaries across more than 60 countries Bosch employs more than 300,000 people and generates revenue of more than €50 billion (2011). Bosch is the world's largest supplier of automotive components (Wikipedia 2013).

In 1999 Bosch founded Bosch Management Support GmbH (BMS), a pioneering retired expert staffing firm for the Bosch group. Triggering the launch of BMS was the experience of Robert Bosch's top management that a growing number of

186   *J. Deller and L. Pundt*

retirees were offered freelance contracts after they had reached retirement. BMS was founded with the objective to offer transparent and fair conditions to those retirees whose expertise was in demand. Therefore, the only business purpose of BMS is the recruitment of retired Bosch experts with limited-time contracts only. BMS offers its services to Bosch units and business partners exclusively. All Bosch contracts with retirees ('senior experts') are handled through BMS.

The BMS competence center is located in Germany. However, after several years of experience, BMS has founded subsidiaries in North America, the United Kingdom, Japan, India and Latin America.

The process of identification of future senior experts begins in their last year with Bosch. About six months before (early) retirement, Bosch employees are contacted in writing about their interest in joining BMS. According to experience about one-third of all Bosch employees are not interested in continuing work in retirement, another third would like to work until legal retirement age, while the last third is interested in continuing as senior experts in retirement. While in the early years of BMS most senior experts had white-collar jobs, the number of blue-collar workers interested in work in retirement is growing now. Those interested in post-retirement work fill in a questionnaire asking for skills, competencies and experiences.

BMS operates a pull-system. Projects are generated based on word-of-mouth advertising as well as BMS sales campaigns with Bosch clients, employees and retirees. Only when a project contract is awarded does BMS use a database to identify and contact qualified candidates and check their availability. When approached, about one out of three senior experts is available for a project. After a candidate is selected by the client, they agree on project details. BMS invoices Bosch and signs a work contract with the expert.

BMS charges a reasonable price for its services. One advantage for Bosch is that external service providers are at least about twice as expensive. BMS margins cover social security contribution and insurance premium. All senior expert-related paperwork is done by BMS. Individual daily rates for senior experts are comparable to the level of regularly employed Bosch staff. BMS retirees either receive a salary based on a regular employment contract or bill BMS as freelancers. While working on a project they continue to receive full company pension. BMS does not employ individuals in partial retirement before retirement age. All income is taxable.

Based on their thorough experience of a long career at Bosch, senior experts are immediately efficient without having to adjust to unfamiliar company cultures or processes. Using BMS as a service provider also has strategic knowledge-management benefits: it helps to keep sensitive specialized know-how inside the company and prevents it from being disseminated to the competition.

In 2012 BMS had an expert pool of 1,646 retirees with a working life experience of 30,000 person years. Some 668 retirees were contracted in 2012 alone. Having sold 60,297 expert working days in 2012 (up from 15,883 in 2009), BMS generated €27.5 million in revenue, on average €456 per person per day.

Transitions from work to retirement in Germany 187

Managers accounted for about a quarter (26 percent) of the days, specialists for the remaining three-quarters (74 percent). BMS experts were active in a broad range of functions, including blue collar: commercial (31 percent), production (28 percent), support (19 percent), development (14 percent) and marketing/sales (8 percent). Technical service offerings include quality assurance, construction support, process analysis and improvement, projects for cost improvement, as well as market analyses. On the person and leadership side, know-how transfer ('mentoring') between home and abroad as well as between BMS senior experts and Bosch junior employees, and the integration of new companies represent another field of expertise. Additional service offerings include temporary substitution of a Bosch employee or manager during their absence from work or before a position is filled again. Singular projects, like event management, can also be assigned, as can the representation of Bosch in public bodies. BMS retirees also work as trainers or presenters.

Customers appreciate the professional placement service as a 'perfect match'. This is reflected in the standard post-project customer satisfaction rating: Mean customer satisfaction in 2012 was 91.8 out of 100 points. Based on the high number of experts, BMS has a potential for high capacity and can offer swift availability of senior experts.

Senior experts perceive fair and transparent conditions and highly value projects in the global Bosch organization. Transferring their expertise leads to high levels of individual satisfaction and self-assessed preservation of personal intellectual capacity. Senior experts also enjoy their individual contribution to the success of the Bosch organization. Motivational facets of senior experts differ across the international units of BMS. While in most countries an individual shortage of financial resources does not play a major motivational role, income from projects is an important motivation for senior experts in India and Japan due to the local income situation in retirement. In contrast money is rather seen as a hygiene factor in Germany, where less senior experts work for financial reasons.

There are several prerequisites for successful implementation of a senior expert model as in Bosch Management Support. First of all, the company culture needs to appreciate the expertise of older employees. Second, the company management must support the concept. Finally, the decision to use BMS services is always made by the cost center manager in charge, irrespective of his or her management level. Contracting with BMS is done only for temporary support, usually in bottleneck situations. All rules are transparent, standardized and comply with the local law. There is no 'hidden agenda' (T. Heinz, personal communication, August 2011; Odendahl 2011; A. Odendahl, personal communication, May 2013).

Recommended actions for organizations, society and politics

This chapter has pointed out several historic lines as well as new, quite dynamic developments that are characteristic for the German labor market. These aspects and developments play an important role for the future of silver work in retirement

188   *J. Deller and L. Pundt*

in Germany. One key motivator from the labor market supporting change seems to be the already existing and predicted shortage of well-trained personnel. An economic interest for organizations is the increased flexibility enabled by employing silver workers according to market needs (Naegele *et al.* 2012). Retirees have several advantages that organizations can benefit from: they are similarly qualified to younger cohorts (Brenke 2013), they are part of larger cohorts as they are part of the baby-boomer generation and many of them are still willing to be active in retirement, as we have shown in this chapter. Not only are they motivated and flexible, a growing number is also continuing to work (mostly part-time) despite unfavorable conditions. To benefit most, organizations should tailor their practices to the needs of individuals. Offering a person–organization fit is a prerequisite for those retirees who are not in financial need to decide to continue to work. BMS can serve as a business concept and role model of how to balance the needs of organizations and individuals. However, to fully utilize the potential, organizations and policy-makers are well advised to rethink current contracts and legal framework conditions. Introducing a new culture of part-time employment around retirement is a challenge for all. Organizations have to learn to meet the interests of their managers and employees to gradually phase out of work without penalizing participants with a stigma. Job designs and job ratings need to be adapted to support rather than punish part-time work. The challenge is to develop transition models for experienced individuals that allow them to work less and longer. Today's block model of the partial retirement scheme does not lead in this direction. It should be the exception rather than the rule. Policy-makers as well as social partners, employers and unions should also look into new regulations allowing for options to continue work even after retirement with the same employer. Under the given regulations employers are very reluctant to keep retirees on their workforce since they understand it to be very hard to cease an employment contract that has been prolonged into retirement. Therefore, they usually arrange for fixed-term and project-based contracts in a different unit of the organization that is not subject to a labor agreement with unions. Some also choose to offer freelance contracts not subject to social security. Policy-makers have a variety of additional challenges ahead. Besides introducing a flexible legal pension framework allowing for a simultaneous tailored mix of work *and* pension income they should come up with a new model of full integration of silver work into the labor market. Employees in retirement age can not only contribute to their own financial situation, they could also better support those who are not able to continue to work. A logical way to reach this objective is to include silver work in the social security system. By contributing to social security, silver workers could not only profit from a higher pension in later years, they could also continue to contribute to a solidarity system supporting those in need.

We tried to show that in order for gradual or phased retirement to become the norm in Germany, the prerequisite for new forms of retirement, such as a 'new retirement paradigm', 'redefined retirement', 'de-institutionalization' or 'individualization' of retirement need to be realized on different levels. To support

Transitions from work to retirement in Germany   189

this development, Deller *et al.* (2009) have developed recommendations for organizations, society and politics:

1   Organizations should reposition strategic HR management with the objective to systematically mobilize and integrate silver workers supporting business needs. This should include flexible structures regarding working time and design as well as appropriate advanced training to provide an attractive organizational environment.
2   A culture of appreciation for seniors needs to be developed in both society and organizations: the still-prevalent 'mania for youth' seems to be limited in time – not because of the forecasted changes in population structure alone. Deller *et al.* (2009) expect a growing recognition of individual long-time experience, substantial expertise and superior social competencies. Implementing the above-mentioned structures and values of organizational culture will not only be a key to attract silver workers. Also younger parts of the workforce may find these appealing.
3   On the macro level the establishment of a supportive legal framework for silver workers is suggested: the present regulatory system needs to be replaced by definite terms that put post-retirement work on a legal foundation and make it attractive. Policy-makers should therefore create incentive structures that will promote the development of a labor market for post-retirement work, also allowing for income in retirement, a fourth pillar of old-age pension. A new system can also profit from further contributions to social security as an element of solidarity of those who are still working with those who cannot continue.

Outlook

Nonetheless, the empirical quantitative and qualitative research available to date has several shortcomings. The qualitative approach to the environment and working conditions of active retirees in Germany draws its conclusions from a fairly specific sample of individuals who are above the national average when it comes to educational status and financial situation. At the same time, results from quantitative surveys use databases that have not been designed to research work in retirement in depth. Therefore, a representative national sample as well as data from a full census are needed for several reasons to make progress in our understanding of silver work in Germany. First, the numbers of working retirees reported differ depending on the sources used. Reliable information is needed in order to more precisely quantify actual numbers. Data from a full census should represent reliable numbers. Second, though several quantitative surveys have included selected variables that allow us to get a first impression of the role (psychological) variables may play for work in retirement, both psychometric qualities and constructs measured are quite limited. To record further interesting variables, validated scales for the relevant fields should be used, or new constructs and their operationalizations should be developed. For instance, it should

190 *J. Deller and L. Pundt*

be considered whether the construct space of 'appreciation' can be adequately recorded with scales to measure the 'respect' construct. A detailed representative survey is needed that encompasses scales of relevant construct variables for work in retirement. Third, we can only report correlations of the variables measured so far since data from a longitudinal study are not available yet. However, an interesting question is how the willingness to continue in employment and various forms of post-retirement activities is formed over time. To this end, a longitudinal design measuring motivation, socio-economic parameters and willingness to contribute suggests itself, starting in the end phase of traditional working life and extending beyond retirement age. The representative survey should thus have a longitudinal design to allow for causal inferences. In order to better interpret findings from such research, more qualitative research is needed focusing on different groups of individuals who work in retirement. Combining the results of qualitative with those of quantitative surveys will enable us to develop a fuller and more detailed understanding of the field of study.

For the success of silver work in Germany, we need a paradigm shift including individual perspectives as relevant parts of a new form of work. In a way, we are on the forefront of another humanization of work, tailoring it better to the needs of individuals.

Note

1 A part of this chapter has used material from Maxin and Deller (2010).

References

Aleksandrowicz, P., Fasang, A., Schömann, K. and Staudinger, U.M. (2010) 'Die Bedeutung der Arbeit beim vorzeitigen Ausscheiden aus dem Arbeitsleben' [The meaning of work in early retirement], *Zeitschrift für Gerontologie und Geriatrie*, 43: 324–9.

Bangali, L. (2008) *Active Ageing between Labour Market and Retirement: Externalization and Integration – Two Contradictory Patterns for Ageing Workforce in Germany*, WIP Working Paper No. 39, Tübingen, Germany: Universität Tübingen. Online. Available at: http://tobias-lib.uni-tuebingen.de/volltexte/2008/3252/pdf/WiP39.pdf (accessed May 24, 2013).

Brenke, K. (2013) *Immer mehr Menschen im Rentenalter sind berufstätig [More persons working in retirement]*, DIW Wochenbericht No. 6, Berlin: Deutsches Institut für Wirtschaftsforschung. Online. Available at: www.diw.de/documents/publikationen/73/diw_01.c.415345.de/13-6-1.pdf (accessed September 1, 2013).

Brussig, M. (2010) *Anhaltende Ungleichheiten in der Erwerbsbeteiligung Älterer; Zunahme an Teilzeitbeschäftigung [Persistent Diversity in Labour Participation of Older Persons: Increase in Part-time Work]*, Duisburg, Germany: Universität Duisburg Essen. Online. Available at: www.iaq.uni-due.de/auem-report/2010/2010-03/auem 2010-03.pdf (accessed May 2, 2013).

Brussig, M. and Wübbeke, C. (2009) 'Policy-making in ageing labour markets: The case of hidden early retirement in Germany', in M. Kuhn and C. Ochsen (eds.), *Labour Markets and Demographic Change*, Wiesbaden, Germany: VS Verlag für Sozialwissenschaften.

Transitions from work to retirement in Germany 191

Brussig, M., Knuth, M. and Wojtkowski, S. (2009) *Altersteilzeit: Zunehmend Beschäftigungsbrücke zum späteren Renteneintritt* [*Part-time Employment Prior to Retirement: Increasingly Bridge Employment to Later Entry into Retirement*], Duisburg, Germany: Universität Duisburg Essen. Online. Available at: www.iaq.uni-due.de/auemreport/2009/2009-02/auem2009-02.pdf (accessed May 2, 2013).

Bundesagentur für Arbeit (2013a) *Geringfügig entlohnte Beschäftigte nach Altersgruppen* [*Minor Employment by Age Groups*], Nürnberg, Germany: Bundesagentur für Arbeit.

Bundesagentur für Arbeit (2013b) *Sozialversicherungspflichtig Beschäftigte nach Altersgruppen* [*Employees Subject to Social Insurance Contribution by Age Groups*], Nürnberg, Germany: Bundesagentur für Arbeit.

Bundesinstitut für Bevölkerungsforschung (2008) *Daten, Fakten, Trends zum demographischen Wandel in Deutschland* [*Data, Facts and Trends for Demographic Change in Germany*], Wiesbaden, Germany: Bundesinstitut für Bevölkerungsforschung und Statistisches Bundesamt.

Deller, J. and Maxin, L.M. (2008) ' "Silver Workers": Eine explorative Studie zu aktiven Rentnern in Deutschland' ['Silver Workers': An explorative study of active retirees in Germany], *Arbeit*, 17: 166–79.

Deller, J. and Maxin, L.M. (2009) 'Berufliche Aktivität von Ruheständlern' [Occupational activity of retirees], *Zeitschrift für Gerontologie und Geriatrie*, 42: 305–10.

Deller, J. and Maxin, L.M. (2010) 'Silver Work: Zum Stand beruflicher Aktivitäten im Ruhestand in Deutschland' [Silver Work: Occupational activities in retirement in Germany], *Informationsdienst Altersfragen des Deutschen Zentrums für Altersfragen*, 37(2): 3–9.

Deller, J., Liedtke, P.M. and Maxin, L.M. (2009) 'Old-age security and *Silver Workers*: An empirical investigation identifies challenges for companies, insurers, and society', *Geneva Papers on Risk and Insurance*, 34: 137–57.

Deutsche Rentenversicherung (2012) *Rentenversicherung in Zahlen 2012* [*Old-age Pension Insurance in Numbers 2012*], Berlin: Deutsche Rentenversicherung.

Eurofound (2012) *Income from Work after Retirement in the EU*, Luxembourg: Publications Office of the European Union. Online. Available at: www.eurofound.europa.eu/pubdocs/2012/59/en/2/EF1259EN.pdf (accessed August 31, 2013).

Gramke, K., Fischer, D., Schlesinger, M. and Schüssler, R. (2009) *Arbeitslandschaft 2030. Auswirkungen der Wirtschafts- und Finanzkrise* [*Work Landscape 2030: Impact of Market and Financial Crisis*], Munich: Vereinigung der Bayerischen Wirtschaft e.V.

Gruber, J., Milligan, K. and Wise, D.A. (2009) *Social Security Programs and Retirement around the World: The Relationship to Youth Employment, Introduction and Summary*, Cambridge, MA: National Bureau of Economic Research. Online. Available at: www.nber.org/papers/w14647 (accessed May 2, 2013).

Hochfellner, D. and Burkert, C. (2013) 'Berufliche Aktivität im Ruhestand' [Occupational activity in retirement], *Zeitschrift für Gerontologie und Geriatrie*, 46: 242–50.

Lehr, U. and Kruse, A. (2006) 'Verlängerung der Lebensarbeitszeit: eine realistische Perspektive?' [Extending working life: A realistic perspective?], *Zeitschrift für Arbeits- und Organisationspsychologie*, 50(4): 240–7.

Maxin, L.M. and Deller, J. (2010) 'Activities in retirement: Individual experience of Silver Work', *Comparative Population Studies*, 35: 801–32.

Micheel, F. and Panova, R. (2013) 'Entwicklung der Erwerbstätigkeit Älterer in Deutschland: Rückblick auf die letzten zwei Jahrzehnte' [Development of old-age employment in Germany: Review of the last two decades], *Bevölkerungsforschung aktuell*, 34: 6–12. Online. Available at: www.bib-demografie.de/SharedDocs/Publikationen/DE/

192   *J. Deller and L. Pundt*

Download/Bevoelkerungsforschung_Aktuell/bev_aktuell_0113.pdf?__blob=publicationFile&v=5 (accessed May 24, 2013).

Micheel, F., Roloff, J. and Wickenheiser, I. (2010) 'The impact of socioeconomic characteristics on older employees' willingness to continue working in retirement age', *Comparative Population Studies*, 35: 869–902.

Moog, S. and Raffelhüschen, B. (2010) 'Herausforderungen der Legislaturperiode für die Tragfähigkeit der Renten- und Pflegeversicherung' Pflegeversicherung' [Challenges for the election period concerning the capacity of old-age pension scheme and long term care insurance], *Vierteljahrshefte zur Wirtschaftsforschung*, 79: 27–43.

Naegele, G. and Krämer, K. (2002) 'Recent developments in the employment and retirement of older workers in Germany', *Journal of Aging & Social Policy*, 13: 69–92.

Naegele, G., Maylandt, J. and Mörbitz, L. (2012) *Income from Work after Retirement: the German Case*, Dortmund, Germany: Institute of Gerontology at Technische Universität Dortmund.

Odendahl, A. (2011) 'Wissen einfangen und nutzen, bevor es verloren geht: eine Antwort am Beispiel der Bosch Management Support GmbH' [Using knowledge before it gets lost: an answer using the example of Bosch Management Support GmbH], paper presented at 1. Wirtschaftswissenschaftliches Forum Essen, Germany, September 2011. Online. Available at: http://wissenschaftliches-forum.fom.de/fileadmin/fom/downloads/Demografietagung/Vortraege/5.5.1_Praxis_Odendahl.pdf (accessed April 9, 2013).

Pimpertz, J. and Schäfer, H. (2009) 'Was kostet der vorzeitige Ausstieg aus dem Erwerbsleben?' [What are the costs of early retirement?], *IW-Trends*, 36.

Scherger, S., Hagemann, S., Hokema, A. and Lux, T. (2012) *Between Privilege and Burden: Work Past Retirement Age in Germany and the UK*, ZeS-Working Paper No. 4/2012, Bremen, Germany: Universität Bremen, Zentrum für Sozialpolitik. Online. Available at www.zes.uni-bremen.de/lib/download.php?file=b6c53d42c9.pdf&filename=ZeS-AP_2012_4.pdf (accessed May 11, 2013).

Statistik der Bundesagentur für Arbeit (2013) *Altersteilzeit nach dem Altersteilzeitgesetz (AtG) – Dezember 2012 [Partial Retirement in the Partial Retirement Law (German AtG)]*, Nürnberg, Germany: Statistik der Bundesagentur für Arbeit. Online. Available at: http://statistik.arbeitsagentur.de/Statistikdaten/Detail/201212/iiia4/altersteilzeit-altersteilzeit/altersteilzeit-d-0-pdf.pdf (accessed August 31, 2013).

Wang, M., Zhan, Y., Liu, S. and Shultz, K.S. (2008) 'Antecedents of bridge employment: A longitudinal investigation', *Journal of Applied Psychology*, 93: 818–30.

Wanger, S. (2009) *Altersteilzeit: Beliebt, aber nicht zukunftsgerecht [Partial Retirement: Popular But Not Sustainable]*, IAB-Kurzbericht No. 8. Online. Available at: http://doku.iab.de/kurzber/2009/kb0809.pdf (accessed May 2, 2013).

Wanger, S. (2010a) 'Die Altersteilzeit im Zusammenspiel individueller und betrieblicher Einflussfaktoren' [Partial retirement interacting with individual and occupational influencing factors], *WSI Mitteilungen*, 63: 395–403.

Wanger, S. (2010b) 'Wer nutzt die Altersteilzeit? Eine Analyse der Inanspruchnahme nach betrieblichen, persönlichen und beruflichen Merkmalen' [Who is using partial retirement? An analysis of the use by occupational, personal, and career criteria], in T. Salzmann, V. Skirbekk and M. Weiberg (eds.), *Wirtschaftspolitische Herausforderungen des demografischen Wandels*, Wiesbaden, Germany: VS Verlag für Sozialwissenschaften.

Wikipedia (2013) 'Robert Bosch GmbH'. Online. Available at: http://en.wikipedia.org/wiki/Robert_Bosch_GmbH (accessed April 25, 2013).

Part II

Bridge employment in North America

10 Bridge employment in the United States

Mo Wang, Lee Thomas Penn, Agustina Bertone, and Slaviana Stefanova[1]

Increasingly, researchers have found it beneficial to conceptualize retirement as not a one-time event, but a dynamic process that includes elements of retirement planning, retirement decision-making (e.g., early retirement, full retirement, or bridge employment), and post-retirement transition and adjustment (Wang *et al.* 2011). Research also shows that each retirement situation is unique to the individual (Wang and Shultz 2010; Wang 2007). Indeed, what it means to 'retire' can be interpreted in many ways, such as (1) lack of paid employment, (2) receipt of pension and/or retirement benefits, (3) exit from one's main employer, (4) reduced work hours, (5) hours worked or earnings received from work below some arbitrary cutoff, (6) changing employers late in one's career, (7) self-assessment of being retired, and (8) some combination of the previous definitions (Denton and Spencer 2009). For many individuals retirement can mean complete withdrawal from work, re-entering the workforce in another capacity, or even continuing to work past the age of qualification for social security benefits and pensions.

The choice to work during retirement is gaining popularity with retirees in the United States (Cahill *et al.* 2013). In fact, working in retirement has become more common for Americans than complete work withdrawal (Cahill *et al.* 2006). In the literature, working in retirement is known as bridge employment, which is defined as the labor-force participation patterns observed among older workers as they leave their career jobs and move toward complete labor-force withdrawal (i.e., full retirement; Shultz 2003). The capacity in which the retiree works can vary in the amount of hours worked, the amount of responsibility, and familiarity of work tasks (Wang and Shultz 2010).

One form of bridge employment that has gained attention is phased retirement (Drago *et al.* 2009). In phased retirement, an individual continues to work in the same career and work setting, yet works fewer and more flexible hours (Wang *et al.* 2013). This arrangement allows the individual to maintain a sense of continuity in retirement life (Zhan *et al.* 2009). It also is an appealing arrangement for employers because they are able to preserve their skilled workers and needed talent (Wang and Shultz 2010). Another form of bridge employment that researchers are beginning to study closely is encore retirement. Retirees engaging in encore careers use their accumulated knowledge and skills to work

196 *M. Wang* et al.

toward meaningful community improvement (Simpson *et al.* 2012). Here, the individual often chooses to devote some or all of their time in retirement toward a greater good and not for pay. An example would be a volunteer social worker (Simpson *et al.* 2012).

Typically, researchers distinguish between all forms of bridge employment using two criteria: namely, by career and organization. In career bridge employment, an individual takes on a job in the same field or industry as the pre-retirement job (Davis 2003; von Bonsdorff *et al.* 2009; Wang *et al.* 2008). For example, a lawyer may choose to retire and continue to work as a lawyer in some capacity, or conversely the lawyer may choose to work in a new career, such as in business as a manager. Another category of bridge employment is organizational bridge employment, which is whether an individual takes on a bridge job in the same company or in a different company (Jones and McIntosh 2010; Zhan *et al.* 2013). Thus, bridge employment can be categorized into five distinct types in the current literature: career bridge employment in the same organization, career bridge employment in a different organization, non-career bridge employment in the same organization, and non-career bridge employment in a different organization, as well as full retirement (i.e., complete labor-force withdrawal).

The goal of this chapter is to present a thorough analysis of bridge employment in the United States. First, we will examine the prevalence and current trends of bridge employment in the United States. We will then explore the psychological and contextual antecedents of bridge employment. Following that, we will summarize the potential outcomes of bridge employment. Finally, we will conclude the chapter with a discussion of future directions for research in U.S. bridge employment.

Prevalence of bridge employment in the United States

In the United States, the population is aging. In 2010, the Administration on Aging reported that 40.2 million individuals in the United States were at the retirement age of 65 or older, which has greatly increased from the 3.1 million individuals in 1900. Proportionally, the 65-years-or-older population represented 4.1 percent of the total U.S. population in 1900 and 13 percent of the total U.S. population in 2010, an increase of 8.9 percent in only 110 years (U.S. Census Bureau, International Database). By 2050, the number of Americans 65 years or older is expected to increase to 88.5 million (Vincent and Velkoff 2010) and represent 20.2 percent of the total U.S. population (U.S. Census Bureau, International Database). The reasons for these growing trends are decreased fertility and mortality rates over the course of the last century (Wheaton and Crimmins 2013). Combined with the fact that the oldest baby-boomers started to reach retirement age in 2011, there are expected to be 85 dependants per 100 workers in 2040 (Wheaton and Crimmins 2013).

The rising proportion of retirees threatens the stability of the Social Security system. Currently, there are approximately three workers contributing to Social

Bridge employment in the United States   197

Security for every one retiree, yet that ratio will decrease to approximately two workers for every one retiree by 2030 (Giandrea *et al.* 2008). In an attempt to lessen the strain on workers contributing to Social Security, the U.S. government has raised the qualifying age for full benefits from 65 to 67 (Wheaton and Crimmins 2013). The government has also raised the amount of credit awarded for delayed retirement from 3 percent per year of delay to 8 percent (Cahill *et al.* 2013). Furthermore, employers have begun to favor defined contribution (DC) retirement plans, in which the employee has the choice of investment options from multiple employers, over defined benefit (DB) retirement plans, in which the employer is responsible for making the investment (Rau and Adams 2013; Wheaton and Crimmins 2013). Because the DC plans carry over from employer to employer and can continue as long as the employee chooses, there is less incentive for an employee to retire at any given age (Wheaton and Crimmins 2013).

As a result of these trends, individuals are increasingly working up to and past retirement age. For many, this takes the form of bridge employment. Cahill *et al.* (2006) found that over half of Americans aged 50+ transitioned to bridge employment after leaving their full-time career jobs. Similarly, other longitudinal studies have found that anywhere from 30 to 50 percent of individuals experience post-retirement employment (Maestas 2010; Pleau 2010; Warner *et al.* 2010). In fact, Chen and Scott (2005), using data from the Health and Retirement Study (HRS), found that after eight years in retirement transition (1994–2002), 40.1 percent of retirees indicated that they were engaged in at least one form of working in retirement, and of that amount 19 percent were engaged in working full-time. Further, the idea of working into retirement is increasingly becoming an intentional choice. The Pew Research Center (2006) found that 77 percent of U.S. workers expect to work for pay after retirement, and Sass *et al.* (2010) found that 40 percent expect to work past age 65. In one study, 38 percent of workers aged 50–65 indicated that they would be interested in phased retirement alone (Brown 2005).

Not only is the amount of individuals engaging in bridge employment increasing, but they are also becoming more diverse. Traditionally, the retirees engaging in bridge employment in the United States have been male. Studies from various sources suggest that women are less likely to re-enter the labor force after self-identifying as retired (Maestas 2010; Moen *et al.* 2000; Pleau 2010; Singh and Verma 2003). Still, between 1980 and 2010, the labor-force participation rates for both retired men and women in the United States rose (8 percent for men aged 65–69 and 11.8 percent for women aged 65–69) and are projected to continue to rise (Wheaton and Crimmins 2013). Furthermore, while the majority of workers aged 55 or older in the United States is Caucasian (78.9 percent in 2010), the retirement-age population is becoming more ethnically diverse (Wheaton and Crimmins 2013). By 2040, Caucasians will represent only about 60 percent of the retirement-age labor force, while Asian Americans, African Americans, and especially Hispanic Americans will represent the other 40 percent. As such, the aging working population is

198 *M. Wang* et al.

becoming more heterogeneous, yet this may present a societal problem because of cumulative disadvantages. Research shows that decisions throughout the life of one's career can compound to affect the availability of later career alternatives and retirement choices (Hayward *et al*. 1998). Because of the indirect influences of society and organizational climates (e.g., availability of promotions and retirement plans, etc.), women and ethnic minorities may not have the same financial security in retirement as whites or males (O'Rand 1996). Older populations indeed show higher rates of income inequality than other age groups (Easterlin *et al*. 1993), and women and minorities are more susceptible to poverty after the age of 65 (Burkhauser *et al*. 1994; Farley 1988). It can only be seen what effect the rising education rates of these groups will have on retirement outcomes in the coming years.

Changes in the work environment are also affecting the rise in bridge employment rates in the United States. For one thing, jobs themselves are becoming less physically demanding and more cognitively and psychosocially demanding (Wang *et al*. 2009). This contributes to rising rates in bridge employment in two ways: (1) the physical decline of aging is less likely to prevent an individual from performing work tasks; and (2) cognitively challenging tasks keep individuals interested in work (Hayward *et al*. 1989). Many organizations in the United States are also realizing the benefits of maintaining their experienced workers and are thus implementing technology and retirement transition training programs, offering flexible hours, and providing family-leave and assistance programs for those past retirement age (Wang *et al*. 2009, 2013). Unfortunately, age discrimination may still be an issue in some work cultures, which discourages some individuals from continuing to work past retirement age (Wang *et al*. 2013).

Overall, the population of the United States is getting older and continuing to work past retirement age. For many, this work takes the form of bridge employment. Such a growing phenomenon warrants study by psychologists. Specifically, by studying antecedents, we can more accurately predict bridge employment choices. By studying outcomes, we can facilitate better transition to retirement for older workers and prevent individuals at risk from poor outcomes.

Antecedents of bridge employment

There are various factors that precede a person's decision to choose bridge employment. These antecedents can be categorized into micro, meso, and macro levels (Wang and Shultz 2010; Szinovacz 2013). Micro-level factors encompass demographic factors (e.g., age, gender, and education), as well as financial status and health. In the meso level, work environment, work role, and one's thoughts and attitudes about one's occupation are accounted for. In the macro level, organizational-level policies, the local job market, and the regional economy are considered. Extensive research has shown that all of these antecedents influence one's decision-making regarding bridge employment (e.g., Adams and Rau 2004; Kim and Feldman 2000; Wang *et al*. 2008).

Micro-level antecedents

Age

Wang *et al.* (2008) have shown that demographic factors, such as age, education, total wealth, and self-reported health are individual factors that predict bridge employment. Age has been found to be negatively associated with choosing bridge employment within one's career or outside of one's field (Adams and Rau 2004; Kim and Feldman 2000; Wang *et al.* 2008). The older a worker is, the less likely it is that he or she will participate in bridge employment. Research by Hesketh and Griffin (2007) showed that subjective life expectancy, or how long an individual expects to live, more strongly predicts the age at which he or she prefers to retire than other factors, such as income and self-reported health. Their research also demonstrated that those who believed they would live longer made plans to retire later. We speculate that subjective life expectancy affects whether an individual remains in the workforce through a bridge job, as higher subjective life expectancy means that an individual is more physically capable and can work longer. Conversely, as a person ages, he or she is likely to face more health complications, such as cognitive decline and physical impairments. These may lower subjective life expectancy ratings. As a result, one might want to have time to enjoy doing things unrelated to the workforce toward the end of one's life, such as devote time to grandchildren or an unfinished personal project. Further research is necessary to fully understand the mechanisms of age and subjective life expectancy in influencing bridge employment decisions.

Education

The education a person has received also impacts his or her decision to take on bridge employment. Years of education completed has been found to be positively related to taking bridge employment (Wang *et al.* 2008). Kim and DeVaney (2005) showed that retirees with undergraduate or graduate degrees were more likely to participate in bridge employment than those without higher degrees. Greller and Stroh (2004) found that even a general education led to more opportunities to be employed in different career fields after retiring from one's career occupation. Moreover, persons with higher levels of education are likely to have more choices in selecting a bridge job and are also more likely to easily adapt to a switch into a new career field (Wang *et al.* 2009). This is because people who have attained higher levels of education have more transferable skills across careers than those who are less educated. Therefore, those with less education might not have the option of choosing a bridge job outside of their lifetime career after retirement due to a lack of skills required in a different field.

Health

Research has shown that health is an important antecedent in choosing to engage in bridge employment. It has been found that changes in self-reported health are related to an employee's subjective estimate of how much longer he or she will stay in the workforce (McGarry 2004). Furthermore, health has been found to be positively correlated with taking bridge employment (Wang *et al.* 2008), which could be a result of having the stamina and energy to continue being a productive, contributing member of the workforce.

Following the same idea, those individuals who experience a negative health shock are less likely to engage in bridge employment (Maestas 2010). We speculate that this could be due to the inability to carry out required tasks in one's occupation or because such a physical or mental impairment requires intensive recovery time. Additionally, elderly workers facing deterioration of health may have more limited jobs that they can take in bridge employment (Adams and Rau 2004; Jex *et al.* 2007). Cahill *et al.* (2006) found that among workers employed full-time in the past, those who expressed having fair or poor health were less likely to engage in bridge employment after their career job in comparison to those who reported having good health.

Personality

Little research has been conducted on the role of personality and its direct effects on bridge employment decisions. However, personality has been researched in relationship to retirement in general. Löckenhoff *et al.* (2009) found that along the Big Five personality traits, those low in conscientiousness were found to retire earlier than persons who displayed higher levels of conscientiousness. Furthermore, personality has been found to be related to how satisfied a person is with their career (Judge *et al.* 2002). Hence, we speculate that personality might affect a person's tendency to choose career bridge employment over bridge employment in another field. However, no empirical research has been conducted to examine this relationship. In another study, Blekesaune and Skirbekk (2012) found that personality predicts different retirement paths for men and women in a Norwegian population. While neuroticism predicted disability and earlier retirement in women, this finding was not replicated in the sample of men. Thus, it is likely that gender and personality may interact in influencing one's bridge employment decisions. Further research would benefit from exploring such an effect.

Cognitions about bridge employment

A large amount of research has been conducted on micro-level individual attributes that affect a person's decision to take bridge employment over other retirement options. In particular, researchers have examined cognitions about retirement at the individual level. It has been found that people who actively

Bridge employment in the United States 201

think more about retirement are less likely to participate in both career bridge employment and bridge employment in a different field (Wang *et al.* 2008). This is purportedly because full retirement can be a disruptive process if an individual has not prepared to replace the social, cognitive, and financial resources maintained through work (Wang *et al.* 2008). As such, the individual can either prepare for retirement or keep working to smooth the adjustment process. Indeed, those satisfied with their jobs were more likely to choose career bridge employment instead of full retirement (Wang *et al.* 2008). Furthermore, Weckerle and Shultz (1999) found that older workers who felt that their retirement was voluntary were less likely to take bridge employment. However, people's negative thoughts about retirement are positively related to bridge employment seeking behaviors (Adams and Rau 2004).

Individual motives as a proximal antecedent of bridge employment

Individual motive plays an important role in the decision to engage in bridge employment. Indeed, retirement in any form is not a uniform, one-time event but a dynamic and personal life stage (Wang *et al.* 2011). Therefore, it is important to capture individual motive at a given time point as a proximal antecedent to understand their bridge employment decisions. In addition, there are many different motivators that can lead an individual to engage in bridge employment (see Table 10.1).

One dimension of bridge employment motives is whether the individual is being pushed toward or being pulled by bridge employment. Push factors are

Table 10.1 Motives to engage in bridge employment

	Push factors	*Pull factors*
Career and job	• Involuntary retirement • Loss of career/ professional identity	• Flexibility of hours • Learn new skills • Commitment to organization • Equal opportunity employer • Maintain health insurance • Impact community • Dream career/career calling
Personal	• Still at young age • Desire to retire with spouse • Supporting dependants • Lack of retirement planning	• Supplementary income • Maintain social needs • Maintain life structure

202   *M. Wang* et al.

negative aspects about the individual's current situation that drive the retiree toward finding new work. Pull factors are appealing aspects that draw the individual toward the new bridge job. These push and pull aspects can also be conceptualized into career and job vs. personal categories. In this way, bridge employment motives can be categorized into a 2×2 taxonomy that contains four quadrants (see Table 10.1). The first is the quadrant of push career and job factors, which encompasses involuntary retirement and loss of professional identity. Involuntary retirement forces an individual out of his or her current job, thereby pushing a capable retiree into bridge employment jobs. Loss of career or professional identity associated with retirement may also be difficult for certain retirees, which may push them into taking bridge employment. The next quadrant covers pull career and job factors. These are appealing aspects of the bridge employment job that draw the individual, including flexibility of work hours, learning new skills, commitment to the organization if it is an organizational bridge employment job, working for an equal opportunity employer, maintaining health insurance, impacting the community, and having the chance to pursue one's dream career or career calling. The third quadrant covers personal factors in the individual's life that push the individual toward a bridge job. These include young age (e.g., the individual is faced with a retirement decision and feels too young to fully retire), the desire to retire at the same time as one's spouse, the need to support dependants, and lack of retirement planning. Finally, an individual can be drawn toward acquiring a bridge job for many personal reasons. This quadrant includes such reasons as the need for supplementary income, the need to maintain social resources (e.g., social interaction with co-workers and customers), and the need to maintain one's routine or life structure. Future empirical studies can further shed light on the potential interactions among these motives and how they influence one's bridge employment decisions.

Meso-level antecedents

Work environment

At the meso level there are various job and organizational factors that can play an influential role in a person's decision regarding bridge employment. For example, previous studies have shown that retirement income satisfaction, career options, devotion to one's job and organization, and career possibilities predict an individual's plans for career bridge employment (e.g., Heindel *et al.* 1999). Employees may engage in career bridge jobs because they are committed to their organizations (Adams and Beehr 1998) or because they feel devoted and content with their profession (Shultz 2003). On the other hand, workers who believed the job market to be in good condition, desired having better use of their job-related skills, and had less concerns about changes in their employment benefits were more inclined to engage in bridge employment in a career outside of their field (von Bonsdorff *et al.* 2009). Moreover, female workers who had more

Bridge employment in the United States   203

non-work interests were found to be more likely to transfer to a bridge job in a different field than to hold a career bridge job (von Bonsdorff *et al.* 2009). Because of a lack of other activities outside the workforce, women might feel inclined to engage in a bridge job in their career to continue being active and feel a sense of purpose in their lives.

Additionally, researchers have also found that flexible schedules and a statement describing equal employment opportunities increased retirees' likelihood of taking bridge employment (Rau and Adams 2005). We suspect that flexible schedules may allow elderly workers to transition from full-time jobs to full retirement more easily, whereas an inflexible schedule might discourage older employees from continuing to work if it means their schedule will remain exactly as it was during full employment, especially if the job is stressful. Furthermore, organizations that produce a statement of equal opportunities for workers may encourage the elderly to remain in the workforce because they do not feel they are discriminated against or are viewed as less capable in comparison to younger workers. In other words, such a statement may make elderly employees feel appreciated and qualified in their work, further reassuring them of their competencies in their field despite growing older. Weckerle and Shultz (1999) found that older workers who felt that their employer preferred younger workers for a promotion were less likely to consider bridge employment after retirement, and Szinovacz *et al.* (2013) found that employees who felt that their employers chose younger workers for promotions were much less likely to anticipate working after 62 years of age. These research findings suggest the same explanation: employees that feel valued by their employer may be likely to consider bridge employment with the same employer if they feel they are being treated fairly and respectfully.

Wang *et al.* (2008) further found that work stress is negatively associated with participating in bridge employment, meaning that individuals who retire from jobs with more stressful working conditions are less likely to engage in bridge employment and are more likely to choose full retirement. We speculate that stressful working conditions may cause a person to view retirement as an escape and make working seem less desirable.

Family

Family factors have also been suggested as affecting bridge employment decisions. Kim and Feldman (2000) found that if one's spouse was still working, a retiree was more inclined to engage in a bridge job, whether inside or outside of his or her familiar career fields. Their research also showed that one's need to support other family members (e.g., spouse, children, or parents) was positively related to the decision to take on bridge employment. Specifically, a person's desire to pursue bridge employment may come as a result of needing to relieve a financial burden at home (i.e., helping children through college, taking care of elderly parents). On the other hand, Wang *et al.* (2008) found no relationships between marital quality and marital status and a retiree's decision to pursue a

204 *M. Wang* et al.

bridge job. This suggests that family variables may be distal predictors of bridge employment decisions, but further empirical research is still needed to confirm this theorizing.

Macro-level antecedents

Labor market and the economy

Research has demonstrated a contradiction among the retirement patterns of older workers during periods of economic instability. While some research has shown an increase in time of postponement of retirement during hard economic times (Goda *et al.* 2010; Munnell *et al.* 2009), other research shows a decline in employment and increased retirement rates (Coile and Levine 2009, 2011; von Wachter 2007). This seemingly contradictory finding is relevant to bridge employment because it suggests that elderly employees might seek to extend their time in the workforce in the form of a bridge job due to an unstable economy and its personal financial repercussions. However, an individual may actually only participate in bridge employment if he or she can acquire a job in spite of the decline in unemployment that results from economic situations, such as a recession. Therefore, a retiree's participation in bridge employment may depend on both the financial pressure he or she faces as well as the job-market conditions at the time of retirement.

In addition, Szinovacz and colleagues (2013) found that fluctuation in the stock market significantly impacted retirement expectations among part-time retirees, suggesting that such fluctuations may shape retirement expectations mostly among employees in bridge jobs or on the brink of retirement. Furthermore, their research suggests that debt influences retirement plans, often making adults push their retirement age past 65 (Szinovacz *et al.* 2013). As such, we expect that if an individual has high debt at the end of their career, they may consider a bridge job instead of retiring to pay off their debt.

Cultural norms

Cultural norms and expectations may also shape and influence an individual's decision to participate in bridge employment. Szinovacz *et al.* (2013) speculated that cultural differences in how and whether a person should go about retiring affect one's retirement decision. For example, cultural norms may expect a person to stop working when they are no longer as capable because otherwise he or she may be a burden to the organization he or she works in. Another perspective may be that time off during retirement is time that one earns and deserves for playing an active role in the workforce, so they may enjoy the end of their lives (Szinovacz *et al.* 2013). Therefore, we suspect that such cultural expectations are transferrable to bridge employment decisions because an individual might continue to work through a bridge career due to societal and cultural influences.

Outcomes of bridge employment

Bridge employment may influence the life of an individual in various ways and various life domains. Research has studied bridge employment individual outcomes in the forms of financial well-being, physical health, and psychological well-being. Research has also focused on meso- and macro-level outcomes of bridge employment in terms of its impact on family factors and community.

Financial well being

Bridge employment has become a vital tool for maintaining financial well-being in retirement. For the better part of the twentieth century, older Americans relied on the three-legged stool of retirement income, which consisted of employer-provided pensions, Social Security, and personal savings (Cahill *et al.* 2013). However, with the introduction of 401(k) plans, the 1980s marked the beginning of a gradual shift in favor of a 'do-it-yourself' approach to labor-force exit (Munnell 2007; Munnell *et al.* 2004). Thus, the retirement income stool was forced to evolve a fourth leg: labor-market earnings. With cuts to Social Security and stricter Medicare and Medicaid restrictions and coverage, Americans are relying more on personal savings by waiting longer to retire and following a trend of gradual retirement and bridge employment (Cahill *et al.* 2013). Thus, financial well-being has become one of the primary concentrations in bridge employment research. According to a study conducted by the Families and Work Institute and the Sloan Center on Aging and Work at Boston College (Brown *et al.* 2010), 20 percent of those employed at age 50 and older who defined themselves as retired were engaging in paid employment. Additionally, 75 percent of those employed at age 50 and older expected to have paid employment during retirement (Wang *et al.* 2013).

Bridge employment is ideal for retirees who find themselves in poor financial situations. It mitigates their financial burden and provides the added income toward retirement funds (Quinn 2010). Though the causal relationship between fiscal well-being and bridge employment is unclear, one can postulate that an outcome of paid employment after retirement is that it substantially boosts the fiscal well-being of those who have minimal financial resources during retirement (Zhan *et al.* 2009).

In some instances, salary is not the primary reason for seeking bridge employment. Johnson *et al.* (2009) found that older workers in later career stages are trading financially lucrative careers in favor of work that is more personally fulfilling or fosters growth and learning. In order to pursue a more gratifying but lesser paying position after retirement, economic stability is an essential prerequisite. However, not all retirees can afford to choose a personally rewarding job over a financially sound job (Wang *et al.* 2013).

As we demonstrated above, it is clear that bridge employment is often utilized for financial reasons among American retirees (e.g., Kim and Feldman 2000; Wang *et al.* 2008). However, no empirical studies have been conducted to determine whether retirees who engage in bridge employment fare better financially

206   *M. Wang* et al.

than those who do not. Studies examining the financial outcomes of bridge employment are distinctly absent from previous literature (Wang and Shultz 2010), therefore more empirical research must be conducted on this topic.

Physical health

A longitudinal investigation conducted by Zhan *et al.* (2009) found that the prevailing trend among U.S. retirees who engaged in either bridge employment in a different field or career bridge employment suffered from significantly fewer major diseases than those who retired completely from the workforce. Similarly, both forms of aforementioned bridge employment demonstrated a negative relation to functional limitations in comparison to full retirement (Zhan *et al.* 2009; Griffin and Hesketh 2008). Additionally, using data from the HRS, Dave *et al.* (2006) found a causal relationship between complete exit from the labor force and deterioration in physical and mental health, whereas these effects were mitigated in individuals that held bridge employment. These findings suggest that the physical and/or cognitive tasks associated with employment and job behavior aid in maintaining retirees' physical well-being and functional level (Wang and Shultz 2010), though access to health coverage provided by employers may also play a part (Stanton 2006).

It is important to note that the above findings support continuity theory, which emphasizes the importance of maintaining consistency in lifestyle and patterns over time (Atchley 1989). As such, retirees engaging in bridge employment are less likely to encounter the disruptive effects that may be associated with retirement transition. Rather, it is plausible that they will maintain their pre-retirement patterns of physical and mental activity through working, thus mitigating the experience of health decline (Zhan *et al.* 2009). Consistent with continuity theory, retirees engaging in bridge employment would be more motivated to achieve consistency and maintain, or even improve, their levels of well-being and satisfaction (Zhan *et al.* 2009).

Psychological well-being

The role transition from work to full retirement and associated potential role loss are important to consider when it comes to retirees' psychological well-being. Role theory often views retirement as taking away retirees' work-role identity (Bush and Simmons 1990). Supporters of this theory postulate that role loss can result in lowered levels of well-being as depression, anxiety, and stress are oftentimes byproducts of the retirement transition (Thoits 1992). This is especially true for retirees who strongly identified themselves with their work roles (e.g., Quick and Moen 1998; Reitzes and Mutran 2004). For many, continuing to work in the form of bridge employment can mitigate the negative outcomes of work-role loss for retirees, as it helps maintain the work role (Wang and Shultz 2010).

There is little consensus among researchers concerning the true impact of retirement transition on the psychological well-being of retirees. Some studies

Bridge employment in the United States 207

have found that when compared to other workers, retirees report higher rates of depression and loneliness alongside low life satisfaction, happiness, and psychical health (e.g., Atchley and Robinson 1982; Kim and Moen 2002; Richardson and Kilty 1991; Ross and Drentea 1998). Conversely, studies have also shown retirement to positively impact stress levels, life satisfaction, and health (e.g., Calasanti 1996; Ekerdt *et al.* 1983; Midanik *et al.* 1995). Meanwhile, a third set of studies has demonstrated retirement to be a relatively neutral event in an individual's life, causing little impact on one's well-being (e.g., Gall *et al.* 1997; Stull 1988). Wang (2007) postulated that these discrepancies might be due to individual differences among retirees and the cross-sectional design that researchers often employ. Using growth mixture modeling analysis, Wang (2007) found that U.S. retirees might actually demonstrate three distinct psychological well-being change patterns upon entering retirement life. These entail a maintaining pattern (e.g., psychological well-being remains stable before and after the retirement transition), a U-shape pattern (e.g., psychological well-being initially declines and then rises), and a recovery pattern (e.g., psychological well-being begins low and improves over time). Pinquart and Schindler (2007) independently demonstrated the same change patterns with a representative German sample as well. The practical implications of Wang's study (2007) were threefold. First, it provided a feasible method for predicting change patterns within psychological well-being as observed during the retirement transition and adjustment process. Second, the study found that a decline in retirees' health impacted their psychological well-being more profoundly than financial decline; this provides policy-makers with new insight into how to best aid individuals during retirement. Finally, this study demonstrated the close association between bridge employment and the maintaining pattern of the psychological well-being change during retirement adjustment, suggesting that having a bridge job may protect retirees from risks involved in the retirement transition and adjustment processes.

In terms of different types of bridge employment, U.S. retirees engaging in career bridge employment have actually been shown to have better ratings of mental health than those who took full retirement, but not those who engaged in bridge employment in a different field (Zhan *et al.* 2009). This may be because bridge employment in a different field may require additional adjustment due to unfamiliarity to the job and work environment, which may bring on additional stress and uncertainty for retirees. Thus, it is likely that career bridge employment is particularly beneficial for retirees to maintain positive mental health levels.

Family outcomes

As we mentioned earlier, work roles may be weakened during the role transition from pre-retirement employment to bridge employment. However, in this process, the role of the family member is often strengthened (Barnes-Farrell 2003). Studies have consistently demonstrated that married retirees who identify

208   M. Wang et al.

strongly with their family roles have an overall more positive experience during retirement (Calasanti 1996; Reitzes et al. 1996). However, if marital problems arise, the retiree's perceptions of retirement hassles escalate (Bosse et al. 1991). In this way, continuing to work in the form of bridge employment may present a means of maintaining a work–family role balance in retirement in the sense that bridge employment offers a separate social circle and social activities for retirees, though further research is still needed.

Previous research also suggests that U.S. married couples prefer to retire concurrently (Cahill et al. 2013). Bridge employment is rapidly becoming a means of allowing couples to retire jointly. For example, one partner can engage in bridge employment while she waits for her partner to retire the following year. In a study conducted by Johnson (2004), 20 percent of married couples retired within the same year as one another and 30 percent within two years of one another. Being married in retirement contributed to higher levels of psychological well-being when compared to retirees who were single or widowed (e.g., Pinquart and Schindler 2007). Interestingly, this effect dissipated in instances where the other spouse is working (e.g., Moen et al. 2001; Wang 2007).

Having few dependants also appears to equate to better mental well-being when entering older ages (e.g., Kim and Feldman 2000; Marshall et al. 2001). In recent decades individuals have begun to postpone having children until later years; it is no longer unusual for people in their forties or fifties to have young children. Thus, the flexibility in work hours and having greater control over one's schedule, as bridge employment often provides, aids in resolving the conflict between work and family needs in addition to providing supplementary income (Wang et al. 2013).

Community and organizational impact

Predominately, bridge employment holds positive outcomes for those who choose to engage in it; however, it can be equally advantageous for employers and the nation as a whole.

As employees age, their priorities may shift away from lucrative careers and high social status in favor of more meaningful work that provides a sense of purpose outside of economic success. Research on the meaning of work found that up to 95 percent of people reported a willingness to continue in work activities despite not having to for economic purposes (Harpaz and Fu 2002). There is great consensus among research that individuals who find meaning in their work are far more satisfied with their jobs (Pratt and Ashforth 2003). Sometimes this may manifest itself in the form of volunteerism, devotion to passing on the knowledge, or giving back to one's organization.

Individuals with high levels of career commitment may choose to give back to their company or profession by mentoring the next generation of employees within their career field. Older workers' desire to pass on their knowledge and skills to younger generations is known as generativity motivation (Dendinger et al. 2005). Thus, working past retirement age in the form of bridge employment

Bridge employment in the United States 209

is one method that allows individuals to contribute to the greater good (Simpson *et al.* 2012). Such motivation is mutually beneficial for the retiree who engages in meaningful work and their employer who will benefit from a new generation of well-trained employees. Similarly, retirees who strongly identify with or are emotionally attached to their previous employer can engage in bridge employment within their pre-retirement company for the sole purpose of contributing to efficiency and work output of the organization (Zhan *et al.* 2009).

From a national perspective, bridge employment is economically advantageous not only for the individual but for the nation. Given the current U.S. Social Security system, the longer individuals choose to remain in the workforce, the longer they pay payroll taxes and contribute to economic production, and the less time they will spend in receiving Social Security payment from the government. In addition, extended employment typically brings various benefits such as health insurance and additional retirement savings, which helps bring relief to overburdened governmental subsidies and public programs (Cahill *et al.* 2013).

Future research directions

Although research on bridge employment in the United States has been on the rise in recent years, there are still many areas that remain to be studied extensively. One way in which U.S. bridge employment can be further explored is by depicting the longitudinal trends of bridge employment. In other words, it is important to see how retirees' bridge employment engagement may change over time and whether it is associated with the level of adjustment they reach in their retirement lives. After all, bridge employment, as a form of productive activity in retirement, is not a one-time event but a dynamic phenomenon. Future studies focusing on investigating antecedents and outcomes of bridge employment would also benefit from longitudinal studies that examine retirees before, during, and after engaging in bridge employment.

Another way in which future research effort will benefit is through further examining the antecedents of the different types of bridge employment (e.g., career vs. non-career and organizational vs. non-organizational). Our postulation of motives for bridge employment examines the proximal psychological antecedents for engaging in general bridge employment. However, further research is necessary for testing their various associations to different types of bridge employment. In addition, different motives may channel different distal antecedents' effects on bridge employment decisions. In addition, the same antecedent may have different impacts on different bridge employment choices through different proximal motives.

Finally, there is a lack of thorough research on demographic diversity and bridge employment. With the aging population becoming more diverse (Wheaton and Crimmins 2013) and older populations showing higher rates of income inequality than other age groups (Easterlin *et al.* 1993), it is important that researchers examine the trends of bridge employment in relation to gender and ethnic trends in labor-force participation.

210   *M. Wang* et al.

Note

1 Author note: the third author and the fourth author of this chapter share equal contribution.

References

Adams, G.A., and Beehr, T.A. (1998) 'Turnover and retirement: A comparison of their similarities and differences', *Personnel Psychology*, 51: 643–65.

Adams, G.A., and Rau, B.L. (2004) 'Job seeking among retirees seeking bridge employment', *Personnel Psychology*, 57: 719–44.

Administration on Aging (2010) *A Profile of Older Americans: 2009*. Online. Available at: www.aoa.gov/AoAroot/Aging_Statistics/Profile/index.aspx (accessed April 10, 2013).

Atchley, R.C. (1989) 'A continuity theory of normal aging', *The Gerontologist*, 29: 183–90.

Atchley, R.C., and Robinson, J.L. (1982) 'Attitudes toward retirement and distance from the event', *Research on Aging*, 4: 299–313.

Barnes-Farrell, J.L. (2003) 'Beyond health and wealth: Attitudinal and other influences in retirement decision-making', in. G.A. Adams and T.A. Beehr (eds.), *Retirement: Reasons, Processes, and Results*, New York: Springer.

Blekesaune, M., and Skirbekk, V. (2012) 'Can personality predict retirement behaviour? A longitudinal analysis combining survey and register data from Norway', *European Journal of Aging*, 9: 199–206.

Bosse, R., Aldwin, C.M., Levenson, M.R., and Workman-Daniels, K. (1991) 'How stressful is retirement? Findings from the Normative Aging Study', *Journal of Gerontology: Psychological Sciences*, 46: 9–14.

Brown, K.S. (2005) 'Attitudes of individuals 50 and older toward phased retirement', *AARP Knowledge Management*, 1–30.

Brown, M., Aumann, K., Pitt-Catsouphes, M., Galinsky, E., and Bond, J.T. (2010) 'Working in retirement: A 21st century phenomenon', *National Study of the Changing Workforce 2008*. Online. Available at: http://familiesandwork.org/site/research/reports/workinginretirement.pdf (accessed March 30, 2013).

Burkhauser, R.V., Duncan, G.J., and Hauser, R. (1994) 'Sharing prosperity across the age distribution: A comparison of the United States and Germany in the 1980s', *The Gerontologist*, 34: 150–60.

Bush, D.M., and Simmons, R.G. (1990) 'Socialization processes over the life course', in M. Rosenberg and R.H. Turner (eds.), *Social Psychology: Sociological Perspectives*, New Brunswick, NJ: Transaction.

Cahill, K.E., Giandrea, M.D., and Quinn, J.F. (2006) 'Retirement patterns from career employment', *The Gerontologist*, 46: 514–23.

Cahill, K.E., Giandrea, M.D., and Quinn, J.F. (2013) 'Bridge employment', in M. Wang (ed.), *The Oxford Handbook of Retirement*, New York: Oxford Library of Psychology.

Calasanti, T.M. (1996) 'Gender and life satisfaction in retirement: An assessment of the male model', *Journal of Gerontology: Social Sciences*, 51: 18–29.

Chen, Y.P., and Scott, J. (2005) *Phased Retirement: Who Opts for It and Towards What End?*, Washington, DC: AARP. Online. Available at: http://assets.aarp.org/rgcenter/econ/2006_01_retire.pdf (accessed May 6, 2008).

Coile, C., and Levine, P.B. (2009) *The Market Crash and Mass Layoffs: How the Current*

Economic Crisis May Affect Retirement, NBER Working Papers, Cambridge, MA: National Bureau of Economic Research. Online. Available at: http://nber.org/papers/w15395 (accessed March 3, 2013).

Coile, C.C., and Levine, P.B. (2011) 'Recessions, retirement, and Social Security', *American Economic Review: Papers and Proceedings*, 101: 23–8. Online. Available at: http://dx.doi.org/10.1257/aer.101.3.23 (accessed April 4, 2013).

Dave, D., Rashad, I., and Spasojevic, J. (2006) 'The effects of retirement on physical and mental health outcomes', *NBER Working Papers 12123*, National Bureau of Economic Research, Inc.

Davis, M.A. (2003) 'Factors related to bridge employment participation among private sector early retirees', *Journal of Vocational Behavior*, 63: 55–71.

Dendinger, V.M., Adams, G.A., and Jacobson, J.D. (2005) 'Reasons for working and their relationship to retirement attitudes, job satisfaction and occupational self-efficacy of bridge employees', *International Journal of Aging and Human Development*, 61: 21–35.

Denton, F.T., and Spencer, B.G. (2009) 'What is retirement? A review and assessment of alternative concepts and measures', *Canadian Journal on Aging*, 28: 63–76.

Drago, R., Wooden, M., and Black, D. (2009) 'Who wants and gets flexibility? Changing work hours preferences and life events', *Industrial and Labor Relations Review*, 62: 394–414.

Easterlin, R.A., Macunovich, D.J., and Crimmins, E.M. (1993) 'Economic status of the young and old in the working-age population, 1964 and 1987', in V.L. Bengston and W.A. Achenbaum (eds.), *The Changing Contract across Generations*, Newbury Park, CA: Sage.

Ekerdt, D.J., Bosse, R., and LoCastro, J.S. (1983) 'Claims that retirement improves health', *Journal of Gerontology*, 38: 231–6.

Farley, R. (1988) 'After the starting line: Blacks and women in an uphill race', *Demography*, 25: 477–95.

Gall, T.L., Evans, D.R., and Howard, J. (1997) 'The retirement adjustment process: Changes in the well-being of male retirees across time', *Journal of Gerontology: Psychological Sciences*, 52: 110–17.

Giandrea, M.D., Cahill, K.E., and Quinn, J.F. (2008) *Self-employment Transitions among Older American Workers with Career Jobs*, Working Paper, Washington, DC: U.S. Bureau of Labor Statistics.

Goda, G.S., Shoven, J.B., and Slavov, S.N. (2010) *Does Stock Market Performance Influence Retirement Expectations?*, Cambridge, MA: National Bureau of Economic Research. Online. Available at: http://ssrn.com/abstract=1648011 (accessed March 13, 2013).

Greller, M.M., and Stroh, L.K. (2004) 'Making the most of "later career" for employers and workers themselves: Becoming elders, not relics', *Organizational Dynamics*, 33: 202–14.

Griffin, B., and Hesketh, B. (2008) 'Post-retirement work: The individual determinants of paid and volunteer work', *Journal of Occupational and Organizational Psychology*, 81: 101–21.

Harpaz, I., and Fu, X. (2002) 'The structure of the meaning of work: A relative stability amidst change', *Human Relations*, 55: 639–68.

Hayward, M.D., Friedman, S., and Chen, H. (1998) 'Career trajectories and older men's retirement', *Journal of Gerontology: Social Sciences*, 53: 91–103.

Hayward, M.D., Grady, W.R., Hardy, M.A., and Sommers, D. (1989) 'Occupational influences on retirement, disability, and death', *Demography*, 26: 393–409.

212 *M. Wang* et al.

Heindel, R.A., Adams, G.A., and Lepisto, L. (1999) *Predicting Bridge Employment: A Test of Feldman's (1994) Hypotheses*, Poster presented at the 14th annual conference of the Society for Industrial and Organizational Psychology, Atlanta, GA.

Hesketh, B., and Griffin, B. (2007) 'Self-estimates of life expectancy as an influence on intended retirement age', in G.G. Fisher (ed.), *International Perspectives on Older Workers: Work and the Retirement Process*, symposium conducted at the 22nd Annual Conference of the Society for Industrial and Organizational Psychology, New York.

Jex, S.M., Wang, M., and Zarubin, A. (2007) 'Aging and occupational health', in K.S. Shultz and G.A. Adams (eds.), *Aging and Work in the 21st Century*, Mahwah, NJ: Erlbaum.

Johnson, R.W. (2004) 'Do spouses coordinate their retirement decision?', *Center for Retirement Research*, 19: 1–8.

Johnson, R.W., Kawachi, J., and Lewis, E.K. (2009) *Older Workers on the Move: Recareering in Later Life*, Washington, DC: AARP Public Policy Institute.

Jones, D.A., and McIntosh, B.R. (2010) 'Organizational and occupational commitment in relation to bridge employment and retirement intentions', *Journal of Vocational Behavior*, 77: 290–303.

Judge, T.A., Heller, D., and Mount, M.K. (2002) 'Five-factor model of personality and job satisfaction: A meta-analysis', *Journal of Applied Psychology*, 87: 530–41.

Kim, H., and DeVaney, S.A. (2005) 'The selection of partial or full retirement by older workers', *Journal of Family and Economic Issues*, 26: 371–94.

Kim, J.E., and Moen, P. (2002) 'Retirement transitions, gender, and psychological well-being: A life-course model', *Journals of Gerontology: Series B: Psychology Science and Social Science*, 57: 212–22.

Kim, S., and Feldman, D.C. (2000) 'Working in retirement: The antecedents of bridge employment and its consequences for quality life in retirement', *Academy of Management Journal*, 43: 1195–210.

Löckenhoff, C.E., Terracciano, A., and Costa, P.T., Jr. (2009) 'Five-factor model personality traits and the retirement transition: Longitudinal and cross-sectional associations', *Psychology and Aging*, 24: 722–8.

McGarry, K. (2004) 'Health and retirement: Do changes in health affect retirement expectations?', *Journal of Human Resources*, 39: 624–48.

Maestas, N. (2010) 'Back to work: Expectations and realizations of work after retirement', *Journal of Human Resources*, 45: 719–48.

Marshall, V.W., Clarke, P.J., and Ballantyne, P.J. (2001) 'Instability in the retirement transition: Effects on health and well-being in a Canadian study', *Research on Aging*, 23: 379–409.

Midanik, L.T., Soghikian, K., Ransom, L.J., and Tekawa, I.S. (1995) 'The effect of retirement on mental health and health behaviors: The Kaiser Permanente Retirement Study', *Journal of Gerontology: Social Sciences*, 50: S59–S61.

Moen, P., Erikson, M.A., and Dempster-McClain, D. (2000) 'Social role identities among older adults in a continuing care retirement community', *Research on Aging*, 22: 559–79.

Moen, P., Kim, J.E., and Hofmeister, H. (2001) 'Couples' work/retirement transition, gender, and marital quality', *Social Psychology Quarterly*, 64: 55–71.

Munnell, A.H. (2007) 'Working longer: A potential win-win proposition', in T. Ghilarducci and J. Turner (eds.), *Work Options for Older Americans*, Notre Dame, IN: University of Notre Dame Press.

Munnell, A.H., Cahill, K.E., Eschtruth, A., and Sass, S.A. (2004) *The Graying of*

Bridge employment in the United States 213

Massachusetts: Aging, the New Rules of Retirement, and the Changing Workforce, Boston, MA: The Massachusetts Institute for a New Commonwealth.

Munnell, A.H., Muldoon, D., and Sass, S.S. (2009) 'Recessions and older workers', *Center for Retirement Research Brief IB# 9–2*. Chestnut Hill, MA: Center for Retirement at Boston College.

O'Rand, A.M. (1996) 'The precious and the precocious: Understanding cumulative disadvantage and cumulative advantage over the life course', *The Gerontologist*, 36: 230–8.

Pew Research Center (2006) 'Working after retirement: The gaps between expectation and reality', September 21. Online. Available at: http://pewresearch.org/pubs/320/working-after-retirement-the-gap-between-expectations-and-reality (accessed March 10, 2013).

Pinquart, M., and Schindler, I. (2007) 'Changes of life satisfaction in the transition to retirement: A latent-class approach', *Psychology and Aging*, 22: 442–55.

Pleau, R.L. (2010) 'Gender differences in post-retirement employment', *Research on Aging*, 32: 267–303.

Pratt, M.G., and Ashforth, B.E. (2003) 'Fostering meaningfulness in working and meaningfulness at work: An identity perspective', in K.S. Cameron, J.E. Dutton, and R.E. Quinn (eds.), *Positive Organizational Scholarship*, San Francisco: Berret-Koehler.

Quick, H.E. and Moen, P. (1998) 'Gender, employment, and retirement quality: A life course approach to the differential experiences of men and women', *Journal of Occupational Health Psychology*, 1: 44–64.

Quinn, J.E. (2010) 'Work, retirement, and the encore career: Elders and the future of the American workforce', *Generations*, 34: 45–55.

Rau, B.L., and Adams, G.A. (2005) 'Attracting retirees to apply: Desired organizational characteristics of bridge employment', *Journal of Organizational Behavior*, 26: 649–60.

Rau, B.L., and Adams, G.A. (2013) 'Aging, retirement, and human resources management: A strategic approach', in M. Wang (ed.), *The Oxford Handbook of Retirement*, New York: Oxford Library of Psychology.

Reitzes, D.C., and Mutran, E.J. (2004) 'The transition into retirement: Stages and factors that influence retirement adjustment', *International Journal of Aging and Human Development*, 59: 63–84.

Reitzes, D., Mutran, E., and Fernandez, M. (1996) 'Preretirement influences on postretirement self-esteem', *Journals of Gerontology*, 51: S242–S249.

Richardson, V., and Kilty, K.M. (1991) 'Adjustment to retirement: Continuity vs. discontinuity', *International Journal of Aging and Human Development*, 33: 151–69.

Ross, C.E., and Drentea, P. (1998) 'Consequences of retirement activities for distress and the sense of personal control', *Journal of Health and Social Behavior*, 39: 317–34.

Sass, S.A., Monk, C., and Haverstick, K. (2010) 'Workers' response to the market crash: Save more, work more?', *Center for Retirement Research at Boston College*, 10–3, February. Online. Available at: www.globalaging.org/pension/us/2010/CrashRetire.pdf (accessed February 3, 2013).

Shultz, K.S. (2003) 'Bridge employment: Work after retirement', in G.A. Adams and T.A. Beehr (eds.), *Retirement: Reasons, Processes, and Results*, New York: Springer.

Simpson, M., Richardson, M., and Zorn, T.E. (2012) 'A job, a dream, or a trap? Multiple meanings for encore careers', *Work, Employment & Society*, 26: 429–46.

Singh, G., and Verma, A. (2003) 'Work history and later-life labor force participation: Evidence from a large telecommunications firm', *Industrial & Labor Relations Review*, 56: 699–715.

214   *M. Wang* et al.

Stanton, M.W. (2006) *The High Concentration of U.S. Health Care Expenditures*, Research in Action, 19, AHRQ Publ. No. 06-0060, Rockville, MD: Agency for Healthcare Research & Quality.

Stull, D.E. (1988) 'A dyadic approach to predicting well-being in later life', *Research on Aging*, 10: 81–101.

Szinovacz, M.E. (2013) 'A multilevel perspective for retirement research', in M. Wang (ed.), *The Oxford Handbook of Retirement*, New York: Oxford Library of Psychology.

Szinovacz, M.E., Martin, L., and Davey, A. (2013) 'Recession and expected retirement age: Another look at the evidence', *The Gerontologist*. Online First: Available at: http://gerontologist.oxfordjournals.org/content/early/2013/02/26/geront.gnt010.abstract (accessed April 17, 2013).

Thoits, P.A. (1992) 'Identity structure and psychological well-being: Gender and marital status comparisons', *Social Psychology Quarterly*, 55: 236–56.

United States Census Bureau (2012) *U.S. Population Projections: 2012 National Population Projections*. Online. Available at: www.census.gov/population/projections/data/national/2012.html (accessed March 27, 2013).

Vincent, G.K., and Velkoff, V.A. (2010) *The Next Four Decades: The Older Population in the United States – 2010 to 2050* (Current Population Reports P25–1138), Washington, DC: U.S. Census Bureau.

von Bonsdorff, M.E., Shultz, K.S., Leskinen, E., and Tanksy, J. (2009) 'The choice between retirement and bridge employment: A continuity and life course perspective', *International Journal of Aging and Human Development*, 69: 79–100.

von Wachter, T. (2007) *The Effect of Economic Conditions on the Employment of Workers Nearing Retirement Age*, Chestnut Hill, MA: Center for Retirement Research. Online. Available at: http://dx.doi.org/10.2139/ssrn.1294717 (accessed February 10, 2013).

Wang, M. (2007) 'Profiling retirees in the retirement transition and adjustment process: Examining the longitudinal change patterns of retirees' psychological well-being', *Journal of Applied Psychology*, 92: 455–74.

Wang, M., and Shultz, K.S. (2010) 'Employee retirement: A review and recommendations for future investigation', *Journal of Management*, 36: 172–206.

Wang, M., Adams, G.A., Beehr, T.A., and Shultz, K.S. (2009) 'Career issues at the end of one's career: Bridge employment and retirement', in S.G. Baugh and S.E. Sullivan (eds.), *Maintaining Focus, Energy, and Options through the Life Span*, Charlotte, NC: Information Age Publishing.

Wang, M., Henkens, K., and van Solinge, H. (2011) 'Retirement adjustment: A review of theoretical and empirical advancements', *American Psychologist*, 66: 204–13.

Wang, M., Olson, D.A., and Shultz, K.S. (2013) *Mid and Late Career Issues: An Integrative Perspective*, London: Routledge Academic.

Wang, M., Zhan, Y., Liu, S., and Shultz, K.S. (2008) 'Antecedents of bridge employment: A longitudinal investigation', *Journal of Applied Psychology*, 93: 818–30.

Warner, D.F., Hayward, M.D., and Hardy, M.A. (2010) 'The retirement life course in America at the dawn of the twenty-first century', *Population Research & Policy Review*, 10: 893–919.

Weckerle, J.R., and Shultz, K.S. (1999) 'Influences on the bridge employment decision among older USA workers', *Journal of Occupational and Organizational Psychology*, 72: 317–30.

Wheaton, F., and Crimmins, E.M. (2013) 'The demography of aging and retirement', in M. Wang (ed.), *The Oxford Handbook of Retirement*, New York: Oxford Library of Psychology.

Zhan, Y., Wang, M., Liu, S., and Shultz, K.S. (2009) Bridge employment and retirees' health: A longitudinal investigation', *Journal of Occupational Health Psychology*, 14: 374–89.

Zhan, Y., Wang, M., and Yao, X. (2013) 'Domain specific effects of commitment on bridge employment decisions: The moderating role of economic stress', *European Journal of Work and Organizational Psychology*, 22: 362–75.

11 Promoting active aging

The Canadian experience of bridge employment

Tania Saba

Introduction

Population aging is an inevitable phenomenon and will be at the center of debates over the next 20 years. From 2011 to 2030, the median age in Canada will rise from 39.9 years to 44.8 years. As underlined by Statistics Canada, Quebec is the province with the fastest aging population. The median age in Quebec has already reached 41.4 years and 15.7 percent of the population is aged 65 and over. In fact, statistics from July 1, 2011, showed that for the first time, people aged 65 and over outnumbered those aged 15 and under, the numbers being 1,253,600 and 1,241,700 respectively (Statistics Canada 2013). This new reality puts Quebec among the leaders of aging societies. In fact, the province ranks second after Japan.

One of the major concerns caused by an aging population is the question of whether the working population will be productive enough to maintain economic growth as well as the serious impacts on workplaces. On the one hand, employers are preoccupied with employee loyalty and skills development issues as the risk of labor shortages in public and private organizations is intensifying. At the same time, while striving to maintain a skilled and productive workforce, organizations and governments must take into account the formidable challenges posed by an aging generation and find diversified and innovative solutions.

In Canada, the time has come to encourage private and public agencies to promote active aging. Valuing, developing and transmitting the knowledge of older employees have become pressing concerns. Some individuals who are approaching retirement are faced with easy-to-make decisions, while others must come to terms with the harsh reality of conditions that are unfavorable to retirement. Developing an active aging strategy requires considering employers' attitudes regarding older people, individuals' perceptions of their end of career and efforts made by governments which may very well cause the balance to tip in favor of either active aging or a withdrawal from the labor market.

Although there is an extensive body of literature – of an economic, political and organizational nature – on workforce aging and its impacts, the express call to encourage active aging is recent (OECD 2012; Saba 2010). It mainly stems from public agencies and, in this sense, much remains to be done in terms of

The Canadian experience of bridge employment 217

gaining a better understanding of the organizational and individual issues involved in order to support this effort and achieve an effective linkage between market needs and government initiatives. Indeed, the end-of-career trajectories of both men and women remain unpredictable and often uncertain. How can we better understand end-of-career trajectories? This chapter seeks to answer this question by focusing particularly on bridge employment.

This chapter will present the major individual, organizational and governmental considerations in envisaging end of career from the perspective of introducing a viable strategy for active aging. First, we will retrace the history of how end-of-career management has been viewed in Quebec and Canada. Second, we will present the underlying principles and motives behind end-of-career behaviors. Third, we will examine various end-of-career trajectories and describe the types of bridge jobs taken up by retiring Canadian workers and the frequency of this practice. This chapter will end with recommendations for the future, explaining the importance for employers, governments and older workers to link up their efforts in order to be able to assess the advantages and risks associated with bridge employment.

A history of the way end-of-career management in Quebec and Canada has been viewed

Three major approaches emerge from research and the evolution of policies and public programs for retirement and the regulation of the end of career of older workers. They emphasize a resolutely monolithic view of the way end of career should be perceived and managed.

The 1990–1997 period: a marked preference for early retirement

An examination of statistics shows that, except for self-employed workers, a marked trend toward a lower retirement age for all workers started after 1976. The retirement age fell to its lowest level in Canada and Quebec between 1990 and 1997. Large numbers of public-sector employees with more than 20 years' seniority took advantage of the most advanced retirements, with their average retirement age decreasing from 58.8 years to 56.9 years. High deficits in the public sector and the profusion of generous early-retirement offers aimed at reducing the workforce in the private sector help explain this enthusiasm for early retirement. During this period, early retirement was more pronounced in some sectors, namely, education, public administration and health. The combination of higher median ages and lower retirement ages caused significant succession problems and labor shortages in the affected sectors. This pressure caused by early retirement was more intense in Quebec, a province characterized by both greater population aging and retirements at a lower age than in other Canadian provinces (Saba and Guérin 2002; Institut de la statistique du Québec 2013). In Quebec and Canada, however, the much-desired model of retirement at age 55 remained more of an illusion than a reality during this period, since

218   *T. Saba*

individuals who could retire early were, on average, older than 55. This privilege was reserved for individuals who had access to generous pension funds and a sufficient number of years of seniority to be able to take advantage of these funds.

The trend toward a lower retirement age during this period was widespread among most OECD countries constrained by the same demographic reality (Table 11.1). The multitude of public policies promulgated in the 1980s in several European countries were aimed at encouraging older employees to retire so as to avoid laying off younger employees and thereby opening up job opportunities for the young unemployed (Saba and Guérin 2004).

The 1997–2001 period: pleas for phased retirement and arrangements of working conditions – the beginnings of a longer working life

As a result of the observed dramatic repercussions of premature retirement among workers approaching retirement age, support for early retirement began to diminish over the following years. Pleas for physical and temporal work arrangements and phased retirement largely echoed in organizations and were supported by some government initiatives. Phased retirement is an option that allows workers to gradually reduce their working time, in anticipation of full retirement. This reduction can take the form of a decrease in the daily, monthly or yearly working time and can be staggered over several years. Moreover, phased retirement can include partial or total, immediate or deferred compensation measures for incurred income losses (CCTM 2002).

In support of praises for the benefits of phased retirement, Statistics Canada's reports (Schellenberg *et al.* 2005) showed that, during this period, a significant number of workers over the age of 50 worked more than 50 hours per week in some sectors, namely, the primary sector, health, administration and social sciences, as well as in some professions. Moreover, greater flexibility in work-time arrangements appeared to limit health problems, facilitate the transmission of the knowledge of older workers and accommodate those wishing to improve their work/life balance.

As of 1997, claims decrying the risks of early retirement as well as the economic recovery began to reverse the downward trend in the employment rate among people aged 55. A slight increase was observed between 1997 and 2001 (Carrière and Galarneau 2011) (see Figure 11.1).

From 2001 to date: reversed retirement trends and calls for the retention of older workers

From 2001 onwards, statistics showed a rise in the employment rate of workers aged 55 and over (Figure 11.1). In fact, the employment rate among these workers increased by 12 percent between 1997 and 2010, reaching 34 percent by the end of this period (Carrière and Galarneau 2011). As of 2005, a growing awareness among the stakeholders began to challenge the policies, practices and

Table 11.1 Average effective age of retirement of men in selected OECD countries

	1970–1975	1975–1980	1980–1985	1985–1990	1990–1995	1991–1996	1992–1997	1993–1998
Australia	65.8	64.1	62.6	62.5	62.3	62.2	61.9	61.8
Austria	66.4	64.8	62.5	62.7	60.9	60.8	60.8	61.0
Belgium	64.2	61.5	60.6	58.5	58.3	57.9	58.5	58.5
Canada	65.4	64.9	63.6	63.3	62.5	62.5	62.5	62.2
Denmark	65.9	65.5	65.9	65.4	62.9	62.7	63.1	62.7
Finland	66.5	65.9	63.0	61.3	60.6	61.2	60.0	60.3
France	65.1	63.5	61.2	60.0	59.3	59.5	59.6	59.5
Germany	–	–	–	–	–	60.3	60.6	61.0
Greece	66.5	65.9	65.2	63.7	63.2	63.4	63.8	62.6
Italy	63.4	61.9	62.6	61.8	59.6	59.8	59.6	59.9
Japan	71.4	70.7	69.9	70.4	70.9	70.8	70.5	70.1
Korea	66.2	68.4	66.4	70.0	70.6	69.6	69.6	68.7
Spain	66.8	64.8	63.5	62.9	60.7	60.9	61.4	61.5
Sweden	66.1	65.3	64.3	64.2	62.7	63.8	63.7	64.0
United Kingdom	67.4	66.0	62.8	62.8	62.0	62.0	62.3	61.7
United States	66.9	66.4	65.8	64.7	64.2	64.4	64.7	64.8

Source: OECD (2006).

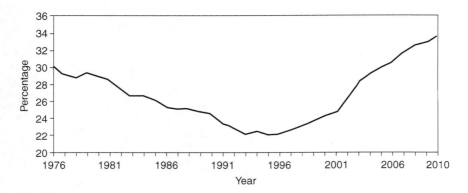

Figure 11.1 Employment rate trend for people aged 55 and over reversed in the mid-1990s (source: Statistics Canada, Labour Force Survey, 1977 to 2008, in Carrière and Galarneau 2011).

attitudes that discouraged older people from working. Government reports and studies from the International Labour Office (ILO) and the OECD deplored the fact that policies and attitudes were not adapted to reality and emphasized the need to review them in order to encourage the extension of working life. The practices in effect not only prevented older workers from choosing when and how to retire but were also onerous for organizations, the economy and society. There were concerns that if nothing was done to promote better employment prospects for older workers, the number of retirees per worker in OECD countries would double over the next 50 years. Living standards would be threatened and very strong pressures would be exerted on the funding of social protection systems. The OECD insisted that employment be made a more attractive and rewarding option for older workers. It suggested that strong financial incentives be linked with the extension of working life and that mechanisms that are financially conducive to early retirement be abolished. It pushed for the adoption of methods of recruitment and wage determination that encourage employers to hire and retain older workers. It suggested helping, supporting and encouraging aging workers in order to improve their employability (OCDE 2006a).

Growing trends since 2005

An examination of recent statistics shows that the average retirement age in Canada has increased (Table 11.2), but nevertheless remains stable at 62 years and is thus lower than that in the 1970s. Moreover, the rate of employment among Canadians aged 55 and over has markedly increased for several years, nevertheless without a significant increase in the average retirement age. How can this phenomenon be explained?

It was observed that both men and women entered into full-time employment later in life. On the other hand, among people aged 55 and over, only the

The Canadian experience of bridge employment 221

Table 11.2 Changes in average retirement age, Canada, men and women

Categories of workers	2008	2009	2010	2011	2012
All retirees	61.4	61.9	62.1	62.3	62.9
Public-sector employees	59.6	60.1	60.1	60.7	61.0
Private-sector employees	62.0	62.4	62.8	62.9	63.3
Self-employed workers	65.4	66.2	65.8	65.9	66.4

employment rate of men fell between 1976 and 1997 while that of women rose during this period and beyond. The increase in the employment rates observed among men aged 55 to 69 as of the mid-1990s may be an indication that men in this age group are delaying their retirement. Among women, the increase in the employment rate is likely the result of two trends: delayed retirement and the arrival of cohorts with higher employment rates.

There remains a fairly strong trend toward early retirement in the public sector (Table 11.2). According to Carrière and Galarneau (2011), the average retirement age does not accurately reflect how workers' retirement behaviors have evolved because it does not take age structure into account. The first of the baby boomers turned 50 in 1990, making those aged 50 and over younger and bringing down the average retirement age given the great number of young retirees who belonged to a generation that was well-off in terms of pension funds and working conditions. All baby boomers will reach the age of 60 some time between 2006 and 2026, making those aged 50 and over older and increasing the average retirement age by approximately 1.5 years. Thus, it is possible that there has been an apparent but artificial extension of working life among older workers.

The average retirement age thus does not accurately reflect how workers' retirement behaviors have evolved. Carrière and Galarneau (2011) suggest constructing expected working-life tables based on data from Statistics Canada's Labour Force Survey, using a method similar to that used to calculate life expectancy. These working-life tables show a significant increase in delayed retirement as of the mid-1990s, which is consistent with the increase in the employment rate among older Canadians during this same period. The expected years of employment for men and women appears to have been even higher in 2008 than in 1977; that is, 16 years vs. nearly 14 years, respectively. These estimates confirm that, in 2008, Canadians tended to retire later than in 1977.

For both men and women, the statistics indicate that the expected length of retirement has stabilized after increasing considerably from 1977 to the mid-1990s (see Figure 11.2). Given the increase in life expectancy, this relative stability confirms that the number of years spent in employment from age 50 onwards has been increasing for nearly 15 years. Considering that this trend has prevailed for a substantial number of years, it cannot be mainly attributed to an unfavorable economic context (Carrière and Galarneau 2011). Rather, the statistics appear to indicate a reversed trend that is yet to be explained.

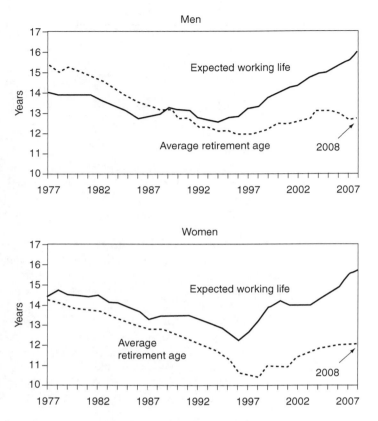

Figure 11.2 Years of employment before retiring and average retirement age, by gender (source: Statistics Canada, Labour Force Survey, 1977 to 2008, in Carrière and Galarneau 2011).

New trends in the behavior of older workers approaching retirement have emerged and become established, including that of extending their working life, which appears either as a return to work or a willingness to take up bridge jobs.

Bridge employment

A tentative definition

Bridge employment is an important pillar for the examination of ends of career and the promotion of active aging since it redefines retirement through its impact on the transition process into retirement (Ulrich and Brott 2005; Wang 2007). It is defined as the pattern of labor-force participation exhibited by older workers as they leave their career jobs and move toward complete labor-force withdrawal

(Shultz 2003). Bridge jobs can take various forms: part-time jobs, self-employment or temporary employment after full-time employment ends and before permanent retirement begins (Feldman 1994). Bridge employment is classified into two main types: career bridge employment, which corresponds to taking up jobs in the same field, profession or industry sector, and non-career bridge employment, which refers to taking up jobs in a different field (Feldman 1994; Shultz 2003; Pengcharoen and Shultz 2010). Bridge employment can provide extra income for those who do not have enough pension income or savings in their later years. It can also help older workers balance work and leisure time while remaining engaged in economically and socially productive activities. Bridge employment can therefore contribute to the well-being of individuals and their families (Wang *et al.* 2008).

The motives underlying the recourse to bridge employment

Given that the phenomenon of bridge employment appears to be on the rise, it is important to grasp the motives and antecedents behind it and the public policies that regulate it in order to assess its advantages but also its potential risks. Understanding these theories and antecedents can put into perspective the behavior of Canadians approaching retirement and better anticipate their decision to stay active or retire.

The theories behind the choice of bridge employment

Four theoretical perspectives were used in seeking to distinguish the motives that prompt individuals to retire from those that drive them to opt for bridge employment or extend their working lives beyond the age at which they are eligible to retire. The theories based on resource conservation, continuity, roles and life course appear to constitute valuable explanatory frameworks (Quick and Moen 1998; Wang 2007; Wang *et al.* 2008). The theories aim to provide both a rational framework for interpreting employees' behaviors toward the end of their career and a review of all antecedents that have an impact on the decisions made when approaching retirement (Wang *et al.* 2008).

Resource Conservation Theory. Resource conservation theory is based on a reasoning that individuals aim to gain, maintain, protect and conserve things they appreciate (resources) (Hobfoll 2001). Hobfoll (2002) defines resources as things that are valued in their essence, such as good health, or that act as a means to achieve valued goals, such as money. The end of a career is a period of multiple changes that is similar to the end of adolescence in terms of the numerous new and major transitions involved (Hobfoll 2011). Of course, the significant loss of resources incurred at the end of a working life is critical and individuals seek to compensate for this loss by mobilizing personal resources (Wang *et al.* 2008). Thus, retirees are likely to return to the labor market, in career-related jobs or different jobs, thereby drawing on their skills to compensate for expected or actual losses at retirement.

224   *T. Saba*

Continuity theory. Continuity theory as proposed by Atchley (1989, 1999) is based on the premise that people who retire remain the same psychologically. They continue to like the same things and to have the same temperament, attitudes and preferences. They thus appreciate maintaining their engagement in the same activities and are likely to want to take up comparable jobs if work constitutes a value and an important accomplishment in their lives (Beehr 1986; Richardson and Kilty 1991; Schmidt and Lee 2006). Retirement is not considered to be a disruptive event but rather an opportunity to maintain a certain lifestyle (Quick and Moen 1998). This theory suggests that individuals who have been highly involved in and devoted to their work will tend to maintain a degree of continuity by participating in activities they appreciate (Atchley 1989). Indeed, remaining active in the labor market provides a natural way to maintain one's daily routine and engage in social interactions. On the other hand, Kim and Feldman (2000) rightly claim that retirement can be an opportunity to engage in activities that are valued in a different way than through labor-market participation.

In brief, continuity theory argues that an individual's self-identity and self-concept do not differ considerably before and after retirement or during the transition to retirement. The foundations of continuity theory thus contribute to explaining the tendency to want to continue working at retirement age (Atchley 1989; Davis 2003; Doeringer 1990; Feldman 1994; Gall *et al.* 1997; Kim and Feldman 2000; Wang 2007).

Role theory. The theory of roles is an approach grounded in both sociology and social psychology and considers that a large part of an individual's daily activities conform to a socially defined category (for example, mother, manager, teacher). For each social role, there is a set of rights, duties, expectations, norms and behaviors that a person must face and fulfill. The model is based on the premise that people behave in a predictable way, reacting to a specific context, and that this behavior is mainly induced by the social role a person holds (Von Bonsdorff *et al.* 2009).

Life-course theory. The life-course theory examines the socio-historical importance of the events and experiences that shape the behavior of individuals throughout their lives and even through several generations (Elder 1994, 1998; MacLean and Elder 2007). The life-course literature presents a theory, characterized by a longitudinal perspective, that seeks to explain how individuals and their cohort members are shaped by the social and historical contexts they have experienced. Retirement can be viewed as a transition phase in an ongoing life trajectory (Wang 2007). The decision to withdraw from the labor market could be influenced by a series of events that have marked the life of an individual (Elder 1998). This theory mainly advocates breaking down the life course into key moments (timing) and argues that the choices made by an individual are interdependent. Timing refers to the period, the social condition and the background history that lead to various choices throughout the life trajectory. Social interdependence in human lives refers to the interaction between the social worlds and the networks that connect individuals, their daily life and their

The *Canadian experience of bridge employment* 225

reactions to the more striking societal changes (Elder 1998). The life-course perspective emphasizes the influence of individual attributes, job-related psychological variables and family-related variables on decisions related to retirement (Wang *et al.* 2008). The life-course theory also provides a useful perspective for distinguishing between men's behaviors and women's behaviors regarding decisions concerning retirement, the transition toward retirement or extending their working life (Quick and Moen 1998).

Antecedents

While it is true that the retirement process has been the subject of numerous studies, a consensus on the antecedents related to early retirement among Canadian retirees is yet to be reached (Saba 2010; Gobeski and Beehr 2009).

Based on extensive literature reviews, researchers have identified a diverse array of motives for older workers to continue working (Armstrong-Stassen 2008; Bal and Visser 2011; Weckerle and Shultz 1999; Kooij *et al.* 2011) and have classified these work-related motives into three categories: security motives, social motives and growth motives. Griffin and Hesketh (2008) suggested that work-related variables which act to delay retirement are also likely to influence whether or not a person engages in work activity in retirement. Drawing on the work of Mor-Barak (1995), Armstrong-Stassen *et al.* (2012) identified four primary motives for Canadian retirees to return to the workforce: financial, social, personal fulfillment and generative – defined as the opportunity to share one's knowledge and skills with the younger generation.

Three work-related attitudes that appear relevant to retirement and bridge employment are career attachment, work attachment and job satisfaction, and continuity theory helps to predict their effects (Gobeski and Beehr 2009). These effects or underlying variables include: job-related strain, intrinsic job characteristics, occupational goal attainment, job-related skills, local unemployment rate, poor health, age and retirement age.

Canadian public policies that have an influence on bridge employment

The implications of an aging population for employers include both labor and skills shortages due to the loss of older experienced workers through retirement and fewer younger workers to fill the void (Park 2011). One way to address these projected shortages is for older people to come out of retirement and re-enter the workforce (Carrière and Galarneau 2011; van Dalen *et al.* 2010). The challenge for public policy-makers is how to encourage retirees to return.

In Canada, retirement income is based on three pillars. The first two pillars relate to public funds. The first is Old Age Security and the Guaranteed Income Supplement; the second is the Canada Pension Plan (CPP) and Quebec Pension Plan. These first two elements form a foundational base of income for individuals in retirement. In addition to these two elements, the privately administered

226 *T. Saba*

Registered Pension Plans (RPPs) and Registered Retirement Savings Plans (including individual and group RRSPs) constitute the third pillar of the Retirement Income System (Baldwin *et al.* 2011).

In two reports published in 2006, the OECD (OCDE 2006a, 2006b) deplored the fact that Canadian legislation hampers the employment of aging workers. Since 2007, several measures have been adopted to increase the labor-market participation of people aged 55 and over, as stated in an OECD report produced in 2012. Actions were implemented to strengthen financial incentives to maintain the employment of aging workers, abolish employment barriers on the side of employers and improve the employability of aging workers.

Since 2010, three important initiatives have been put forward in Canadian legislation as part of the financial incentives used to encourage aging workers to remain in the labor market. The first is *Increasing flexibility for combining pensions with work income*. Specifically, the amendments made to the CPP in 2010 to increase the flexibility with which pensions can be combined with work income are being phased in gradually over a six-year period. As of January 2012, *contributors can begin receiving their CPP retirement pension without any work interruption*. Also as of January 2012, individuals under the age of 70 who work while receiving their CPP retirement pension can increase their retirement income by continuing to contribute to the CPP in order to earn the new Post-Retirement Benefit (PRB). The contributions are mandatory for working recipients of the CPP retirement pension under the age of 65. After the age of 65, the contributions are voluntary until age 70. Employers must contribute if workers do.

The second initiative helps the partners of low-income pensioners get back into the labor market. Allowance beneficiaries can choose to work to increase their income and still continue to receive allowance benefits, although their benefit will be reduced on the basis of the other income they earn (OECD 2012).

The third initiative focuses on phased retirement. Amendments to income tax regulations were passed in 2007 to allow for phased retirement under defined-benefit registered pension plans. Individuals can receive up to 60 percent of their pension while at the same time continuing to increase pension benefits through continued contributions. In 2009, changes were made to the Pension Benefits Standards Act to permit phased retirement in *federally regulated defined-benefit pension plans*. Some provinces made changes to their legislation to specifically address phased retirement for those with provincially regulated defined-benefit plans (OECD 2012).

The focus on abolishing barriers was conveyed through recommendations to abolish mandatory retirement where it was still in force, with exceptions made for workers who are subject to specific conditions and who fall under federal or provincial jurisdiction, depending on the case.

As regards improving the employability of older workers, Canadian government initiatives have consisted in increasing transfers to the provinces so as to improve accessibility to training programs that are generally aimed at workers seeking employment. The provinces have established programs that mainly target older workers. The Canadian government has also implemented measures to facilitate self-employment among aging workers (OECD 2012).

Bridge employment in Canada

Given the above, it is not surprising to note that, in Canada, bridge employment has been increasing markedly since 1999. Statistics Canada, drawing on the same definitions as those outlined above, including that of Ruhm (1990), specifies that '"Bridge employment" refers to any paid work after an individual retires or starts receiving a pension'. Unlike in the United States, where bridge employment has been widely studied, there has been a yawning gap in research in this area in Canada, but this gap was partly addressed by a first important study published in 2008 (Hébert and Luong 2008; Cahill *et al.* 2007; Giandrea *et al.* 2009). This study first presents cross-sectional analyses using the Survey of Labor and Income Dynamics to show the prevalence of bridge employment among Canadians aged 50 to 69 between 1999 and 2004. Then, a longitudinal examination of a group of older workers over the same period shows transitions into and out of bridge employment and retirement.

Hébert and Luong (2008) estimate that approximately 7.9 percent of persons aged 50 to 69 held bridge jobs in 1999, and this percentage rose to 9.7 percent in 2004 (Figure 11.3). However, the number of workers in bridge employment increased by more than 40 percent over this period as the size of this age group increased due to the aging of the baby-boom cohorts. The prevalence of bridge employment varied greatly by age, ranging from a low of 2 percent among those aged 50 to 54 to a peak of 18 percent for those aged 65 to 69 in 2004.

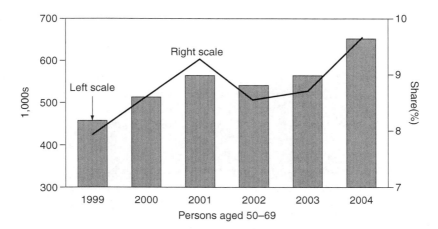

Figure 11.3 Bridge employment increased more or less steadily from 1999 to 2004 (source: Statistics Canada, Survey of Labour and Income Dynamics, 1999 to 2004, in Hebert and Luong 2008).

228   T. Saba

Hébert and Luong (2008) drew pertinent conclusions regarding the profile and behavior of individuals in bridge employment. They estimated that the 'survival rate' among those who retire directly after a career employment is 61 percent after one year and 47 percent after four years. The conditional probability of interrupting retirement and taking up work again was therefore highest within the first year of retirement, at nearly 40 percent, while it was 10 percent or less from the second to the fourth year of retirement. Consequently, retirees who re-enter the labor market are more likely to do so during the first year following their retirement. After this first year, the probability of returning to the labor market appears to be much lower, at least until the fourth year. However, it is important to note that the survival rate did not take the retirees' age into account, and therefore, this rate could be higher for younger retirees who have a better chance of finding a job after a longer period of retirement. The estimated time that individuals remained in bridge employment was two to three years.

Data from Statistics Canada show that bridge employment generally corresponds to an individual choice. Hébert and Luong (2008) found that access to bridge employment does not vary according to gender, unlike the decision to retire. Surprisingly, individuals with a university education are more likely to return to the labor market and take up a bridge job (Park 2011). Well-paid workers with an employer-sponsored pension plan appear to be more likely to leave their career employment, activate their pension benefits and continue working in a bridge job. Thus, bridge jobs are not necessarily aimed at people who cannot financially afford to retire. Many of these jobs are held by people who choose to remain in the labor market given their interests and the skills they have to offer. Interestingly, workers living in rural areas or small communities were nearly twice as likely to take up a bridge job as workers living in large urban centers.

Bridge jobs are not accessible to all those who would like to take advantage of them (Adams and Rau 2004; Rau and Adams 2005). Carrière and Galarneau (2012) reported that a great number of Canadians continue to be forced to retire. Involuntary retirement can be prompted by a layoff, sickness, a disability or the fact of having to care for a family member, any of which can force an individual to leave the labor market permanently.

Older workers who return to the labor market in a self-employed capacity have a specific profile. According to Uppal (2011), these older individuals tend to have a high income and a university degree and often engage in this activity to create a family business. They mainly confine themselves to three industries (primary goods, customer services and business services). The professional profile of self-employed older workers is thus less diversified.

As for older workers seeking employment, a great number look for jobs even outside their local area and, thus, are not very different from younger unemployed individuals. They are more likely to accept jobs with poorer conditions than those of their previous jobs and are generally very pessimistic about the possibility of finding a job within three months following their loss of employment, in fact twice as pessimistic as young workers whose unemployment rates are generally higher. They associate this difficulty with their age (Bernard 2012).

Conclusion

The aging of the Canadian population has created a context that is conducive to labor shortages, has exacerbated the dependency ratios on young people and intensified the pressure on public funds and health services (Park 2011). From now to 2021, nearly one out of four workers will be aged 55 and over. Labor-market participation up to age 65 appears to be one ready solution to limit the impacts of population aging in Canada for at least the next 35 years. However, the average retirement age in Canada is still around 62 years and has changed very little since 1996. Canadians do not appear to want to postpone their retirement age. There is much speculation on this issue and a probable change in policy is imminent that will raise the age at which retiring workers can access public pension funds from 65 to 67. However, in contrast with the United States, this remains a work in progress and the social disadvantages associated with increasing the age of access to public retirement funds are significant. These disadvantages include, among others, the risk of impoverishment among a vulnerable group of workers who tend to experience difficulty finding stable employment after a certain age and who have not received relevant workplace training to overcome the obsolescence of their knowledge and acquire the skills that are sought in the labor market.

Are people aged 55 and over willing to consider remaining employed longer by taking up bridge jobs and, thus, returning to the labor market?

First, it should be acknowledged that the statistics seem to indicate that they are. Although the average retirement age has remained relatively stable since 2001, it should be noted that the labor-force participation rate, the expected number of years before retirement, and the percentage of people returning to the labor market among those aged 55 and over are increasing continuously.

Second, the theoretical frameworks help to explain the decision to enter into bridge employment. With regard to the theoretical considerations, continuity theory, conservation theory and role theory provide different and yet interesting perspectives that treat retirement as an opportunity for individuals to maintain their roles, lifestyle and social contacts as they approach retirement, while avoiding the negative outcomes of retirement (Quick and Moen 1998; Von Bonsdorff et al. 2009; Wang et al. 2008). Furthermore, in explaining bridge employment in a Canadian context, Armstrong-Stassen et al. (2012) pushed the utility of continuity theory further, by examining its ability to understand not just bridge employment, but also the specific type of bridge employment that people accept. They believe that the important issue defining continuity is not the actions of retirees (e.g. taking up a bridge job), but rather the fact that retirees continue to have the same psychological makeup after retirement as before retirement (same attitudes, temperament, preferences and skills). These authors found that retirees will be more likely to want to return to work for their former employer, particularly when they have the ability to work in jobs that are meaningful, with mentoring opportunities and with a modified work role. Experienced retirees can share their expert knowledge with younger workers through mentorship

230   T. Saba

programs that appropriately match the skills and personality of young workers with returning retired workers.

The life-course theory, for its part, calls into question retirement as an endpoint of working life. To date, the focus of retirement research has been on identifying the factors that predict older workers' decision to retire from the workforce and the factors related to retirement adjustment and satisfaction. The factors associated with the decision of retired people to return to the labor force have received little attention (Saba 2010; Maestas 2010). This is due, in part, to the fact that unretirement is a relatively recent phenomenon. Historically, when people retired from the workforce, they remained retired. However, in most developed countries, there has been a growing trend toward retired people returning to paid employment. In fact, Brown *et al.* (2010: 4) suggested that working in retirement may become the 'new normal'. Statistical analyses clearly show that retirement is a process rather than a one-time event. Numerous older workers who have started receiving a pension remain in the labor market in one way or another for about two or three years before they stop working completely. Moreover, a great number of those who stop working for pay subsequently re-enter the labor market, most often within the first year after retiring. Consequently, it could be argued that considering work and retirement as distinct phases in the life course does not accurately reflect the reality of a large proportion of older adults.

Third, enhanced understanding has been gained into the motives prompting individuals to opt for bridge employment and whether this phenomenon is generalized or restricted to individuals with distinct profiles. Recent studies have shown that some characteristics are crucial. Higher compensation, a university education and an employer-sponsored pension plan are associated with an increased probability of leaving a career job for a bridge job. Given these characteristics, this transition appears to result from a choice rather than from necessity. Moreover, given the limits of the data from Statistics Canada, it was impossible to determine whether individuals who re-entered the labor market after a retirement period shared similar profiles. A previous study indicated that financial considerations were an important motive for retirees to return to the labor market, in particular for those who retired due to downsizing, job loss or illness (Carrière and Galarneau 2011, 2012; Schellenberg *et al.* 2005).

Fourth, public policies that regulate the financial implications of returning to work and extending working life beyond retirement age have evolved since 2007. The federal and provincial governments have implemented legislative programs both in Canada and Quebec to allow older workers to extend their careers or return to the labor market. This strategy mainly involves bringing down the barriers to employees' return to work and allowing them to continue contributing to their retirement fund in order to benefit from it later. These adjustments will ensure that there are no unfair advantages or disadvantages in taking up one's pension before or after the age of 65, and so strengthen the financial incentives to carry on working. Other initiatives have facilitated phased retirement and introduced some flexibility for employees and employers. In recognition that

The Canadian experience of bridge employment   231

retirement tends to be a process rather than a one-time event, this change will help avoid an interruption in the income of workers and disruptions in the supply of human resources. Retired individuals can subsequently return to work or older workers who remain in the workforce can start earning more. These changes also provide employers with more flexibility to retain older workers (OECD 2012).

Should it be concluded that bridge employment is a solution that helps to compensate for labor shortages, meets the needs of individuals and employers and is supported by governments?

Given the profile of individuals who take advantage of bridge jobs during a time when labor-market participation is progressing markedly among people aged 55 and over and even among those aged 65 and over, bridge employment – defined as a choice made by individuals who have retired from a career job to take up another job for a time before taking full advantage of retirement – is a favored alternative that is not necessarily accessible to a great number of workers aged 55 and over who cannot afford to leave their jobs even when they have reached retirement age. Bridge employment as a means of preventing early withdrawal from the labor market and maintaining a skilled workforce is certainly an attractive alternative that is easily accessible to young retirees. However, this solution cannot be described as a panacea for extending working life.

Given the observed adverse effects of the early-retirement packages offered in the 1990s, it is evident that encouraging older workers to remain in the labor force is desirable (Saba and Guérin 2005). However, active aging strategies must include various measures to match the diverse aspirations of people at the end of their careers. Indeed, there are limits to individuals remaining in the labor market beyond the normal retirement age. Individuals whose health is more fragile or who strongly wish to retire must be able to benefit from arrangements, including gradual withdrawal from work. These arrangements can involve physical accommodations, adaptations to work schedules or job content and the possibility to perform new roles and responsibilities in accordance with a reduced workload. These arrangements are strongly recommended so that the workload of older workers can be reduced and their knowledge can be transmitted to younger generations before their permanent retirement. Retirement in the form of early retirement, normal or phased retirement must remain an option and must be an integral part of active aging strategies. It is still an important aspiration that allows workers to withdraw from the labor market for various reasons, such as pursuing leisure activities, doing volunteer work or taking care of their health or family members.

Bridge jobs are arrangements and must not be confused with employee-retention initiatives that aim at continuity in the development of individuals and rely on the long-term contribution of older workers. Bridge employment thus represents one measure among others to retain employees. Whether bridge employment corresponds to an individual choice or an arrangement made for a person who can no longer continue working under the same conditions, it has its own *raison d'être*; however, it cannot replace a more comprehensive vision aimed at promoting an effective strategy for active aging. Such a strategy cannot

232   T. Saba

be carried out in isolation and cannot be successful without coordination among organizational and individual initiatives and public policies. The promotion of active aging begins in organizations through succession planning that must be based on an exhaustive diagnosis so as to take the interests and capacities of individuals into account, introduce a culture of skills training and development that is accessible to all, reconcile the demographic realities, individual differences and specific characteristics of workplaces and take account of labor-market realities. Organizational initiatives related to the management of the aging workforce must be without discrimination (Urwin 2006; Karpinska *et al.* 2013). They must result in measures such as the introduction of practices related to training, promotion, mobility and knowledge transfers or aimed at fostering the autonomy of older workers and increasing the responsibilities and special assignments that are accessible and applicable to them (Callanan and Greenhaus 2008). Actions taken by organizations must be supported by public policies that encourage the employment of people aged 55 and over, focus on the employability of this age group, bring down the barriers to employment and reducing unemployment among older people. Envisaging ends of career that are acceptable to the individual, society and the organization is a process that cannot be achieved without a real desire on the part of all stakeholders to find solutions aimed at developing the employability of older workers and fostering active aging.

References

Adams, G. and Rau, B. (2004) 'Job seeking among retirees seeking bridge employment', *Personnel Psychology*, 57: 719–44.

Armstrong-Stassen, M. (2008) 'Organisational practices and the post-retirement employment experience of older workers', *Human Resource Management Journal*, 18: 36–53.

Armstrong-Stassen, M., Schlosser, F. and Zinni, D. (2012) 'Seeking resources: Predicting retirees' return to their workplace', *Journal of Managerial Psychology*, 27: 615–35.

Atchley, R.C. (1989) 'A continuity theory of normal aging', *The Gerontologist*, 29: 183–90.

Atchley, R.C. (1999) 'Continuity theory, self, and social structure', in C.D. Ryff and V.W. Marshall (eds.), *The Self and Society in Aging Processes*, New York: Springer Publishing Company.

Bal, P.M. and Visser, M.S. (2011) 'When are teachers motivated to work beyond retirement age? The importance of support, change of work role and money', *Educational Management Administration & Leadership*, 39: 590–602.

Baldwin, J.R., Frenette, M., Lafrance, A. and Piraino, P. (2011) *Income Adequacy in Retirement: Accounting for the Annuitized Value of Wealth in Canada*, Statistics Canada Catalogue no. 11F0027M, Ottawa, Ontario. Economic Analysis (EA) Research Paper Series, No. 074: 1–36.

Beehr, T.A. (1986) 'The process of retirement: A review and recommendations for future investigation', *Personnel Psychology*, 39: 31–55.

Bernard, A. (2012) 'La recherche d'emploi chez les chômeurs ages' [The job search of the older unemployed], *Catalogue de Statistique Canada: L'emploi et le revenu en perspective* [*Perspectives on Labor and Income*], No. 75-001-X: 1–16.

Brown, M., Aumann, K., Pitt-Catsouphes, M., Galinsky, E. and Bond, J.T. (2010)

The Canadian experience of bridge employment 233

Working in Retirement: A 21st Century Phenomenon, Boston: Boston College, The Sloan Center for Aging and Work.

Cahill, K.E., Giandrea, M.D. and Quinn, J.F. (2007) *Down Shifting: The Role of Bridge Jobs after Career Employment*, Research Report, Boston College: The Center on Aging & Work/Workplace Flexibility, No. 6.

Callanan, G.A. and Greenhaus, J.H. (2008) 'The baby boom generation and career management: A call to action', *Advances in Developing Human Resources*, 10: 70–85.

Carrière, Y. and Galarneau, D. (2011) 'Reporter sa retraite: une tendance récente?' [Delayed retirement: A new trend?], *Catalogue de Statistique Canada: L'emploi et le revenu en perspective [Perspectives on Labor and Income]*, No. 75-001-X: 3–18.

Carrière, Y. and Galarneau, D. (2012) 'Combien d'années avant la retraite?' [How Many Years before Retirement], *Catalogue de Statistique Canada: Regards sur la société canadienne*, No. 75-006-X: 1–9.

Conseil consultatif sur la main-d'œuvre et le travail (CCTM) (2002) *Adapter les milieux de travail au vieillissement de la main-d'œuvre: stratégie du Conseil consultatif [Adapting Workplaces to the Aging of Workers]*, Discussion Paper (research conducted by Patrice Jalette and Daniel Villeneuve), Montréal: CCTM.

Davis, M.A. (2003) 'Factors related to bridge employment participation among private sector early retirees', *Journal of Vocational Behavior*, 63: 55–71.

Doeringer, P.B. (1990) *Bridges to Retirement: Older Workers in a Changing Labor Market*, Ithaca, NY: ILR Press.

Elder, G.H., Jr. (1994) 'Time, human agency, and social change: Perspectives on the life course', *Social Psychology Quarterly*, 57: 4–15.

Elder, G.H., Jr. (1998) 'The life course as developmental theory', *Child Development*, 69: 1–12.

Feldman, D.C. (1994) 'The decision to retire early: A review and conceptualization', *Academy of Management Review*, 19: 285–311.

Gall, T.L., Evans, D.R. and Howard, J. (1997) 'The retirement adjustment process: Changes in the well-being of male retirees across time', *Journal of Gerontology*, 52B: 110–17.

Giandrea, M.D., Cahill, K.E. and Quinn, J.F. (2009) 'Bridge jobs: A comparison across cohorts', *Research on Aging*, 31: 549–76.

Gobeski, K.T. and Beehr, T.A. (2009) 'How retirees work: Predictors of different types of bridge employment', *Journal of Organizational Behaviour*, 30: 401–25.

Griffin, B. and Hesketh, B. (2008) 'Post-retirement work: The individual determinants of paid and volunteer work', *Journal of Occupational and Organizational Psychology*, 81: 101–21.

Guérin, G. and Saba, T. (2003) 'Stratégie de maintien en emploi des cadres de 50 ans et plus' [Strategies for extending employment of managers 50 years and older], *Relations industrielles/Industrial Relations*, 58: 590–617.

Hébert, B.P. and Luong, M. (2008) 'Bridge employment', *Catalogue de Statistique Canada: Perspectives on Labor and Income*, No. 75-001-X: 5–12.

Hobfoll, S.E. (2001) 'The influence of culture, community, and the nested-self in the stress process: Advancing conservation of resources theory', *Applied Psychology: An International Review*, 50: 337–421.

Hobfoll, S.E. (2002) 'Social and psychological resources and adaptation', *Review of General Psychology*, 6: 307–24.

Hobfoll, S.E. (2011) 'Conservation of resource caravans and engaged settings', *Journal of Occupational and Organizational Psychology*, 84: 116–22.

234 T. Saba

Institut de la statistique du Québec. Online. Available at: www.stat.gouv.qc.ca (accessed May 24, 2013).

Karpinska, K., Henkens, K. and Schippers, J. (2011) 'The recruitment of early retirees: A vignette study of the factors that affect managers' decisions', *Ageing & Society*, 31: 570–89.

Karpinska, K., Henkens, K. and Schippers, J. (2013) 'Retention of Older Workers: Impact of Managers' Age Norms and Stereotypes', *European Sociological Review*, published online June 18, doi:10.1093/esr/jct017

Kim, S. and Feldman, D.C. (2000) 'Working in retirement: The antecedents of bridge employment and its consequences for quality of life in retirement', *Academy of Management Journal*, 43: 1195–210.

Kooij, D.T.A.M., de Lange, A.H., Jansen, P.G.W., Kanfer, R. and Dikkers, J.S.E. (2011) 'Age and work-related motives: Results of a meta-analysis', *Journal of Organizational Behavior*, 32: 197–225.

MacLean, A. and Elder, G.H., Jr. (2007) 'Military service in the life course', *Annual Review of Sociology*, 36: 175–96.

Maestas, N. (2010) 'Back to work: Expectations and realizations of work after retirement', *Journal of Human Resources*, 45: 718–48.

Mor-Barak, M.E. (1995) 'The meaning of work for older adults seeking employment: The generativity factor', *International Journal of Aging and Human Development*, 41: 325–45.

OCDE (2006a) *Vieillissement et politiques de l'emploi* [*Aging and Employment Policies*], Paris: OCDE.

OCDE (2006b) *Vieillissement et politiques de l'emploi: Vivre et travailler plus longtemps* [*Aging and Employment Policies: Living and Working Longer*], Paris: OCDE.

OECD (2006) *Aging and Employment Policies.* Online. Available at: www.oecd.org/employment/emp/ageingandemploymentpolicies-statisticsonaverageeffectiveageofretirement.htm (accessed June 1, 2013).

OECD (2012) *OECD Thematic Follow-up Review of Policies to Improve Labor Market Prospects for Older Workers.* Online. Available at: www.oecd.org/els/emp/Older%20workers_Canada-MOD.pdf (accessed March 15, 2013).

Park, J. (2011) 'Retraite, santé et emploi chez les personnes de 55 ans et plus', [Retirement, health and employment among those 55 plus], *Catalogue de Statistique Canada: L'emploi et le revenu en perspective* [*Perspectives on Labor and Income*], No. 75-001-X: 3–14.

Parker, O. (2006) *Too Few People, Too Little Time: The Employer Challenge of an Aging Workforce*, Ottawa: The Conference Board of Canada.

Pengcharoen, C. and Shultz, K.S. (2010) 'The influences on bridge employment decisions', *International Journal of Manpower*, 31: 322–36.

Quick, H.E. and Moen, P. (1998) 'Gender, employment and retirement quality: A life course approach to the differential experiences of men and women', *Journal of Occupational Health Psychology*, 3: 44–64.

Rau, B.L. and Adams, G.A. (2005) 'Attracting retirees to apply: Desired organizational characteristics of bridge employment', *Journal of Organizational Behaviour*, 26: 649–60.

Richardson, V. and Kilty, K.M. (1991) 'Adjustment to retirement: Continuity vs. discontinuity', *International Journal of Aging and Human Development*, 33: 151–69.

Ruhm, C.J. (1990) 'Bridge jobs and partial retirement', *Journal of Labor Economics*, 8: 582–601.

The Canadian experience of bridge employment 235

Saba, T. (2010) 'Promouvoir une stratégie viable en faveur d'un vieillissement actif' [Promoting a viable strategy in favor of active aging], *Vie et vieillissement*, 8: 31–8.

Saba, T. and Guérin, G. (2002) 'La gestion des cadres de 50 ans et plus au lendemain des mises à la retraite massives [Managing workers 50 years and older following massive early retirement], in F. Lamonde, M. Audet, M. Bernard, R. Laflamme and A. Larocque (eds.), *La gestion des âges*, Québec: PUL.

Saba, T. and Guérin, G. (2004) 'Planifier la relève dans un contexte de vieillissement: conjuguer les préférences individuelles, les politiques publiques en matière de retraite et les enjeux organisationnels' [Succession planning in an aging workplace: Considering individual preferences, public policies and organizational issues], *Gestion: Revue internationale de Gestion*, 29: 54–63.

Saba, T. and Guérin, G. (2005) 'Extending employment beyond retirement age: The case of health care managers in Quebec', *Public Personnel Management*, 34: 195–213 [Citation of Excellence by Emerald Management Reviews, UK].

Schellenberg, G., Turcotte, M. and Ram, B. (2005) 'Post-retirement employment', *Perspectives on Labor and Income*, 6: 14–17.

Schmidt, J.A. and Lee, K. (2006) 'Voluntary retirement and organizational turnover intentions: Differential associations with commitment constructs in work and non-work settings', Paper presented at the Annual Meeting of the Society for Industrial and Organizational Psychology, Dallas, TX.

Shultz, K.S. (2003) 'Bridge employment: Work after retirement', in G.A. Adams and T.A. Beehr (eds.), *Retirement: Reasons, Processes, and Results*, New York: Springer.

Statistics Canada (2010) 'Labour Force Survey, 1976 to 2010', in Carrière Y. and Galarneau D. (2011), *Delayed retirement: A new trend? Perspectives on Labour and Income*, Statistics Canada, Catalogue no. 75-001-X, p.4.

Statistique Canada (2013) Online. Available at: www.statcan.gc.ca/daily-quotidien/110928/dq110928a-eng.htm (accessed May 24, 2013).

Ulrich, L.B. and Brott, P.E. (2005) 'Older workers and bridge employment: Redefining retirement', *Journal of Employment Counseling*, 42: 159–70.

Uppal, S. (2011) 'Le travail autonome chez les personnes âgées' [Seniors' self-employment], *Catalogue de Statistique Canada: L'emploi et le revenu en perspective* [*Perspectives on Labor and Income*], No. 75-001-X: 3–15.

Urwin, P. (2006) 'Age discrimination: Legislation and human capital accumulation', *Employee Relations*, 28: 87–97.

Van Dalen, H.P., Jenkens, K.I., Henderikse, W. and Schippers, J. (2010) 'Do European employers support later retirement?', *International Journal of Manpower*, 31: 360–73.

Von Bonsdorff, M.E., Shultz, K.S, Leskinen, E. and Tansky, J. (2009) 'The choice between retirement and bridge employment: A continuity theory and life course perspective', *International Journal of Aging and Human Development*, 69: 79–100.

Wang, M. (2007) 'Profiling retirees in the retirement transition and adjustment process: Examining the longitudinal change patterns of retirees' psychological well-being', *Journal of Applied Psychology*, 92: 455–74.

Wang, M., Zhan, Y., Liu, S. and Shultz, K.S. (2008) 'Antecedents of bridge employment: A longitudinal investigation', *Journal of Applied Psychology*, 93: 818–30.

Weckerle, J.R. and Shultz, K.S. (1999) 'Influences in the bridge employment decision among older USA workers', *Journal of Occupational and Organizational Psychology*, 72: 317–29.

Part III

Bridge employment in the Asia-Pacific region

12 The role of partial retirement in organizational policy-making in Australia

Philip Taylor, Christopher McLoughlin and Catherine Earl

Background

The Australian economy emerged relatively unscathed from the global financial crisis and unemployment is low by current international standards. A shortage of skilled workers to fill vacancies may become a frustration for employers, and in the coming years the aging of the population will constrain labor-supply growth. Some occupations and industries are already feeling pressures from the demographic shift in labor supply, in particular those with aging workforces, poor working arrangements or conditions, or unattractive (e.g., remote) locations. As a result, and in order to contain fiscal costs, Australia is implementing a raft of measures that aim to raise participation by older workers. Recent public policy has aimed at prolonging working lives through both pension reforms and labor-market policy. The intention has been to tighten the eligibility for early retirement while increasing incentives to carry on working. For instance, the Federal Government's Transition To Retirement (TTR) scheme allows a worker to commence an account-based pension while still working. TTR provides an opportunity to ease into retirement and take advantage of tax concessions. While an individual is still working, employer and member contributions will continue to be paid into their superannuation account. However, under the TTR rules, it is possible to withdraw some or all of a superannuation fund and turn it into a retirement income stream to compensate for a reduced income resulting from a move from full-time to part-time work. Until recently, an individual could only access their superannuation once they reached the age of 65 or retired.

Changing age demographics and sustainability of social security systems mean that the strategies adopted in the mid to late twentieth century to create early retirement pathways are no longer tenable and need to be reoriented toward the employability of older workers (Flynn *et al.* 2013). Nonetheless, external pressures affect the management of older workers in employer policies that continue to favor the flexibility of early retirement (Conen *et al.* 2011; Vickerstaff *et al.* 2003). Retirement is no longer an abrupt or single event, but constitutes a process or phase. In the United States, for instance, one study found that 60 percent of employees surveyed left full-time work after the age of 50, and 53 percent of employees aged over 55 moved into a bridge job (Cahill *et al.* 2006).

240   *P. Taylor* et al.

In Australia, 54 percent of women and 38 percent of men shifted to partial retirement (Thomson 2007). Some 80 percent of baby boomers in Australia preferred a phased retirement pathway in their current field of employment or a similar job (Humpel *et al.* 2009). Reduced hours are also widespread among men and women across industry sectors in Europe, with more older workers than younger workers employed part-time (Kantarci and van Soest 2008).

Partial retirement is much promoted in the literature. Commentators such as Reday-Mulvey (2013) point to benefits for both older workers and employers. For the employer, for instance, it is said to reduce the employment costs of older workers, reduce absenteeism and retain skills and experience, while for the employee it is said to provide a flexible transition to retirement, support adaptation to changing abilities, reduce stress and increase recuperation time and increase choice and life satisfaction. From a public policy perspective there are also potential benefits to the public purse in terms of increased tax revenues and reduced welfare payments.

Despite evidence for its popularity among workers, many employers are skeptical about following the lead of government policy in terms of prolonging working lives and in this regard their attitudes are 'hardwired' and slow to change (van Dalen *et al.* 2010). Problems judged by human resource managers (surveyed in Western Europe) as major obstacles in introducing phased retirement initiatives did not generally stem from a lack of support from the workforce (18 percent), but rather centered on 'hidden extra costs' (32 percent), 'inadequate commitment by top management' (31 percent), and 'resistance by lower- and middle-management' (28 percent) (Smolkin 1996, in Kantarci and van Soest 2008: 119). Evidence is lacking as to why employers implement policies of partial retirement. It is known that progressive organizations that already engage in flexible work schedules are generally the ones that are also open to implementing phased retirement initiatives (Hutchens and Grace-Martin 2006). But part-time retirement often appears to be considered a form of early retirement, albeit part-time. Alternatively it might be viewed as capturing and retaining important knowledge that might otherwise disappear overnight (Taylor 2002). Research carried out in the United States of America indicates that opportunities for phased retirement are greatest in health, education and social services and are lowest in other parts of public administration. Transport, communications and utilities are likely to not permit phased retirement, while the construction industry is very supportive of phased retirement (Hutchens and Grace-Martin 2006). While the government sector in the USA tended to be 'particularly unreceptive' to phased retirement on account of the difficulties with federal law, pensions and other factors (Hutchens and Grace-Martin 2006), phased retirement is common in the public sector in the Netherlands (Kantarci and van Soest 2008).

In this chapter we report evidence on the extent of part-time retirement in Australian workplaces, comparing industry sectors and assessing its role in human resource policy-making. In particular we report on analysis that attempts to elucidate whether it is just another form of early retirement, or whether it

The role of partial retirement in Australia 241

forms part of strategies aimed at lengthening working lives and contributing to organizational well-being.

Methodology

The data on which this chapter is based come from an Australian project that considered the employment of older workers in a globalizing economy.[1] This project included a CATI survey of 2,000 Queensland employers with more than 50 employees (29 percent response rate, i.e., 590), carried out in 2010. The survey instrument contained a range of questions about attitudes and behaviors toward older workers and concerning wider issues of labor supply, including questions about retirement.

Employers with more than 50 employees were surveyed, accessed for a telephone interview through two rented business lists, one general and another focused on large organizations that are frequently updated and verified for accuracy by their owners. Responding organizations were selected at random from these lists and were contacted until the objective of a 30 percent response rate was achieved. The survey covered all employment sectors. On average each interview was completed in 35 minutes. Queensland employers were surveyed due to the involvement of the Queensland Government as a funding partner on the grant. Queensland, as with the rest of Australia, has been experiencing low levels of unemployment with concerns about labor shortages.

Large organizations, with 200 or more employees, accounted for 53 percent of responding organizations, with organizations with between 50 and 199 employees accounting for the remaining 47 percent. Also, organizations were classified as either 'for profit', constituting 73 percent of the sample, while the remaining 27 percent were government and not-for-profit organizations (17 percent and 10 percent respectively). Organizations' gender balance was slightly skewed toward males. On average, 57 percent of employees were male, although the spread of the percentage of genders in responding organizations was normally distributed across the sample. The distribution of age groups within organizations also showed that, on average, 20 percent of employees were over 50 years of age and 27 percent were younger than 30 years of age, with the remaining 53 percent aged between 30 and 50. Finally, the respondents representing participating organizations were characterized as predominantly male (64 percent) with an average age of 45 years but with ages ranging from 22 to 69.

Respondents indicated their occupation, with 41 percent in human resources manager/officer or other recruitment functions, 17 percent in director, managing director, chief executive officer or financial officer roles, 14 percent were regional or department managers, 12 percent in general manager roles and 10 percent were heads or directors of a department. Also, approximately 6 percent of the sample was employed in administrator or 'other' roles. This sample is considered to be largely representative of medium and large organizations in Queensland and also Australia, an assertion based on the consideration that participating organizations were selected at random within Queensland from business lists and a response rate of approximately 30 percent can be considered to be 'substantially higher than the response rate generally found in corporate surveys' (Henkens et al. 2008).

Policies concerned with issues of workforce aging

Figure 12.1 presents the percentage of organizations that had adopted policies in response to workforce aging. Although it was common for them to adopt a multifaceted approach to the engagement of older workers (see Figure 12.2), Figure 12.1 clearly indicates that some policies were more popular than others. Notably, part-time retirement was more popular than early retirement (32 percent vs. 15 percent of employers implementing such policies). A part-time retirement policy was almost as popular as a reduction of working hours before retirement (implemented by 32 percent and 33 percent of employers, respectively). However, there was a range of policies that were more popular than part-time retirement. These included coaching and mentoring, continuous career development supported by training, and retirement planning. It is suggested that the wide adoption of these policies may be linked to three factors, including the level of commitment of resources required to implement them, the ease of engagement

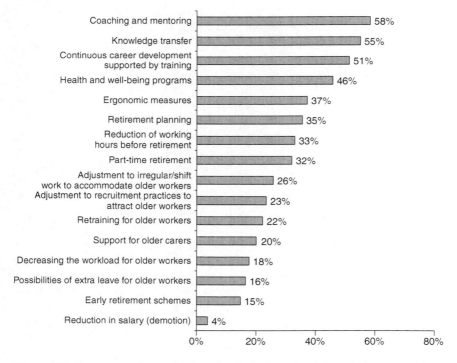

Figure 12.1 Percentage of organizations that had adopted policies relating to workforce aging.

The role of partial retirement in Australia 243

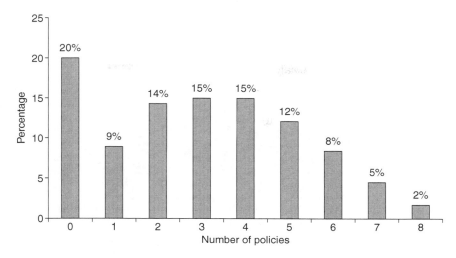

Figure 12.2 Percentage of responding organizations by the number of older-worker-oriented policies used by the organization.

of older workers with these policies and the extent that policies may be viewed by employers as a source of intergenerational conflict within organizations. For example, the most popular policy of coaching and mentoring requires relatively few resources as it is likely to be formally or informally practiced in corporate succession planning. Second, it is likely to provide valued status to older workers and thus to engage them and, third, it demonstrates a clear pathway for younger workers to view their career advancement and thus it can be argued that it discourages intergenerational conflict. We would also argue that the high incidence of policies concerning mentoring and knowledge transfer may reflect a recognition that older workers are keepers of wisdom and expertise that the organization needs to capture before the worker departs.

Figure 12.2 presents the percentage of responding organizations by the frequency of older-worker policies implemented. It is notable from this figure that one in five responding organizations had not adopted any of these policies. The majority had applied one or more policy responses, with almost 60 percent having adopted between two and five older-worker-oriented policies. The remaining 15 percent of responding organizations adopted between six and eight policies.

Partial retirement and other older-worker-oriented policies

Figure 12.3 presents the percentage of responding organizations that had adopted, would consider adopting and would not consider adopting a part-time retirement policy by the number of older-worker-friendly policies adopted. This

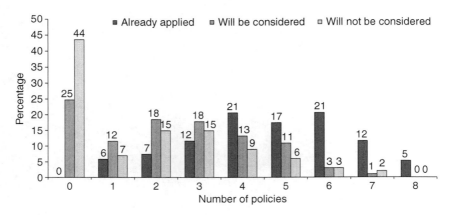

Figure 12.3 Percentage of responding organizations that had adopted, would consider adopting and would not consider adopting a part-time retirement by the number of older-worker-oriented policies adopted.

figure helps contextualize the importance of a part-time retirement policy among organizations most active in the engagement of older workers. One in three responding organizations (N=190) utilized part-time retirement. Seventy percent (N=133) of them also adopted four to seven other older-worker-oriented policies. More than half (56 percent) of the organizations that applied four to seven of these policies had adopted the part-time retirement response. Almost half of the organizations that had not adopted or would not consider adopting part-time retirement had not employed any other older-worker-oriented policies. For the organizations that would consider adopting part-time retirement in future, more than 70 percent had employed fewer than three other older-worker-oriented policies. These findings suggest that part-time retirement is one of the primary policy responses employers use to engage older workers.

Figure 12.4 presents the percentage of total number of organizations that had adopted each of the older-worker policies that had also employed a part-time retirement policy. Included in the labels of the older-worker-friendly policies are the total numbers of responding organizations that had adopted each of the policies to indicate the overall popularity of this policy response compared to the adoption among employers who had a part-time retirement policy. It is evident from this figure that, on the one hand, the policy responses most readily adopted by employers with a part-time retirement policy also have some connection to part-time retirement. For example, 'a reduction in working hours before retirement' has similarities to part-time retirement. Also, 'reduction in salary (demotion)' could be caused by the shift from full-time to part-time work. On the other hand, policy responses that were least readily adopted by employers with a part-time retirement policy appeared to have connections to empowerment and the facilitation of continued working. For example, 'supporting older carers', 'health and well-being

The role of partial retirement in Australia 245

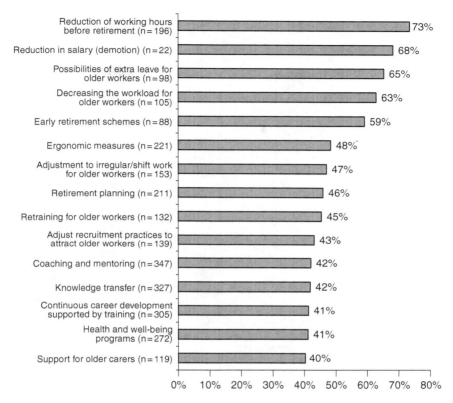

Figure 12.4 Percentage of the total number of organizations that had adopted each of the older-worker-friendly policies that had also employed a part-time retirement policy.

Note
Included in the labels of the older-worker-friendly policies are the total numbers of responding organizations that had adopted each of the policies.

programs' and 'continuous career development supported by training' had the lowest proportion of adoption concurrently with a part-time retirement policy. Taken together this suggests employers adopted an integrated strategy toward older workers when part-time retirement was utilized.

Table 12.1 presents the probability that an employer who used part-time retirement would have adopted another of the older-worker-friendly policies, 95 percent confidence interval for the probability and the variance explained in adoption of each policy by the adoption of part-time retirement. For example, employers that used part-time retirement were 21 times more likely to have a policy of reduced working hours for workers approaching retirement than employers that did not use this. Based on the sample used in this study we can be 95 percent certain that this increased probability of having a policy of reduced

246   *P. Taylor* et al.

Table 12.1 Probability that an employer that used part-time retirement would have adopted another of the older-worker-friendly policies, 95% confidence interval for the probability and the variance explained in adoption of each policy by the adoption of part-time retirement

	Exponential Beta	95% CI low	95% CI high	Nagelkerke R Square
Reduction of working hours before retirement	21.251	13.665	33.047	0.452
Possibilities of extra leave for older workers	5.542	3.49	8.801	0.152
Decreasing the workload for older workers	4.995	3.2	7.796	0.139
Reduction in salary (demotion)	4.873	1.953	12.163	0.077
Early retirement schemes	3.862	2.419	6.166	0.094
Coaching and mentoring	3.368	2.282	4.971	0.09
Ergonomic measures	3.291	2.298	4.713	0.096
Knowledge transfer	2.925	2.016	4.244	0.075
Retirement planning	2.662	1.862	3.807	0.066
Continuous career development supported by training	2.486	1.736	3.56	0.056
Adjustment to irregular/shift work to accommodate older workers	2.441	1.667	3.573	0.051
Health and well-being programs	2.199	1.548	3.123	0.044
Retraining for older workers	2.135	1.434	3.178	0.035
Adjustment recruitment practices to attract older workers	1.905	1.286	2.82	0.026
Support for older carers	1.59	1.049	2.409	0.012

working hours for workers approaching retirement is between 13 and 33 times more likely among the responding organizations with a part-time retirement policy. Also, organizations indicating that they used part-time retirement explained 45 percent of the variation in participants' adoption of reduced working hours for workers approaching retirement. From this table we can conclude that employers who used part-time retirement policies were at least twice as likely to use almost any of the other policies (except 'Adjustment to recruitment practices to attract older workers' and 'Support for older carers') than those that did not use part-time retirement. This finding further supports the proposition that when employers began to attempt to engage with older workers they used a multifaceted approach and one of the primary policy responses they used was offering part-time retirement.

Table 12.2 presents the results of principle components analysis of items pertaining to human resource strategies, including part-time retirement. Of note, part-time retirement loads together with variables concerning the promotion of a

Table 12.2 Principle components analysis structure: human resource strategies

	*Component**	
	1	*2*
Part-time retirement	0.719	
Reduction of working hours before retirement	0.739	
Early retirement schemes	0.495	
Possibilities of extra leave for older workers	0.765	
Decreasing the workload for older workers	0.672	
Continuous career development supported by training		−0.675
Health and well-being programs		−0.597
Knowledge transfer		−0.813
Coaching and mentoring		−0.84

Notes
* Components are: 1 'Older worker flexible withdrawal strategies' and 2 'General human resource strategies'.

flexible end to working life. The variable with the highest loading on this factor is the possibility of extra leave for older workers. Altogether, these findings are supportive of Hutchens and Grace-Martin's (2006) findings that flexible work schedules and part-time retirement go hand in hand.

Partial employment and industry

Figure 12.5 presents the percentage of each industrial sector that had adopted part-time retirement. Industry comparisons on the uptake of part-time retirement policies appear to reflect existing positive/negative perceptions regarding older workers, particularly at the low adoption end. For example, both the information and telecommunications and retail sectors present themselves as being youthful. The high incidence of physically demanding work in the manufacturing sector may explain the apparent weaker orientation toward older workers who may be regarded as less physically capable than younger workers, despite their greater experience and higher skill levels. Conversely, high-skill industries appear at the high proportion of adoption of part-time retirement end of the continuum. Those such as education and training and professional, scientific and technical services that are likely to have large proportions of high-skill workers appear to have the most frequent adoption of part-time retirement policies. This conforms to the findings of other studies regarding occupation types and prolonged working lives. The two industrial sectors with the next highest proportions of part-time retirement uptake are those that could be expected to have large numbers of workers in physically demanding roles: transportation, postal and warehousing and construction. Their uptake of part-time retirement is surprising and worthy of a follow-up study.

248 P. Taylor et al.

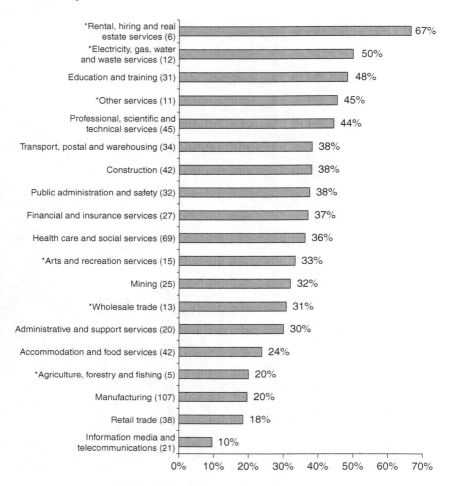

Figure 12.5 Percentage of each industry group that had adopted part-time retirement.

Note
The number of respondents in each industry group is noted in the category labels and * denotes an industry group that had insufficient sample sizes to make inferences based on normative values.

Part-time retirement and employers encouraging later retirement

Employers participating in the study were asked, 'In the case your establishment faces a shortage of personnel – now or in the near future – would you encourage employees to retire later?' Of the 595 respondents, 34 percent (N=203) indicated that they had already began to encourage their employees to retire later, 44 percent (N=260) indicated that this response would be considered in the future and the remaining 22 percent (N=132) responded that their organization would not encourage workers to retire later. Among the 203 respondents that were already encouraging employers to retire later, almost half (N=95, 47 percent) coupled this response with a part-time retirement policy. Approximately 40 percent (N=86) of the employers that were encouraging employees to retire later indicated that they would consider a part-time retirement policy in the future. Finally, approximately 10 percent of those organizations that were encouraging their employees to retire later indicated that they would not consider using a part-time retirement policy. These proportions are presented in Figure 12.6.

Of the 132 employers that indicated they were not encouraging their employees to retire later, approximately 20 percent (N=26) had adopted a part-time retirement policy and 46 percent indicated they would consider adopting this policy in the future. Binary logistic regression indicated that organizations that encouraged employees to retire later, compared to all other respondents, were more than two-and-a-half times more likely to have a part-time retirement policy.

These findings suggest that although part-time retirement was likely to be used by employers to retain the workers that were approaching retirement, a small percentage of responding organizations (5 percent of the whole sample) were adopting part-time retirement while not encouraging their workers to retire later, presumably adopting this policy as a form of early retirement.

Concluding remarks

Our analysis indicates that when Australian employers implemented older-worker policies they used a multifaceted approach and one of the primary policy responses they were using was part-time retirement. Among our employers, approximately one-third had adopted part-time retirement as a policy response,

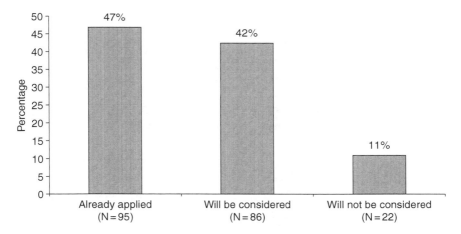

Figure 12.6 Percentage of employers that are encouraging employees to retire later by the adoption of part-time retirement policies.

250 *P. Taylor* et al.

which positions this measure (along with other flexible retirement measures) as being rather less common than others targeting issues of workforce aging. It appears to form part of a suite of policies linked to flexible retirement that firms are enacting, such as reduced hours or demotion. It is being deployed in organizations that both wish to reduce headcount and ones that wish to retain expertise, although rather more frequently the latter. This indicates that part-time retirement is largely associated with a prolongation of working lives. One caveat here is the period when this study was undertaken. The interviews took place at a time of strong growth in the Australian economy. In weaker economies where skill and labor shortages are not such a concern, a different finding may have been observed. That part-time retirement was most commonly deployed in knowledge-intense sectors such as education is perhaps no surprise, although this does raise the question of what happens to those workers who do not have ready access to flexible retirement options in sectors such as manufacturing and retail. Understanding why such sectors might be disinclined to promote part-time retirement is important. Many workers in such industries would likely benefit from the opportunity to phase in to retirement. With the demise of early retirement, many such workers may find themselves caught in the hinterland between full-time work and full retirement, having no third choice that might allow them a gradual exit from the paid workforce.

Note

1 This project was supported by the Australian Research Council (LP0884065), the Australian Population Institute, Success Factors and the Department of Employment, Economic Development and Innovation in Queensland.

References

Cahill, K.E., Giandrea, M.D. and Quinn, J.F. (2006) 'Retirement patterns from career employment', *The Gerontologist*, 46: 514–23.

Conen, W.S., Henkens, K. and Schippers, J. (2011) 'Are employers changing their behavior toward older workers? An analysis of employers' surveys 2000–2009', *Journal of Aging & Social Policy*, 23: 141–58.

Flynn, M., Upchurch, M., Muller-Camen, M. and Schroder, H. (2013) 'Trade union responses to ageing workforces in the UK and Germany', *Human Relations*, 66: 45–64.

Henkens, K., Remery, C. and Schippers, J. (2008) 'Shortages in an ageing labor market: An analysis of employers' behaviour', *International Journal of Human Resource Management*, 19: 1314–29.

Humpel, N., O'Loughlin, K., Wells, Y. and Kendig, H. (2009) 'Ageing baby boomers in Australia: Evidence informing actions for better retirement', *Australian Journal of Social Issues*, 44: 399–415.

Hutchens, R. and Grace-Martin, K. (2006) 'Employer willingness to permit phased retirement: Why are some more willing than others?', *Industrial and Labor Relations Review*, 59: 525–46.

Kantarci, T. and van Soest, A.H.O. (2008) 'Gradual retirement: Preferences and limitations', *De Economist*, 156: 113–44.

Reday-Mulvey, G. (2013) *The Four Pillars Programme. What Have We Been Able to Achieve?* Online. Available at: www.genevaassociation.org/PDF/Working_paper_series/GA_E&D_395_02_REDAY-MULVEY_Life,Four_pillars,GA,Retirement.pdf (accessed May 15, 2013).

Taylor, P. (2002) *New Policies for Older Workers*, Bristol: The Policy Press.

Thomson, J. (2007) *The Transition of Older Australian Workers to Full and Partial Retirement.* Online. Available at: www.economics.unimelb.edu.au/downloads/wpa-pers-07/1005.pdf (accessed May 15, 2013).

van Dalen, H., Henkens, K. and Schippers, J. (2010) 'How do employers cope with an ageing workforce? Views from employers and employees', *Demographic Research*, 22: 1015–36.

Vickerstaff, S., Cox, J. and Keen, L. (2003) 'Employers and the management of retirement', *Social Policy and Administration*, 37: 271–87.

13 The Japanese approach to bridge jobs

Chikako Usui, Richard A. Colignon and Dan Rosen

Introduction

The Japanese labor market is increasingly paradoxical. A shrinking and aging population should produce a natural downsizing of the labor market with a corresponding opening of job opportunities, yet the job market for new, young employees has in fact become increasingly severe. Similarly, the lingering economic recession coupled with an aging and shrinking population should naturally adjust employment markets through attrition (retirement); however, the job market for young workers has actually been shrinking. High levels of unemployment have persisted, not only because of job scarcity due to recessions but also because of job mismatch. Job mismatch for older workers typically occurs when their skills become obsolete and unable to meet employers' expectations. In Japan, though, the problem is acute even among recent college graduates. This mismatch involves the expectations of corporate recruiters and college graduates.

As for older workers, mandatory corporate retirement practices coupled with government concerns over the future cost of supporting an aging population have produced a labor-market gap between regular career employment and full retirement. To ameliorate this gap and a labor-market mismatch involving older workers, policy-makers have turned to the use of bridge jobs.

Older workers in Japan have one of the highest rates of labor-force participation among industrially advanced countries. Among people 60–64 years of age, 57.3 percent of Japanese are in the labor force, compared to 55.2 percent in the United States, 44.4 percent in Germany, and 18.9 percent in France. Among those aged 65–69, the rates are 36.3 percent, 31.4 percent, 8.6 percent, and 4.9 percent, respectively (Table 13.1). Considering men individually, 70.9 percent of those age 60–64 and 46.2 percent of those 65–69 are economically active in Japan.

Despite this, labor-force participation among older workers has been steadily declining as the challenge of job mismatch has increased. There are redundant workers (an oversupply of employees and not enough jobs) in office, production, and construction work. Many firms have begun outsourcing office functions overseas, and no one expects growth in office work. In contrast, there is a labor

The Japanese approach to bridge jobs   253

Table 13.1 Labor-force-participation rates among older persons (male and female combined)

Country	Age					
	20–24	*55–59*	*60–64*	*65–69*	*70–74*	*75+*
	(%)					
Japan	68.3	75.2	57.3	36.3	22.8	8.3
(male)		(88.5)	(70.9)	(46.2)	(30.1)	(13.6)
United States	71.4	73.3	55.2	31.4	18.0	7.4
Germany	70.3	77.5	44.4	8.6	2.7	1.2
France	62.2	65.2	18.9	4.9	1.2	0.4

Source: Japan Labor Policy Institute (2012) (Online: www.works-i.com/?action=repository_ uri&item_) and Cabinet Office, Japanese Government (Online: www8.cao.go.jp/kourei/ whitepaper/w-2012/gaiyou/s1_4_1.html).

shortage among professional and technical jobs in the health sectors and caregiving services. Older workers often find themselves without the skills or experience that is relevant to these expanding sectors. Moreover, many older workers find themselves incapable of meeting the physical demands of caregiving responsibilities.

The challenge of job mismatch among older workers and their growing need for bridge jobs have put the interests of corporations and policy-makers at odds. Corporations have generally required workers to retire at age 60 in order to provide flexibility in internal labor markets. Faced with a rapidly expanding burden exacerbated by a stagnant economy and shrinking tax revenues, the government has responded by raising the age to 65 at which people become entitled to full public pensions. Bridge employment has emerged as a partial solution.

In this chapter we discuss the institutional factors that have created the conditions for the development of bridge jobs in Japan. First, we examine the increasing mismatch between labor-force participation and job availability. Second, we discuss the government response to the increasing burden of an aging population and its reconsideration of labor-market policy. Finally, we consider the development of a stratified bundle of employment paths for older workers that serve to bridge the gap between the end of their career jobs and the beginning of full retirement.

Mandatory provision of bridge jobs until age 65

The Japanese government reformed public pensions in 2000 by raising the age to 65 when people become entitled to full pension benefits. This change began in 2013 and will be in full effect by 2025. Males born between 1953 and 1955 will become eligible to receive their earnings-related portion of the public pension (equivalent to Social Security in the United States) at age 61 (instead of age 60).

254   *C. Usui* et al.

The entitlement age will be raised every three years until 2025. Thus, starting in 2013, workers who have reached the mandatory corporate retirement age of 60 will have to wait for at least one year to receive public pension benefits. To cope with this gap, the government has advised companies to retain workers either by changing the mandatory corporate retirement age to 65 or by providing bridge jobs until employees become eligible for full pensions. Starting April 1, 2013, the policy – the extension of mandatory corporate retirement or provision of bridge jobs until one reaches 65 – became mandatory. The idea of re-employing or re-hiring workers after they reach the mandatory corporate retirement age is an old, well-established practice in Japan. The re-employment system (or re-hiring system or continued employment system) has developed along with an employment system based on lifetime employment, seniority-based promotion, and mandatory corporate retirement. Workers are hired 'fresh out of school' and are promoted by seniority, experience, and in-house training. The Japanese education system has been geared to support lifelong careers at a given company/corporation. Although the number of core workers afforded these benefits is shrinking, it remains a core institution among large firms (Matanle and Mitsui 2011).

This employment system shields workers from the risks of unemployment. Salaries are determined by seniority rather than by market-based pay rates. Workers earn higher salaries as they get older. Thus, older workers tend to be overpaid relative to their productivity, while younger workers experience the reverse. Earnings and statuses peak in their late forties to early fifties. Large firms then demote employees in the managerial ranks to non-managerial posi-tions (i.e., remove managerial compensation) once they reach their early to mid fifties. When workers reach the mandatory corporate retirement age of 60, firms provide re-employment opportunities to those with accumulated skills and experience. Mandatory retirement provides a mechanism for removing costly layers of workers and making room for younger ones. Once workers go through a ritual retirement at age 60, they are then re-employed and assigned to new positions that are lower in status and wages. Many workers are re-hired in con-tractual or part-time positions at subsidiaries or affiliates and are given entirely different responsibilities. Often, they do not retain regular worker status or union membership at the home company.

The new law mandates employment (bridge jobs) to all workers until they reach age 65 or a change in the mandatory corporate retirement age to 65. Most companies opt for bridge jobs. As might be expected, the larger the company, the greater the resistance to the legislation. For large companies, mandatory retirement has been a vital personnel tool, meaning that employers are not inclined to raise the retirement age.

The use of mandatory corporate retirement is lawful and universal among large firms. The age changed from 55 to 60 in 1994. Although the idea and prac-tice of mandatory retirement may seem unfair, it is also found in countries such as France, Ireland, and Sweden (Department for Work and Pensions 2010). In contrast, mandatory retirement has been abolished and is not permitted at any age in places such as the United States, Canada, and New Zealand.

The Japanese approach to bridge jobs 255

Another reason that large firms are reluctant to keep older workers is that they are products of a generalist-oriented job training system (among white-collar workers) emphasizing personnel management skills. This leaves older workers without specialized and transferable technical skills. The personnel system is built on frequent re-assignments and transfers that build personnel management skills rather than strategic management skills or new technical skills. Large companies shuffle and re-shuffle regular white-collar employees every few years (*jinji-ido*). Moving from one section or division to another or from one branch to another allows them to climb job ladders and move to higher-status positions. From the employee's point of view, this in-house training system leads to an accumulation of expertise and networks that are company-specific. Little of it would be of interest to other employers.

Stratification of bridge jobs by company size and employment status

The situation is quite different among smaller companies. They contend with chronic labor shortages of young college graduates and skilled workers because they are less able to offer competitive salaries, promotion opportunities, and job security. The mandatory retirement age at many small firms is 70. Some have no retirement age at all. Table 13.2 is a summary of the results of a government survey conducted in June 2011. It found that 59.9 percent of small firms (31 to 50 employees) and 46.9 percent of medium-sized firms (51 to 300 employees) have established mechanisms for retaining workers until age 65. In contrast, only 24.3 percent of large firms (employing more than 300 people) have developed these mechanisms (Ministry of Health, Labor, and Welfare 2012b, 2012c). A closer inspection of these figures (see Table 13.2) shows that among small and medium-sized firms (31–300 employees), 34.3 percent have continued employment for older workers, 14.4 percent have mandatory retirement at 65 (instead of 60), and 2.9 percent have no mandatory retirement. Combined, these figures show that 51.7 percent of small and medium firms have mechanisms for employing older workers until they reach age 65. Among large firms, 18.3 percent have

Table 13.2 Prevalence of re-employment system until age 65 measured by % firms with re-employment system until age 65, 2011

Company (number of employees)	% firms
All firms (31+)	48.8
Small firms (31–50)	59.9
Medium firms (51–300)	46.9
Small + medium firms (31–300)	51.7
Large firms (301+)	24.3

Source: Ministry of Health, Labor, and Welfare (2012b, October 18), Press Release (Online: www. mhlw.go.jp/stf/houdou/2r9852000002m9lq-att/2r9852000002m9q0.pdf).

256   *C. Usui* et al.

continued employment for older workers, 5.6 percent have mandatory retirement at 65, and 0.4 percent have no age limit. These figures, when combined, yield 24.3 percent.

The difference between how larger firms and smaller firms relate to the labor market on issues of retirement and retention of older workers illustrates Japan's stratified employment system.

One way Japan reproduces its stratification through the labor market is represented in the patterns/paths of bridge jobs. The bridge jobs are mediated by (1) the home company; (2) government employment agencies (e.g., Hello Work; Silver Human Resources Service Center); or (3) self-employment (finding a bridge job on one's own).

As of April 1, 2013, the law requires the retention of older workers until age 65, except for those who take voluntary retirement. Although most firms long ago instituted bridge jobs, it is not clear if and how they will meet the requirements of the new legislation. This is because enforcement of the law relies on administrative guidance involving non-codified, extralegal regulation. Government agencies work with companies to induce compliance. Notably, there is no fine for violations. However, when a company fails to comply with the law, the government (in this case the Ministry of Health, Labor, and Welfare) will disclose the name of the offender in public (Ministry of Health, Labor, and Welfare 2012c). This leverages public opinion to gain corporate compliance.

As late as June 2012, 48.8 percent of companies with 31 or more workers reported that they had instituted new or additional mechanisms/arrangements to meet the government requirements. This represents 51.7 percent of small and medium firms and 24.3 percent of large firms. The government report does not include data for firms with fewer than 30 employees.

Home company re-hires

The major path for finding bridge jobs is through the home company. This path applies to those who have been employed as regular employees, not non-regular (part-time, temporary, or contractual) workers. According to government data, 80 percent of all male workers are regular employees but only 44.7 percent of females are. In other words, 20 percent of all male workers and 55.3 percent of all females are non-regular employees. Moreover, among workers 55–59 years of age, 85.7 percent of men and 40 percent of women are regular employees (see Table 13.3). Theoretically, they will have access to bridge jobs arranged by their home companies upon reaching official and ritual retirement at 60.

These bridge jobs bring about substantial reductions in pay, are sometimes part-time, and may not be related to their skills or experience. The positions are typically offered at smaller subsidiaries or affiliates of the home company. Thus, these bridge jobs are associated with a substantial loss of status and wages. Yet, these transitions have become institutionalized, providing security and continuity in employment.

This re-employment pattern is not without complications. Until recently, large firms were able to eliminate labor excess through generous voluntary early

The Japanese approach to bridge jobs   257

Table 13.3 Older workers by employment status

Age	Male worker status (%)							
	Regular	Non-regular	Part-time	Temporary	Dispatched	Contract	Executives	Other
All ages	80.0	20.0	(3.1)	(6.9)	(2.0)	(3.9)	(2.2)	(1.7)
55–59	85.7	14.3	(2.7)	(2.7)	(1.0)	(3.9)	(2.1)	(1.7)
60–64	44.5	55.5	(12.3)	(9.1)	(1.8)	(10.9)	(17.3)	(3.7)
65–69	27.4	72.6	(22.8)	(16.7)	(2.8)	(10.2)	(13.2)	(6.5)

Age	Female worker status (%)							
	Regular	Non-regular	Part-time	Temporary	Dispatched	Contract	Executives	Other
All ages	44.7	55.3	(33.7)	(8.6)	(4.2)	(4.6)	(1.7)	(2.3)
55–59	40.0	60.0	(47.6)	(3.4)	(1.4)	(3.3)	(2.0)	(2.2)
60–64	28.2	71.8	(51.2)	(6.2)	(1.6)	(4.2)	(4.2)	(4.3)
65–69	28.4	71.6	(52.0)	(6.9)	(1.7)	(2.4)	(2.8)	(5.7)

Source: Statistical Bureau, Ministry of Internal Affairs and Communication (Tokyo, Japan) *2007 Employment Status Survey*, Table I-8 (Online: www.stat.go.jp/english/data/shugyou/pdf/sum2007.pdf).

retirement packages, often including severance pay of 24 months of salary. The benefits of these packages have decreased as economic conditions have deteriorated. Currently, they only rarely include more than 12–18 months of salary. Moreover, large companies no longer have enough positions in subsidiaries and affiliates into which to move older workers. There are abundant anecdotes about subsidiaries returning transferred employees to the parent firm.

Many companies go to extraordinary measures to force workers to resign. Often these techniques involve 'power harassment'. Until recently, Japanese companies were hesitant to shed redundant workers, so they developed elaborate ways to force people out. Creating '*madogiwa-zoku*' or 'window sitters' is a method that emerged in the 1980s. These are typically middle managers who have managerial titles but no subordinates or responsibilities. They are ostracized and placed by the window, where they while away their workdays. These idle workers have effectively been confined to a kind of in-house retirement until they quit (see, for example, Rosen 2013).

Another common example of power harassment is imposing inconvenient job transfers that necessitate living away from one's family or assigning taxing travel schedules. These corporate bullying techniques are used to exert psychological pressure to make workers leave. In December 2012, news stories said that the government was investigating five large firms (Panasonic, Sharp, Asahi Life Insurance, Sony, and NEC) for putting unwanted workers in a special room, called *oidashi-beya* (the room to force people out) (see, for example, Brasor 2013). The room is packed with workers who had poor performance evaluations and those who declined the company's 'tap on the shoulder' (suggesting that they take early retirement). They were given tedious or humiliating daily tasks that made them want to quit.

258   *C. Usui* et al.

As the recession continued, however, many corporations began direct layoffs of massive numbers of workers as part of restructuring. In 2002, for example, Nippon Telegraph and Telephone Corp. reached an agreement with its union and transferred some 110,000 regular employees, about half of its workforce, to subsidiaries. The arrangement included a provision under which workers aged 51 and over would be fired from NTT, then re-hired at subsidiaries with salary cuts of as much as 30 percent (Matus 2002). Sharp in 2012 carried out a large restructuring involving the termination of 20 percent of its regular workers through voluntary early retirement. The company had not carried out a restructuring of that scale since the 1950s, but its poor performance in recent years finally led to this restructuring. In March 2013, Samsung purchased 3 percent of Sharp's shares and became the largest foreign shareholder of Sharp (BBC News 2013). Similarly, Renesas, one of the world's largest semiconductor system suppliers for mobile phones and automotive appliances, announced it would reduce its regular work force by 25 percent (more than 10,000 workers) and transfer another 500 to its major stockholder companies, including Hitachi and Mitsubishi (*Asahi Shimbun* 2012). Panasonic in 2012 reduced the size of its worldwide employees by 10 percent (about 3.6 million layoffs). It continued its restructuring to cut costs and return profitability, including 10,000 layoffs before the end of March 2013.

Some bridge jobs do in fact involve upward mobility, to executive positions. Only 2.1 percent of male workers age 55–59 are corporate executives, but the figure is 17.3 percent at 60–64 and 13.2 percent age 65–69 (Table 13.3). Similarly, while only 2 percent of female workers aged 55–59 are corporate executives, the percentage is 4.2 percent at age 60–64 and 2.8 percent at 65–69. The conclusion to be drawn is that some workers rise to corporate executive positions after reaching the mandatory retirement age and remain at that level for a couple of years. They are then removed to allow later cohorts ascending an escalator system. This pattern clearly illustrates Japan's tiered employment system. This elite form of re-employment highlights employee stratification. It stands in contrast to the treatment of regular employees both as to compensation and status.

Stratification by employment status and company size

Japan has two classes of workers: regular (or standard) employees (s*eisha-in*) and non-regular (non-standard) employees (*hi-seisha-in*). The new legislation mandating continued employment of older workers until the age of 65 applies to regular employees only. In 2007, of workers in the 55–59 age group, 85.7 percent of men and 40 percent of women were regular employees (Table 13.3). Thus, it is reasonable to assume that after the legislation takes effect in 2013, nearly these same percentages of men and women will be included in the 'privileged class' of older workers who will benefit from the re-hiring system from their home companies. This would leave 14 percent of men workers and 60 percent of women workers in that age group without such recourse. They must seek jobs on their own to remain active in the labor force beyond age 60.

The contrast between large firms and small to medium firms shows the reality of long working life is much harder at large corporations. More than half (54 percent) of small firms and 48 percent of medium firms have adjusted to the legislation so that they now have the mechanisms in place to keep older workers employed until 65 (Ministry of Health, Labor, and Welfare 2012b). Among large firms, the figure is roughly half of that: 24.3 percent. The Ministry of Health, Labor, and Welfare's annual survey of companies with 31 or more workers shows the extent to which they have met the mandate to provide jobs to older workers until they reach 65 years of age.

Government-sponsored labor-clearing houses

In sharp contrast to regular employees who are given bridge jobs by their home company until they reach age 65, bridge job options for non-regular employees are limited. These are the workers who have been non-regular employees. They have had temporary, intermittent, precarious work and will continue on that path in old age. In addition, there are those who have been displaced or quit regular jobs and have become non-regular workers. Two major labor-clearing houses connect these older individuals to bridge jobs: Hello Work and the Silver Human Resources Service Center. Both have offices throughout the country. Hello Work is a public employment service center that operates a nationwide network of offices without regard to age or nationality. It also offers job training.

Hello Work

Roughly half of all job-seekers at Hello Work were displaced workers: the other half were those who left their main career jobs voluntarily, according to a national survey of 20,000 workers conducted by the Ministry of Health, Labor, and Welfare in November 2001–January 2003 (Fuess 2010). The survey provides insights to workers who lost jobs, causes of job losses, and the outcomes. Personnel reductions or bankruptcy accounted for nearly 50 percent of all the displacements. People in their fifties bore the brunt of the job losses.

Hello Work was designed to assist displaced blue-collar and older workers when it was established in the 1980s. However, the number of displaced has increased in recent decades. Job seekers at Hello Work now include displaced managers, specialists, technicians, and recent college graduates. Japan's unemployment rose sharply in the late 1990s and reached an all-time high of 5.5 percent in 2001. Initially, there were two distinct groups of job-seekers: older workers who lost their jobs as the result of corporate restructuring (staff cuts) or bankruptcy (grouped as 'job losers' by Fuess); and younger dissatisfied employees looking to switch jobs. The split between those who found a job ('early finder') and those who had not was even. Nearly 85 percent of early job-finders were age 30 or younger.

In contrast, among those aged 55 and older, fewer than one-third were early job-finders. Thus, older persons faced more difficulties in finding work.

260   *C. Usui* et al.

Companies typically place age restrictions on their job advertisements, a practice that is legal in Japan. According to another study, the number of available jobs for workers in their mid-thirties as opposed to mid-fifties with the same qualifications is four to one (Matus 2002).

Fuess (2010) reports that of the 20,000 job-seekers who came to Hello Work in November 2001, 35.9 percent were early job-finders, 17.3 percent were late finders, and 27.8 percent became repeat failures. The remaining 19 percent included those who found jobs but failed to keep them. According to Fuess,

> the youngest job seekers had the highest likelihood of job finding and keeping. For those aged 24 and below, 46.5 per cent found jobs early and kept them. In contrast, barely one-quarter of the 55–59 age group and not even one-fifth of the 60+ age group, could find and retain jobs. Late finders tended to be middle-aged and repeated failures were directly related to age. Whereas the youngest job hunters were least likely to fail and fail again (only 16.9 per cent), the oldest searchers were most likely to fail repeatedly (57.0 per cent of the 60–64 age group and 60.9 per cent of the 65+ age group).

As the economy has stagnated over the last two decades, the number of job-seekers has exceeded the number of jobs available. Our interviews with municipal government officials in various prefectures lead to the same conclusion: job options for late-middle-age and older persons are very limited. Very few companies recruit workers beyond age 50, except for two types of jobs: taxi drivers and security guards. The scarcity of employment opportunities for older workers in the open market serves as a reminder that those who have regular positions are a privileged class. The types of bridge jobs offered by their home companies may not be what they hope for, but – in general – older workers who are regular employees are hanging onto whatever they can get.

Silver Human Resources Service Centers

Despite the encouraging title, Hello Work has little to offer older persons. So, they often make their way to the doorsteps of Silver Human Resources Service Centers. The results there are also often disappointing. The Centers are semi-public (non-governmental) organizations established by municipal governments to serve people who are aged 60 or older seeking part-time/temporary jobs and/ or job training. These jobs are not meant to bring steady income. Rather, they are sporadic, temporary, and short-term in nature. The wages are low (below minimum wage) because the aim of the jobs is to promote active, healthy aging. They are not meant to be bridge jobs.

The first Silver Human Resources Service Center was established in Tokyo in 1975. Such centers proliferated across the country with the amendment to the Employment Stabilization Law of 1986. Each center acts as an intermediary contractor between companies or individuals who place job orders and older persons

The Japanese approach to bridge jobs   261

seeking temporary work. Older persons register at their municipal center, and the center allots the work to registered members based on qualifications and preferences. Available jobs include general work (indoor and outdoor cleaning, building janitorial work, weeding, flyer-distribution), facility maintenance (e.g., attendants at parking lots or community centers), specialized work (e.g., teaching, translation, editing, and driving), skilled work (e.g., professional gardening, carpentry, and repairs), office work assistance, door-to-door work (e.g., collection of subscription fees), and domestic services (e.g., housekeeping assistance). Members are paid by the Center according to criteria determined by type of work and hours.

The three most common types of jobs contracted are general work, facility maintenance, and domestic services. For example, 2005 data published by the Federation of Tokyo Silver Human Resources Center in the Tokyo area indicate that general work constituted 40.8 percent of all the work orders they received, followed by facility maintenance work with 32.9 percent and services, 14.9 percent (International Longevity Center Japan 2006).

According to one estimate, the financial disbursement averages about 40,000 yen a month (approximately $400/month) (International Longevity Center Japan 2006). However, in many centers, the number of available jobs has declined in recent years, while the number of job-seekers has increased. This reveals the effects of the prolonged recession. More than 25 percent of the center members seek jobs out of economic need (Ministry of Health, Labor, and Welfare 2013). According to another report, 3,332 Silver Human Resources Service Centers in 2009 had 791,859 members and total sales of 307,000,000,000 yen (about $3.07 billion). Had every member received a job, the amount per person would have been just 387,700 yen (about $3,877 a year).

These two reports illustrate the manners in which bridge jobs are stratified by employment status. Older persons who have built their working careers as regular employees are accorded greater job security until they reach age 65, while those who had temporary, intermittent, precarious work will continue on that path in old age.

Self-employment

Joining an existing family business or returning to a family farm is a common type of self-employment among older persons in Japan. While self-employed persons and family business workers comprised 11.1 percent of the total labor force in 2011, the self-employment sector accounted for 20.1 percent of workers age 55–64, and 51.6 percent among workers age 65 and over. Japan's rate of self-employment is one of the highest among advanced countries, but it has been declining rapidly. Self-employed persons made up 22.3 percent of the labor force in 1990 but decreased to 11.1 percent by 2011. During the same period, it declined from 8.8 to 7 percent in the United States and 15.1 to 13.9 percent in the United Kingdom (OECD 2011). The current legislation of requiring companies to keep older workers employed until they reach 65 is expected to further diminish Japan's self-employment (Cabinet Office of Japan 2012).

262   C. Usui et al.

The options for those who leave their home companies voluntarily or have been terminated before reaching mandatory retirement are limited. About one-fourth of regular employees leave their home companies voluntarily at 60. Some pursue self-employment, but job start-ups for people of their age are not very common.

Discussion and conclusion

Our examination of bridge jobs and the social forces pressing their development show several key features of Japan's institutional structure. As a result of population aging and slow economic growth, all advanced countries have initiated policy reforms for curtailing financial burdens in maintaining public pensions. Different countries have adopted measures such as increasing the age at which public pension benefits become available, increasing the amount of public pension contributions (social security tax), reducing pension benefits, and postponing cost-of-living adjustments.

Although Japan has adopted measures of this type in preparation for baby boomers reaching the mandatory corporate retirement age of 60, the prolonged recession during the past two 'lost decades' has heightened worries about its ability to produce the output necessary to support the baby-boomer population. Demographic trends and economic performance have eroded the capacity to support life-long employment. These pressures have strained the key political relationship between government and large corporations. The bridge job law exists within this context.

By our estimate, the law covers roughly 64 percent of those aged 55–59 (or 87 percent of male workers). Large corporations have criticized the legislation and have publicly expressed their opposition to putting resources into keeping older workers. Policy-makers will have to find ways to induce cooperation if the law is to be effective. Toyota, for example, has re-employed 70 percent of its workers reaching the mandatory corporate retirement. With the new legislation, it has announced that it will consider a diverse menu of employment options, including the reduction of working hours for assembly jobs and the creation of new jobs such as grounds-keeping and office-clearing (*Asahi Shimbun* 2013).

Large corporations are already retaining excess workers on their payrolls. The government has been reluctant to allow layoffs of older workers because these would spike the 'official' unemployment rate. Higher unemployment increases social anxiety. Government officials prefer asking companies to give older workers make-work and providing subsides to companies to do so. Thus, Japan's official unemployment, which reached a peak of 5.4 percent in 2002, was 4.5 percent in 2012, a remarkably low rate compared to that of other advanced countries. However, when excess staffing and hidden in-house unemployment (*shanai shitsugyo*) is factored in, Japan's employment is believed to exceed 10 percent. In 2010, three million unemployed workers and at least five million excess workers were kept by companies in the labor force of 62 million. Thus, instead of the official unemployment rate of 4.8 percent in 2010, the real unemployment

The Japanese approach to bridge jobs 263

Table 13.4 Unemployment rate (%)

Country	Year							
	2000	2002	2004	2006	2008	2010	2011	2012
Japan	4.73	5.36	4.72	4.12	3.97	5.03	4.8	4.4
United States	3.97	5.78	5.54	4.61	5.80	9.63	9.0	8.1
Germany	8.00	8.70	10.52	10.19	7.60	7.06	6.0	5.5
France	9.08	8.91	9.26	9.24	7.82	9.73	9.8	10.3

Source: Japan Institute for Labor, Policy, and Training, *Databook of International Statistics 2012* (Online: www.jil.go.jp/kokunai/statistics/databook/2012/04/p139_t4-2.pdf).

Notes
Figures for 2011 and 2012 are from OECD, *Economics: Key tables from OECD*. ISSN 2074–384x (Online: www.oecd-ilibrary.org/economics/harmonised-unemployment-rates_2074384x-table6).

rate would have been 12.9 percent (Ikeda 2010). The Ministry of Finance in 2009 stated in its official publication that the number of redundant workers exceeded six million (Kyodo News 2009; Ministry of Economy, Trade, and Industry 2011). This point – that the Japanese official unemployment rate is misleading – has been known for some time. The Economic White Paper published in 1999 indicated that if the redundant staffing were laid off, the unemployment rate would rise from 3 to 8 percent in that year (see Table 13.4).

This chapter pointed to continuing challenges with Japan's old institutions predicated on economic growth and stability, lock-step hiring, and seniority-based promotion. Corporate job training and the education system have been geared to support life-long careers. But this expectation is clearly out of sync with the reality of global economic competition. The landscape of Japanese labor markets is stratified by employee status and company size along with the result of historical and recent accommodations between business and government. The accommodations involving bridge jobs promise to engender new developments in corporate re-employment. Interviews with corporate leaders and managers indicate that large companies may revise promotion systems and wage structures so that salaries would peak in the mid-forties instead of early fifties. They also would provide mid-career job training at earlier ages, leaving only the selected few for further promotions.

Japan's future depends on whether new growth industries will emerge and raise economic productivity. It is as much the weakness of the economy as the demographics that makes population aging a social problem. Without economic growth, available jobs will remain scarce, including bridge jobs for older workers.

References

Asahi Shimbun (2012) 'RUNESASU Keiei nan' (Financial troubles with RUNESASU), July 10. Online. Available at: www.asahi.com/business/update/0731/TKY2012073 10587.html?ref=reca (accessed May 12, 2013).

264 *C. Usui* et al.

Asahi Shimbun (2013) 'Toyota considering new re-employment arrangements', March 18. Online. Available at: www.asahi.com/business/update/0218/NGY2013021 80011. html (accessed May 12, 2013).

BBC News (2013) 'Samsung to buy 3 per cent stake in Japanese rival Sharp', March 6. Online. Available at: www.bbc.co.uk/news/business-21680996 (accessed May 2, 2013).

Brasor, P. (2013) 'No room for subtleties when laying off workers', *Japan Times*, January 26. Online. Available at: www.japantimes.co.jp/news/2013/01/26/national/no-room-for-subtleties-when-laying-off-workers (accessed April 20, 2013).

Cabinet Office of Japan (2012) *Annual Report on the Economic and Financial Conditions of Japan* [*Nenji keizai zaisei houkoku*], Tokyo: Cabinet Office. Online. Available at: www5.cao.go.jp/j-j/wp/wp-je11/h03_01.html (accessed April 15, 2013).

Department for Work and Pensions (2010) *Comparative Review of International Approaches to Mandatory Retirement*, Research Report 674, London: DWP.

Fuess, S.M. (2010) 'Job centers: Are finders keepers? A note from Japan', *Contemporary Economic Policy*, 28: 136–43.

Iida, Y. (2012) 'Older workers welcome variety of jobs after retirement', *Labor Research* [*Rodochosakai*]. Online. Available at: www.chosakai.co.jp/alacarte/a12-09.html (accessed March 15, 2013).

Ikeda, N. (2010) *Why Does Official Unemployment Rate Keep Increasing as Government Policy Tries to Protect Employment?*, President Online, May 31. Online. Available at: http://president.jp/articles/-/7020 (accessed March 15, 2013).

International Longevity Center Japan (2006) *Japan's Silver Human Resource Centers: Understanding an Increasingly Diverse Range of Work Available*. Online. Available at: http://longevity.ilcjapan.org/f_issues/0702.html (accessed May 7, 2013).

Japan Today (2013) *Looming Layoffs: Which Workers Are at Greatest Risks?*, January 25. Online. Available at: www.japantoday.com/category/kuchikomi/view/looming-layoffs-which-workers-are-at-the-greatest-risk (accessed May 5, 2013).

Kyodo News (2009) *In-house Unemployment (Redundant Workers) Exceeds 6 Million, According to the White Paper of Japanese Economy*, July 24. Online. Available at: www.47news.jp/CN/200907/CN2009072401000232.html (accessed March 6, 2013).

Matanle, P. and Matsui, K. (2011) 'Lifetime employment in 21st century Japan: Stability and resilience in the Japanese management system', in S.A. Horn (ed.) *Emerging Perspectives in Japanese Human Resource Management*, Berlin: Peter Lang.

Matus, D. (2002) 'Tough times for Japan's middle-aged workers as companies slash payrolls', Hawaii Business. Online. Available at: www.hawaiibusiness.com/Hawaii-Business/January-2002/Goodbye-Jobs-aHello-Worka (accessed February 5, 2013).

Ministry of Economy, Trade, and Industry (2011) *Sangyo kozo wo enkakuka suru odanteki shisaku no arikata* [*Policy considerations for restructuring Japanese economy*]. Online. Available at: www.meti.go.jp/committee/sankoushin/shinsangyou/003_03_00.pdf (accessed February 19, 2013).

Ministry of Health, Labor, and Welfare (2012a) *Employment Situation of Older Workers*, Table 5. Online. Available at: www.mhlw.go.jp/stf/houdou/2r9852000002m9lq-att/2r9852000002m9q6.pdf (accessed February 19, 2013).

Ministry of Health, Labor, and Welfare (2012b) Press Release, October 18.

Ministry of Health, Labor, and Welfare (2012c) *The Law Governing Employment Stabilization for Older Workers* [*Koreisha koyo antei ho*]. Online. Available at: www.mhlw. go.jp/seisakunitsuite/bunya/koyou_roudou/koyou/koureisha/topics/dl/tp0903-gaiyou. pdf (accessed February 19, 2013).

The Japanese approach to bridge jobs   265

Ministry of Health, Labor, and Welfare (2013, February 27) *Senior Employment with a Framework for Life-Long Social Participation: The First Conference*. Online. Available at: www.mhlw.go.jp/stf/shingi/2r9852000002y1u7.html (accessed January 27, 2014).

Nikkei shimbun (2012) 'Panasonic halving head office work force', May 29. Online. Available at: www.nikkei.com/article/DGXNASDD280RM_Y2A520C1MM 8000/?dg =1 (accessed April 1, 2013).

OECD (2011) *OECD Fact book 2011: Economic, Environmental and Social Statistics – Table Self Employment Rates*. Online. Available at: www.oecd-ilibrary.org/sites/ factbook-2011-en/07/01/04/index.html?contentType=&itemId=/content/chapter/ factbook-2011-61-en&containerItemId=/content/serial/18147364&accessItemIds=&mi meType=text/html (accessed April 1, 2013).

Recruit Work Institute (2012) *Koyo no genjou [Current Conditions of Employment]*. Online. Available at: www.works-i.com/?action=repository_uri&item_id...id (accessed April 14, 2013).

Reisinger, D. (2012) 'Panasonic eyes major layoffs at headquarters', CNET, March 29. Online. Available at: http://news.cnet.com/8301-1001_3-57442700-92/panasonic-eyes-major-layoffs-at-headquarters (accessed April 14, 2013).

Rosen, D. (2013) 'Reserving the window seat', 119 Hogaku Shimpo 165, March.

Wood, A., Robertson, M., and Wintersgill, D. (2010) *A Comparative Review of International Approaches to Mandatory Retirement*, Department for Work and Pensions, Research Report 674. Online. Available at: http://research.dwp.gov.uk/asd/asd5/ rports2009-2010/rrep674.pdf (accessed May 10, 2013).

Conclusions

14 Bridge employment

Lessons learned and future prospects for research and practice

Carlos-María Alcover, Gabriela Topa, Emma Parry, Franco Fraccaroli and Marco Depolo

Population aging is a reality that threatens both developed and developing societies in the medium to long term. The rising number of people making the transition to retirement in the coming decades will jeopardize the stability of pension systems and the welfare of the aged and, last but not least, it puts at risk the retention of the expertise of senior employees and transfer of their skills and knowledge needed for organizations to perform effectively.

Governments and society in the developed and developing countries have essayed a range of responses to these changes in the labor force and the challenges they bring in their wake. Chief among these have been measures designed to keep older workers in their jobs, to delay retirement and to promote gradual retirement (Kantarci and van Soest 2008; Peiró *et al.* 2013). Bridge employment has been one of the most widely used strategies to prolong working life over the last two decades (Cahill *et al.* 2013; Shultz 2003), taking different forms in different countries as explained in the preceding chapters.

The complex series of changes related with population aging has obliged social scientists and policy-makers progressively to reformulate notions of aging, work and careers (van der Heijden *et al.* 2008; Wang *et al.* 2012), resulting in the present heterogeneous array of retirement process concepts, including retirement planning, retirement decision-making, later retirement (i.e., bridge employment) and retirement adjustment and post-retirement activities, to name but a few (Crego *et al.* 2008; Wang 2013). In this regard, we might also mention other social and community-benefit activities carried out by old people, such as volunteering, care activities and unpaid socially productive activities among the aged (Siegrist and Wahrendorf 2009). As Cahill and colleagues (2005: 2) predicted several years ago, 'going forward, traditional retirements will be the exception rather the rule'. In our opinion, this prediction has already come true in many developed countries.

The variety and range of these experiences in turn have consequences for the health, quality of life, income and leisure activities of old people (Topa *et al.* 2014), the investigation and analysis of which has grown increasingly important given the political repercussions of decisions affecting the socio-economic status

270   C.-M. Alcover et al.

of the elderly, and pension and benefits systems (Brugiavini *et al.* 2002; French 2005; Hershey *et al.* 2010; Topa *et al.* 2011). The chapters of this book cast a spotlight on many of these changes.

In this concluding chapter, we weave together common themes from across the chapters in order to present an overview of the complex situation described above. We identify commonalities and differences in bridge employment patterns through the experiences of the countries mentioned in the international overview. Next, we deal with conceptual issues and the practical outcomes of bridge employment patterns in the different socio-economic realities and organizational and work contexts of the countries represented in this book. Finally, we offer an overview of future research and the practical implications of bridge employment for the coming years.

Bridge employment: commonalities and differences across countries

We began our analysis in two European countries with similar socio-economic characteristics, the Netherlands and Sweden, observing that the highest proportion of working people aged over 55 is to be found in Sweden. Compared to an average of 47 percent continued labor-market participation among the 60–64 age bracket in the EU-27, the rate in Sweden is almost 70 percent. Meanwhile, closer examination of those citizens who continue to work beyond the normal retirement age reveals certain common traits. Most of them are well-educated and they tend to affirm that they continue to work because they find it interesting and motivating. In this light, it may be supposed that these people earn above-average salaries and that they will also enjoy generous pensions. Consequently, financial motives are not the main reason why people continue to work. While the people who continue in paid work between the ages of 60 and 70 are more likely to have a high socio-economic status in most European countries (Komp *et al.* 2010), the data confirm that Sweden has the highest rate among women (35.3 percent) and the second highest among men (42.3 percent), behind only Switzerland (51.7 percent).

Despite this bright outlook, barriers to bridge employment also exist in Sweden. These include the difficulty of finding appropriate jobs, which can push some workers into retirement before they would actually wish. Discrimination against older workers also makes itself felt in Sweden. These attitudes on the part of employers, who view older workers as lacking adequate skills for the work they are asked to perform, can make the elderly victims of a form of downsizing that meets with scant resistance either among the trade unions or employees as a whole. In this light, numerous empirical studies have underscored the need for HR management procedures that are more sensitive toward the issue of employee age.

The chapter on the Netherlands by Henkens and van Solinge paints a similar picture. A key feature of the current situation is the way in which systems based on legislation and tax incentives for employers to encourage early retirement

Lessons learned and future prospects 271

among numerous groups of workers are now being rolled back. Early retirement schemes of this kind have now begun to shift toward later retirement proposals, resulting in a change in the share of the labor market represented by people aged over 55 and a progressive rise in the average age of retirement. Nevertheless, other data still show that early retirement incentives are generous for workers between 60 and 62 years of age (Schils 2008). In the Dutch case, 17 percent of men and 10.3 percent of women aged between 60 and 70 remain in paid employment, most of them in some form of bridge employment (Komp *et al.* 2010). These rates are significantly lower than in other countries in the same socioeconomic bracket as the Netherlands, like Denmark (see van Oorschot and Jensen 2009 for a comparative analysis), Germany and Sweden, although they are significantly higher than in France, which has the lowest average rates in Europe at 5.4 percent labor-market participation among men and 7.3 percent among women, or neighboring Belgium with rates of 10.6 percent and 5 percent respectively (Komp *et al.* 2010).

It is precisely with Belgium that the next chapter deals. Its authors begin by noting that less than 2 percent of Belgians over the age of 65 continue in work. This very low rate continues despite efforts by the authorities to raise the rate of activity among the elderly through measures like restrictions on early retirement, support for active aging strategies, promotion of age diversity and recognition of older people's right to work.

Despite these measures, age discrimination continues to be found in Belgium, taking similar forms to the prejudice described by the authors of the chapter on Sweden. However, the impact is greater in Belgium, as labor-market participation in Sweden is above the European average. The age considered 'on time' for retirement is 65 years, so that workers taking early retirement, or who are or become unemployed at the age of 55 or more, are seen as outside the labor market.

In short, the picture in Belgium reveals that waning support for early retirement may have led to an increase in other forms of premature labor-market exit, although it has not necessarily led to any expansion of bridge employment alternatives. The result is that the activity rate among the elderly remains low in comparison both with neighboring countries and with the EU-27 average.

The situation described in Poland is hardly more encouraging, although the country's peculiarities as an ex-Communist nation with a relatively short period of integration in the market economy need to be recognized. The context described by the author features very low rates of employment among old people. Among other reasons, this is due to the inflexibility of the labor market and to the generous benefits offered to workers taking early retirement. Taking both of these factors together, it is not hard to understand that Polish workers are generally keen to escape from job insecurity and take refuge in early retirement. In short, there is still little prospect of older workers seeking to extend their working lives in Poland, a situation that is without doubt attributable to the economic conditions inherited after decades of Communist rule, not to mention more recent policy decisions.

272 C.-M. Alcover et al.

In southern Europe, Spain is a representative example of the general situation in the Mediterranean nations, where a range of factors now threaten the viability of the public pension system. In the first place, the dependency rate is forecast to rise sharply over the next decade, while unemployment has grown to alarming levels. In the second, the rate of labor-market participation by people aged over 55 is low compared to the average for the EU-27, in part because of policies and practices favoring early retirement over the last two decades. In fact, only 18.9 percent of men and just 8 percent of women aged between 60 and 70 are in paid work in Spain, less even than in Greece (26.1 percent and 8.5 percent, respectively) (Komp et al. 2010). In addition, the public pension system is both generous and, until very recently, made it almost impossible to draw a pension and engage simultaneously in paid work, so that the development of bridge employment could hardly offer a more discouraging picture. However, recent government measures to foster later labor-market exit and the results obtained in the Spanish sub-sample of the SHARE survey (Topa et al. 2014) and from the SECOT case study offer a more nuanced view, suggesting that the outlook has begun to change.

In line with general EU trends, especially in northern Europe, the United Kingdom has shifted from high rates of early retirement in recent decades to an increase in the number of people remaining in work beyond the age of 65. This phenomenon may be observed both in part-time and full-time work, and among people returning to the labor market after retirement. In view of the data, the authors of the chapter on the United Kingdom see the identification of barriers and factors supporting longer working lives among old people as a key issue.

Based on the studies carried out, the authors conclude that bridge employment constitutes a transition for British workers to a new stage of their careers in which they expect to continue with their personal development while contributing to society and adding value. These perceptions indicate a clear change in the meaning of retirement as a gradual process and not a cliff-edge end to working life, and they are similar to views found also in the United States, Canada, Sweden, the Netherlands and Australia.

Italy is another representative example of the general situation in the Southern European countries, where a combination of demographic factors and labor-market trends emphasize the salience of aging processes and generational imbalances, with possible effects on the financial sustainability of the pensions system and on the possibility to maintain current employment levels. Thus, the rate for people aged between 55 and 64 in Italy was around 40 percent in 2012.

The three main socio-economic and cultural factors explaining this worrying delay are, first, low labor-market participation by women (the female employment rate in Italy was 47.2 percent, compared with the EU-27 rate of 58.6 percent); second, the older Italian population has an education level below the corresponding European average; and third, the high prevalence of the early retirement policies adopted in the past 20 years (the average effective age of retirement in Italy in the period 2006–2011 was 59.2 years for women and 60.8 for men, despite the retrenchment of early retirement policies and the introduction of measures to raise the pensionable age carried out in recent years).

Lessons learned and future prospects 273

Italy does not have at present specific legislation on bridge employment, and labor laws tend to make it difficult to get the flexibility intrinsically required by bridge employment systems. For instance, data from SHARE show that 67.4 percent of Italian workers moved directly into retirement and 4.8 percent moved to a bridge job, compared to 51.26 and 11.2 percent respectively in the case of German workers (Brunello and Langella 2012). However, the authors show that some forms of pre- and post-retirement adjustments, managed on informal bases or through individual relations, do exist in the Italian labor market.

Among the EU-27, Germany is the paradigmatic model for the development of policies related with employment among older people. In the 1970s, early retirement was increasingly used in corporate restructuring processes and to provide an exit for large numbers of workers to leave the labor market, leaving jobs free for younger job-seekers. Meanwhile the Partial Retirement Act, which was widely applied between 1996 and 2009, allowed workers aged over the age of 55 to reduce their working hours over a period of ten years. The related costs were initially borne by the employer, but were reimbursed by the state if the vacant post was taken by an unemployed youngster. In practice, however, a high percentage of these workers left off working and took early retirement, and a true bridge employment culture failed to develop in Germany, as may be observed from the fact that only 22 percent of men and 13 percent of women in the 60–70 age bracket are in paid employment (Komp *et al.* 2010). This trend is now coming under strong pressure as a result of recent changes in government policy intended to raise the retirement age among older workers in order to reduce the burden on the social benefits system.

These chapters on eight European countries provide an overview of labor-market participation by older workers, bridge employment and the prolongation of working life, and may be considered representative of the diversity existing in this area and of more local socio-economic conditions, legislation and geographical factors. The quantitative and qualitative data used in the in-depth analyses of all eight countries are essentially the same as used by Brunello and Langella (2012) in their recent statistical analysis based on data from the Survey on Health, Ageing and Retirement (SHARE). These researchers found that 10.54 percent of the sample of European males aged 55–70 from 15 countries have moved from a career to a bridge job on their way to (eventual) retirement and 37.4 percent have moved directly from a career job to full retirement. The remaining 52 percent were still in their original occupations. They also found that traditional patterns of retirement (i.e., moving from a career job to permanent withdrawal from the workforce) are still more prevalent in Mediterranean Europe (Italy, France and Spain) than in Northern and Central Europe (Germany, Austria, Switzerland, the Netherlands, Belgium, Denmark and Sweden). Overall, these rates suggest that the transition from a career or full-time job to a bridge job is much less frequent in Continental Europe than in either the United States or Japan (Brunello and Langella 2012), a conclusion that coincides with the data included in the European chapters of this book.

The second part of the book examines the situation in North America (United States and Canada). To begin with, the United States offers the clearest picture

274   C.-M. Alcover et al.

of bridge employment. Cross-sectional and longitudinal studies show that around half of Americans above the age of 50 claim to have had at least one work experience after retirement from their full-time career job. Approximately 20 percent of these people have taken full-time jobs. Furthermore, workers' expectations accord with this reality, insofar as they themselves expect or wish to engage in paid work beyond the age of 65. The firm foundations of this form of labor market exit in the United States is reflected not only in the numbers concerned but also in the variety of bridge jobs, a situation encouraged by highly flexible legislation.

Neighboring Canada shifted progressively away from policies and organizational practices to downsize and cut costs by offering massive early retirement to aging employees, more prevalent in the period between 1990 and 1997 (see also Saba and Guerin 2005). Earlier policies in support of early retirement had resulted in a progressive fall in the retirement age, but a subsequent policy shift in favor of phased retirement has again raised the rate of labor-market participation among the group aged over 55 years to 34 percent. These changes reflect a consolidation of the upward trend in the employment rate among older workers, although this trend will require continued support in Canada and Quebec, for example by means of legislation to make it easier to work and draw a pension, and programs to improve older workers' access to training and education in order to keep their skills up to date.

The third part of the book deals with two countries in the Asia-Pacific region, Australia and Japan, each of which has its own very different socio-economic context and culture. To begin with Australia, the panorama is peculiar, indeed paradoxical. On the one hand, unemployment is very low and workers are urgently needed in some professions and jobs, resulting in the reorientation of measures fostering early retirement toward the employability of old people. However, 54 percent of women and 38 percent of men aged over 55 were partially retired according to 2007 data. The authors' analysis of this apparent contradiction throws some light on the conceptualization of bridge employment, as we shall explain in the next section of this chapter.

The situation of bridge employment in Japan is also paradoxical, although for different reasons than Australia. The contradiction here is based on the collision of two realities. On the one hand, workers aged over 60 encounter increasing difficulties holding on to their jobs, because employers tend to push them to retire in order to gain job-market flexibility, while on the other, government policy imposes a minimum age of 65 years for workers to draw their pensions. Bridge employment provides an alternative that resolves the conflict between these needs. In fact, the percentage of old workers in Japan is one of the highest among all of the developed countries. The authors of this chapter offer a suggestive analysis, which we discuss in the next section.

In light of this brief overview of the conclusions reached by the contributing authors with regard to the existence and development of bridge employment, differences between the countries analyzed affect both the availability of jobs for older workers and the policies implemented by governments, as well as the fit of new employment practices with the predominant values in each national culture.

Lessons learned and future prospects   275

Despite this diversity, all of the analyses appear to concur in pointing to a need for the progressive application of policies to foster the continuation of working life beyond the age of 65. Furthermore, the different authors also propose a range of theoretical reflections to improve our understanding of the bridge employment phenomenon. The next section focuses on these issues.

Conceptual issues and practical outcomes from bridge employment experiences

The contributions made by Henkens and van Solinge to the understanding of bridge employment are based on a longitudinal study of workers aged over 50 in the Netherlands carried out over a period of ten years beginning in 2001. The participants' responses to the survey depict a panorama in which bridge employment emerges as a widespread practice taking a variety of forms, given that almost one-third of retired people participate in the labor market in one way or another. Some of them do so as a means of making a gradual transition to full retirement, but many conserve strong links with the world of work beyond the age of 65. The most frequent form of bridge employment is part-time working, involving either a shorter working day or a shorter week. This flexibility is also applied to contractual relations and to the financial remuneration received by these workers. Contrary to what might be expected, it is not only the better educated and the physically fit who opt for bridge employment but also workers with more limited training and skills, who participate by changing the kind of jobs they do, adopting the *non-career* bridge employment formula or bridge employment in a different field (Wang *et al.* 2008; Zhan *et al.* 2013).

When asked about their reasons for continuing to work, the majority of the better-qualified elderly workers in the Netherlands tend to explain that they enjoy it, although smaller percentages also mention financial motives and their desire to maintain social contacts. In general, physical health is a factor that differentiates those retirees who continue in some form of work for financial reasons from those who do not mention money as the main reason for taking a bridge job.

Based on their own studies and surveys carried out at the national level, Isaksson, Johansson and Palm have confirmed the importance of social relationships at work and the need for personal autonomy as key factors in bridge employment among older workers in Sweden. At the same time, they observe that the intention to retire or to continue working among men and women appears to be affected to differing degrees by psychosocial and health factors. Based on data collected in their own qualitative studies, these authors provide detailed information about the perceptions of workers aged over 60 who continue in employment. The majority of them prefer *career-based* or *organization-based* bridge employment (following the typology proposed by Zhan *et al.* 2013), even when it involves a reduction in working hours or a significant change in the tasks performed. According to the authors, the difficulty of finding a new job in a different firm or business is one of the key reasons for this preference.

276　C.-M. Alcover et al.

People in Sweden receive detailed information on their estimated future pension entitlements annually, and financial planning for retirement is considered a matter of great importance. In this light, the general agreement among survey respondents that the justification for bridge employment goes beyond merely financial reasons is particularly important. The conclusion, then, is that older Swedish workers tend to value other psychological and psychosocial benefits of bridge employment above and beyond strictly financial rewards.

The contribution made from Belgium by Desmette and Vendramin to our understanding of bridge employment is based on the data on workers above the age of 50 collected in EWCS, 2010. The key concept throwing light on bridge employment is the perceived sustainability of work, as defined by the authors. Participants perceived low sustainability where they detected high pressure at work, scant autonomy and limited prospects for career progress. Younger workers also perceived negative health impacts from work, although this image changed among older workers. The work–life balance is perceived as a key component of sustainability, materializing in shorter working hours for many workers aged from 50 to 55 years. In the authors' judgment, these preferences suggest a path to increase the rate of active aging.

Despite the conceptual relevance of this reflection, however, the reality in Belgium also indicates that negative stereotypes of older workers may be a first step toward early retirement or inhibit acceptance of a bridge job. Where measures to ensure preferential treatment of older workers are implemented, they are perceived as less competent by other groups, including potential employers and colleagues. This reveals the existence of a gap between policy or recommended practice and cultural values or social representations. While the former seek to prolong working life, the latter discourage any such extension.

These contradictions had in fact already been noted in earlier studies. They arise because of the survival of long-standing moral structures that seek to strengthen intergenerational relations and exchanges at work and recognize the legitimacy of age differences, at the same time as a burgeoning 'new capitalism' attempts to maximize the efficiency of individual human resources (Roberts 2006). The prestige of 'youth' and the values associated with it (efficiency, innovation, high skill, creativity, flexibility) may unconsciously conflict with the (negative) category of 'old' rather than joining forces with the (positive) category 'mature'. This conflict manifests itself not only among the members of the exogroup (the 'young') but also among those of the endogroup (the 'old'), as shown in a recent study by Bustillos *et al.* (2012). A recent meta-analysis (Bal *et al.* 2011) has confirmed Posthuma's and Campion's (2009) claims regarding the multidimensional and varied nature of perceptions held about older workers, and the complex mix of positive and negative views about them. These perceptions may in turn influence the goals and motivation related to work among older employees (Kanfer *et al.* 2013; Kooij *et al.* 2011; Weiss and Lang 2012), as well as attitudes toward work (Desmette and Gaillard 2008) and the decision whether to continue or to retire.

Zientara's reflections on the situation in Poland corroborate the reality of the negative stereotype. Many Polish employers believe it is easier to instill the

Lessons learned and future prospects 277

values of the market economy into the younger generation than it is to re-educate older people who have spent most of their lives living under a Communist economy associated with less competitive, dynamic and innovative values. The existence of these social representations creates a structural disadvantage for older workers, becoming a special, more subtle form of age discrimination that hinders the implementation and use of bridge employment in its different forms and aggravates the effects of the ageist stereotypes found in other EU countries, described in the chapters of this book.

Analysis of bridge employment in Poland using qualitative methods shows that gradual transitions from work to retirement are extremely rare. Furthermore, most interviewees were strikingly unwilling even to consider the possibility. These data may be a reflection of negative earlier work experiences, resulting in feelings of tedium and fatigue, which would only add to the satisfaction of drawing a pension. These conclusions agree with findings from ten other European countries included in the SHARE study, which show that poor-quality work experiences of aged workers are significantly associated with poor health, lower well-being and intended early retirement (Siegrist *et al.* 2006; Westerlund *et al.* 2009). In this regard, Poland seems to have a long road ahead, both to improve HR practices and to align policy with the needs of the labor market and twenty-first-century society.

In Spain, Alcover and Topa observe that the concept of bridge employment has yet to find its place in the legislation. Though certain Spanish practices may be considered in some ways analogous, it is nevertheless the case that bridge employment has not so far been addressed conceptually and no measures have been designed or implemented either in the labor market or in organizational policy. However, the authors provide both quantitative data from the SHARE study and case-study data based on the SECOT experience. Despite the very small size of the Spanish sub-sample used in SHARE, it is sufficient for the authors to show the importance of bridge job quality as a predictor of desirable outcomes like life and job satisfaction. Meanwhile, analysis of the case study underscores the direct, positive impact of involvement by seniors in business mentoring activities on improvements in the participants' psychosocial quality of life. In short, the very limited data available show that bridge employment experiences, though still few and far between, can reduce the negative psychosocial outcomes associated with abrupt labor-market exit by older workers and offer a useful tool to help meet the challenges posed by the rapid aging of Spain's population and the sustainability of pensions and welfare systems.

From the United Kingdom, Parry and Bown Wilson explore barriers to and supporting factors for bridge employment experiences using a database of interviews with diverse cohorts of workers and surveys of a broader sample. The main barriers include a lack of jobs for senior roles and scant support from immediate supervisors, in some cases revealing the existence of a 'youth' culture within organizations, which offer few career opportunities for old people. These findings concur with the analysis performed in the UK context by Roberts (2006). The evidence confirms the panorama of unfavorable stereotyping against

278   C.-M. Alcover et al.

older workers already noted in other chapters. Key factors to support involvement in bridge employment include a need for career transition role models and external support for older workers in organizations.

In their examination of the reasons why older managers may wish to continue working, the British authors describe experiences designed to change workers' priorities, so that subjective matters become more important than money or promotion. Several of the participants in these schemes also expressed concern about the threatened loss of identity associated with full retirement from the world of work. This reveals the importance for employers of seeking alternative rewards that meet the specific needs of these workers.

In their analysis of the situation in Italy, Depolo and Fraccaroli find that this Mediterranean country does not have at present real and specific legislation on bridge employment, and labor laws tend to make it difficult to get the flexibility intrinsically required by bridge employment modalities. The authors identify and document some informal experiences of pre- and post-retirement adjustment strategies, in which public and private companies and senior workers association are involved.

In general, they support the adaptation posited by Olini (2012) to the Italian situation of the general principles suggested by the European Union to make senior workers better able to cope with the challenge of satisfactorily managing the final stage of their careers in times of crisis: support and update skills, strengthen the culture of learning in the workplace, maintain work opportunities for seniors, increase support for senior jobseekers and reduce the gap in the labor cost between younger and older workers.

Depolo and Fraccaroli conclude that it is difficult to find a consistent exit strategy for Italy similar to those of other countries where bridge employment policies have been implemented. It appears that, apart from the strong governmental intervention on pensions (which has given rise to longer working time before retirement), no institutional and systematic set of interventions is likely to be found and applied. It seems more likely that partial – or at least one-dimensional – approaches and interventions will be the unwritten rule. Indeed, if these informal and ad hoc interventions allow positive outcomes for older workers and organizations, they will always be welcome, while waiting for an (unlikely) articulated frame of reference on bridge employment.

Deller's and Pundt's contribution to our understanding of bridge employment in their chapter on the German context is based on the qualitative findings obtained in the course of interviews with retirees who continued to do paid work of some kind. Among other matters, the results of this study show a high level of career bridge employment, in particular because the tasks involved and contacts made in earlier phases of the participants' careers had a powerful influence on work experiences after the age of 65. The participants stressed the need to design specific HR management policies for older workers in order to foster the emergence of more friendly job designs that were better suited to their needs. In this regard, the data concurred with other studies that suggest that the working environment in Germany does not encourage older workers to continue in

Lessons learned and future prospects 279

employment, mainly because they have only limited access to training and the system of labor relations remains inflexible (Schils 2008). Meanwhile, the need for recognition and acknowledgment again emerges as a key motivation to continue working, concurring with the reflections included in the chapters on Sweden, the United Kingdom and the Netherlands.

From the United States comes clear support for the idea that bridge employment will be one of the key tools to support the financial well-being of old people. Furthermore, empirical findings stress that bridge employment contributes to achieving a good adjustment between the individual and the psychosocial environment over the course of the aging process, replacing an abrupt transition and favoring the continuity of lifestyles, and preventing any abrupt decline in health, well-being or life satisfaction. As a recent study of post-retirement employment trends over the last 33 years (1977–2009) has shown, however, it is not only changes at the organizational and individual levels that have influenced older workers' decisions to continue working or not, but also shifting demographic and economic forces at the macro level, which provide a counterweight to micro-level transformations (Pleau and Shauman 2013).

Wang, Penn, Bertone and Stefanova underline the advantages of bridge employment not only for individuals but also for society as a whole. Given the current Social Security system in the United States, the longer people remain in the labor market, the more they will contribute to economic growth and the less time they will spend living off the savings accumulated in the pension system.

Meanwhile, Saba provides data on the growth of bridge employment in Canada and Quebec based on studies involving participants between the ages of 50 and 69. The cross-sectional studies show an increase in this form of labor-market participation, mainly as a result of the individual choices of older workers. As in the case of the European countries (Komp *et al.* 2010), the best-qualified, highest-paid employees, who will also be the recipients of the most generous pensions, are precisely those who are keenest to seek labor-market re-entry through bridge employment after retirement. This once again indicates that financial needs are not the main motivating factor, as we have already seen in the discussion of the countries of northern Europe. Despite the progressive spread of these practices, however, the author points to the need to distinguish clearly between bridge employment, which in Canada and Quebec seems to remain an individual choice or a one-off agreement between employer and worker, and the necessary implementation of broader policies designed to promote active aging through involvement in work. These policies will require careful assessment of individual motives and abilities, organizational cultures, demographics and labor-market conditions.

The study of the Australian context provided by Taylor, McLoughlin and Earl is based on evidence obtained from the managers of the country's leading firms, taking the organization as the basic analytic unit to identify policies to respond to the challenge of population aging.

Percentage adoption rates for partial adoption vary widely depending on the industry concerned. In this light, the authors argue that different perceptions

280   C.-M. Alcover et al.

exist with regard to older workers. On the one hand, certain industries see themselves as offering 'young men's work', given the physical demands of the job, and are very unwilling to employ older people. On the other hand, the adoption of partial retirement strategies is fairly common in activities that require high levels of education and skills, like teaching and professional services.

Nevertheless, the authors caution against a superficial analysis of their data. When information about firms with partial employment policies is combined with data on those that encourage their employees to opt for early retirement, it turns out that many of them are in fact the same. In short, the picture painted by the Australian data is apparently optimistic, but a closer look at the data reveals that partial retirement is used at least sometimes as a strategy to leverage full early retirement and not as a mechanism to prolong the working lives of older employees.

Finally, the analysis of the reality in Japan offered by Usui, Colignon and Rosen reflects certain peculiarities proper to the situation of the country and suggests some very interesting reflections on the nature of bridge employment. In the first place, large concerns have employed a different strategy to small and medium-sized enterprises in the face of legislative changes. Where large firms have so far been unwilling to hold on to older workers, smaller businesses continue to employ around 34 percent of such people. The authors see this segmentation as illustrating the stratification of the labor market, which is structured around employment status. Those who have built their careers as regular employees enjoy greater security through to retirement, while those who do not achieve this status will not attain it in their old age either. Even so, large firms are still obliged to retain numbers of surplus workers given the government's refusal to authorize mass redundancies, which would have a negative impact on society as a whole by driving up unemployment. In short, the outlook is far from promising in Japan, because the number of available jobs will shrink unless the economy begins to grow, and this constraint also applies to bridge employment. To some extent, then, we may conclude that bridge jobs are subject to the same forces and pressures as any other jobs in a given society at a given time.

Directions for future research and practical implications of bridge employment

Interest in policies and practices related with the prolongation of working life and the continuation of old people in some form of paid work or self-employment, and the importance attached to such measures at the individual, organizational, economic and social levels, are a response to the challenges facing society in the majority of developed and developing countries. Recent studies carried out in countries all over the world have examined the prevalence and effect of policies and practices designed to encourage *late careers* (e.g., Engelhardt 2012), *post-retirement employment* (e.g., Pleau and Shauman 2013), *gradual retirement* (e.g., Kantarci and van Soest 2008), *working longer* (e.g., Munnell and Sass 2008) and *labor-force re-entry* (e.g., Cahill *et al.* 2011;

Lessons learned and future prospects 281

Maestas 2010). While their findings reflect relative disparities in policy measures and the prevalence of such practices depending on the countries and contexts analyzed, the goals they pursue coincide with those we have identified through the contributions made in this book.

The principal objectives targeted by the different forms of bridge employment may be summarized as follows:

1 to address population aging and the need to extend active life in line with the increase in actual life expectancy;
2 to underpin the viability of pension and social benefits systems;
3 to maintain the quality of life, health and welfare of older people before, during and after retirement processes;
4 to retain highly skilled workers in organizations and benefit from the implicit knowledge they possess;
5 to ensure the transmission of knowledge and intergenerational relations and succession;
6 to balance life-cycle stages through phases combining different degrees of productive activity in line with the nature of work and early twenty-first-century society.

As may be observed, the objectives identified emerge at different levels of analysis, a fact that suggests an initial direction for future research. Investigation of the predictors, effects and consequences of bridge employment must take a multi-level and interdisciplinary approach, allowing integration of the diversity of variables and processes involved in the manner indicated by scholars researching the retirement planning, retirement transition and retirement adjustment frameworks (e.g., Adams and Rau 2011; Beehr and Bennett 2007; Hesketh *et al.* 2011; Noone *et al.* 2009; Wang 2007; Wang and Shultz 2010; Wong and Earl 2009).

Meanwhile, the available data do not so far allow any precise evaluation of the extent to which goals have been achieved, and time-series data and longitudinal studies are needed to assess the medium- and long-term effects of bridge employment at the different levels of analysis, and to relate outcomes with the background to and predictors of workers' actual decisions. National and international surveys provide useful data, but we believe it will be necessary to perform specific studies and research projects to triangulate individual, organizational, economic and social factors accurately while taking account of differences between careers and occupations. In this regard, we concur that the dynamic nature of bridge employment needs to be addressed in detail as proposed by Wang and Shultz (2010: 197), who emphasize that 'bridge employment is a longitudinal workforce participation process between one's retirement decision and entering full retirement'. This research standpoint appears ever more necessary given that bridge employment processes involve a range of people, beginning with those who are younger than 60 years of age and ending with those who are over 70. Consequently, bridge employment cannot be viewed

282 C.-M. Alcover et al.

as a single event or a one-time decision-making concept, but must be addressed as a medium- to long-term period in the latter stages of a worker's career, which may itself include different phases (salaried bridge jobs in more than one organization, different work arrangements over the years, bridge self-employment and so forth) occurring over a number of years.

The contributions to this book are drawn from very different geographical, employment and socio-economic contexts, a fact that allows us to identify some gaps in our understanding of the bridge employment phenomenon.

In the first place, policies that set a minimum retirement age seem not to produce the same outcomes in all countries. Given the specificity of socio-economic problems in each region, postponement of the official or statutory retirement age may have different effects in different societies, and the effects of such measures are certainly not linear or easily foreseeable. While they do lighten the cost burden in the social security system, they can also increase unemployment rates among other age groups because it takes longer for vacancies to open up for young people.

Second, the panoramas depicted in the different chapters differ widely depending on variables such as the health of the workers participating in surveys. This is particularly clear in the chapter on the United Kingdom. While the fit and healthy are keen to carry on working, respondents suffering from ill health would generally prefer to shorten their professional lives as much as possible. However, findings on the relations between partial or full retirement and health are contradictory (Coe and Zamarro 2011), revealing both positive and negative impacts. For example, those who labor in poor working conditions, under high levels of stress or who perceive their health as poor will tend to retire, whether fully or partially, as soon as they can, and it is probable that their health will actually improve after retirement (Neuman 2008; van den Berg *et al.* 2010). In contrast, workers who enjoy low levels of stress and perceive their health as good tend to prolong their working lives, either full-time or part-time, and to stay healthy (Liu *et al.* 2009). If they retire early, however, whether voluntarily or involuntarily, their health may suffer negative impacts, as occupational activity benefits older people, at least as regards cognitive functioning (Mazzonna and Peracchi 2012; Rohwedder and Willis 2010) and mental health in men (Butterworth *et al.* 2006). Meanwhile, other studies showed that retirement has a significantly positive impact on self-reported health measures, but no impact on objective health measures, at least in the short-run (Johnston and Lee 2009). This leads us to a matter that has been confirmed in other contexts (Topa *et al.* 2011), which is that relations between health and retirement are not linear, and the two influence each other before, during and after labor-market exit. Furthermore, the reciprocal relations between work and retirement differ widely between countries.

In the third place, future research should address the specifics of the solutions proposed to deal with population aging, an emerging problem now facing the majority of the developed and developing nations. Any solutions therefore need to be analyzed from a local perspective, as the proposed forms of bridge employment must fit the immediate context (Topa *et al.* 2014). In any event, the

Lessons learned and future prospects   283

evidence provided in the chapters of this book calls for some degree of caution to avoid excessive optimism in the interpretation of local solutions, even where outcomes appear very positive, because even successful initiatives may fail if transplanted to another country without due consideration of the original context.

Fourth, future research needs to go deeper into the background and predictors of different forms of bridge employment, examining the factors involved at different analytic levels (Gobeski and Beehr 2009; von Bonsdorff *et al.* 2009; Wang *et al.* 2008). Studies of this kind should be based on existing theories of retirement if these provide a valid explanation of decisions in this area. Otherwise, researchers could formulate specific explanatory models and theories, contributing in this way to our understanding of what are highly complex processes (Zhan *et al.* 2013) involving numerous variables producing multiple interactive and iterative effects.

Fifth and finally, future research should seek to standardize data on different countries, correcting a situation in which there is no agreement on where bridge jobs should be considered in official labor-market statistics, for example. In this regard, we would recommend that researchers should propose precise, internationally useable definitions of the different types of bridge employment, or at least definitions that would allow academics and practitioners to distinguish between particular formats. It would likewise be useful to continue to make progress toward a more refined operationalization of the different forms of bridge employment (Kim and Feldman 2000).

The main practical implications of bridge employment according to the different chapters of this book, and based on our own analysis, are discussed below in relation to the six objectives enumerated at the beginning of this section.

In the first place, bridge employment in all its different forms facilitates the implementation of policies and practices designed to foster active aging (James *et al.* 2010; European Union 2012), eventually enhancing quality of life among the elderly, as well as perceived and general health (Ilmarinen 2006; Maltby 2011).

Second, bridge employment policies help people over the age of 55 to remain in full- or part-time work beyond the usual or statutory retirement age, which may be enhanced by the introduction of permanent benefit reductions for early retirees, as already been implemented, for instance, in Germany (Hanel 2010). As a consequence, aged workers are able to contribute for several more years to public benefits systems, underpinning the viability of public pensions arrangements, and at the same time they may contribute to private retirement schemes to a varying degree depending on the institutional context in each country and the health and family or personal circumstances of each individual. This requires a wide-ranging debate involving government, political parties, trade unions, employers' organizations and other social agents (Phillipson 2013) with the aim of assuring secure jobs for older workers who decide to continue in employment and secure retirement conditions (Hank and Erlinghagen 2011) to prevent rising insecurity and risk for the elderly at the end of their lives.

284   C.-M. Alcover et al.

In the third place, bridge employment alternatives can allow workers and organizations to negotiate flexible, individual formulae to suit the personal characteristics of each employee with a view to the continuation of working life. As Templer and colleagues have recently pointed out, 'to promote the retention of older workers, policies, practices and programs should be customized to the different needs of career, bridge and self-employed individuals' (Templer *et al.* 2010: 479). Although it has not been conclusively shown that work, partial and full retirement and health are positively related, as explained above, it would seem that a good fit between working conditions, individual traits, the level of activities and the continuation of working life may be beneficial for the general health and well-being of old people. In this regard, bridge employment offers considerable advantages given the ability of the formula to adapt to gender differences affecting the transition to retirement, in particular in the case of women, whose career, family circumstances and life histories often have little to do with the traditional male model of continued full-time work (Everingham *et al.* 2007). The different forms of bridge employment, then, offer flexibility in the final stages of working life and at the beginning of retirement to suit the profiles of different groups of women, taking into consideration the possibility that many of their decisions are not the result of an individual process (Loretto and Vickerstaff 2013) but are made in a wider domestic and family context. In sum, organizations will need to consider the different work-related variables in addressing attrition and turnover challenges and formulating human resource forecasts and specific strategies for increasing the retention of older workers (Shacklock *et al.* 2009), and not only take into account gender differences but also differences among retired career – i.e., managerial or professional – women (Armstrong-Stassen and Staats 2012).

A fourth practical implication of bridge employment is its facilitating role in the retention of the most experienced human capital, consisting of people with extensive implicit knowledge and highly developed skills and abilities, whose immediate replacement by a younger worker is not always an easy or smooth process. Workers leaving their jobs merely because they have reached a given age represent a sudden loss of human and social capital for organizations, which can entail financial loss and/or adverse business outcomes, and can even jeopardize the continuity of small and medium-sized enterprises and family firms. Where organizations are able to offer attractive conditions (Rau and Adams 2005) and create specific motivational systems (Claes and Heymans 2008), bridge employment can contribute significantly to the retention of a knowledgeable older workforce, instead of contingent workers (Saba and Guerin 2005), or the return of retirees.

In the fifth place, the continuation of older people in work may underpin the intergenerational handover, facilitating processes of socialization, education and training among the young, not to mention succession processes affecting top management posts discharged by senior employees. All of this can be structured through internal monitoring and coaching programs implemented either formally or informally by organizations, allowing them to create fluid, flexible knowledge-sharing and knowledge-management systems.

Lessons learned and future prospects 285

Bridge employment can also help align people's life-cycle traits with the context and conditions of life today. This is a key practical implication, replacing the model of clearly defined, compartmentalized 'stages' or 'periods' by a new model that favors the ideas of 'process' and 'transition' through the life experience of each individual based on changes in the conditions of his or her life (Elder and Johnson 2003; Peterson and Murphy, 2010; Shultz and Wang 2011). In our opinion, it is necessary to rebalance the stages of active employment and retirement on a more realistic basis given the significant, and ongoing, increase in the life expectancy of people in the majority of developed and developing countries, especially if the aim is to ensure that elderly people are able to maintain similar living standards to those that they enjoyed in the course of their professional lives. However, bridge employment and the extension of working life cannot be made into a panacea to fix the shortfall in retirement income (Cahill *et al*. 2013), and nor should it be presented as an 'obligation' for all older workers, given the need to consider state of health, occupation, family situation and other personal and social factors that might make it inadvisable for an individual to continue working beyond a given age.

One last practical implication concerns the opportunities for self-employment that bridge employment may offer. Self-employment offers real psychosocial advantages that are very much valued by older workers, such as independence and flexible working hours (Giandrea *et al*. 2008a). Furthermore, it is likely that people above the age of 60 who are strongly driven by achievement and independence will actually commit more strongly to self-employment options than to wage-and-salary bridge jobs (Kerr and Armstrong-Stassen 2011). These options have positive consequences for political leaders, as they allow older workers to continue earning and paying social security dues and taxes, and they are also becoming increasingly attractive to employers, who will need to fill an expected shortfall in skilled workers (Giandrea *et al*. 2008a, 2008b). In short, the versatility of bridge employment in practice seems beyond doubt.

Let us end with a note of caution regarding the current and future implementation of bridge employment. This refers to the need to regulate age-based social security benefits and entitlements with great care in view of the years worked and contributions paid, in order to ensure fairness and equality of opportunity and treatment based on the workers' personal characteristics and conditions. The aim must be to seek a fair balance between the obligations and rights of all citizens over the course of their whole lives and to underpin social cohesion and equality in the increasingly complex societies of the twenty-first century.

Both the contributors and the editors of this book have sought in each of its chapters to make a modest input to the debate and to suggest future alternatives for the design and implementation of measures and systems to permit flexible prolongation of working life, an area that is likely to prove vital to the socio-economic stability of future generations. While the future is always difficult to predict, we may nevertheless derive enormous benefits from the effort to achieve certain medium- and long-term outcomes, improving individuals' quality of life,

286   C.-M. Alcover et al.

enhancing the efficiency and sustainability of organizations and ensuring fairness and equality for society as a whole.

References

Adams, G.A. and Rau, B.L. (2011) 'Putting off tomorrow to do what you want today', *American Psychologist*, 66: 180–92.

Armstrong-Stassen, M. and Staats, S. (2012) 'Gender differences in how retirees perceive factors influencing unretirement', *International Journal of Aging and Human Development*, 75: 45–69.

Bal, A.C., Reiss, A.E.B., Rudolph, C.W. and Baltes, B.B. (2011) 'Examining positive and negative perceptions of older workers: A meta-analysis', *Journal of Gerontology Series B: Psychological Sciences and Social Sciences*, 66B: 687–98.

Beehr, T.A. and Bennett, M.M. (2007) 'Examining retirement from a multi-level perspective', in K.S. Shultz and G.A. Adams (eds.), *Aging and Work in the 21st Century*, Mahwah, NJ: Lawrence Erlbaum.

Brugiavini, A., Peracchi, F. and Wise, D.A. (2002) 'Pensions and retirement incentives, a tale of three countries: Italy, Spain and the USA', *Giornale degli Economisti e Annali di Economia*, 61: 131–69.

Brunello, G. and Langella, M. (2012) *Bridge Jobs in Europe*, IZA Discussion Paper no. 6938, Bonn: Forschungsinstitut zur Zukunft der Arbeit.

Bustillos, A., Fernández-Ballesteros, R. and Huici, C. (2012) 'Efectos de la activación de etiquetas referidas a la vejez' [Effects of category label activation about the elderly], *Psicothema*, 24: 352–7.

Butterworth, P., Gilla, S.C., Rodgers, B., Ansteya, K.J., Villamil, E. and Melzer, D. (2006) 'Retirement and mental health: Analysis of the Australian national survey of mental health and well-being', *Social Science & Medicine*, 62: 1179–91.

Cahill, K.E., Giandrea, M.D. and Quinn, J.F. (2005) *Are Traditional Retirements a Thing of the Past? New Evidence on Retirement Patterns and Bridge Jobs*, Bureau of Labor Statistics Working Papers, no. 384, Washington, DC: U.S. Department of Labor.

Cahill, K.E., Giandrea, M.D. and Quinn, J.F. (2011) 'Reentering the labor force after retirement', *Monthly Labor Review*, June: 34–42.

Cahill, K.E., Giandrea, M.D. and Quinn, J.F. (2013) 'Bridge employment', in M. Wang (ed.), *The Oxford Handbook of Retirement*, Oxford: Oxford University Press.

Claes, R. and Heymans, M. (2008) 'HR professionals' views on work motivation and retention of older workers: A focus group study', *Career Development International*, 13: 95–111.

Coe, N.B. and Zamarro, G. (2011) 'Retirement effects on health in Europe', *Journal of Health Economics*, 30: 77–86.

Crego, A., Alcover, C.M. and Martínez-Íñigo, D. (2008) 'The transition process to post-working life and its psychosocial outcomes: A systematic analysis of Spanish early retirees' discourse', *Career Development International*, 13: 186–204.

Desmette, D. and Gaillard, M. (2008) 'When a "worker" becomes an "older worker": The effects of age-related social identity on attitudes towards retirement and work', *Career Development International*, 13: 168–85.

Elder, G. and Johnson, M. (2003) 'The life course and aging: Challenges, lessons and new directions', in R.R. Settersten (ed.), *Invitation to the Life Course*, New York: Baywood Publishing.

Lessons learned and future prospects   287

Engelhardt, H. (2012) 'Late careers in Europe: Effects of individual and institutional factors', *European Sociological Review*, 28: 550–63.

European Union (2012) *Employment Policies to Promote Active Ageing 2012*, Luxembourg: Publications Office of the European Union.

Everingham, C., Warner-Smith, P. and Byles, J. (2007) 'Transforming retirement: Rethinking models of retirement to accommodate the experience of women', *Women's Studies International Forum*, 30: 512–22.

French, E. (2005) 'The effects of health, wealth, and wages on labour supply and retirement behaviour', *Review of Economic Studies*, 72: 395–427.

Giandrea, M.D., Cahill, K.E. and Quinn, J.F. (2008a) *Self-Employment as a Step in the Retirement Process*, Boston: The Sloan Center on Aging and Work: Workplace Flexibility at Boston College. Online. Available at: www.bc.edu/content/dam/files/research_sites/agingandwork/pdf/publications/IB15_SelfEmployment_Retire.pdf (accessed July 30, 2013).

Giandrea, M.D., Cahill, K.E. and Quinn, J.F. (2008b) *Self-employment Transitions among Older American Workers with Career Jobs*, Bureau of Labor Statistics Working Papers, no. 418, Washington, DC: U.S. Department of Labor.

Gobeski, K.T. and Beehr, T.A. (2009) 'How retirees work: Predictors off different types of bridge employment', *Journal of Organizational Behavior*, 30: 401–25.

Hanel, N. (2010) 'Financial incentives to postpone retirement and further effects on employment: Evidence from a natural experiment', *Labour Economics*, 17: 474–86.

Hank, K. and Erlinghagen, M. (2011) 'Perceptions of job security in Europe's ageing workforce', *Social Indicator Research*, 103: 427–42.

Hershey, D.A., Henkens, K. and van Dalen, H.P. (2010) 'What drives retirement income worries in Europe? A multilevel analysis', *European Journal of Ageing*, 7: 301–11.

Hesketh, B., Griffin, B. and Loh, V. (2011) 'A future-oriented retirement transition adjustment framework', *Journal of Vocational Behavior*, 79: 303–14.

Ilmarinen, J. (2006) *Towards a Longer Worklife: Aging and the Quality of Work Life in the European Union*, Helsinki: Finnish Institute of Occupational Health.

James, J.B., Besen, E., Matz-Costa, C. and Pitt-Catsouphes, M (2010) *Engaged as We Age: The End of Retirement as We Know It?*, Boston: The Sloan Center on Aging and Work at Boston College. Online. Available at www.bc.edu/content/dam/files/research_sites/agingandwork/pdf/publications/IB24_EngagedAsWeAge.pdf (accessed July 24, 2013).

Johnston, D.W. and Lee, W.-S. (2009) 'Retiring to the good life? The short-term effects of retirement on health', *Economic Letters*, 103: 8–11.

Kanfer, R., Beier, M.E. and Ackerman, P.L. (2013) 'Goals and motivation related to work in later adulthood: An organizing framework', *European Journal of Work and Organizational*, 22: 253–64.

Kantarci, T. and van Soest, A. (2008) 'Gradual retirement: Preferences and limitations', *De Economist*, 156: 113–44.

Kerr, G. and Armstrong-Stassen, M. (2011) 'The bridge to retirement: Older workers' engagement in post-career entrepreneurship and wage-and-salary employment', *Journal of Entrepreneurship*, 20: 55–76.

Kim, S. and Feldman, D.C. (2000) 'Working in retirement: The antecedents of bridge employment and its consequences for quality of life in retirement', *Academy of Management Journal*, 43: 1195–210.

Komp, K., van Tilburg, T. and van Groenou, M.B. (2010) 'Paid work between age 60 and 70 years in Europe: A matter of socio-economic status?, *International Journal of Aging and Later Life*, 5: 45–75.

288   C.-M. Alcover et al.

Kooij, D.T.A.M., De Lange, A.H., Jansen, P.G.W., Kanfer, R. and Dikkers, J.S.E. (2011) 'Age and work-related motives: Results of a meta-analysis', *Journal of Organizational Behavior*, 32: 197–225.

Liu, S., Shultz, K.S., Wang, M. and Zhan, Y. (2009) 'Bridge employment and retirees health: A longitudinal investigation', *Journal of Occupational Health Psychology*, 14: 374–89.

Loretto, W. and Vickerstaff, S. (2013) 'The domestic and gendered context for retirement', *Human Relations*, 66: 65–86.

Maestas, N. (2010) 'Back to work: Expectations and realizations of work after retirement', *Journal of Human Resources*, 45: 719–48.

Maltby, T. (2011) 'Extending working lives? Employability, work ability and better quality working lives', *Social Policy and Society*, 10: 299–308.

Mazzonna, F. and Peracchi, F. (2012) 'Ageing, cognitive abilities and retirement', *European Economic Review, 56*: 691–710.

Munnell, A.H. and Sass, S.A. (2008) *Working Longer: The Solution to the Retirement Income Challenge*, Washington, DC: Brookings Institution Press.

Neuman, K. (2008) 'Quit your job and live longer? The effect of retirement on health', *Journal of Labor Research*, 29: 177–201.

Noone, J.H., Stephens, C. and Alpass, F.M. (2009) 'Preretirement planning and well-being in later life: A prospective study', *Research on Aging*, 31: 295–317.

Olini, G. (2012) 'Differenziali retributivi tra giovani e anziani' [Differences in pay between younger and older workers], *Newsletter Nuovi Lavori*, 109. Online. Available at: www.nuovi-lavori.it/newsletter/article.asp?qid=1285&sid=115 (accessed July 31, 2013).

Peiró, J.M., Tordera, N. and Potočnic, K. (2013) 'Retirement practices in different countries', in M. Wang (ed.), *The Oxford Handbook of Retirement*, Oxford: Oxford University Press.

Peterson, C. and Murphy, G. (2010) 'Transition from the labor market: Older workers and retirement', *International Journal of Health Services*, 40: 609–27.

Phillipson, C. (2013) 'Commentary: The future of work and retirement', *Human Relations*, 66: 143–53.

Pleau, R. and Shauman, K. (2013) 'Trends and correlates of post-retirement employment, 1977–2009', *Human Relations*, 66: 113–41.

Posthuma, R.A. and Campion, M.A. (2009) 'Age stereotypes in the workplace: Common stereotypes, moderators, and future research directions', *Journal of Management*, 35: 158–88.

Rau, B.L. and Adams, G.A. (2005) 'Attracting retirees to apply: Desired organizational characteristics of bridge employment', *Journal of Organizational Behavior*, 26: 649–60.

Roberts, I. (2006) 'Taking age out of the workplace: Putting older workers back in?', *Work, Employment and Society*, 20: 67–86.

Rohwedder, S. and Willis, R.J. (2010) 'Mental retirement', *Journal of Economic Perspectives*, 24: 119–38.

Saba, T. and Guerin, G. (2005) 'Extending employment beyond retirement age: The case of health care managers in Quebec', *Public Personnel Management*, 34: 195–213.

Schils, T. (2008) 'Early retirement in Germany, the Netherlands, and the United Kingdom: A longitudinal analysis of individual factors and institutional regimes', *European Sociological Review*, 24: 315–29.

Shacklock, K., Brunetto, Y. and Nelson, S. (2009) 'The different variables that affect

Lessons learned and future prospects 289

older males' and females' intentions to continue working', *Asia Pacific Journal of Human Resources*, 47: 79–101.

Shultz, K.S. (2003) 'Bridge employment: Work after retirement', in G.A. Adams and T.A. Beehr (eds.), *Retirement: Reasons, Processes, and Results*, New York: Springer.

Shultz, K.S. and Wang, M. (2011) 'Psychological perspectives on the changing nature of retirement', *American Psychologist*, 66: 170–9.

Siegrist, J. and Wahrendorf, M. (2009) 'Participation in socially productive activities and quality of life in early old age: Findings from SHARE', *Journal of European Social Policy*, 19: 317–26.

Siegrist, J., Wahrendorf, M., von dem Knesebeck, O., Jürges, H. and Börsch-Supan, A. (2006) 'Quality of work, well-being, and intended early retirement of older employees: Baseline results from the SHARE study', *European Journal of Public Health*, 17: 62–8.

Templer, A., Armstrong-Stassen, M. and Cattaneo, J. (2010) 'Antecedents of older workers' motives for continuing to work', *Career Development International*, 15: 479–500.

Topa, G., Alcover, C.M., Moriano, J.A. and Depolo, M. (2014) 'Bridge employment quality and its impact in retirement: A structural equation model with SHARE panel data', *Economic and Industrial Democracy*, 35.

Topa, G., Moriano, J.A., Depolo, M., Alcover, C.M. and Moreno, A. (2011) 'Retirement and wealth relationships: Meta-analysis and SEM', *Research on Aging*, 33: 501–28.

van den Berg, T.I.J., Elders, L.A.M. and Burdorf, A. (2010) 'Influence of health and work on early retirement', *Journal of Occupational and Environmental Medicine*, 6: 576–83.

van der Heijden, B.I.J.M., Schalk, R. and van Veldhoven, M.J.P.M. (2008) 'Aging and careers: European research on long-term career development and early retirement', *Career Development International*, 13: 85–94.

van Oorschot, W. and Jensen, P.H. (2009) 'Early retirement differences between Denmark and the Netherlands: A cross-national comparison of push and pull factors in two small European welfare states', *Journal of Aging Studies*, 23: 267–78.

von Bonsdorff, M.E., Shultz, K.E., Leskinen, E. and Tansky, J. (2009) 'The choice between retirement and bridge employment: A continuity theory and life course perspective', *International Journal of Aging and Human Development*, 69: 79–100.

Wang, M. (2007) 'Profiling retirees in the retirement transition and adjustment process: Examining the longitudinal change patterns of retirees' psychological well-being', *Journal of Applied Psychology*, 92: 455–74.

Wang, M. (2013) 'Retirement: An introduction and overview of the Handbook', in M. Wang (ed.), *The Oxford Handbook of Retirement*, Oxford: Oxford University Press.

Wang, M. and Shultz, K.S. (2010) 'Employee retirement: A review and recommendations for future investigation', *Journal of Management*, 36: 172–206.

Wang, M., Olson, D.A. and Shultz, K.S. (2012) *Mid and Late Career Issues: An Integrative Perspective*, London: Routledge.

Wang, M., Zhan, Y., Liu, S. and Shultz, K.S. (2008) 'Antecedents of bridge employment: A longitudinal investigation', *Journal of Applied Psychology*, 93: 818–30.

Weiss, D. and Lang, F.R. (2012) '"They" are old but "I" feel younger: Age-group dissociation as a self-protective strategy in old age', *Psychology and Aging*, 27: 153–63.

Westerlund, H., Kivimäki, M., Singh-Manoux, A., Melchior, M., Ferrie, J.E., Pentti, J., Jokela, M., Leineweber, C., Goldberg, M., Zins, M. and Vahtera, J. (2009) 'Self-rated health before and after retirement in France (GAZEL): A cohort study', *The Lancet*, 374: 1889–96.

Wong, J.Y. and Earl, J.K. (2009) 'Towards an integrated model of individual, psychosocial, and organizational predictors of retirement adjustment', *Journal of Vocational Behavior*, 75: 1–13.

Zhan, Y., Wang, M. and Yao, X. (2013) 'Domain specific effects of commitment on bridge employment decisions: The moderating role of economic stress', *European Journal of Work and Organizational Psychology*, 22: 362–75.

Author index

Page numbers in *italics* denote tables, those in **bold** denote figures.

Achenbaum, W.A. 211
Ackerman, P.L. 20, 87, 287
Ackers, P. 110
Adams, G.A. 4, 10, 17–23, 36, 48–9, 84–6, 88, 132, 136, 152–3, 197–203, 210–14, 228, 232, 234–5, 281, 284, 286, 288–9
Ajzen, M. 89
Alcover, C.M. 5, 13, 17, 22–3, 69, 88, 120–1, 127, 131–6, 277, 286, 289
Aldwin, C.M. 210
Alley, D. 3, 8–10, 17–18, 116, 132
Alonso, J. 118–19, 133
Alpass, F. 49, 288
Altobelli, J. 11, 21
Angelini, V. 120, 132
Ansteya, K.J. 286
Antón, J.I. 88, 135
Anxo, D. 158, 165
Armstrong-Stassen, M. 8, 18, 49, 92, 100,-2, 104, 109, 139, 151, 225, 229, 232, 284–7, 289
Aronson, J. 80, 88
Arquié, J-C. 89
Arthur, M.B. 140, 151
Arthur, S. 100, 108–9
Ashforth, B.E. 208, 213
Atchley, R.C. 59, 67, 206–7, 210, 224, 232
Audet, M. 235
Auman, C. 87
Aumann, K. 210, 232

Bach, S. 112
Bakker, A.B. 67
Bal, A.C. 276, 286
Bal, P.M. 19, 59, 67, 225, 232
Balcerowicz, L. 93, 95, 110
Baldwin, J.R. 226, 232
Balibar, E. 92, 110

Ballantyne, P.J. 21, 212
Baltes, B.B. 286
Baltes, M.M. 71, 85
Baltes, P.B. 71, 85
Barbier, M. 85
Barnes, H. 92, 101, 102, 108, 110
Barnes, M. 152
Barnes-Farrell, J.L. 207, 210
Baruch, Y. 140, 151–2
Bataille, C.D. 21–2
Baugh, S.G. 23, 153, 214
BBC News 258, 264
Beck, V. 17, 18
Becker, G.S. 33, 48
Beehr, T.A. 6–0, 18, 20, 22–3, 30, 49, 54, 60, 68, 71, 85–6, 88, 128, 130, 132, 136, 152–3, 202, 210, 213–14, 224–5, 232–3, 235, 281, 283, 286–7, 289
Beier, M.E. 20, 287
Bender, K.A. 5, 18, 92, 100, 102, 110
Bengston, V.L. 211
Bennett, M.M. 6–8, 10, 18, 30, 49, 71, 85, 128, 130, 132, 281, 286
Bernard, A. 228, 232
Bernard, M. 235
Bertone, A. 14, 279
Bertrand, F. 71, 78, 81, 83, 85
Besen, E. 287
Bidewell, J. 9, 18
Bilimoria, D. 150, 152
Binstock, R.H. 20
Björkman, B. 111
Black, D. 211
Błaszczyk, B. 110
Bleaney, M. 111
Blekesaune, M. 71, 85, 200, 210
Blundell, R. 92, 102, 110
Boehm, S. 87

292 *Author index*

Bond, J.T. 210, 232
Bongers, P.M. 19
Borghgraef, A. 49
Börsch-Supan, A. 3, 5, 11, 18, 118–19, 130, 132, 166, 289
Bosmans, K. 89
Bosse, R. 208, 210–11
Bowling, N.A. 10, 18
Bwon Wilson, D. 13, 277
Boxall, P. 94, 110
Braeckman, L. 88
Brandes, P. 110
Brandt, M. 166
Brasor, P. 257, 264
Bredgaard, T. 8, 18, 82, 84–5
Brewster, C. 93–4, 112
Brooke, L. 50
Brott, P.E. 10, 23, 140–1, 153, 222, 235
Brown, A. 75, 85
Brown, K.S. 197, 210
Brown, M. 205, 210, 230, 232
Bruch, H. 87
Brugiavini, A. 18, 132, 270, 286
Brunello, G. 51, 67, 273, 286
Brunetto, Y. 9, 22, 288
Buck, H. 136
Budd, J.W. 94, 110
Bumpass, L.L. 48–9
Burdorf, A. 19, 289
Bureau, M-C. 86
Burkhauser, R.V. 198, 210
Burnay, N. 88
Bush, D.M. 206, 210
Business Link 138, 139, 142, 151
Bustillos, A. 276, 286
Butler, R.N. 71, 85
Butterworth, P. 282, 286
Buyens, D. 56–7, 68
Byles, J. 19, 36, 49, 287
Bytheway, B. 71, 85

Cahill, K.E. 4–8, 17–20, 27, 49, 118, 130, 132, 134, 195, 197, 200, 205, 208–12, 227, 233, 239, 250, 269, 280, 285–7
Calasanti, T.M. 207–8, 210
Callanan, G.A. 232–3
Calvo, E. 6, 19, 128, 132
Campion, M.A. 79, 88, 276, 288
Caria, A. 88
Carrière, Y. 218, **220–2**, 225, 228, 230, 233, 235
Casper, L. 49
Catellino, O. 165
Cattaneo, J. 289

Chang, B. 21
Charles, K.K. 92, 100, 102, 110
Charlwood, A. 85
Chen, H. 211
Chen, Y.P. 197, 210
Chiesa, R. 17, 132
Cicchelli, V. 89
Claes, R. 78, 82–3, 85–6, 284, 286
Clark, E. 94, 113
Clark, R.L. 10, 19
Clarke, P.J. 21, 212
Clayton, P.M. 17, 19, 118, 133
Clayton, S. 86
Coe, N.B. 282, 286
Coile, C.C. 204, 210–11
Colcombe, S.J. 87
Colignon, R.A. 16, 280
Conde-Ruiz, J.I. 116–19, 133
Conen, W.S. 39, 49, 239, 250
Conrad, H. 118, 133, 136
Corpeleijn, A. 30, 49
Costa, P.T. Jr. 212
Costigan, P. 152
Coulmas, F. 133, 136
Cox, J. 251
Crego, A. 17, 121, 131–4, 269, 286
Crimmins, E.M. 3, 8–10, 17–18, 33, 49, 116, 132, 196–7, 209, 211, 214
Croda, E. 18, 132
Crosby, F.J. 81, 86
Crosby, J.R. 88
Curryer, C. 49
Czaja, S.J. 20

Dąbrowski, M. 110
Dave, D. 206, 211
Davey, A. 36, 50, 214
Davies, P.G. 88
Davis, F. 92, 110
Davis, M.A. 7, 9, 19
Davis, N. 93, 110
Davoine, L. 75, 86
De Cuyper, N. 88
De Grip, A. 50
De Jong, S.B. 67
de Lange, A.H. 11, 19, 21, 68, 135, 234, 288
de Preter, H. 3, 19
de Vos, A. 68
de Wind, A. 9, 19
de Witte, H. 88–9
Deci, E.L. 61, 66, 68
DeFillippi, R.J. 140, 151
Delay, B. 71, 79, 81, 86

Author index 293

Deller, J. 14, 167–8, 172–**4**, 179, 181–4, 189–91, 278
Dempster-McClain, D. 212
Denaeghel, K. 19, 34, 49
Dendinger, V.M. 19, 208, 211
Dennis, H. 36, 49
Denton, F.T. 195, 211
Depolo, M. 14, 22–4, 68–9, 88–9, 136, 159, 278, 289
Derriennic, F. 89
Desmette, D. 12, 71, 79–81, 83, 86–7, 276, 286
DeVaney, S.A. 7, 20, 199, 212
Dewilde, T. 68
Dharwadkar, R. 95, 110
di Biase, T. 50
Di Pierro, D. 23, 113
Dikkers, J.S.E. 21, 68, 135, 234, 288
Dirven, H.J. 30, 50
Ditlman, R. 88
Dobosz-Bourne, D. 93, 110
Docherty, P. 74, 86
Doeringer, P.B. 6, 19, 22, 92, 102, 110, 224, 233
Doménech, R. 119, 126, 131, 133
Dorn, D. 5, 19, 36, 49, 120, 133
Downing, R.A. 86
Doyal, L. 60, 68
Drago, R. 195, 211
Drentea, P. 207, 213
Duncan, G.J. 210
Dundon, T. 94, 110
Duval, R. 120, 133
Dworschak, B. 136
Dychtwald, K. 92, 102, 110

Earl, C. 15, 279
Earl, J.K. 279, 281, 290
Easterlin, R.A. 198, 209, 211
Ecosse, E. 88
Egorov, V. 95, 111
Ekerdt, D.J. 17, 19, 207, 211
Elder, H.W. 92, 100, 102, 111
Elder,G.H.Jr. 5, 19, 128, 133, 224–5, 233–4, 285–6
Elders, L.A.M. 289
Elovainio, M. 78, 86
Emerick, H. 55, 68
Engelhardt, H. 3, 5, 19, 119–20, 131, 133, 280, 287
Engström, P. 111
Erhel, C. 86
Erickson, T. 110
Erikson, M.A. 212

Erlinghagen, M. 283, 287
Eschtruth, A. 212
Evans, D.R. 211, 233
Everingham, C.5, 19, 284, 287

Farley, R. 198, 211
Farrell, S.K. 79, 86
Feldman, D.C. 7, 9–10, 18–21, 34, 49, 54–5, 60, 68, 71, 86, 130, 134, 139–40, 152, 198–9, 203, 205, 208, 212, 223–4, 233–4, 283, 287
Fernández, A. 111
Fernández, J.J. 121, 127, 134
Fernández, M. 213
Fernández-Ballesteros, R. 127, 134, 286
Fernández-Macías, E. 88
Ferrie, J.E. 289
Fey, C. 93–4, 111
Figurny-Puchalska, E. 113
Filatotchev, I. 95, 111
Finkelstein, L.M. 79, 86
Finnegan, R.P. 111
Fisher, G.G. 212
Fluckinger, C.D. 21
Flynn, M. 141, 151–2, 239, 250
Foden, D. 89
Fonseca, A.M. 111
Forbes 99, 111
Forde, C. 85
Forma, P. 86
Forman, J.D. 92, 111
Forslin, J. 86
Fougère, M. 118, 134
Fouquereau, E. 102, 104, 111
Fraccaroli, F. 14, 17, 23–4, 68, 89, 159, 278
Frank, F.D. 103, 111
Franzé, A. 120, 135
French, E. 270, 287
Frenette, M. 232
Frese, M. 87
Friedman, S. 211
Fu, X. 208, 211
Fukaya, T. 22
Furåker, B. 68
Furunes, T. 57, 68
Fusulier, B. 70, 86

Gaciong, Z. 113
Gaillard, M. 71, 79–81, 83, 86–7, 276, 286
Galarneau, D. 218, **220**, 221, **222**, 225, 228, 230, 233, 235
Galinsky, E. 210, 232
Gall, T.L. 207, 211, 224, 233

294   Author index

Galland, O. 89
Gandini, A. 164–5
García, J.R. 119, 126, 131, 133
García-Pérez, J.I. 121, 134
Gaudart, C. 88
Gawrońska-Nowak, B. 91, 111
Geldhauser, H.A. 8, 22
Gendell, M. 101, 111
George, G. 110
George, L.K. 20
Geuskens, G.A. 19
Ghai, D. 75, 87
Ghilarducci, T. 212
Giandrea, M.D. 5, 7, 18–20, 49, 130, 132, 134, 197, 210–11, 227, 233, 250, 285, 286–7
Gielnik, M.M. 71, 78, 87
Gilla, S.C. 286
Giordanengo, A. 23, 113
Gobeski, K.T. 7, 9, 20, 225, 233, 283, 287
Goda, G.S. 204, 211
Goldberg, M. 289
González, C.I. 116, 133
Góra, M. 99, 111
Grace-Martin, K. 240, 247, 250
Grady, W.R. 211
Gratton, L. 103, 111
Greenhaus, J.H. 232, 233
Greller, M.M. 10, 20, 140, 152, 199, 211
Griffin, B. 8, 18, 20, 199, 206, 211–12, 225, 233, 287
Gruber, J. 3, 20, 169, 191
Guergoat-Larivière, M. 86
Guerin, G. 4, 8, 22, 217–18, 231, 233, 235, 274, 284, 288
Guglielmi, D. 17, 24, 89, 132
Guillemard, A-M. 71, 79, 83, 87

Hagestad, G.O. 36, 50
Hall, D.T. 140, 152
Hall, N. 152
Hallsten, L. 68
Hamel, G. 89
Hanel, N. 283, 287
Hank, K. 283, 287
Hansez, I. 85, 89
Harcourt, M. 69
Hardy, M.A. 211, 214
Harpaz, I. 208, 211
Harper, S. 117, 134
Harvey, C. 112
Harvey, S. 134
Hauser, R.M. 22, 136, 210

Haverstick, K. 19, 132, 213
Havlovic, S. 93–4, 113
Hayward, M.D. 198, 211, 214
Hébert, B.P 227–8, 233
Heilman, M.E. 81, 87
Heindel, R.A. 202, 212
Heller, D. 212
Henderikse, W. 235
Henkens, K. 5, 11, 20, 23, 29, 33–4, 36–8, 49, 50, 121, 134, 136, 214, 234, 242, 250–1, 270, 275, 287
Henretta, J.C. 6, 8, 20, 128, 134
Hershey, D.A. 5, 20, 117, 134, 270, 287
Herz, D.E. 102, 109, 111
Hesketh, B. 18, 20, 199, 206, 211–12, 225, 233, 281, 287
Hess, T.M. 87
Heymans, M. 82, 85, 284, 286
Hirsch, D. 92, 100–1, 111
Ho, J-H. 22, 136
Hobfoll, S.E. 223, 233
Hofferth, S. 49
Hofmeister, H. 212
Holman, D. 75, 87
Horn, S.A. 264
Howard, J. 211, 233
Howorth, C. 112
Huhtanen, P. 69
Huici, C. 286
Huizinga, W.P. 29, 49
Humpel, N. 240, 250
Humphrey, A. 142, 152
Humphreys, C. 152
Hurd, M.D. 36, 49
Hutchens, R. 240, 247, 250
Hutsebaut, M. 89
Huyez-Levrat, G. 71, 86
Huys, R. 89
Hyman, R. 92, 94, 111

Iida, Y. 264
Ikeda, N. 263, 264
Ilmakunnas, P. 140, 152
Ilmakunnas, S. 140, 152
Ilmarinen, J. 7, 17, 20, 90, 101–2, 108, 111, 118, 134, 283, 287
Irving, P. 140–2, 152
Isaksson, K. 12, 54–6, 59, 68, 275
Iweins, C. 80–1, 83, 87
Iyer, A. 86

Jacobson, J.D. 19, 211
James, J.B. 21, 283, 287
Jankowicz, A.D. 93–4, 110–11

Author index 295

Jansen, P.G.W. 21, 67–8, 135, 234, 288
Jenkens,K.I. 235
Jensen, P.H. 271, 289
Jepsen, M. 89
Jex, S.M. 10, 20, 200, 212
Jiménez-Martín, S. 120, 134–5
Jociles, M.I. 120, 135
Johansson Hanse, J. 57, 68
Johansson, G. 12, 54–6, 59, 68, 275
Johns, T. 103, 111
Johnson, M. 5, 19, 128, 133, 285–6
Johnson, R.W. 205, 208, 212
Johnston, D.W. 282, 287
Jokela, M. 289
Jolivet, A. 165
Jones, D.A. 196, 212
Judd, C.M. 89
Judge T.A. 200, 212
Jürges, H. 5, 18, 132, 289

Kadefors, R. 57, 68
Kanfer, R. 11, 17, 20–1, 68, 87, 135, 234, 276, 287–8
Kantarci, T. 4, 6, 10, 20, 240, 251, 269, 280, 287
Karoly, L.A. 7, 24, 130, 137
Karpinska, K. 232, 234
Kawachi, J. 212
Keen, L. 251
Kendig, H. 21, 250
Kerr, G. 285, 287
Kilbom, Å. 68
Kilty, K.M. 207, 213, 224, 234
Kim, H. 7, 20, 199, 212
Kim, J.E. 207, 212
Kim, S. 7, 9–10, 19–20, 34, 49, 54–5, 68, 130, 134, 139–40, 152, 198–9, 203, 205, 208, 212, 224, 234, 283, 287
Kivimäki, M. 86, 289
Kobayashi, E. 22
Kodama, M. 112
Komp, K. 5, 21, 126, 131, 135, 270, 271–3, 279, 287
Kooji, D.T.A.M. 68
Kostoris, F.P.S 165
Koubek, J. 93–4, 112
Kuczyński, G. 94, 96, 100, 114
Kunze, F. 83, 87
Kvale, S. 103–4, 112
Kyodo News 263–4

Laflamme, R. 235
Lafrance, A. 232
Laine, M. 86

Lakey, J. 110
Lamonde, F. 235
Lamura, G. 165–6
Lang, F.R. 289
Langella, M. 51, 67, 273, 286
Larocque, A. 235
Lavigne, M. 95, 112
Lee, K. 224, 235
Lee, M.D. 4, 21–2
Lee, R. 118, 135
Lee, W.-S. 282, 287
Leigh, L. 49
Leineweber, C. 289
Lemaire, C. 85
Léonard, É. 89
Lepisto, L. 18, 212
Leplège, A. 80, 88
Leskinen, E. 23, 214, 235, 289
Lessof, C. 110
Levenson, M.R. 210
Levine, P.B. 204, 210–11
Lewis, E.K. 212
Lewis, P. 113
Liang, J. 22
Lingier, S. 88
Lissenburgh, S. 92, 100–2, 112
Litwin, H.166
Liu, S. 23–4, 50, 69, 89, 192, 214–15, 235, 282, 288–9
LoCastro, J.S. 211
Löckenhoff, C.E. 200, 212
Loh, V. 20, 287
Lokhorst, B. 50
Loretto, W. 101, 112, 284, 288
Louis, M.R. 139, 152
Luong, M. 227–8, 233

McAulay, A. 112
McClelland, C. 75, 87
McGarry, K. 200, 212
McIntosh, B.R. 196, 212
Mackenbach, J. 18, 132
MacLean, A. 224, 234
McNair, S. 101, 112, 139, 141, 152
Macunovich, D.J. 211
Maczynski, J. 94, 112
Maestas, N. 197, 200, 212, 230, 234, 281, 288
Magd, H. 103, 112
Mainiero, L.A. 140, 152
Malchaire, J. 79, 88
Malpede, C. 156, 166
Maltby, T. 283, 288
Marchington, M. 94, 110, 112

296 Author index

Marshall, V.W. 5, 21, 208, 212, 232
Martin, B. 21
Martin, L. 214
Martin, R. 94, 112
Martínez-Íñigo, D. 286
Matanle, P. 254, 264
Matsui, K. 264
Matus, D. 258, 260, 264
Matz-Costa, C. 287
Mazzonna, F. 282, 288
Méda, D. 71, 86, 88
Melchior, M. 289
Melzer, D. 286
Mercenier, J. 134
Mérette, M. 134
Meschi, E. 164, 166
McLoughlin, C. 15, 279
Midanik, L.T. 207, 212
Miklos, S.M. 71, 74, 88
Millet, B. 49
Mirvis, P.H. 140, 152
Mitchell, O.S. 10, 19
Moen, Ph. 11, 21, 34, 50, 100, 102, 104,
    108, 112–13, 140, 152, 197, 206–8,
    212–13, 223–5, 229, 234
Molinié, A.-F. 83, 88–9
Monk, C. 213
Montziaan, R. 50
Morales, J.F. 23, 69, 88, 136
Mor-Barak, M.E. 225, 234
Moreno, A. 23, 289
Moriano, J.A. 22, 23, 69, 88, 136, 289
Morison, B. 110
Morschhäuser, M. 131, 135
Mortelmans, D. 19, 49
Moulaert, T. 86
Mount, M.K. 212
Mueller, F. 104, 112
Muldoon, D. 213
Muller-Camen, M. 250
Munnell, A H. 21, 204–5, 212–13, 280,
    288
Muñoz de Bustillo, R. 75, 88, 118, 127,
    131, 135
Murphy, G. 6, 21, 136, 285, 288
Muszyńska, M.M. 117, 135
Mutran, E.J. 206, 213
Mykletun, R. 57, 68

Naegele, G. 50, 170, 172, 174, 176, 178–9,
    188, 192
Nakai, Y. 9, 21
Nazroo, J. 110
Nelson, S. 288

Neuman, K. 90, 92, 100, 102, 104, 112,
    282, 288
Nonaka, I. 112
Noone, J.H. 5, 21, 281, 288
Notelaers, G. 88

O'Loughlin, K. 21, 250
O'Rand, A.M. 198, 213
Olini, G. 163, 166, 278, 288
Olson, D.A. 23, 214, 289
O'Neil, D. 150, 152
Owen, L. 152

Padula, M. 166
Palm, S. 12, 275
Park, B. 89
Park, J. 225, 228–9, 234
Parker, O. 234
Parker, S. 110
Parkinson, L. 49
Pärnänen, A. 57, 68
Parry, E. 13, 277
Parry, J. 110
Pasini, G. 166
Pasqua, P. 23, 113
Patrickson, M. 42, 49
Paul, M.C. 111
Paumès, D. 89
Payne, S. 60, 68
Pedraza, P. 135
Peeters, M. 55, 68
Peiró, J.M. 4, 17, 21, 269, 288
Peláez, O. 118, 122, 136
Peltokorpi, V. 103, 112
Peng, I. 118, 136
Penn, L.T. 14, 279
Pengcharoen, C. 10, 21, 223, 234
Pentti, J. 289
Peracchi, F. 282, 286, 288
Pérée, F. 85
Pérez-Díaz, V. 126, 136
Peters, S. 85
Peterson, C.L. 6, 21, 136, 285, 288
Pettigrew, T.F. 88
Phillipson, C. 4, 6, 21, 42, 49, 101, 112,
    118, 128, 136, 283, 288
Pickering, K. 152
Pinquart, M. 54, 68, 207–8, 213
Piraino, P. 232
Pitt-Catsouphes, M. 210, 232, 287
Plassman, V. 152
Pleau, R. 5, 6, 21, 197, 213, 279–80, 288
Pond, R. 34, 49
Posthuma, R.A. 79, 88, 276, 288

Author index

Potočnic, K. 21, 288
Pratt, M.G. 208, 213
Principi, A. 165–6
Pueyo, V. 82–3, 88–9
Pugeault-Cicchelli, C. 89
Puig-Barrachina, V. 89
Pundt (Maxin), L. 14, 167–8, 172–4, 179, 181, 182–4, 190–1, 278
Purcell, J. 94, 110
Purdie-Vaughns, V. 88

Quick, H.E. 100, 102, 104, 108, 112, 206, 213, 223–5, 229, 234
Quinn, J.F. 4, 18–21, 49, 132, 134, 205, 210–11, 213, 233, 250, 286–7

Rahhal, T.A. 87
Raley, R.K. 48–9
Ram, B. 235
Ransom, L.J. 212
Rashad, I. 211
Rau, B.L. 10, 21, 36, 48, 84–5, 117, 135, 197–203, 210, 213, 228, 232, 234, 281, 284, 286, 288
Raymo, J.M. 4–5, 7, 11, 22, 71, 88, 136
Reday-Mulvey, G. 240, 251
Reeuwijk, K.G. 19
Reisinger, D. 265
Reiss, A.E.B. 286
Reitzes, D.C. 208, 213
Remery, C. 250
Réveillère, C. 88
Reynolds, S.L. 49
Richardson, M. 213
Richardson, V. 207, 213, 224, 234
Richiardi, M. 23, 113
Rivas, L.A. 135
Rivière, H. 88
Roberts, I. 276–7, 288
Robertson, M. 265
Robinson, I. 49
Robinson, J.L. 207, 210
Rodgers, B. 286
Rodríguez, J.C. 126, 136
Rohwedder, S. 282, 288
Rosen, D. 16, 257, 265, 280
Rosenberg, M. 210
Ross, C.E. 207, 213
Rousseau, D.M. 67–8, 151
Rudolph, C.W. 286
Rudolph, P.M. 92, 100, 102, 111
Ruhm, C.J. 6, 22, 33, 49, 227, 234
Ryan, R.M. 61, 66, 68
Rymsza, M. 91, 112–13

Saba, T. 4, 8, 15, 22, 216–18, 225, 230–1, 233, 235, 274, 279, 284, 288
Sachs, J.D. 110
Sahin-Dikmen, M. 152
Saito, Y. 49
Sánchez-Martín, A.R. 134
Sapelli, G. 165–6
Sarchielli, G. 24
Sargent, L.D. 9, 21–2
Sass, S.A. 10, 19, 21, 132, 197, 212–13, 280, 288
Saunders, M. 104, 113
Schad-Seifert, A. 133, 136
Schalk, R. 5, 10, 22–3, 120, 136, 289
Schellenberg, G. 218, 230, 235
Schils, T. 271, 279, 288
Schindler, I. 54, 68, 207–8, 213
Schippers, J.J. 49–50, 234–5, 250–1
Schlosser, F. 46, 49, 139, 151, 232
Schmidt, J.A. 224, 235
Schneider, F. 121, 136
Schreurs, B. 72, 88
Schroder, H. 250
Scott, J. 197, 210
Seitsamo, J. 69
Settersten, R.R. 19–20, 36, 50, 133–4, 286
Shacklock, K. 9, 22, 284, 288
Shani, A.B. 86
Sharit, J. 20
Shauman, K. 5, 6, 21, 279–80, 288
Shimizutani, S. 4, 22
Shoven, J.B. 211
Shultz, K.S. 4–9, 10, 17–24, 46, 49–50, 69, 85, 89, 130, 132, 136–7, 192, 195, 198, 201–3, 206, 212–15, 223–5, 234–5, 269, 281, 285–6, 288–9
Siegrist, J. 18, 132, 269, 277, 289
Siemianowicz, J. 91, 93, 113
Siermann, C. 30, 50
Sillence, J. 112
Simmons, R.G. 210
Šimová, Z. 9, 22
Simpson, M. 196, 209, 213
Simpson, P. 140, 152
Sinervo, T. 86
Singh, G. 197, 213
Singh-Manoux, A. 289
Skirbekk, V. 192, 200, 210
Skorupińska, K. 91, 111
Slavov, S.N. 211
Smeaton, D. 92, 100–2, 112, 138, 142, 152
Smith, A. 4, 21, 101, 118, 136
Smith, D.B. 50, 102
Smith, P.W. 34, 49

298 Author index

Smolenaars, E. 28, 50
Snell, A.F. 21
Söchert, R. 131, 135
Soghikian, K. 212
Soidre, T. 54, 68
Solem P.E. 71, 85
Sommers, D. 211
Soulsby, A. 94, 113
Sousa-Poza, A. 5, 19, 36, 49, 120, 133
Spasojevic, J. 211
Spencer, B.G. 195, 211
Spencer, D. 85
Spiegel, P.E. 92, 100, 113
Staats, S. 8, 18, 284, 286
Steele, C.M. 80, 88
Steels, J. 152
Stefanova, S. 14, 279
Stephens, C. 49, 288
Sterns, H.L. 71, 74, 88
Stevenson, D. 49
Stinglhamber, F. 87
Stratford, N. 152
Stroh, L.K. 10, 20, 199, 211
Stull, D.E. 207, 214
Sugihara, Y. 22
Sugisawa, H. 22
Sullivan, S.E. 23, 140, 152–3, 214
Sutinen, R. 86
Sweeney, M.M. 22, 71, 88, 136
Sweet, S. 152
Symonides, B. 103, 113
Szinovacz, M.E. 5, 22, 36, 50, 198, 203–4, 214
Sztompka, P. 96, 113

Tajfel, H. 80, 88
Tansky, J. 23, 235, 289
Tavener, M. 49
Taylor, C.R. 111
Taylor, M.A. 8, 22
Taylor, P.E. 15, 36, 50, 57, 69, 240, 251, 279
Taylor, R. 110
Tekawa, I.S. 212
Templer, A. 284, 289
Terracciano, A. 212
Thoits, P.A. 206, 214
Thomas, K. 36, 49
Thomson, J. 240, 251
Thornhill, A. 113
Tischner, J. 92–3, 113
Tittenbrun, J. 95–6, 113
Topa, G. 5, 8, 10–11, 13, 22–3, 54–5, 60, 69, 71, 88, 115–16, 118, 120, 122, 124,
126–8, 130, 132, 134, 136, 269–70, 272, 277, 282, 289
Tordera, N. 21, 288
Touranchet, A. 89
Tremblay, D-G. 86
Treu, T. 162–3, 166
Troos, F. 82, 84–5
Tropp, L.R. 88
Truxillo, D.M. 17, 23
Tuckett, A. 112
Tung, R. 93–4, 113
Tuomi, K. 69
Turcotte, M. 235
Turner, J. 212
Turner, J.C. 80, 88
Turner, R.H. 210
Tyszkiewicz, J. 113

Ulrich, L.B. 10, 23, 140–1, 153, 222, 235
Uotinen, V. 111
Upchurch, M. 250
Uppal, S. 228, 235
Urwin, P. 232, 235
Usui, C. 16, 280

Vahtera, J. 289
Valenduc, G. 75, 84, 89
Van Dalen, H.P. 29, 30, 50, 134, 225, 235, 240, 251, 287
van den Berg, T.I.J. 282, 289
van der Beek, A.J. 19
vander Hallen, P. 70, 89
van der Heijden, B.I.J.M. 4, 17, 19, 23, 269, 289
Van Dijk, H. 68
Van Emmerik, I.J.H. 88
Van Ginneken, P.J. 29, 50
van Groenou, M.B. 21, 135, 287
Van Hootegem, G. 89
Van Koningsveld, D.B.J. 29, 50
Van Loo, J. 42, 50
Van Loo, K. 78, 83, 86
van Looy, D. 19
van Oorschot, W. 271, 289
van Soest, A.H.O. 4, 6, 10, 20, 240, 251, 269, 280, 287
Van Solinge, H. 11, 23, 33–6, 38, 49–50, 121, 136, 214, 270, 275
van Tilburg, T. 21, 135, 287
van Veldhoven, M.J.P.M. 23, 289
Vandekerckhove, T. 89
Vandenbrande, T. 71, 75, 82, 89
Vandenbroucke, G. 70, 89
Vanroelen, C. 89

Author index 299

Vegeris, S. 152
Velkoff, V.A. 196, 214
Vendramin, P. 12, 71, 74–5, 82, 84, 86, 88–9, 276
Verma, A. 197, 213
Vickerstaff, S. 6, 23, 239, 251, 284, 288
Villamil, E. 286
Villosio, C. 9, 23, 92, 100–1, 113, 156, 166
Vincent, G.K. 196, 214
Visser, M.S. 225, 232
Vogt, G. 133, 136
Volkoff, S. 82–3, 89
von Bonsdorff, M.E. 9, 23, 59, 69, 196, 202–3, 214, 224, 229, 235, 283, 289
von dem Knesebeck, O. 289
von Nordheim, F. 5, 23, 120, 136
Von Wachter, T. 204, 214
Vough, H.C. 21–2

Wahrendorf, M. 269, 289
Walker, A. 57, 69
Wang, M. 4–9, 10, 14, 17, 19–24, 27, 46, 50, 52–4, 59, 69, 71, 82, 89, 145, 153, 172, 192, 195–208, 210, 212–15, 222–5, 229, 235, 269, 275, 279–86, 288–9, 290
Warner, D.F. 19, 197, 214, 287
Warner-Smith, P. 19, 287
Warr, P. 102, 113
Warren, J.R. 22, 136
Weber, G. 18, 101, 113, 132, 166
Weckerle, J.R. 9, 23, 130, 137, 201, 203, 214, 225, 235
Weisner, R. 49
Weiss, D. 276, 289
Welle, B. 81, 87
Wells, Y. 250
Westerholm, P. 68
Westerlund, H. 277, 289

Westerman, M.J. 19
Wheaton, F. 196–7, 209, 214
White, P. 101, 112
Wilkinson, A. 69, 94, 110, 112
Willis, R.J. 282, 288
Wink, P.21
Wintersgill, D. 265
Wise, D.A. 3, 20, 49, 191, 286
Wolsko, C. 89
Wong, J.Y. 281, 290
Woo, W.T. 110
Wood, A. 265
Wood, G. 57, 69
Wooden, M. 211
Woodfield, S. 152
Wooldridge, A. 90, 113
Workman-Daniels, K. 210
Wright, M. 111

Yao, X. 24, 215, 290
Ybema, J.F. 19
Yin, R.K. 103, 113
Yzerbyt, V. 87

Zacher, H. 87
Zamarro, G. 282, 286
Zaniboni, S. 9, 24
Zappalà, S. 9, 24, 78, 89
Zarubin, A. 20, 212
Zhan, Y. 9, 10, 23–4, 50, 54–5, 69, 89, 192–6, 205–9, 214–15, 235, 275, 283, 288–90
Zientara, P. 13, 90–4, 96, 99–103, 113–14
Zikic, J. 21
Zinni, D. 49, 232
Zins, M. 289
Zissimopoulos, J.M. 7, 24, 137
Zorn, T.E. 213

Subject index

Page numbers in *italics* denote tables, those in **bold** denote figures.

absenteeism 96, 161, 240
Accenture 159, 165n1
Administration on Aging 196, 210
Age and Employment Network, The
(TAEN) *see* The Age and Employment
Network (TAEN)
age biases and stereotyping 56–7, 67,
79–81, 143, 276–7; *see also* age
prejudice
age diversity 70–1, 79–81, 83, 271
age management 12, 57, 67, 82–3, 103,
162
age prejudice 57, 80–1, 131, 163, 271
ageism 56–7, 71, 80–1, 83, 103, 106 ; age
discrimination 10, 57, 71, 131, 138, 158,
198, 271, 277
age-related performance 71, 81, 149, *183*,
257; functional age 71, 81
aging 12, 70, 74, 97, 115, 131, 155,
216–17, 227, 229, 272; active 13, 15,
70–2, 79, 82, 84, 125, 129, 131, 216,
222, 231–2, 253, 271, 276, 279, 283;
and careers 17, 269 (*see also* career);
changes in population composition 3,
14, 72, 90–1, 115, 118–19, 129, 155,
196–7, 209, 216–17, 225, 229, 239,
252–3, 262–3, 269, 277, 279, 281–2;
demography 13, 70, 74, 127;
ergonomics of 83; occupational health
and 17; physical and functional changes
with 81, 198; and work 4, 17, 269;
workers 78, 84, 226–7, 274 (*see also*
older workers); workforce 12, 16, 27,
47, 57, 74, 78, 138, 216, 232, 239, **242**,
250
Asahi Shimbun 258, 262
Asia-Pacific region 11, 237, 274
Assolombarda 163

Australia *4*, 11, 15–16, 130, *219*, 239–50,
272, 274
Austria *219*, 273
autonomy 7, 10, 48, 61, 78, 130–1, 141,
146, 275; task 75–6, **76**, 78, 82; at
work **58**, 62, 66, 75–6, **76**, 94, 141, 232,
276

baby boomers 16, 196, 221, 240, 262;
baby-boom generation 227
Barclays Wealth 141
Belgium 12–13, 70–84, 85n5, 163, *219*,
271, 273, 276
blue-collar workers 186
Brazil 3, *4*
BRICS group 3, *4*
Bridge employment (definition,
conceptualization and modalities) 6–16,
27, 38–40, 46–7, 52, 63, 70, 82, 138,
150–1, 168, 170–1, 185, 195–8, 209,
222–7, 269, 275, 280–6; antecedents of
36–8, 54–5, 196, 198, 209; attitudes
about 9, 13, 71, 139, 146; barriers or
restrictions 11, 56–9, 142–3, 158, 270,
277; benefits 10–11, 276, 279; bridge
job 7, 31, *32*, 36–8, 42, 56, 61, 127, 196,
199, 202–4, 207, 228–30, 238, 256, 259,
262, 273, 275–7; *career-consistent* 7,
52, 55, 66, 78, 140, 196, 200–2, 206–7,
222, 275, 278; cognitions about 200–1;
consequences 55–6, 281; decision 8, 34,
44, 61, 141, 199–204, 209, 228;
extrinsic motives 28, 43, 61–2; financial
reasons 28, 43, 45, 48n 54, 206; health
34, **35**, 45, 47, 54–5, 78, 127, 199–200,
206; individual factors 33, 43, 54, 141,
200; institutionalbarriers 122, 142,
158, 171, 277; intrinsic motives 5, 28,

Subject index 301

45, 47, 48n 61–2, 65–6, 130, 179; macro-level antecedents of 15, 71, 198, 204; micro-level antecedents of 15, 71, 198–202; meso-level antecedents of 15, 71, 198, 202–4; *non-career* 7, 52, 55, 140, 196, 200–2, 206–7, 222, 275; organizational 196; outcomes 15–16, 196, 205–9, 270; pull motives to engage in 54, 141, 201–2; push motives to engage in 54, 71, 80, 141, 201–2, 204, 270; research on 196, 209, 280–6
Bureau of Labor Statistics 9, 18, 20, 134, 211, 286–7

Cabinet Office of Japan 261, 264
Canada *4*, 7, 11, 15, 118, 120, 130, 216–32, 254, 272–4, 279
career 5–7, 28, 33, 53, 63, 66–7, 73, 83, 92, 98, 104, 138, 146, 149–51, 195, 198–208, 282–4; career job (or career employment) 6–7, 27–8, 30–1, 36, 38–42, 47–8, 52, 61, 66, 195, 222–3, 228–31, 253, 259, 272–4; commitment 8, 208; counseling 17; development 17, 83, 242, 245, *246–7*; end-of-career 15, 64, 70, 78, 216–17, 222–3, 232; identity 140, 146–7; management 140; mid and late career 4, 59, 83, 198, 200, 205, 263; mobility; opportunities 75, *76*, 78, 83, 140, 151, 159, 277; progression 13, 139–41, 143, 145–9, 243, 276; stability 9; stage 139, 145, 147, 151; switch 40; transitions 13, 139–40, 142–5, 149–51, 278
Central Statistical Office 97–9, 110
Center for equal opportunities and opposition to racism 79, 85
changing nature of work and retirement 4, 7, 28–9, 51, 140, 146, 170, *184*, 254
China 3, *4*, 115
civil servants 84n2, 173, **174**
coaching **242**, 242–3, **245–7**, 284
communism 92–5; communist system 92, 94
community 15, 150, 196, *201*, 202, 205, 208, 265, 269
Conseil consultatif sur la main-d'œuvre et le travail (CCTM) 218, 233
Convention Collective de Travail 86
continuity theory 59, 206, 224–5, 229
cultural factors 11, 14, 155, 157, 272; cultural norms 12, 15, 54, 56, 60–1, 67, 142, 204; cultural values 12, 51, 93, 142, 274, 276

defined benefit plans 197, 226; defined contribution plans 197
demographics of aging 13–14, 33, 90, 109, 115, 120, 127, 154, 158, 218, 232, 239, 263, 272; changes 162, 167–8, 239, 279; diversity 15, 209; factors (as antecedents of bridge employment) 43, 198–9; transition 3; trends 16, 92, 97, 115–17, 175, 232
Denmark 120, 158, *219*, 271, 273
dependency rate 13, 115, 117, 129, 272
disability 28, 72, 82, 200, 228; disability legislation 28; disabled workers 71, 125
diversity 57, 70, 163, 273

early retirement 4–5, 8, 12–14, 29–31, 40, *44*, 64, 71–2, 78–80, 82–4, 85n4, 96, 98, 120, **123–4**, 125, 131, 138, 156, 168–9, 186, 195, 217–18, 220–1, 231, **242**, **245**, *246–7*, 249–50, 270–4, 276–7; antecedents 34, 42, 71, 80, 225, 280; benefits 8, 29, 271; consequences 82; incentives for 91, 96, 120–2, 217, 231, 239–40, 270–1, 274; involuntary or forced 28–9, 45, 82, 120–1, 127; pull factors 82; push factors 82; voluntary 29, 82, 120, 258
economic crisis 84n4, 120, 156–8, 162–4; and recession 16–17, 29, 53, 99, 141, 204, 252, 258, 260–1
education 12, 29, 33, **34**, **40**, *44*, 47, 57–8, 63, 78, 119, 131, 155–6, 163–4, **175–6**, 198, 217, 230, 240, 247, **248**, 250, 254, 263, 272, 274, 280, 284; as antecedent of bridge employment 15, 33, 41, 43, 45, **46**, 53–4, 175, 178, 181, 189, 198–9, 228; *see also* older workers, educational level
ELSA Study 5
employability 7, 14–15, 97, 101, 132, 165, 168, 170, 226, 232, 239, 274
employers 7, 15–16, 38–40, 46–7, 55, 57–8, 63–4, 67, 80, 96–7, 108–9, 118, 126, 130, 138–43, 149, 164, 169–71, 178, **180**, 188, 195, 197, 203, 206, 208, 216–17, 220, 225–6, 230–1, 239–46, **249**, 252, 254–5, 270, 274, 276, 278, 283, 285
Employers Forum on Age and Cranfield University 151
employment: career 6–7, 27, 30, 140, 228, 252; conditions 34, 38–9, 47–8, 75, *76*, 97–8, 124, 128, 171, 186, 254, *257*;

302   *Subject index*

employment *continued*
 flexible 9; full-time 27, 125, 170, 203,
  220, 223; life-long 16, 254, 262;
  insecurity 91, 96; paid 30, 32, 38–9, 45,
  47, 127, 172–3, **174**, 176, 178, 195, 205,
  230, 271, 273; part-time 8, 51–2, 103,
  106, 125, 138, 169, 178, 188, 247, 256,
  260, 280; post-retirement 5, 102–3, *105*,
  107, 109, 154, 178, 197, 279; rate 12,
  51–3, 98, 119, 155, 169, 174–5, 204,
  218, **220**, 221, 271–2, 274, 280;
  re-employment 8, 30, 254, *255*, 256,
  258, 263, 280; relations 6; stable 47,
  229; temporary 8, 27, 38, *39*, 51–2, 125,
  184, 223, 256, *257*, 259–61
entrepreneurship 91, 93, 129;
  entrepreneurs 1289 163; entrepreneurial
  behavior 10; *see also* self-employment
ethnic minorities 198; ethnic
  discrimination 57
Eurofound, European Foundation for the
  Improvement of Living and Working
  Conditions 72, 75, 172
Europe, European countries 4–5, 8, 11–14,
  51–2, 62, 72–3, 85n5, 90–2, 95, 99, 102,
  107–9, 115–21, 126, 129–31, 138,
  154–6, 160, 163–4, 218, 240, 270–3,
  277–9, 283
European Working Condition Survey
  (EWCS) 71–3, 75–6, 78–84, 85n5, 276
Eurostat 51, 90, 98, **116**, 118, 155, 160,
  175
externalization 14, 168, 179

family issues 3, 6, 8, 60, 74, 79, 107, 128,
  147, 164, 173, 174, 198, 257, 261,
  283–4; in retirement 10, 13, 48, 54–5,
  64, 84, 148, 150, 156, 225, 228, 231; in
  bridge employment decision 9, 15, 127,
  141, 203–4, 285; outcomes in bridge
  employment 205, 207–8
female labor force participation 9, 155,
  157, 169, 202, *253*, 256, 258, 272
fertility 3, 91, 97, 154, 196; total fertility
  rate 154
financial planning 66, 276; in retirement
  276; in bridge employment decision 12,
  28, 43, 45, 54, 64, 179, *180*, *183*, 198,
  201, 204–5, 230, 270, 275–6
financial well-being (as outcome of
  bridge employment) 15, 127, 141,
  205–6, 279
Finland 57, 59, 219
flexibility 7, 12, 29, 53, 67, *76*, 84, 108,

  159, 188, 218, 226, 230–1, 239, 253,
  271, 274–6; of bridge employment 12,
  38, 41–2, 47, 61–2, 65–6, 159, 201–2,
  208, 273, 278, 284; flexible work 5, 7,
  12, **58**, *65*, 92, 103–6, 108, 130, 138–9,
  142–4, 149, 178, *184*, 240, 247, 285
flexicurity 164
France *4*, 11, 73, 120, 130, 156, 158, 163,
  219, 252, *253*, 254, 263, 271, 273

gender 54, 81, 155, 200, 209, 227–8, 241;
  gender differences 59, 62, 66–7, 141,
  284; *see also* female labor force
  participation; women
generational gap 162
German Aging Survey 172, 176–7, *180*
German Socio-Economic Panel 172, 176
Germany 3–*4*, 14, 73, 99, 121, 155–6, 158,
  167–90, *219*, 252–*3*, *263*, 271, 273, 278,
  283

health and retirement 7, 9, 12–13, 15, 33,
  37, *44*–5, 47–8, 54, **56**, 59, 64, 71, 74–5,
  77–8, 90–1, 101–2, 115, 119–21, 130–2,
  142–4, 149–50, 161, 164, 178–9, 181,
  200–2, 206–7, 209, 217, 223, 231, 240,
  242, **245**, *246*–*7*, **248**, 253, 260, 269,
  275–6, 281–4; mental 10, 55, 77, 127,
  129, 206–7; objective 282; perceived 8,
  43–*4*, 83, 199, 279; physical 15, 77,
  127, 200, 275; poor health 28, 34, 45,
  60, 71, 103, 108, 164, 200, 225, 277,
  282; problems 34, 38, 47, *65*, 98, 101–2,
  105–6, 108, 200, 207, 218, 279; risk for
  77; status 3, 34–**5**, 55, 83, 168, 198, 285
Health and Retirement Study (HRS) 5, 8,
  197, 206
Higher Council for Employment 70, 87
human capital 33, 40, 43, 155, 160, 284
human resources 231, 276; HR
  management 8, 17, 79, 83; HR managers
  83, 104, 240–1; HR policy and practices
  10, 79, 240, 246–*7*, 284

Iceland 51, 98
identity: personal 10, 151, 224, 278;
  career, professional or work 59–60, *65*,
  80–1, 140, 146–7, 150, *201*–2, 206;
  social 10, 80, 122, 131, 151
idiosyncratic deals 67
income in retirement 5–6, 8, 27, 40, 47,
  52–4, 60, 62, 66–7, 70, 84n2, 102,
  108–9, 117, 121, 127, 129, 141, 150,
  157–8, 162–4, 179–9, 186–9, 198–9,

Subject index   303

201–2, 205, 208–9, 218, 223, 225–8, 231, 239, 260, 269, 285
India 3–4, 115, 186–7
Institut de la statistique du Québec 217, 234
Instituto Nacional de Estadística 116–18, 134–5
International Longevity Center Japan 261, 264
intergenerational relationships at work 71, 79, 83, 129, 183, 243, 276, 281, 284
Ireland 254
Istituto Nazionale di Statistica 154, 157, 166
Italy 3–4, 11, 14, 117, 130, 154–65, *219*, 272–3, 278

Japan 3–4, 11, 16, 51, 90–1, 115, 117–19, 121, 130, 186–7, 216, *219*, 252–63, 273–4, 280
Japan Today 264
job: and cognitive or mental demands 73, 81, 101, 130, 199, 206; and physical demands **58**, 73, 80, 82, 101, 130, 199, 206, 280; and psychosocial demands 7, 53, 71, 162, 198; characteristics and stressors 8, 10, 48, 53–4, 59, 101, 121, 149, 168, 203, 207, 225, 282; involvement 59–60, 184, 279; loss 230; performance 94, 96, 149, *183*, 258; satisfaction 8, **41**, 54–5, 59, 94, 100, 127, 141, 143, 149, 161, 225, 277; quality 75–6, 82, 277

Labor Clearing Houses 259
labor force 5–6, 8, 10, 16, 28–30, 36, 41, 50, 70, 82, 90–1, 118, 156, 170, 175, 195–7, 205–6, 209, 222, 229–31, 252–3, 258, 261–2, 269, 280; withdrawal 6–7, 27, 30, 33, 222; *see also* workforce
labor markets 5, 13, 17, 27, 61, 75, 90–1, 96–7, 106, 115, 162–3, 167, 187–9, 204–5, 239, 252–3, 263; and older workers 6, 8, 11, 13–15, 28, 31–4, 36, 39–40, 47, 51–3, 57, 59, 61, 66, 70, 73, 78, 83, 92, 100–3, 108, 118, 121–31, 140–4, 154–9, 168–72, 175–6, 216, 223–4, 226, 228–32, 256, 270–80, 282–3; re-enter 9, 27, 36, 38, 43, 45–6, 223, 228, 232; stratification 256, 258, 280
labor supply 239, 241
life course perspective 60, 225; life course

stages and trajectories 6, 12, 36, 47, 52, 60, 128, 230
life course theory 59–60, 223–5, 230
life expectancy 3, 8, 30, 90, 97, 99, 102, 107, 116, 118, 122–2, 138, 154–5, 167, 170, 221, 281, 285; subjective 199
life satisfaction 5, 10, 127, 131, 179, 207, 240, 279
lifelong learning 101, 131
longitudinal studies 197, 209, 274, 281

managers 57, 73, 93–4, 96, 145, 148–9, 151, 159–60, 178, *180*, 187–8, 241, 257, 259, 263, 278–9; *see also* HR managers
marital status **35**; in bridge employment 34–6, **35**, **43–4**, 203; in retirement 203
mature job seekers 9, 259–61
mentoring 125, 128, 145, 160, 187, 208, 229, **242–3**, **245–7**, 277
migration trends 3; emigration 118; immigration 118

Netherlands, the 11, 27–48, 73, 158, 240, 270–3, 275, 279
Netherlands Interdisciplinary Demographic Institute (NIDI) 11
New Zealand 254
NIDI Work and Retirement Panel 28, 20, 46–7
Norway 51, 57, 98–9, 120, 200

occupational health 17
older adults 9, 11, 27–8, 30, 33, 36, 46, 140, 230; *see also* older workers
older workers: active coping styles 80, 84; attitudes and bias against 10, 57–8, 67, 79–81, 83, 101, 143, 247, 270, 276; capabilities and competence 142–3, 159, 228, 243, 252–4; career mobility and stability 13, 139, 143–51, 217; cognitive ability 81, 101, 199, 282; coping strategies 9, 32, 80, 162; educational level **40**, **46**, 43; employability 7, 15, 67, 73–5, 226, 232, 239; employment rates 5, 12–13, 33, 51, 59, 70, 81–2, 91, 98, 119, 232, 240, *257*, 274; extrinsic motives 28, 61; family situation 34–5, 43, 48, 79, 145; financial position 43, 48, 144, 205; intrinsic motives 61–2, 130; learning opportunities 9, 101, 163, 202, 205, 278; married 47; motivation 10–11, 14, 62, 79, 130, 225; opportunities for 36, 66, 70, 142, 260;

304　Subject index

older workers *continued*
　participation in workforce 78, 155,
　　158–9, 168–70, 195, 230–1, 239, 253,
　　258, 260–2, 269, 273, 283, 285;
　　productivity 10, 39, 81, 101, 254;
　　retention of 118, 124–6, 138, 218, 220,
　　231, **242**, 244–**5**, 256, 284; skills 10, 63,
　　161, 202, 208, 252–3, 255; socio-
　　economic status 5, 126, 131, 164,
　　269–70; training 71, 101, 145, **242**,
　　245–*6*, 274; well-being 10, 15, 17, 36,
　　48, 55, 60, 74, 80, 84, 117, 129–31, *183*,
　　205–8, 223, **242**, **245**, *246–7*, 277, 279,
　　284; working conditions 12, 54, **56**,
　　58–9, *65*, 74–6, 79–83, 85n5, 121,
　　158–9, 161–2, 183–*4*, 218, 221, **245**,
　　246–7, 282, 284; *see also* aging
　　workers; senior workers
organizational behavior 17
organizational climate 160, 198
organizational commitment 8, 94, 96, 103
organizational culture 57, 103, 145, 189,
　279
organizational downsizing 55, 57, 121,
　174, 230, 270; and restructuring 38, *44*,
　121, 141, 144

Pacto de Toledo *123–4*, 125–6, 135
Partial Retirement Act 169, 273
pension 8, 28–31, 43–5, 47, 52–4, 60–2,
　66–7, 70, 72, 82, 84n2, 98–9, 107–9,
　123–6, 141, 143, 151, 157–8, 165, *178*,
　196, 218, 221–3, 227, 262, 274, 276–7;
　public pension systems 3, 8, 13, 30,
　90–2, 98–101, 115, 117–22, 127, 129,
　131, 138–9, 156–9, 166, 169–70, 174–8,
　188–9, 225–6, 229–30, 239, 253–4, 262,
　269–72, 279, 281; pay-as-you-go system
　3, 28–9, 99, 117, 167, 170; private
　pensions 52, 66, 99, 283
Pensions Policy Institute 142, 152
personality 15, 200, 230; Big Five
　personality traits 200
Pew Research Center 197, 213
Poland 13, 90–109, 158, 271, 276–7
policy-makers 17, 46, 55, 67, 90, 109, 118,
　188–9, 207, 225, 250, 252–3, 262, 269
poverty 101, 157, 198; rates 176
power harassment 257
private sector 16, 47, 98, 143, 146, 217,
　221
procedural justice 81, 94
psychological needs 61, 66
psychological well-being 15, 48, 205–8

public policy 17, 109, 239–40
public sector 47, 53, 59, 72, 142–3, 217,
　221, 240

qualitative analysis 14, 168, 172, 179, 181,
　189–90, 275, 277–8; qualitative data 10,
　173
quality of life 8, 13, 80, 84, 129, 283, 285;
　in retirement 269, 277, 281
quality of working life 127, 149
quantitative analysis 109, 178–9, 189–90;
　quantitative data 179, 273, 277
Quebec 15, 216–17, 225, 230

resource conservation theory 223
Recruit Work Institute 265
recruitment 10, 107, 186, 220, 241, **242**,
　245–*6*
replacement 5, 93, 161, 167, 284; rates 29,
　48, 98
retention practices 124, 142, 218, 231,
　256, 269, 284
retirement: adjustment 84, 195, 201, 207,
　230, 269, 273, 278, 281; as process 201,
　207; attitudes about 9, 71, 80, 91, 148,
　225, 229, 276; consequences 60, 102,
　154, 158, 269; couples and partners 34,
　36, 38, 60, 64, 208, 226; decision
　making in 100, 195, 269, 282; delay 9,
　101, 197, 221, 225, 269; expectations 6,
　29, 130, 148, 204, 274; flexible 13, 115,
　124–6, 138, 250; forced 28, 36, 38, 82,
　100, 121, 228; full 7, 11, 16, **31**, 34, 46,
　70, 80, 82, 127, 129–31, 169–72, 195–6,
　201, 203, 206–7, 218, 250, 252–3, 273,
　275, 278, 281–2, 284; gradual 6, 10,
　51–2, 56, 205, 269, 280; health in 10,
　28, 34, 38, 45, 55–**6**, 64–*5*, 71, 77, 83–4,
　102–8, 121, 127, 130, 141, 164, 178,
　181, 200–2, 206–7, 225, 231, 275,
　281–4 (*see also* health and retirement);
　institutional context of 27–8, 119, 121,
　130, 253, 283; mandatory age of 7, 17,
　36—8, 52, 61, 63, 84n3, 159, 226,
　254–6, 258, 262; mental health in 55,
　127, 129, 206–7, 282; normal age of 17;
　partial 6, 9, 14, 124–5, 128, 138, 145,
　178–82, 186, 188, 239–40, 243, 280;
　planning 12, 51, 54–6, 60–1, 195,
　201–2, 242, **245**–*6*, 268, 281; phased 6,
　15, 27, 145, 188, 195, 197, 218, 226,
　230–1, 240, 274; physical health in 127,
　205–6, 275; postponing 13, 52, 155; pull
　factors 54, 82, 141; push factors 82;

Subject index   305

satisfaction in 92, 100, 102, 107–9, 230; thoughts about 201; timing of 33, 52–3, 55; well-being in 10, 55, 131, *183*, 205–8, 223, 279; *see also* early retirement
rights: human 92, 161; labor or work 75, 142, 161, 285; pension 30; social 285; to work 70
role theory 59, 206, 224, 229
Russia 3–*4*, 95

salary 40, 48, 52–3, 64, 98–9, 124, 157, 160, 163–4, 186, 205, *257*–8; demotion and reduction in **242**, 244–**5**, *246*
SECOT (Spanish Seniors for Technical Cooperation) 128–9, 272, 277
selection bias 78, 84
self-employment 6–7, 38, 40, 130, 150, 172, 223, 227, 256, 261–2, 280–1, 285; *see also* entrepreneurship
seniors workers 13, 34, 65, 91, 97, 101–3, 108, 128–9, 159, 163, 189, 277–8; *see also* older workers
shadow economy 121
sickness absence 53, 67
silver work 168, 171-, 174, 187–8, 190; silver workers 179, 181, 183–5, 188–9
social cohesion 285
social identity theory 80
social justice 75
social protection 75, 220
social psychology 224
social relationships at work 58, 63, 66, 141, 275
social security benefits 195, 285
Social Security systems 3, 7–10, 82, 97, 99, 117, 8, 121–6, 130–1, 138, 156–7, 163, 169, 172, 174, 186, 188–9, 195–7, 205, 209, 239, 253, 272, 279, 282, 285
social and organizational support 13, 55, 60–1, 75–*6*, 139, 143–5, 149, 185, 187, 240, **242**, **245**–*7*, 277–8
Spain 11, 13, 115–32, 164, *219*, 272–3, 277
stress 8, 10, 41, 48, 53–5, 59, 80, 101, 106, 121, 149, 159, 164, 203, 206–7, 240, 279, 282
Survey of Health, Ageing and Retirement in Europe (SHARE) 5, 119, 126–7, 164, 272–3, 277
Sweden 12, 51–67, 98, 119, 158, *259*, 254, 270–3, 275–6, 279
Swedish Pensions Agency 56, 68
Switzerland 270, 273

The Age and Employment Network (TAEN) 153
technology 149; age and 144; use by older workers 198
trade unions 29, 99, 118, 126, 270, 283

unemployment 12, 29, 56, 72, 85n4, 94, 96, 99, 103, 106, 120–1, 164, 169, 204, 232, 239, 241, 252, 254, 259, 272, 274, 280; in-house 262; rates 4, 16, 97, 106, 118, 156, 225, 228, 262, *263*, 282; benefits 28–9, 96, 98, 108, 121
United Kingdom *4*–5, 11, 13, 73, 118–19, 121, 130, 138–51, 158, 186, *219*, 261, 272, 277, 279, 282
United States 4, 7–9, 11, 15, 27, 51, 90, 102, 115, 118, 120–1, 130, 195–210, *219*, 227, 229, 239–40, 252–4, 261, *262*, 272–4, 279
United States Census Bureau *4*, 214

voluntary social work 196; volunteering 269

wage 14, 47, 75, 94, 220, *263*; reduction 39, 162, 254, 256, 260
wage-and-salary work 6, *39*, 285
welfare state 27; system 3, 51–2, 54, 119, 131–2, 158, 167, 240, 277
well-being 5, 10, 17, 36, 55, 60, 74, 80, 127, 130–1, 164, 183, 223, **242**, **245**, *246*–*7*, 277, 284; financial 127, *205*, 279; physical 129, 206; psychological 15, 48, 129, 205–8
white-collar workers 52, 61, 67, 255
women 4, 51–3, 76–9, 117–19, 128–9, 143, 145, 150, 155–6, 175, 198–201, 220, 225, 256, 258; and retirement 5, 12, 33, 36, 66–7, 72–4, 84n3, 91, 97–9, 127, 167, *177*–8, 180, 197, *221*–**2**, 240, 275, 284; and bridge employment **34–5**, **37**, 43, 53–6, 59–62, 76, 126, 203, 270–4; *see also* female labor force participation
work ability 7, 20, 101, 288
work attitudes 7, 13, 54, 139, 146, 225, 276; age and 71, 77, 276; and bridge employment decision 198, 225, 229, 240; entrepreneurial 7, 130; in retirement 80, 91, 225
work motivation 13, 47, 139, 208; in older workers 7, 14, 59, 61–3, 65, 67, 79, 141–2, 145, 157, 179, 182–3, 187, 190, 209, 276, 279, 284
work sustainability 73–4, 78, 82–3

306 *Subject index*

workforce: re-entry to 6, 8, 9, 23, 32–4, 36, 38, 43, 45–7, 121, 124, 195, 197, 225, 228, 230, 279–80; withdrawal 6–7, 27, 29, 31, 70–1, 81, 139, 172, 188, 203, 206, 230, 273

working arrangements in mid and late career: alternative 5–6, 128, 138, 149, 198, 278; contingent 10, 130, 284; flexible 8, 10, *65*, 103–4, 139, 145

working conditions: psychosocial factors in 58–9, 67, 75; *see also* older workers

working life 11, 60, 70, 84, 98, 119, 127, 139, 146, 149, 157, 181–2, 186, 190, 230, 272, 284; prolongation or extension of 4–5, 7, 9, 17, 27, 36, 43, 67, 99, 101, 122, 126, 128–31, 142, 157, 169–70, 218, 221–5, 230–1, 259, 269, 273, 275–6, 280, 284–5

work-life balance 71, 74–5, 78–9, 84, 276

World Bank 91, 97, 113

World Economic Forum 91, 97, 113

young workers 61, 228, 230, 252; unemployment 63, 120, 129, 156; *see also* intergenerational relationships at work